Being Israeli
The Dynamics of Multiple Citizenship

A timely study by two well-known scholars offers a theoretically-informed account of the political sociology of Israel. The analysis is set within its historical context, as the authors trace Israel's development from Zionist settlement in the 1880s, through the establishment of the state in 1948, to the present day. Against this background the authors speculate on the relationship between identity and citizenship in Israeli society, and consider the differential rights, duties, and privileges that are accorded different social groups –Jews and Palestinians, Europeans and Middle Eastern Jews, men and women, religiously Orthodox and non-religious Jews – and how these have evolved. In this way they demonstrate that, despite ongoing tensions, the pressure of globalization and economic liberalization has gradually transformed Israel from a warlike welfare society to one more oriented towards peace and private profit. This unexpected conclusion offers some encouragement for the future of this troubled region. However, Israel's position towards the peace process is still subject to a tug-of-war between two conceptions of citizenship: liberal citizenship on the one hand, and the combination of colonial republicanism and an ever more religiously defined ethno-national citizenship on the other.

GERSHON SHAFIR is Professor of Sociology at the University of California, San Diego. His publications include *Land, Labor, and the Origins of the Israeli–Palestinian Conflict, 1882–1914* (1989, 1996) and *Immigrants and Nationalists* (1995). He is the editor of *The Citizenship Debates* (1998). Yoav Peled is Associate Professor in the Department of Political Science, Tel Aviv University. His book, *Class and Ethnicity in the Pale: The Political Economy of Jewish Workers' Nationalism in Late Imperial Russia* was published in 1989 and he co-edited *Ethnic Challenges to the Modern Nation-State* (2000). Both authors have co-edited *The New Israel: Peacemaking and Liberalization* (2000).

Cambridge Middle East Studies 16

Editorial Board
Charles Tripp (general editor)

Julia A. Clancy-Smith   Israel Gershoni   Roger Owen
Yezid Sayigh   Judith E. Tucker

Cambridge Middle East Studies has been established to publish books on the nineteenth- and twentieth-century Middle East and North Africa. The aim of the series is to provide new and original interpretations of aspects of Middle Eastern societies and their histories. To achieve disciplinary diversity, books will be solicited from authors writing in a wide range of fields including history, sociology, anthropology, political science and political economy. The emphasis will be on producing books offering an original approach along theoretical and empirical lines. The series is intended for students and academics, but the more accessible and wide-ranging studies will also appeal to the interested general reader.

Being Israeli

The Dynamics of Multiple Citizenship

Gershon Shafir

University of California, San Diego

Yoav Peled

Tel Aviv University

CAMBRIDGE
UNIVERSITY PRESS

CAMBRIDGE UNIVERSITY PRESS
Cambridge, New York, Melbourne, Madrid, Cape Town, Singapore, São Paulo

Cambridge University Press
The Edinburgh Building, Cambridge CB2 2RU, UK

Published in the United States of America by Cambridge University Press, New York

www.cambridge.org
Information on this title: www.cambridge.org/9780521792240

First published 2002

A catalogue record for this publication is available from the British Library

Library of Congress Cataloguing in Publication data
Shafir, Gershon.
  Being Israeli: the dynamics of multiple citizenship / Gershon Shafir, Yoav Peled.
    p.   cm. – (Cambridge Middle East studies)
  Includes bibliographical references and index.
  ISBN 0 521 79224 X (hardback) – ISBN 0 521 79672 5 (paperback)
  1. Citizenship – Israel.   2. Civil society – Israel.   3. Political culture – Israel.
  I. Peled, Yoav. II. Title. III. Series.

  JQ1830.A91 S53 2002
  323.6′095694–dc21   2001037490

ISBN-13 978-0-521-79224-0 hardback
ISBN-10 0-521-79224-X hardback

ISBN-13 978-0-521-79672-9 paperback
ISBN-10 0-521-79672-5 paperback

Transferred to digital printing 2005

To the memory of Yonathan Shapiro
trailblazer, teacher, friend

To the memory of Yonathan Shapiro
trailblazer, teacher, friend

Contents

Acknowledgments

This book has been many years in the making, and during these years we have incurred many intellectual and material debts to friends, colleagues, and institutions. Many people have read parts of the manuscript at the various stages of its development and have given us valuable comments and suggestions. They are, in alphabetical order, José Brunner Israel Gershoni, Zvi Gitelman, Dov Khenin, Gal Levy, Ian Lustick, Roger Owen, Michael Shalev, Yehuda Shenhav, Oren Yiftachel, and Arnona Zahavi. We would also like to thank the many people, too numerous to be mentioned by name, who provided us with research assistance, or with whom we consulted in less formal ways over the years. Special thanks are due also to the people who have kindly consented to be interviewed for this study. Their names appear in the bibliographical section of the book.

Institutionally, we owe a debt of gratitude for their financial help to the Israel Science Foundation, the Joint Committee on the Near and Middle East of the US Social Science Research Council and the American Council of Learned Societies, the Gershon Gordon Faculty of Social Science and the Department of Political Science, both at Tel Aviv University, and the Academic Senate Committee on Research at the University of California, San Diego.

In addition to these joint thanks we would each like to give special thanks to people and institutions who have helped each one of us personally: Shafir would like to thank the Department of Sociology and Anthropology at Tel Aviv University, where he spent a very fruitful sabbatical year in 1994–5, as well as the University of California's Institute on Global Conflict and Cooperation for its continued support. Peled would like to thank the Center for Judaic Studies at the University of Pennsylvania, and its Director, David Ruderman, for enabling him to spend a most stimulating and productive year there as a Fellow, in 1996–7. A crucial part of his contribution to this book was written during that year. Most especially, Peled would like to thank Horit Herman-Peled, without whose love, companionship, and constant intellectual challenge the effort he invested in this book would have been neither possible nor worthwhile.

Finally, we would like to express our gratitude to our editor at Cambridge University Press, Marigold Acland, for bearing with us through so many missed deadlines and for her unfaltering support for this book, to three anonymous reviewers whose comments and criticisms helped us improve the manuscript, and to Mary Starkey, our copy-editor, for being both diligent and good-natured in the execution of the very complicated project of tri-continental copy-editing.

This book is a real joint product, the culmination of many years of intellectual cooperation. We have each contributed to it equally, and the order in which our names appear on the cover was determined by lot. We dedicate the book to the memory of Yonathan Shapiro who, in different ways, was a friend, teacher, and mentor to us both.

Abbreviations

AWU	African Workers' Union
AY	Agudat Yisrael
BOI	Bank of Israel
CBS	Central Bureau of Statistics
DMC	Democratic Movement for Change
DOP	Declaration of Principles
DT	development town
EESP	Emergency Economic Stabilization Plan
FCC	Federation of Chambers of Commerce
FDI	foreign direct investment
FSU	former Soviet Union
HMO	health-maintenance organization
IDB	Israel Discount Bank
IDF	Israeli Defense Force
ILA	Israel Land Administration
IMC	Israel Management Center
JNF	Jewish National Fund
ISI	import-substitution industrialization
LSM	Labor Settlement Movement
MAI	Manufacturers' Association of Israel
MIC	military–industrial complex
NII	National Insurance Institute
NIS	New Israeli Shekel
NRP	National Religious Party
ONA	Omnium Nord Africa
OT	occupied territories
OWM	Organization of Working Mothers
PLO	Palestine Liberation Organization
PLP	Progressive List for Peace
PM	prime minister
PNF	Palestinian National Front

SES   socio-economic status
TASE   Tel Aviv Stock Exchange
WB   World Bank
WIZO   Women's International Zionist Organization
WWC   Women Workers' Council
WWM   Women Workers' Movement
WZO   World Zionist Organization

1 Introduction

For some time now, Israel's main political and moral dilemma has been described as the need to choose between the two cardinal principles of its political culture: the particularistic commitment to being a Jewish state and the universalist commitment to being a Western-style democracy. The former course would seem to indulge the desire for a homogenous nation-statehood by excluding Palestinians from equal citizenship, whereas the latter would gratify the aspiration for democratization by making Israel the state of all of its citizens (see *Tel Aviv University Law Review* 1995; Mautner et al. 1998; Margolin 1999; Gavison 1999; David 2000). Though such an overly formalistic depiction of these two political principles and their partisans highlights their deep-seated mutual hostility, it masks the tensions within each one of them. Thus, the Jewish element in the Jewish–democratic formula involves a contradiction between Zionism as a secular nationalist movement, seeking self-determination for the Jewish people, and Judaism as both a religious tradition and, in its Orthodox version, a state religion.[1] Nor does the Jewish–democratic distinction recognize the systematic ethnic stratification of Israeli Jews. Similarly, the meaning of democracy is hardly self-evident in the Israeli context. It ranges from an older formalistic arrangement of electoral procedures to a newer substantive liberal conception, focused on a working civil society. Most importantly, the Jewish–democratic dichotomy glosses over the way in which the tension between these two principles has been encompassed by a third – the colonial character of the Zionist state- and nation-building project. It is still not possible to set apart Israeli citizenship and, therefore, Israeli democracy, from its colonial beginnings and continued colonial practices.

---

[1] President of the Supreme Court Aharon Barak made this distinction explicit: "In my opinion, Zionism on the one hand, and Jewish *halacha* (religious law) on the other hand, left their imprint on Israel's Jewish character" (Margolin 1999: 12). This statement was made at a symposium, one of many in recent years, devoted to the potential contradictions between Israel's Jewish and democratic character.

In this book we offer a different conceptualization of Israel's social and political structure, a conceptualization that recognizes three, not two, partly contradictory political goals and commitments. We define these as colonialism, ethno-nationalism, and democracy, and argue that they have presupposed and built on one another, even as they struggled for political mastery in the Yishuv (pre-statehood Jewish community in Palestine) and in Israel. The history of Israel, then, is the history of the pursuit of these contradictory goals and of their evolution in relation to one another and to outside forces with which the Zionist movement and Israeli society have had to contend.

At least between the mid-1930s and the mid-1970s, Zionist state-building efforts were shaped by the evolving ideological hegemony and political dominance of the Labor Settlement Movement (LSM), more conventionally known as Labor Zionism (for our choice of the term see chap. 2 below). This protracted period ended, officially, in 1977, when Labor was unable to form a government after the general elections held that year and Likud proceeded to establish Israel's first right-wing government. In actual fact, however, Labor's hegemonic position had been eroding for at least a decade, ever since, in the wake of the 1967 Arab–Israeli war, it became paralyzed by conflicting pulls. As against the lure of the past – the state-building project of piecemeal colonial expansion and settlement over which it had presided almost since the beginning of the century – stood the draw of a "New Israel" – an emergent civil society whose key actors sought to scale back the state-building efforts, pursue vigorous economic development, and trade the territories captured in 1967 for accommodation with the Palestinians and the Arab world.

Since 1977 neither the incorporation of the nationalist right wing into the post-hegemonic political process nor the simultaneous beginning of the peace process have healed the divisions in Israeli society between left and right, secular and religious Jews, Ashkenazim (Jews hailing from Europe) and Mizrachim (Jews hailing from the Muslim world), Jews and Palestinian Arabs. Indeed, the coincidence of the decline of the LSM and ascendance of the political and ideological right, on the one hand, with the peace process on the other has intensified contention and discord. But this fragmentation and conflicts are still played out within the parameters set by the legacy of the period of LSM dominance – a Eurocentric colonial project that excluded most Mizrachim, Palestinian Arabs, and women from its benefits, and presented its successors with the pressing task of decolonization.

The current phase in Israeli history is characterized by partial and halting decolonization, otherwise known as the peace process, set in motion and accompanied by wide-ranging liberalization and by a counter-movement of swelling religious nationalism and fundamentalism. But this phase cannot be understood without its predecessor – the period of state building under LSM dominance. We will begin our analysis, therefore, with the latter and then proceed to the former. Our key research questions will be: How have the triple objectives of colonialism, ethno-nationalism, and democracy been combined, both conceptually and in practice, over the past century; and how has this combination accomplished the task of incorporating a plethora of antagonistic social groups into the institutions of an evolving society? In other words, we will seek to uncover and explain the ways in which the LSM, and later on the Israeli state as well, sought to meet the universalizing requirements of democratic institution building while engaged in an exclusionary, ethno-nationalist colonial struggle with the Palestinians. We will further ask: How has the balance between the three objectives shifted over time and how has their new arrangement impacted on significant social and political transformations, such as the peace process?

In seeking to answer these questions we chose to place the theoretical tradition built around the concept of "citizenship" at the center of our analysis. Citizenship, as the legal and political framework for achieving full membership in society, has been a central axis of Western political philosophy. Its long conceptual and institutional history forms a bridge between Antiquity and the modern era, linking the civic and political self-conception of the Greek polis and the Roman Empire with the French Revolution and the Enlightenment's emphasis on the equal moral worth of all individuals. As an intellectual and political tradition citizenship has been repeatedly revised and updated. Its historical meaning is thus much broader than the meaning conveyed by its most widespread contemporary use – political citizenship in the nation-state – and it consists today of a string of identifiable schools of thought, or "citizenship discourses."

In the next section of this introduction we will present the three citizenship discourses that are currently predominant – liberal, republican, and ethno-nationalist, and comment on their interrelationships. After that we will introduce neo-institutionalist theory as the prism through which we will apply our analysis of citizenship to the Israeli context. Then we will show how the allocation of Israeli citizenship rights, duties, and privileges through the relevant institutions has comprised an "incorporation regime," and then will examine how different social groups have been incorporated into the Yishuv and Israeli society in a number of "waves." In the final section we will briefly review the main areas in which, we believe, our study of citizenship can address those aspects ignored or even made invisible by functionalism, elitism, and cultural pluralism, the most important theoretical frameworks on which synthetic studies of Israeli society have so far been based.

Citizenship discourses

The liberal discourse of citizenship accents personal liberty and private property, as it views individuals, and only individuals, as the bearers of universal, equal, and publicly affirmed rights. The individual, in either the utilitarian or contractual liberal view, is the sovereign author of her life who pursues her private rational advantage or conception of the good, and is not beholden to the community. The role of politics in this approach remains negative: only to aid and protect individuals from interference by governments, and by one another, in the exercise of the rights they inalienably possess. In return for this protection, individuals undertake certain minimal political obligations – obey the law, pay taxes, vote periodically, serve in the military. Thus, in the liberal view, citizenship, like society itself, is an accessory, not a value in its own right.

Liberalism's strength lies in its ability to tolerate religious, cultural, and political diversity by creating a self-limiting political realm respectful of individual rights and an institutional framework within which polarizing disputes are avoided by permitting the political expression of only those conceptions of the good that are not monopolistic. Even the socially conscious liberal theorists, such as John Rawls, emphasize that no notion of liberal justice may be viewed as a comprehensive moral doctrine but only as a practical *modus vivendi* which allows the emergence of an overlapping consensus of moral principles between opposing doctrines (Rawls 1971; 1993).

Having predominated in the West for about two centuries, the liberal notion of citizenship is being challenged now by the two other traditions, republicanism and ethno-nationalism. Philosophically, these challenges are directed at the individualist conception of the self that is at the heart of the liberal theory of citizenship – the conception that Michael Sandel has aptly characterized as an "unencumbered self" (Sandel 1984). Since the liberal state is supposed to be neutral with respect to its citizens' conceptions of the good, and treat all of them as equal, regardless of their ascriptive and other affiliations, liberal theory must constitute the citizen as an abstract, universal subject stripped of all particularity.

Both republican and ethno-nationalist thinkers have argued that by stripping citizens of all particularity liberal theory has also stripped them of their identity and, therefore, of their ability to form a community. As Maurice Roche has put it, citizens of a liberal state are, and must remain, strangers to one another (Roche 1987: 376–7). For a community can be constituted only by a conception of the good that is morally antecedent to the individual choices of its members, a requirement that contradicts the most basic tenet of liberalism, the priority of right over good (Sandel 1982; 1984). While republicans and ethno-nationalists share this critique of liberalism, they disagree about the moral purpose that a meaningful human community can and should be constituted by. Republicans, or communitarians, contend that the moral community should foster civic virtue, an idea whose origins lie in the ancient Greeks' view of politics as the hub of human existence and as life's supreme fulfillment. For communitarians politics is a communal affair, and citizenship is an enduring political attachment. Citizens are who they are by virtue of participating in the life of their political community, and by identifying with its purposes. Members of such a community experience their citizenship not intermittently, as merely protective individual rights, but rather as active participation in the pursuit of a common good. If we amplify political life by demanding more from the citizen, argue the communitarians, her existence will be richer and she will lead a more fulfilling and morally inspired life.

Republican views of citizenship display a clear aristocratic bias, since they assume that only a minority is capable of the moral transformation that places devotion to the common good ahead of the pursuit of individual interests. An example is the association of citizenship with the military duty of protecting one's city in ancient Greece. Greater obligations are accompanied by exceptional privileges. Active participation is the core of the citizens' civic virtue and the criterion entitling them to a larger share of the community's material and moral resources (Sandel 1982; Taylor 1989; Oldfield 1990).

Republican theorists further challenge the liberal view of civil society and offer their own, alternative conception. Both conceptions posit civil society as existing "over against the state, in partial independence from it, [and as including] those dimensions of social life which cannot be confounded with, or swallowed up in the state" (Taylor 1990: 95). The liberal conception, which originated in Locke, has elaborated "a richer view of society as an extra-political reality" (Taylor 1990: 107), manifested primarily in a self-regulating economy and in the existence of public opinion not beholden to the state. However, the "flight from the public into the narrower and less significant sphere of private satisfactions" (Taylor 1990: 113) entailed by this view, and the neo-liberal revolutions for which it has served as a banner since the 1970s, have caused serious apprehensions among those concerned with republican virtue. As against the Lockean tradition, republicans have therefore drawn on a different tradition of civil society, one informed by civic republicanism and rooted in the political thought of Montesquieu and Tocqueville. In this tradition freedom is guaranteed not by the marginalization of politics but rather by its proliferation and fragmentation in numerous independent public associations (Weintraub 1979; Taylor 1990: 114; Seligman 1995).

Ethno-nationalism, a version of the nationalist doctrine that originated in German Romanticism and spread from there, is interested not in civil society, but in a different kind of community: the nation or ethnic group. In the ethno-nationalist, or *völkisch*, approach, citizenship is not an expression of individual rights or of contribution to the common good, but of membership in a homogenous descent group (Greenfeld 1992). The community, in this view, is not conceived of as existing outside the state, or over against it in some way, but rather as expressed in and embodied by the state. Thus, the tension between the individual and the state, or between the community and the state, that characterizes liberal and republican thinking, respectively, is absent from the ethno-nationalist discourse. Instead, this discourse integrates non-political, cultural elements into the concept of citizenship. It portrays nations as radically different from one another because their members possess distinct cultural markers, such as language, religion, and history. Since nations are thus inscribed into the identity of their members, ethnic nationalism denies the possibility of cultural assimilation (Brubaker 1992).

Of these three conceptions of citizenship, the individualist liberal one is the most inclusive, at least in principle. However, the actual practice of liberal citizenship is frequently in competition with and sometimes systematically overshadowed by alternative approaches. In most societies two or more discourses of citizenship, superimposed on one another, vie for dominance. As Judith Shklar and Rogers Smith have shown, even in the United States, where the Lockean liberal tradition has long been held to dominate political life, its sway fluctuated throughout history and was continuously contested in theory.

Shklar's eloquent essay *American Citizenship* suggests that the value of American citizenship has been historically defined in relation to those who have been denied full membership in the society – slaves, native-born white male wage-workers, and all women. In disenfranchising these groups, the American political community was "actively and purposefully false to its own vaunted principles" (Shklar 1991: 14). But she also lets on that the excluded groups were not truer to these principles. While their struggle for the right to vote and to earn was motivated by a primordial human desire for "social standing" or recognition, a desire that goes beyond the instrumental significance of these rights, white women and factory workers justified their demand for the franchise by wishing to be set apart from, and above, slaves (Shklar 1991: 16–17).

In his *Civic Ideals*, Rogers Smith takes the argument one step further. He claims that the systematic violation of American liberal and republican citizenship ideals in practice must mean that they cannot be privileged analytically either. Thus, civic ideologies containing inegalitarian and exclusionary ascriptive elements, far from being merely the products of prejudice and expediency, have offered competing principles of citizenship in the United States. In his view, these frequently ignoble ascriptive principles (akin to the ethno-nationalist version of citizenship in our terminology) are civic myths which were put forth by elites with the intention of satisfying the dual political imperative of imagining the identity of the people and the legitimacy of its leaders. Thus, Smith offers a "multiple traditions" view of American citizenship, which presents its history as the chronology of the relationships between these competing traditions and their ever-evolving complex and confused compromises, as well as the great eras of democratization and subsequent setbacks, to which they have given rise under changing historical circumstances (Smith 1997: 6, 13–35).

The coexistence, not only of multiple citizenship rights, but also of alternative citizenship traditions or discourses within the same society, poses a number of important questions for sociologists and political theorists. Given the conflicting approaches of these discourses to issues of inclusion and exclusion, what is left of the universalist claims made on behalf of citizenship as full and equal membership in society? If alternative citizenships mean multiple "doors" of entry to membership in society, and doors open to some are closed for others, what are the principles governing the arrangement of these doors? To put the question in the broadest theoretical terms, what is the relationship between citizenship and stratification?

In developing our framework for tackling these questions, we adopt Smith's radical view of "multiple traditions" of citizenship within a single polity. His persuasive application of this pluralist approach to a history customarily described as the greatest triumph of liberal citizenship makes equal sense for many-times segmented Israel, a country that has never even claimed to belong to all of its citizens. We will, however, avoid two of Smith's premises. First, we do not wish to narrow our study of alternative traditions of citizenship to elite perspectives and, as Shklar has sought to do, will seek to round it out by the study of mass movements and popular discourses of citizenship. Second, Smith's characterization of American citizenship as a "none too coherent compromise among the distinct mixes of civic conceptions" (Smith 1997: 6) does not apply to Israel. We believe that there was a coherence to the multiplicity of Israeli citizenships – they were arranged in a hierarchical fashion around the hub of the LSM's republican discourse – as we will argue towards the end of this introduction.

We share Shklar's view that citizenship needs to be framed as a relational entity, a standing or, better yet, a social status. We also agree with her that the true nature of a community is revealed as much by who has been denied full membership in it as by who has been wholeheartedly included. Although her perspective retains a normative concern with exclusion from citizenship, she does not adopt an either/or perspective on citizenship, but inspires us to consider degrees of membership and the relative position of different groups within a seemingly unitary legal framework. Such an approach highlights the internal stratification of citizenship by demonstrating that, in practice, in addition to full citizens, second-, and indeed third- and fourth-class citizens, as well as non-citizens, may exist under a single democratic political authority. While we wish to broaden our perspective beyond the twin rights, to vote and to earn, we agree with Shklar that focusing on such rights is the methodological key to evaluating the degree of membership in, or incorporation into, society.

We do take issue, however, with Shklar and Smith's respective premises that primordial needs compel demands for citizenship and that ascriptive politics are necessary for sustaining political communities. In the US, women's and workers' main rhetorical justification in their struggle for citizenship, as Shklar herself pointed out, was not primordial. They viewed citizenship not as a universal standing but as a privilege that would place them above slaves. Similarly, civic myths do not necessary require ascriptive political imperatives; the latter are just one version, the ethno-nationalist or *völkisch* in this case, of citizenship. The actual historical commingling of civic and ascriptive beliefs does not prove that they are inseparable.

In addition to the lessons learned from Shklar and Smith, we will draw on two additional theoretical sources in the sociological literature on citizenship. T. H. Marshall's historical classification, in his seminal essay "Citizenship and Social Class" (Marshall 1973) will allow us to differentiate between different citizenship rights and connect such rights with social conflict and stratification. Yasemin Soysal's *The Limits of Citizenship* (Soysal 1994) is focused on the relationship between immigrants and the institutions that incorporate them into their host societies through the differential allocation of rights. We adopted this approach, but expanded it to all members of society.

The republican, liberal, and ethno-nationalist theories of citizenship offer normative versions of the "good society," emphasizing the diverse values of freedom, virtue, community, and identity. In 1949 T. H. Marshall offered a sociological perspective on citizenship in the context of the British Labour Party's program of universal provision of welfare services. His approach overlaps with the liberal theory of citizenship, but goes beyond it in a social-democratic direction. Marshall surveys and analyzes the expansion of the rights of citizens as a process of incorporating the working class in twentieth-century Britain into the community of the modern nation-state. The accession to rights, he argues, removes fences between groups previously separated by legal barriers or social custom. New rights make the possession and wielding of previously established rights more effective and, therefore, each time citizenship is expanded it becomes stronger and richer. Marshall's classification of rights is not a prescriptive, or normative, catalog of worthwhile legal or moral claims, but a historical and sociological listing of entitlements that had been won and recognized as legitimate. As a historical study it also introduces into the study of citizenship the element of social change that was missing from the more one-dimensional and static normative approaches.

We will use Marshall's classification as the groundwork for comparing the extent and kinds of equality and inequality that the normative republican, liberal, and ethno-nationalist citizenship discourses have entailed for those to whom they have been extended in Israel. In the section below on Israel's incorporation regime we will demonstrate how we plan to use Marshall's list of citizenship rights to illustrate the stratification of social groups that have entered into society through the different "doors" offered by these three discourses.

Marshall divided the expansion of citizenship into three related, but historically and institutionally separate, stages: civil rights, political rights, and social rights. These rights had accumulated in the eighteenth, nineteenth, and twentieth centuries respectively, in different social institutions that guarantee and dispense them: courts of law, representative legislatures, and the welfare state.

(1) Civil rights are the rights necessary for individual freedom: liberty of the person, freedom of speech, thought and faith, freedom of occupation and of movement in pursuit of that occupation, the right to own property and conclude valid contracts, and the right to due process of law. The institutions entrusted with safeguarding civil rights are the courts of justice.

(2) Political rights ensure participation in the exercise of political power as voter or representative in parliaments and councils of local government.

(3) Social rights make possible the attainment of a modicum of economic welfare and security and, as Marshall elegantly put it, "the right to share to the full in the social heritage and to live the life

of a civilized being according to the standards prevailing in society" (Marshall 1973: 72). These rights are guaranteed by schools and social service institutions.

The importance of Marshall's contribution consists in going beyond the idea that membership in a community is predominantly a political matter: his theory is at once legal, political, economic, and social. Marshall's theory is sociological as well, in that it points out that rights become meaningful only in particular institutional contexts and that they serve different social interests. Institutions, argued Marshall, embed, ensure, and dispense citizenship rights. Still, there is a rich body of empirical studies that criticize Marshall's work for presenting the English case as a universal model and the expansion of citizenship as a linear and irreversible process. These critical studies have opened up a debate over the possible relationships between the different types of rights and, correspondingly, over different types of modern societies. For example, Michael Mann has shown that modernizing absolutist elites granted civil rights, provided, and sometimes even pioneered, limited social rights, but bestowed only sham political citizenship on their subjects. In other cases social citizenship rights have served to constrain, or were even conceived of as a substitute for, civil citizenship. For example, fascism and communism provided no civil or political rights but went furthest toward social citizenship, fascist regimes hesitantly and communist ones aggressively (Mann 1987). Even in Britain, it has been argued, highlighting internal regional variation and giving greater emphasis to the impact of political culture and the public sphere would alter the picture of the evolution of citizenship rights as it was painted by Marshall (Sommers 1993). It has also been shown that for women, including English women, some social rights had in many cases preceded the granting of the two other kinds (Sarvasy 1997: 61).

We feel no need to adopt Marshall's sequence of rights or his analysis of the way they came about. We share, however, his view that citizenship operates as a framework for the incorporation of new groups into the state. Social rights, especially, gave birth to, and were protected by, a whole range of institutions, from medical insurance schemes to unemployment benefits, in the process transforming the state itself into a welfare state.

Marshall's historical account provides a first step for understanding the relations between the sequential expansion of citizenship rights and the dynamics of institutional change. Civil rights enabled the stable and predictable engagement of individuals in the capitalist market; social rights, by contrast, sought to curtail the full commodification of individuals by using the regulatory and distributive powers of the state to limit the purview and sway of the market. The exercise and protection of civil and social rights by their respective institutions thus led to serious clashes. Notwithstanding Marshall's cumulative approach, then, the balance between the institutions safeguarding the two kinds of rights, and concomitantly the very boundaries of the state and, therefore, the sphere and sweep of political rights, have been redrawn over time (Spulber 1997).

The allocation of rights, duties, and privileges to the various social groups constitutes what Soysal (1994) has called an "incorporation regime." This regime defines how resources are allocated to the different social groups by state and para-state institutions, and legitimizes this allocation through a particular conception of citizenship, which we call "citizenship discourse." To understand a particular incorporation regime, therefore, we must be familiar with its main allocative institutions and with the citizenship discourse, or discourses, that prevail in its political culture. Changes in the incorporation regime take place when the interests of various social groups, or the relations of power between them, are modified. These modifications frequently occur in response to changes in the international economic and normative orders and are manifested both institutionally and in terms of the prevailing conception(s) of citizenship.

Citizenship, then, is rarely made of one cloth, and using it as our prism for analyzing Israeli society will require that we examine the different ways of conceptualizing it in their mutual and manifold relationships. By focusing on citizenship, a cumulative tradition of rights and obligations, we can offer a synthetic and in-depth focus on the major structural, institutional, and normative ways of constructing social order and identity and on the way these have fared in the long term, rather than presenting an overview of the hurly-burly of shifting political divisions. In doing that we propose to follow and extend the line leading from Marshall to Soysal in understanding citizenship not only as a bundle of formal rights, but as the entire mode of incorporation of individuals and groups into society. For such an understanding directs our attention to a whole gamut of specific social institutions and raises meaningful empirical questions as to the method, variety, scope, and dynamics of memberships and incorporation.

Neo-institutionalist theory

Our sociological and political study of Israeli citizenship is presented in the context of institutions and institutional regimes, offering a neo-institutionalist perspective on Israeli society. Whereas the study of citizenship has been approached mainly by political and legal theorists from a normative perspective (although, as we saw, it did spawn a sociological branch as well), neo-institutionalist analysis, as formulated in the recent work of John W. Meyer, Douglass North, and others, seeks to identify "institutional effects," that is, offer explanations "that feature institutions as causes" which "simultaneously empower and control" social actors (Jepperson 1991: 153, 146; North 1990; 1998; Meyer 1994; Meyer et al. 1997). For example, Immergut (1992) suggests that the impact of "veto groups" on the political process is filtered through "veto points," namely the locations where groups are allowed to participate in decision making.

Institutions are conventionally defined in terms of norms and values as well as implicit and explicit routines and practices which produce predictable duties and customs. An institutional perspective on citizenship thus allows us to study norms, namely embedded or "institutionalized" rights. Institutionalization frequently signals a stage in which previously contested positions and resources have become depoliticized and decommodified, and are thus viewed as "rights." Institutions play another crucial role: they ensure "rights to rights": they enable and empower citizens to exercise rights they already ostensibly possess. Since even formally universal citizenship rights are frequently not implemented, access to institutions enable citizens to exercise these rights *de facto*, whereas uneven access to institutions might render the same rights meaningless. A focus on citizenship as exercised through institutions promises, therefore, to be an effective analytical tool for our purposes.[2]

New institutionalist theory, however, suffers from a serious shortcoming. By demonstrating how the outcomes of political struggles "are mediated by the institutional setting in which they take place" (Ikenberry 1988: 222–3), institutional analysis is bound to focus on the stable,

---

[2] While we adopt neo-institutionalist analysis as a conceptual link between our analyses of citizenship discourses and the incorporation regime, we do have some important disagreements with this approach. Meyer, for example, argues that the high level of institutional homogeneity found among modern societies is due to the impact of global cultural forces. We see no reason to underestimate the equally potent influence of economic and legal globalization but, even more significantly, believe that the focus on diffusion obscures the struggle between the supporters and opponents of globalization, as well as the vastly different impact of such homogenization on the relative standing of groups located differentially vis-à-vis the resources made available or withdrawn by globalization. North sees social institutions as a means of enhancing performance under given circumstances by reducing transaction costs, and argues that, by so doing, institutions also constrain and shape the range of choices subsequently available to societies and individuals. Whereas Meyer's institutional theory focuses too narrowly on issues of legitimation and social reproduction, downplaying if not ignoring outright their tension with issues of efficiency and goal attainment, North allows us to consider the centrality of these concerns for institutional inertia and transformation (see Powell and DiMaggio 1991: 27). At the same time, while North's economic approach exhibits a built-in bias about efficiency and progress, he seems to ignore distributive issues and distributive justice in general. We feel that these issues are central to understanding the role played by institutions in societies and, in contrast to North's mostly descriptive approach to institutional diversity, also seek to explain the social conditions which propel particular societies to follow their distinct tracks.

or "institutionalized," aspects of the political order. Thus, for the very reasons that studying institutions gives us insight into various aspects of social continuity – homogenization, path dependency, and inertia – the types of social change that may be analyzed and explained through neo-institutionalist analysis remain limited.

Historical institutionalists, who are most sensitized to look beyond the inertia, or "stickiness," of institutions, have highlighted alternative ways in which institutional change occurs. The general assumption behind the analysis of institutional change is that societies comprise several institutional orders and their contradictions allow social actors, during times of social crisis, to try and redefine the institutional logic by which routine actions are conceptualized and regulated (Friedland and Alford 1991). Thelen and Steinmo identify four sources of endogamous change, or institutional dynamism: (1) "previously latent institutions" may suddenly become active and salient; (2) "old institutions [may be] put in the service of different ends"; (3) old actors may decide, frequently under the influence of external changes, to "adopt new goals within the old institutions"; (4) once institutional change has transpired, actors may adjust their strategies to better influence the transformed institution (Thelen and Steinmo 1992: 16–17).

One of the pioneering neo-institutionalist theories seeking to explain institutional transformation is found in Stephen Krasner's approach, which submerges the single institution in the concept of "regime," a set of explicit or implicit principles, norms, rules, and decision-making procedures, around which the expectations of actors converge in order to coordinate policies on issues of common concern (Krasner 1983). The development of institutions after all, as Paul Starr has argued, "takes place within larger fields of power and social structure" (Starr 1982: 8).

Krasner's own explanation of institutional regime change is a model of "punctured equilibrium." Periods of stable institutional life are punctured by crises that lead to the radical restructuring of institutions and to a new period of stability (Krasner 1983). Such crises result from the transformation of the institution's external environment. Krasner emphasized the cultural aspect of his idea of institutional regime, but it is possible to round it out with T. J. Pempel's definition, in which a regime is "a sustained fusion between the institutions of the state and particular segments of the socio-economic order." Regimes, according to Pempel, are based on institutionalized interactions between various social sectors – particularly those that are central to economic activity – with key state institutions (Pempel 1992: 120).

If pushed to account for significant change, neo-institutionalists, as Krasner's example demonstrates, invariably feel compelled to look for explanations outside the institution, first in its relationships with other institutions, and subsequently in external circumstances, namely in the state as a whole or in the international context. Such an outward-looking perspective becomes even more imperative if we are not satisfied with focusing on the consequences of institutional change and wish to explain their causes as well. Neo-institutionalists, however, do not study the dynamic of external circumstances: these serve as the baseline from which they chart institutional change. While our study of the institutions of Israeli citizenship is not the place to offer such an analysis either, we will identify the broader dynamics and theoretical frameworks within which we nest institutions and institutional theory.

Following Immanuel Wallerstein, we suggest that "national states are not societies that have separate, parallel histories, but are parts of a whole" (Wallerstein 1979: 53). It is futile to study one society in isolation from others, since they are interdependent and form a world system which is more than the sum of its parts. Change in one part of the system affects changes in others and, therefore, requires analysis through a global perspective.

The global phenomenon relevant to our study is the series of waves of colonial expansion which, as Bergesen and Schoenberg have argued, resulted from rivalries between great powers wanting to enhance their strategic and economic positions, and, conversely, decolonization, which corresponded to the arrogation of international hegemony by a single power (Bergesen and Schoenberg 1980). The impact the international dynamic has on a single society varies with local conditions and may be illustrated by the fact that whereas the Zionist colonial undertaking occurred at the tail-end of the European colonial drive (which, by then, was focused on Africa), in the current globalization wave Israel stands much nearer to the front of the line. But in both cases, Zionism and Israel are less uncommon than any view of "Israeli exceptionalism" would entail. They respond to the same opportunities and constraints as other societies, although, naturally, the choices each society makes are filtered through its special circumstances and affected by its institutional traditions.

International forces do not determine but influence and constrain the choices of social groups. Under current conditions of globalization, for example, there is a shift in the relative weight of social resources from political to economic. This is not to contend that politics have become irrelevant, or that political aspirations and concerns cannot override economic interests; far from it. But in the 1990s and early 2000s it is becoming costlier to assert the primacy of political and attendant legitimational concerns over economic ones, and the efforts of putting together coalitions to oppose global economic and cultural forces have become more difficult to sustain. Interventionist or developmental states, as well as extensive welfare states, find that they are overextended and under pressure from interested groups to privatize and scale down their activities. Overall, the margin of their relative autonomy in domestic policy areas is frequently reduced.

We argue that the balance of citizenship discourses, rights, and corresponding institutions and incorporation regimes reflects the way in which global changes, mostly economic, but also political, legal, and cultural, enhance the ability of those domestic institutional actors better positioned to take advantage of them to renegotiate their standing vis-à-vis the state and other groups. International changes transform domestic political alliances and through them state structures. Institutional change is likely to take place at such times of "punctured equilibrium" because the crisis of the state provides institutional entrepreneurs with more autonomy and incentive to satisfy their mobilized constituencies. Institutional change, therefore, is frequently the focal point of processes that redress the relationships between social groups and state structures in response to changes in the international sphere and are ultimately reflected in citizenship rights and modes of incorporation.

"Citizenship" is not viewed in this study as an autonomous sphere, purely discursive or causally independent. It is treated, rather, as a "dependent variable" that registers and embodies institutionalized changes originating in a long causal sequence, leading from global and international transformations, through social groups and alliances, to state structures and institutional entrepreneurship. In examining the ways in which the links in this causal chain are enabled, and enable further change, the most important distinctions we will be looking for are: (1) whether the international system is dominated by a single great power, seeking to promote global economic homogenization in its own image, or whether it is a multi-polar system, leading to colonial-type political conflict; (2) whether there is a hegemonic social movement or group that dominates the state, or a pluralistic order in which state and social groups are relatively autonomous; (3) whether major institutions are articulated with each other to form a coherent and rigid "regime," or whether there are multiple institutional orders within a civil society and how "sticky" or flexible institutions are in general; and (4) what are the relationships between the alternative citizenship discourses through which these institutional arrangements are conceptualized and legitimated?

As a consequence of our approach, we do not feel compelled to enter into the debate over the changing boundaries between the state and society. Changes affecting citizens frequently take the form of an institutional reconfiguration in which previously important institutions lose their prestige and resources, while others might grow in stature. Such changes in the articulation of the relations between the many institutions of the state will affect access to citizenship rights. For our purposes, therefore, the state's internal organization is more significant, and easier to determine, than whether state boundaries are shrinking or expanding.

Though state and society are analytically separate concepts, the former comprising political actors and most institutions and the latter social groups and movements, neither is an enclosed sphere. In fact, they meet where, we suggest, citizenship resides, namely, in the overlapping domain of rights, obligations, and institutions. It is here, as we argued earlier, that we find some of the most enduring traditions and frameworks of the social order. Our neo-institutionalist approach to citizenship thus allows us to span two analytical divides that famously challenge sociological and political studies: the divide between state-centered and society-centered approaches, and also the divide between studies that focus on ideas or culture and norms as their main explanatory factors and those that focus on material interests and conflicts. Citizenship occupies an intermediary position between state and society, as it normatively regulates the relationships between the state and individual and collective members of society. Institutions of the kind we will be discussing in this book translate the normative determinations of citizenship into concrete material acts and serve as arenas where distributional conflicts take place. The results of these conflicts are then reflected back onto, and codified by, changes in the prevailing notions of citizenship. In bridging these spheres, citizenship in its institutional manifestations serves as a synthetic tool for the analysis of enduring social structures and long-term changes.

Israel's incorporation regime

We can trace the evolution of the Israeli incorporation regime in four major phases, as new groups were added, differential citizenship rights were either granted or denied, obligations were expected and imposed, and particular institutions were established to administer the resulting *mélange*. While each stage has been associated with the entry, or exit, of new groups, the three citizenship discourses – republican, ethno-national, and liberal – coexisted, in various combinations, through all phases.

The first phase began with the onset of Zionist colonization in Palestine in 1882. The frequently heard argument that Zionist settlement in Palestine differed radically from European colonialism rests on the narrow basis of the claim that, in the terms used by frontier theorists D. K. Fieldhouse (1966) and George Fredrickson (1988), the Zionist movement did not create in Palestine either an "occupation" or a "mixed settlement colony." Moreover, its experiment with "plantation-type colony," during the period of the First Aliya (1882–1903), was rejected by the worker-settlers of the Second Aliya (1904–14), who founded the LSM. This rejection, however, did not stem from moral objections to colonialism. It stemmed, rather, from economic and demographic considerations: the failure of the plantation-type colony to provide employment for a sufficiently large number of Jewish immigrants, given the preference of Jewish plantation owners for lower-priced, indigenous Palestinian labor. But while the Labor Zionists rejected other colonial models, they had their own favored settlement strategy – "homogeneous settlement colony" – that was also a variant of European colonization (see Shafir 1989).

The LSM was constituted from early on as a republican virtue enterprise, organized to achieve a common moral purpose – the success of the Zionist colonial project. The civic virtue associated with the LSM, *chalutziyut* (pioneering), was a composite of two virtuous qualities, corresponding to the two bases of legitimation invoked by the Zionist settlers: Jewish historical rights in Palestine and the redemptive activity of the pioneers, consisting of physical labor, agricultural settlement, and military service. To be virtuous meant, therefore, being a secular nationalist Jewish *chalutz*. Thus the foundation was laid for distinguishing between the civic virtue and consequent rights and privileges, not only of Jews and Arabs, but also of different groupings within the Jewish community, based on their presumed contributions to the project of Zionist redemption (Eisenstadt 1968; Horowitz and Lissak 1978; Peled 1992).

The most unique institutions of *chalutziyut* – the various cooperative bodies, above all the kibbutz and later on the moshav, the paramilitary organization of the *Hagana*, and the all-encompassing, powerful proto-state of the Histadrut (the General Federation of Hebrew Workers in Eretz Israel), as well as the Jewish National Fund (JNF), an organ of the World Zionist Organization (WZO) – formed a coherent institutional regime in support of the colonial project. This institutional regime was democratic, in that the individual rights of Jews, even those not belonging to the LSM, and the procedural rules of democracy, were largely respected in it; it was social, in that it was concerned most of all with the social rights of its "citizens." Both features were mandated by the Yishuv's semi-voluntary nature (enjoying "authority without sovereignty," in the language of conventional Israeli sociology) and by the need to keep all Jews, and all Jewish social sectors, within its bounds, both physically and politically.

The second phase in the history of Israel's incorporation regime began with the achievement of statehood in 1948. This phase saw the mass immigration of both Ashkenazi and Mizrachi Jews, and the expulsion and flight of the majority of Palestine's Arab population. A new ethos, *mamlachtiyut*, was invoked to legitimate this phase, an ethos that emphasized the shift from sectoral interests to the general interest, from semi-voluntarism to binding obligation, from foreign rule to political sovereignty. Equal application of the law was of paramount importance if the state was to assert its authority over the various Jewish social sectors, which had enjoyed a large degree of autonomy in the Yishuv (Peled 1992).

Israel's first premier, David Ben-Gurion, was the great exponent of *mamlachtiyut* and of its key element, the uniform rule of law:

Only in a state in which everyone – citizen, soldier, official, minister, legislator, judge and policeman – is subject to the law and acts according to the law; only in a state in which there is no arbitrariness, neither of ministers or rulers, nor of representatives of the people, and also not of individuals and political leaders – only in a state such as this is freedom guaranteed to the individual and to the many, to the person and to the people. (Cited in Medding 1990: 138)

By virtue of the ethno-nationalist Law of Return, enacted in 1950, Jewish immigrants became Israeli citizens upon arrival, and received broader and more substantial rights than the Palestinians citizens. Among Jewish immigrants, Ashkenazim had better access to state institutions than Mizrachim, although there was some internal differentiation within these two groups as well, depending largely on their time of arrival. In this context, the "1948 Palestinians," those who remained within the "Green Lines" of Israel's armistice borders, were granted Israeli citizenship, albeit within a weak and formalistic liberal framework that made them into lesser citizens. Moreover, most of the rights conveyed by this lesser citizenship were suspended in fact by the military government that was imposed on Israel's Palestinians citizens in 1948 and was to last until 1966.

Overall, republicanism continued to predominate and its sway was extended by the new state. As understood in the context of *mamlachtiyut*, the uniform rule of law did not entail a neutral liberal state or a universal conception of citizenship. The state was to continue to be committed to the values of *chalutziyut* and to demand such commitment from its citizens. As phrased by Ben-Gurion:

Even if in their private lives they act as *chalutzim*, both the individual, and the organizations of individuals, will fail if they do not put their *chalutzic* activity in the service of the state, and if the state's financial, organizational and legislative power is not committed to the *chalutzic* tasks that are thrust upon us. (Cited in Medding 1990: 136)

Mamlachtiyut, then, was not meant to displace the pioneering legitimating ethos or abandon the colonial project. Quite the contrary: it was meant to endow them with the organizational and political resources of a sovereign state. And individuals and social groups were to continue to be treated by the state in accordance with their contributions to the common good as defined by the Zionist vision (Peled 1992). This continuity can best be seen by the fact that, side by side with new state institutions, the LSM's and the WZO's older institutions, responsible for the colonial state-building undertaking, continued to operate. Some of the newly created institutions, among them the Supreme Court and the Bank of Israel, remained feeble, since they did not fit into the preexisting institutional regime and remained on its margin.

In the third phase, a new colonial drive opened with the conquests of the 1967 war. The Palestinian Arab population of the Gaza Strip and the West Bank were brought under Israeli military rule, and East Jerusalem and the Golan Heights were brought under Israeli sovereignty as well. Increasingly massive Jewish colonization was undertaken in these newly conquered areas and their Palestinian residents remained as non-citizens under Israel's military rule. The seeds were thus planted for the hostility and later active resistance, mostly of the 1948 refugees living in camps in Gaza and the West Bank, as well as outside Israel. It was this resistance that shaped the primary political organ of Palestinian nationalism, the Palestine Liberation Organization (PLO), and led, eventually, to the beginning of accommodation between Israel and the Palestinians in 1993.

The fourth phase, which began around 1985, with the decline and end of the Cold War and the rise of the US to a position of global hegemony, and which continues at the time of writing, is characterized not only by the addition of new social groups – immigrants from the former Soviet Union and from Ethiopia and labor migrants from all corners of the globe – but by a profound reevaluation of the incorporation regime itself. The republican mode of incorporation, which was hegemonic during the first three phases, has fallen into crisis and its decline has led to direct conflict between liberal and ethno-nationalist citizenship aspirations, the latter more clearly than ever attired in religious garb.

The first severe political challenge to republicanism and call for liberalization from within the LSM itself came as early as 1965, with the secession from Mapai of the Israel Workers' List (Rafi), headed by none others than David Ben-Gurion, Moshe Dayan, and Shimon Peres. This was a time when the crisis of the developmental state had led to the most severe economic recession which, however, came to an abrupt halt due to the prosperity that followed the territorial acquisitions of 1967. The boom period that followed the 1967 war caused the demands for liberalization to be suspended until after the 1973 war, the war that ended that period of prosperity.

The first serious effort to deal with the economic crisis through liberalization, the Emergency Economic Stabilization Plan of 1985, took place at almost the same time as the onset of sustained Palestinian resistance to the occupation – the first intifada – in 1987. The immediate impetus for overhauling the old incorporation regime came, then, simultaneously from the most privileged and the most oppressed groups in the society – the veteran Ashkenazi elite interested in liberalization and the non-citizen Palestinians seeking emancipation from Israeli rule. Other social groups have been playing secondary roles, whether in supporting liberalization or in opposing it.

Two distinct types of institutional change, each with far-reaching consequences for citizenship, have occurred as part of the liberalization process. The first type undermined the high level of institutional coherence and stability that typified the LSM's institutional regime, a regime that crystallized in the Yishuv and allowed the LSM to shape the contours of, and later assume control over, the Israeli state as well. With the decline of the LSM and republican citizenship, state institutions, and those institutions for which the state provided funding and legal standing, no longer formed a coherent institutional regime. The LSM's own institutions, however, demonstrated considerable stickiness, to the point where they came to be viewed as anathema not only by those excluded from their benefits, but even by a growing segment of the LSM establishment itself. The latter viewed these institutions as obstacles both to the effective management of the economy and to the Labor Party's ability to reconnect with the electorate and return to power after 1977. The opponents of the LSM's institutional regime within the Labor party took over the LSM's flagship institution, the Histadrut, in the 1994 elections and stripped it of its remaining power and prestige by allowing the nationalization of its Sick Fund (HMO).

The second type of change was the emergence of institutional entrepreneurship, both liberal and religious, on an unprecedented scale, and the accumulation of power in the hands of new institutions. Whereas during the first three phases of the incorporation regime the LSM institutions played the key roles in society, during the fourth phase institutions such as the Supreme Court, the Bank of Israel, the Finance Ministry, and the more diffuse bodies of the business community, which had been weak and marginal before, came to occupy the center stage. As against these liberal institutions, new or newly empowered religious institutions, many of them associated with the Mizrachi *charedi* party, Shas, have come to represent the pull of ethno-nationalism. Thus, one way in which Israelis experience the current crisis is through the pull-and-tug of openly competing institutions.

Ideologically, the decline of the republican discourse – the primary ideological tool of social cohesion – has resulted in fierce competition for supremacy between the partisans of the two other discourses – liberal and ethno-nationalist – each of which appears now as a comprehensive alternative in its own right. This competition is evident in the deepening of political fragmentation and instability in Israeli society, the most pronounced and tragic manifestation of which was the assassination of Prime Minister Yitzhak Rabin in November 1995. The brief tenures in office enjoyed by three of Rabin's successors to date – Shimon Peres, Benjamin Netanyahu, and Ehud Barak – are yet another indication of this political fragmentation and instability.

The liberalization of Israeli society both resulted from and was meant to enhance Israel's integration into the processes of economic globalization. The peace process, which began with the Egyptian–Israeli peace signed in 1979 and reached a turning point with the Oslo Accords of 1993, is part and parcel of the broader processes of globalization and liberalization. Both the global system that Israel is increasingly integrated with and the economically powerful social groups within Israeli society that seek globalization and liberalization speak the language of liberal citizenship and Lockean civil society (although in Israel this language still carries many marks of its Zionist birth).

The ascendancy of the liberal discourse came, however, at the price of seriously weakening social citizenship rights. Moreover, liberalization, the weakening of state and other welfare institutions as against market-based interests, should be distinguished from democratization, allowing larger numbers of people greater access to decision-making institutions. In Israel, some aspects of liberalization are having democratizing effects, in that they substitute market-based for ascriptive criteria in determining access to various resources. Other aspects of liberalization, however, both economic and political, have contra-democratic effects, especially with respect to people belonging to the lower socio-economic strata. This process of disempowerment is driving many Israelis, both Jews and Palestinians, to seek support in particularistic ethnic and religious organizations. As a result, the fourth phase is distinguished also by the emergence of demands for a new kind of citizenship rights – group cultural rights (cf. Beyer 1994).

To conclude this section, we propose to view the trajectory of the development of Israeli citizenship as a process of evolution from a colonial frontier to a civil society. A frontier is "a territory or zone of interpenetration between two previously distinct societies" (Lamar and Thompson 1981: 7), characterized by a more or less open conflict over territory between differentially incorporated social groups. According to Lamar and Thompson, "probably the nearest contemporary approach to the kind of frontier ... where rival societies compete for control of the land, is to be found in Israel" (1981: 312). As mentioned above, civil society has been variously defined: liberals see it as a society where a sphere of private, largely economic activity exists autonomously of the state, while republicans see it as a society where a sphere of voluntary public activity exists autonomously of both the state and the market (Taylor 1990; Cohen and Arato 1992; Seligman 1992; 1995).[3] By all accounts, during its fourth phase of development Israel has been moving from a state-dominated society to a civil society in the former, liberal sense of the term (Ezrahi 1997; Hirschl 2000b; Peled and Ophir 2001).

As a latecomer among frontier societies, Israeli society was state dominated, because it was engaged in a massive, publicly financed and organized colonial settlement project. It operated under the cross pressures of demographic, military, political, and legitimational necessities and, like the Yishuv before it, achieved a workable accommodation between the exclusivist goals of Zionist nation building and the integrative imperative of democratic state building. This was done through the use of the republican discourse of citizenship to legitimate the colonial practices by mediating between the exclusionary and integrative tendencies of the ethno-national and liberal discourses respectively. The result was a hierarchical and fragmented incorporation regime, wherein different groups – citizens and non-citizens, Jews and Palestinians, Ashkenazim and Mizrachim, men and women, religious and secular – were placed in accordance with their conceived contribution to the Zionist cause.

Conceptually, the differential allocation of entitlements, obligations, and domination as between the different social groups can be thought of as having proceeded in a number of stages: First, the liberal discourse of citizenship functioned to separate the citizen Jews and Palestinians from non-citizen Palestinians in the occupied territories and abroad, whether these Palestinians were conceived of as refugees or as stateless, non-citizen subjects of Israel's military occupation. Then the ethno-nationalist discourse of inclusion and exclusion was invoked (often under the guise of the republican discourse), in order to discriminate between Jewish and Palestinian citizens within the area of the sovereign state of Israel. Lastly, the republican discourse was used to legitimate the different positions occupied by the major Jewish groupings: Ashkenazim versus Mizrachim, men versus women, secular versus religiously orthodox.

The key to this multiple and hierarchical citizenship framework, and to the complex incorporation regime for which it provided legitimation,

---

[3] The term "civil society" is often used to describe not the whole society but only that sphere of autonomous activity within it, however defined.

was the hegemony of the LSM. That hegemony lasted from around the mid-1930s till about the mid-1960s, sustained by the perceived effectiveness of the LSM's colonial strategy in ensuring the attainment of national sovereignty. As the colonial project fulfilled, and thereby exhausted, itself it ceased to serve the dominant interests in society, which began to promote liberalization and the institutions of civil society in the narrow sense of the term. The liberalization of Israeli society was stimulated by the fact that the international environment presented opportunities that a relatively liberal society could more easily take advantage of. Thus, the transition from frontier to civil society saw the decline of the institutions of republican citizenship and the strengthening of institutions that represent either a Jewish ethno-nationalist or a liberal citizenship discourse, resulting in a sustained struggle between them. To put it differently, the end of the colonial state-building period, and the decline of its attendant republican citizenship, released and compelled the proponents of the Jewish and the democratic commitments to battle between themselves. Significantly, however, the legacy of the state-building period still drives and constrains the line-up and alliances of the social groups involved in this struggle.

Alternative theoretical perspectives on Israeli society

So far, four groups of studies of Israeli society of the scope attempted in this book have been published: by S. N. Eisenstadt (1968; 1985), by his students Dan Horowitz and Moshe Lissak (1978; 1989), by Yonathan Shapiro (1976; 1977; 1996a), and by Sammy Smooha (1978). If we consider the theoretical perspectives informing these studies, their number will go down even further, to three: functionalism (Eisenstadt, Horowitz and Lissak), elitism (Shapiro), and cultural pluralism (Smooha). The questions we would like to pose in this concluding section of the introduction are how have issues of membership and its institutional effects been analyzed through these perspectives, and in what ways can our neo-institutionalist study of Israeli citizenship and the Israeli incorporation regime improve on these analyses?

Crisis and overburden: the theoretical impasse of functionalism

The functionalist school has a strongly systemic, quasi-organic view of society, seeing it as a composite of specialized roles, each contributing its share to the proper functioning of the whole. The most crucial task of any social system, in this view, is to maintain its own integrity and stability, a task assigned primarily to a consensual culture which synchronizes individual interests with society's needs. The state (variously referred to as "polity," "political system," or "center") is viewed as standing above the fray of civil society, entrusted with regulating, through its rational and neutral bureaucracies, the competition between the various social interests for material and symbolic resources. This conceptual framework is notoriously conservative, since it allows no analytical room for legitimate conflict over the definition of the governing normative consensus itself, hence no room for significant, non-disruptive social change. When the demands of non-elite groups (or "peripheries") outstrip the resources available to the state and / or its ability to mediate between the different claims, perforce the system is viewed as "overloaded" or "overburdened."

Functionalist analysis is framed by the existing social order and views the prevailing culture as the main integrative mechanism in society. It therefore tends to take the prevailing self-image of society as authoritative. In our case, this tendency meshed very well with the personal commitment of most Israeli sociologists to Labor Zionism, which was the dominant ideology throughout the formative period of the society, as well as their own formative years as individuals.[4] Zionist ideology, in the version promoted by the LSM, was thus elevated to the status of an objective depiction of reality in the dominant paradigm of Israeli sociology. In fact, the protracted period of dominance of functionalist analysis in Israel, which lasted into the 1980s, long after its demise in Europe and the US, is to be explained by the close identification of its practitioners with the "national interest" (Shapiro 1985; for a detailed historical-sociological analysis of the different schools of Israeli sociology see Ram 1995).

The coincidence between functionalist sociology and Labor Zionism was expressed most clearly through the theory of modernization. The view of modernization as an essentially benign process, consisting in the peaceful diffusion of universalist values and modern institutions from Europe to the rest of the world, was very congenial to the theorists, practitioners, and academic interpreters of Zionism. It helped explain the Zionists' behavior towards both the Palestinians and non-European Jews in a way that did not seem to violate the LSM's commitment to universalist, even socialist, values. Another aspect of modernization theory, namely its view of "modern" (i.e. European) culture as active, and all "traditional" cultures as passive, led to the description of the Yishuv and the state of Israel as at once Jewish, Western, democratic, and "revolutionary."

---

[4] Nowhere is the fusion between personal (understanding of) experience and sociological argument more evident than in Dan Horowitz's posthumously published autobiographical essay (Horowitz 1993).

Modernization theory also served to downplay the inevitability of the conflict with the Palestinian Arab population that ensued from Zionist immigration and colonization. Both the LSM and Israeli functionalist sociologists relied, rhetorically at least, on the prospects of future economic benefits to counter the lure of Arab nationalism. They argued that the Palestinian masses were to benefit from the modernization of Palestine, brought on by Zionist immigration and settlement, and therefore had no rational reason to oppose it. Unfortunately, the Palestinians, like many traditional peoples elsewhere, refused to avail themselves of this opportunity for improvement and chose to fight Zionist settlement instead. This tragic shortsightedness was the main factor responsible for the Jewish–Palestinian conflict.

This argument is inconsistent, however, with another argument, repeated *ad nauseam* by Israeli functionalist sociology, namely that Zionist settlement in Palestine, in spite of its self-evident similarities with other colonial movements, was not a colonial venture imposed on the Palestinian inhabitants. Rather, it was an attempt to establish a modern European society side by side with the local population, without either displacing or exploiting it. Ironically, whereas the first argument asserted that Labor Zionism was to have beneficial effects on Palestinian society, the second held that it was to have no impact at all (Gorni 1968; Lissak 1996; Shafir 1996a: xi–xii; Horowitz and Lissak 1978: 16–17; Aronsohn 1997; Tsahor 1997).

So impressed have Israel's functionalist sociologists been with the idea of two societies coexisting side by side in the same country that even when Jews and Palestinians lived together under one political sovereignty, as many of them have done continuously since the beginning of Zionist settlement, they never viewed them as belonging to the same society. This has been true with respect to both Israel's Palestinian citizens and the non-citizen Palestinians residing in the territories occupied in 1967. The Jewish–Arab conflict, in all of its manifestations, was thus externalized, and was seen, like the Palestinians themselves, as an "issue" affecting Israeli society from without, rather than as a constitutive element in the structuring of the emergent society, which was viewed as exclusively Jewish (Deutsch 1985; Ehrlich 1987). While the political reasons for such myopic views are self-evident, this inward-looking bias has been enhanced by functionalist sociology's excessive preoccupation with demarcating borders between societies; in fact, "boundary maintenance" is viewed by functionalism as one of the central functions of every organization.

Yet another use of modernization theory was the analysis of, and policy recommendations for, the relationships between the veteran, pre-1948

Jewish population of Palestine and the Mizrachi immigrants who joined it in the 1950s. The key concepts informing this analysis were "culture-contact" and "absorption through modernization," referring to the view that non-European immigrants came to Israel without having undergone modernization in their countries of origin and with only lukewarm commitment to Zionism in its secular, let alone socialist, form. They thus faced serious problems of adjustment to the norms of the receiving society and these have affected their ability to be "absorbed" by its institutions (Lissak 1999).

Simultaneously, and again inconsistently, functionalist sociology uncritically repeated the LSM's own self-depiction as a "service elite," whose universal aspect rested on its promise to extend the benefits of modernization to other Jewish immigrants. This promise notwithstanding, when efforts to "resocialize" the Mizrachim turned out to have been a failure, this failure was laid at the Mizrachim's own doorstep, not at that of their LSM mentors. Thus, not unlike the Palestinians, the Mizrachim have been conceptualized as adding to the polity's burdens, especially since the second generation, more assertive than their immigrant parents, came of voting age in the mid-1970s.

According to functionalist analysis the crumbling of the LSM, and its replacement by Likud at the helm of government in 1977, resulted from the cumulative weight of the claims placed on the universalist, democratic center of society, which was too open to the conflicting demands of the peripheries. The crisis of overburden came to a head with the Arab–Israeli war of 1967. Until then, so the argument goes, the tension created by the dual commitment to Jewishness and to democracy was manageable by the "center," since the major issues of the society's collective identity – territorial, demographic, and cultural – had been decided by the end of the Arab–Israeli war of 1948. The 1967 war reopened these issues (many of which were now defined in terms of citizenship and its attendant rights) by extending Israel's boundaries to include the entire territory of Mandatory Palestine with its then close to two million Palestinian inhabitants (Eisenstadt 1985: 356–83).

The reopening of these most crucial issues of societal identity gave rise to intensive conflicting demands pulling in two opposite directions. The national and religious right have demanded that the newly occupied territories, particularly the biblically significant West Bank, be formally incorporated into Israel, and their Palestinian inhabitants either expelled or retained as non- or second-class citizens. The universalist, secular left has been demanding that at least the most populous areas of the occupied territories be relinquished, so as to maintain the demographic balance between Arabs and Jews in Israel, and with it the balance between the country's commitments to Jewishness and to democracy. Since the fault line between these two camps passed within the ruling Labor Party itself (Beilin 1985), the party, and the state with it, have fallen into a crisis of "overburden" (Horowitz and Lissak 1989). This crisis was manifested in paralysis and inaction over the most crucial issues facing the country, and eventually in Labor's loss of its dominant position in the society in 1977.

The main empirical evidence supporting the notion of Israel as an over-burdened polity was provided by the ten-year apparent stalemate in Israeli policy towards the occupied territories (1967–77) and by the highly inflationary economic policies pursued by Likud during its first two terms in office (1977–84). Ample evidence indicating that the Israeli state was perfectly capable of bold and innovative action, such as the 1982 invasion of Lebanon and the 1985 pull-out from there; the Emergency Economic Stabilization Plan of 1985, which brought rampant inflation to an abrupt halt and expedited the process of economic liberalization; and most importantly, the 1979 peace agreement with Egypt, were all but ignored in mainstream sociological analyses of the period. The peace treaty with Egypt, for example, was mentioned only in passing and without any theoretization in the two main texts of the dominant paradigm (Eisenstadt 1985: 510–11; Horowitz and Lissak 1989: 196–7, 201).

Likud's coming to power in 1977 signified, for functionalist analysis, the victory of irrational, primordial, anti-democratic nationalism over the modern, universalist, democratic ethos of the LSM. All the more so since Likud, it was argued, had come to power on the strength, primarily, of the votes of Mizrachi Jews, whose political culture was particularistic, authoritarian, and anti-modern (see Peled 1990). These political character traits manifested themselves in the policies adopted by Likud-led governments: massive settlement in the occupied territories; the 1982 invasion of Lebanon, designed to destroy the PLO and settle the Palestinian question by force; and a populist economic policy which resulted in disastrous hyper-inflation by the time Labor came back to power, in partnership with Likud, in 1984.

The problem with this conceptualization of the political transition of 1977 is that Israeli society, like the Yishuv before it, had always been characterized not by universalism but by differentially allocated rights, duties, and privileges to the various social groups. As Shafir (1989) has already shown with respect to the formative period of the Yishuv (1882–1914), and as we will show further in this book, the LSM's universalist rhetoric and partially universalist state-building practices masked highly exclusionist policies, with respect to Palestinians, Mizrachi Jews, and all women. The functionalists' center-oriented analysis failed to see this because it took the universalistic promises of the LSM at face value. As a result, it misrepresented both the overall layout of Israeli society and the causes underlying Labor's political downfall.

The functionalists' conceptualization of Israel's state crisis (and of the loss of power by the LSM, which for them amounted to the same thing) involved a contradiction, then. If incorporation under the LSM was as universalist as functionalism made it out to be, its extension to new groups should not have led to the weakening of the LSM, but rather to its strengthening, and the very problem of overload would not have emerged. As it turned out, however, according to functionalist analysis not only did the demands for universal citizenship directed at Israel's allegedly most universalistically assimilationist institutional complex – the LSM – lead to a regime-level crisis, they also seem to have led, incongruously, to the victory of particularist citizenship frameworks and political parties over universalism itself.

In sum, our objection to the functionalist perspective is twofold. First, its exaggerated attribution of universalism (liberalism in our terminology) to Israel's citizenship regime conceals a pervasive multidimensional citizenship framework which stratifies, rather than assimilates, its citizens. Second, its systemic approach, which views society as practically an organism, overemphasizes the importance of boundary maintenance, leading to an inward-looking, insular perspective on society. Thus, Israel's creation is construed as purely a nationalist project, in ignorance of its attachment to the coattails of nineteenth-century European colonialism. These two limitations converge in the externalizing of central aspects of Israel's and the LSM's colonial dimension. Most importantly, the Jewish–Arab conflict is treated as external to the society, rather than as a defining aspect of its history and as the key to understanding the LSM as a hegemonic movement ridden with contradictions.

A theoretical perspective that views Israel, or any other society, as a closed, insular system will have great difficulties in explaining its development, especially in the current period. Borders between societies have always been porous, and they are becoming even more so with globalization. Nation-states and social groups are increasingly influenced by global processes, which enable and constrain their choices. The current socioeconomic liberalization that is taking place in Israel, and its attendant decolonization, were inspired simultaneously by the incentives offered by the current wave of globalization and by internal pressures to redefine Israel's multilevel citizenship incorporation regime. The dilemma of democracy and Jewishness is indeed one of the problems that haunt this project; but to comprehend it, we need to study "Israel in the world."

The challenge of elite theory

For many years the functionalist paradigm dominated the field of Israeli sociology and provided the social scientific perspective and terminology for the self-understanding of Israeli society. Since the mid-1970s, however, it has not had the field to itself. Two important challenges, one guided by elite theory, the other by cultural pluralism, have confronted the dominant paradigm at precisely the point that underlies the notion of overburden. Far from being too democratic, these challengers argued, the problems of Israeli society stem, at least in part, from its being not democratic enough.

Yonathan Shapiro, in a study of Achdut Haavoda (the major Jewish workers' party in Palestine in the 1920s and early precursor of the present Labor Party), sought to refute the image of the Labor Zionist leadership as a "service elite," dedicated to the creation of a universalist society and egalitarian polity. Following in the footsteps of Roberto Michels and C. Wright Mills, Shapiro argued that the party leadership behaved like any other power elite, seeking to maintain, enhance, and extend its power over the party, the LSM, the Jewish community in Palestine and, eventually, the WZO. In order to do that the leadership built an impressive bureaucratic apparatus which helped it gain control over the funds funneled into Palestine by the WZO and use them to enhance its dominance over the emerging Yishuv. Socialist values were used by the leadership for legitimational and mobilizational purposes, but were never taken seriously as guidelines for political action (Shapiro 1976; for a critique of Labor Zionist ideology, rather than its practices, see Sternhell 1998).

Although democracy was espoused by the LSM's leadership, it was democracy in the procedural sense only. The semi-voluntary nature of the Yishuv, where state power was in the hands of the British, and the voluntary nature of the LSM itself, forced the leadership to rely on democratic procedures. Substantive democracy, however, which Shapiro identified with liberal democracy, was another matter altogether. Such a democracy required, according to Shapiro, the existence of autonomous rival elites– professional, intellectual, economic – that could serve as counter-weights to the political elite. It was precisely the development of such autonomous elites, however, that the Labor leadership feared most and did everything in its substantial power to stifle. As a result, Israel has notoriously lacked the network of viable, autonomous economic, professional, intellectual, and civic associations the presence of which makes for the existence of civil society (Shapiro 1976; 1977; 1996a).

The second generation of the LSM leadership was so overshadowed by the generation of founders that when, in the course of time, it succeeded the latter to the throne, its narrow, technocratic outlook made it incapable of performing its leadership role. On top of that, this second generation was confronted with the consequences of its predecessors' treatment of Mizrachi Jews as second-class citizens and disdain for the interests of middle-class groups. The resentment of these two social sectors, coupled with the new elite's incompetence, enabled the right-wing, populist Likud to take over in 1977 (Shapiro 1984; 1989).

Shapiro was the first major dissident from functionalist orthodoxy in Israeli sociology. His work constituted a breakthrough in the study of Israeli society, as he focused not on the ideology of the pioneering generation, but rather on its institutional practices, and introduced the notions of power, conflict, and generational change into Israeli sociological discourse (see Sternhell 1999).

Although he transformed the central concern of Israeli sociology and political science from state building to democratization, Shapiro's work remained limited in two important ways. First, his elitist theoretical perspective, a perspective that made him focus on elite politics in the narrow sense of the term, led him to neglect non-elite sectors of the society. Ironically, then, Shapiro, who was very critical of the Labor Zionist "center," remained center-oriented in his own analysis and excluded from his purview the struggle of both Mizrachim and Palestinians for extended citizenship rights. Second, though Shapiro's approach was not inward looking or insular – he identified the source of the LSM's success in constructing its impressive bureaucratic apparatus in its ability to gain control over the funds raised from world Jewry by the WZO – he did not extend this outward-looking perspective to external influences beyond the Jewish circles of the WZO.

The cultural pluralist formulation

The other major challenge to the dominant paradigm to appear in the 1970s was articulated by Sammy Smooha, from the theoretical perspective of cultural pluralism, as developed by M. G. Smith, Leo Kuper, and others (Smooha 1978). Smooha was the first major Israeli sociologist to include the Mizrachim and Israel's Palestinian citizens as integral elements in his definition of Israeli society. This society, he argued, was formed around three major cleavages: a national cleavage between Jews and Arabs, an ethnic cleavage between Ashkenazi and Mizrachi Jews, and a cultural cleavage between religiously Orthodox and non-observant Jews. Lately Smooha has added a fourth cleavage – the class cleavage between rich and poor (Smooha 1993a).

These three (or four) cleavages are not symmetrical in their degree of antagonism, in their invidiousness, and in their intractability. Ranking highest in all three parameters is the national cleavage between Jews and Palestinians. The status of its Palestinian citizens makes Israel, according to Smooha, an "ethnic democracy," a "third-rate" democracy to be distinguished from the majoritarian and consociational models above it, and from *Herrenvolk* democracy below it. An ethnic democracy combines "the extension of political and civil rights to individuals and certain collective rights to minorities with institutionalized dominance over the state by one of the ethnic groups" (Smooha 1990: 391; see also 1992: 21; 1997; 2000; for critiques see Ghanem et al. 1999; Sa'di 2000; Jamal 2000; Gross 2000a).

Smooha shares with the functionalists their recent notion that the Israeli polity is motivated by two contradictory political commitments: to the Jewish character of the state and to its democratic form of government (Smooha 1990: 391–5). This contradiction, however, can account for only two of the three cleavages he has identified, those between Jews and Palestinians and between Orthodox and secular Jews. The Ashkenazi–Mizrachi cleavage, namely the exclusion of Mizrachim, can obviously not be explained by the contradiction between Jewishness and democracy, since both principles are inclusionary with respect to both groups.

Smooha's perspective then is wanting in two areas. First, though his pluralist approach made him pioneer the rejection of LSM-centered sociology, his approach lacks any systemic element. In the best tradition of the theory of cultural pluralism, Smooha's cleavages exist side by side, without forming a coherent structure that could serve as a basis for a comprehensive analysis of the society as an integrated whole. While he aptly characterized Jewish–Palestinian relations within the formal bounds of Israeli sovereignty as "ethnic democracy," he failed to realize that this regime could be sustained only as part of a larger incorporation regime that included all other social cleavages and was legitimated with the help of all discourses of citizenship prevailing in the society. Thus the Ashkenazi–Mizrachi cleavage was shaped by both of the other cleavages: within the colonial state-building project the LSM viewed Mizrachim as second-class participants in the struggle against Palestinian Arabs, while the secular–Orthodox cleavage provided Mizrachim with a legitimate way of expressing their socio-economic grievances as a second-class Jewish group.

In addition, Smooha also adopted the insular perspective, according to which Israeli society is defined by the armistice boundaries of 1949, which mark the official extent of Israeli state sovereignty, and not by social realities as they existed at the time of the Yishuv and again since 1967. As a result, there is one major cleavage that Smooha's analysis misses altogether: the Israeli–Palestinian conflict.[5] This conflict partially overlaps with the one between Israeli and Palestinian citizens of Israel, but Smooha, who has pioneered the study of Israel's Palestinian citizens as a constitutive element of the society, has treated them as an Israeli social group and separated them, analytically, from all other Palestinians and from the broader Israeli–Palestinian conflict.

Conclusion

Since Shapiro and Smooha made their critical theoretical breakthroughs in the mid-1970s, a whole generation of critical social scientists has emerged and has come to intellectual and professional maturity. These social scientists are critical in a dual sense: of the practices of the Zionist leadership and the state of Israel, and of the traditional, that is, functionalist mode of analyzing Israeli society. Together with the "new historians," these social scientists form one side in the so-called "post-Zionism debate" (Ram 1995; Lissak 1996; Silberstein 1996; 1998; Weitz 1997).

The theoretical insights and empirical findings of the critical social scientists have completely transformed the face of Israeli social science. Baruch Kimmerling has pointed to the great importance of territory, frontier, and boundaries in the theory and practice of Zionism, and has shed new light on crucial issues such as the relationships between Judaism as an ideology and an identity and the Israeli–Arab conflict. Shlomo Swirski pioneered the study of the Mizrachim from their own point of view, rather than that of the Ashkenazi elite, and analyzed the history of the Israeli education system from that perspective. Michael Shalev and Lev Grinberg have studied the political economy of Israel and the role of the LSM in forming and managing it for many decades, and Shalev, primarily, has also focused on the Israeli welfare state. Oren Yiftachel, a geographer, has applied spatial analysis to the study of ethnic relations in Israel, both Jewish–Palestinian and intra-Jewish, and to the study of the Israeli state. Uri Ben-Eliezer has studied military–civilian relations, particularly in the crucial, formative decades of the 1930s and 1940s.

The present study, which, to the best of our knowledge, is the first attempt to present a comprehensive analysis of Israeli society from the

---

[5] In his seminal work Smooha mentioned five cleavages: the three mentioned here plus Jewish–Palestinian relations and interreligious relations among Israel's Palestinian citizens. The latter two cleavages were not discussed in the book (or in Smooha's later work), however, for "lack of data" (Smooha 1978: 4).

"new" or "critical" perspective, would not have been possible if not for the work of these and many other scholars, in the fields of sociology, political science, anthropology, history, geography, law, and other fields. We share with these scholars a number of crucial basic assumptions: that, as a unit of analysis, "Israeli society" includes both Jews and Palestinians; that the boundaries of this unit should extend to the limits of Israel's effective rule; that interests, rather than ideas, are the prime moving power of history; and that social and historical analysis should focus, therefore, on actions and their results, rather than on intentions and their ideological justifications.

What we offer in this book, then, is a novel theoretical approach to the historical–sociological analysis of the Yishuv and Israeli society, and potentially to the analysis of other societies as well. Our approach is informed by the insights of critical Israeli social science, but goes beyond them in terms of both comprehensiveness and theoretical ambition. While presenting this theoretical approach we simultaneously employ it to trace the broad outlines of Israel's development from the beginning of Zionist settlement in Palestine in 1882, through the Oslo Accords of 1993, to the present.

We share the view that Israel's political culture and institutions have been marked by tensions between exclusionary and inclusionary goals, but these tensions are not limited to the conflict between a universalist framework of citizenship, which would make Israel into a state of its citizens, and a Jewish ethno-nationalist and increasingly religious citizenship discourse, which would exclude Palestinians from equal citizenship. These are but two of the three citizenship discourses, each with its corresponding set of institutions, that make up Israel's incorporation regime. The third discourse is the republican discourse of civic virtue invoked by the LSM in the service of the colonial project of state building. As we will show below, colonialism has operated as an exclusionary principle with respect to all social groups, with the exception of the dominant Ashkenazim, and on occasion Orthodox Jews. Moreover, in contradistinction to both functionalism and cultural pluralism, we will argue that the inclusionary principle of democracy and the exclusionary principle of Jewish nationalism could coexist only because, and only insofar as, they were mediated by republicanism as part of the colonial project of building the nation-state and attaining national citizenship.

In general, we do not view the cleavages of Israeli society (or most other societies) as standing each one by itself and dividing the society into distinct and separate groups. We view these cleavages as forming a complex and internally connected regime of groups, in which the relations of one group with another circumscribe its association with all other groups as well. Inclusion and exclusion do not operate in isolation from each other, but in tandem as a single whole: while a group may be excluded from a given and favored citizenship discourse, its members' compliance is frequently attained through their incorporation in the society through another, less favored one.

Where multiple citizenship discourses coexist, as they do in Israel, equality on the most basic level of citizenship is used to depoliticize other, unequal forms of incorporation and thus justify the system of stratification. This interdependence also means that when one discourse of citizenship changes, so must the others. As we argue below, in recent years the republican discourse, or principle, has been seriously weakened in Israel, while the liberal and nationalist discourses, or principles, have been revitalized: the former under the influence of global liberalism and the latter by being infused with religious sentiments and dogmas. The weakening of the republican discourse has left the other two in an unmediated polarity, which accounts for the crisis atmosphere that characterizes Israeli politics at the present time.

Part 1

Fragmented citizenship in a colonial
frontier society

2 The virtues of Ashkenazi pioneering

The genesis of virtue

The most distinguishing characteristic of the Jewish Labor Movement in Palestine was that it was not a labor movement at all. Rather, it was a colonial movement in which the workers' interests remained secondary to the exigencies of settlement. Keeping this observation in mind will allow us to properly describe the movement's institutional dynamics and understand the variety of citizenship forms it fostered. It will also save us the mental acrobatics undertaken by the movement's cadres and historians in order to fit this colonial movement into the Procrustean bed of an "a-typical" labor movement.[1] Though they preferred to use Labor Movement as a common label, a more accurate alternate term – *hityashvut ovedet*, freely translated as Labor Settlement Movement (LSM) – was also employed and will serve as our own designation.

A colonial society is any new society established through the combination, to various degrees, of military control, colonization, and the exploitation of native groups and their territorial dispossession, justified by claims of paramount right or superior culture (Shafir 1996b: 193). Some forms of colonialism were undertaken only to exploit native resources and populations. But when colonialism also involved colonization, namely territorial dispossession and the settlement of immigrant populations, its impact was much more far reaching and destructive for the natives. This difference explains why parties to conflicts generated by colonization are usually so intransigent.[2] As a late colonial project, Zionism, including Labor Zionism, was a national colonial movement. It sought to procure a Jewish majority in Palestine and create the political,

---

[1] Israel Kolatt points out that "one of the distinguishing characteristics of the Eretz Israeli labor movement is its being a settlement movement" (Kolatt 1994a: 260). But it is doubtful whether one can call a settlement movement a labor movement at the same time.

[2] In general, settlement colonialism can be distinguished from empire building by its practice of dispossession. For a systematic typology of colonies and the way Zionism fits into this framework, see Shafir 1989: 8–10; 1996c: 229–31.

economic, and cultural institutions that could serve as the infrastructure of a Jewish nation-state. This distinguished Zionism from many colonial movements that operated during the heyday of European colonialism, a fact utilized by Zionist spokespeople in order to dissociate Zionism from colonialism altogether. However, many other colonial movements had sought to create entirely new societies, and imported for that purpose individuals of all classes – both landowners and agricultural workers. Such endeavors, termed by Fredrickson "pure settlement colonies," usually sought to found colonial societies out of clearly defined populations: English, north-west European, or simply "whites," making even Zionism's ethno-nationalist dimension less exceptional than it is made out to be (Fredrickson 1988; Smith 1988; Roediger 1991).

Fewer than 3 percent of the more than two million Jews who left Eastern Europe between 1882 and 1914 chose to immigrate to Palestine. The vast majority chose other colonial destinations – the USA, South Africa, Latin America – or settled in Western Europe (Shafir 1995). Most members of the LSM were Eastern European Jewish immigrants and refugees lacking independent means or marketable skills, seeking to escape poverty, oppression, and anti-Semitism, searching for employment from which they had been displaced in their homelands, and in some cases seeking to farm the land as well. Only between 1924 and 1929 did the first wave of middle-class Polish Jews with some resources to invest – the Fourth Aliya – arrive in Palestine.

The suitability of the impoverished Jewish masses for the national project was not self-evident: it became obvious only once they were harnessed to the settlement project. The Israeli LSM was formed not through class struggle, like most socialist movements, but in the national confrontation between the Zionist settler-immigrants and the Arabs of Palestine. This confrontation involved Jewish colonization of land and the creation of employment for new immigrants, on the one hand, and resistance to such immigration and settlement – in short, anti-colonial struggle – on the part of the Palestinian Arab population, on the other. Colonization – the creation of colonies that were expected to add up to a pure settlement colony – was consequently identified as the national project, as the epitome of Zionism itself. The LSM assumed its leading role in Zionist state building by organizing its members and institutions in response to the challenge of the national–colonial conflict.

The colonial role, identity, and institutions of the LSM were forged in the context of a two-way struggle the Jewish settler-immigrants of the Second Aliya (1904–14) conducted against both the Arabs of Palestine and the Jewish private landowners (or "colonists") of the First Aliya (1882–1903). With the Palestinian Arabs they struggled for the control of land and labor; with the older immigrant-settlers they struggled over the proper aims and methods of Zionist settlement in Palestine.

The Second Aliya immigrants sought in the vineyards and orange groves of the First Aliya year-round jobs, which were their only source of income and for which they demanded higher wages than those paid to Palestinian workers, because they were used to a higher, "European," standard of living. They were also more adept at collective organizing and bargaining than the indigenous Palestinian workers, because labor union activity had begun among Jewish workers in Eastern Europe in the 1880s (Peled and Shafir 1987; Peled 1989). As a result, Jewish workers had to contend with the threat of displacement by the cheaper and unorganized Palestinians, whom the Jewish planters preferred to employ over their co-religionists. (For an analysis of such "split labor market" dynamics see Bonacich 1972.) In the context of this uneven competition, attempts at joint Jewish–Arab labor organizing invariably came to naught. Rather, the very opposite course of action gained currency: Jewish agricultural workers organized for the "conquest of labor" or "Hebrew Labor." To enhance their position, they emphasized their shared Jewishness with the planters, but to no avail. With greater success they stressed the nationalist dimension of their goals, which they shared with the WZO. Only a laboring class, they argued, could produce the numerical Jewish mass necessary for the security of the Zionist project in Palestine.

The ensuing close relationship between the various institutions of the WZO and the Second Aliya focused on the facilitation of immigration, absorption, and settlement, and in Michael Shalev's telling formulation, represented "a practical alliance between a settlement movement without settlers and a worker's movement without work" (Shalev 1990; see also Shalev 1996). The cooperation between the WZO and the workers' movement, which had begun in 1905 with the onset of the former's direct involvement with land purchase and colonization, was transformed into a pragmatic alliance at the WZO's London conference in 1920 (Shafir 1989). This made possible the mobilization of the resources of the Zionist movement on the LSM's behalf. In the alliance between the organized sectors of the Eastern European Jewish agricultural laborers in Palestine and the WZO, the former were transformed from workers into settlers, as the mantle of colonization was thrust on their shoulders, while the WZO became a truly popular movement.

The LSM now saw an opportunity to establish a "closed shop" of truly national dimensions by seeking the "conquest of labor" (in fact, of the labor market) through the "conquest of land" purchased on its behalf by the WZO. Cooperative methods that evolved in the former stage were now applied to colonization and institutionalized as the defining characteristic of the new economic sector. This new LSM economy could employ only Jews, since it was constructed atop two institutional pillars: the Jewish National Fund (JNF), the land-acquisition arm of the WZO established in 1901, and the agricultural workers' Histadrut, established in 1920.[3] The aims of the JNF and the Histadrut were the removal of land and labor, respectively, from the market, closing them off to Palestinian Arabs. More accurately, the JNF's strategy required the initial openness of the land market, while Jewish purchases were effected, and its subsequent closure, in order to retain the "redeemed" land under national Jewish ownership (Kimmerling 1983: 14). Thus, the newly founded LSM economic sector was based on practices of national exclusion.

Whereas the First Aliya sought to establish a society based on Jewish supremacy, the Second Aliya's method of colonization was grounded in separation from the Palestinian Arabs who, consequently, would cease to pose the threat of displacement in the labor market. Since the Jewish organized workers identified their interest as a homogenous Jewish society, their strategy instituted the priority of demography over territory. (Other strands within Zionism, most notably Jabotinsky's Revisionists, have retained the priority of territory to this day.) Thus, although they were initially, like all Zionists, territorial maximalists, in 1937, in 1947, and again in 1993 and 2000, a growing segment within the LSM expressed its willingness to accept the partition of Palestine between a Jewish and a Palestinian (or, earlier, preferably a Transjordanian) state. Partition was acceded to precisely because it alone was capable of reducing the obstacles posed by Palestinian demographic preponderance.[4] In order to increase the ratio of Jewish population to unit of land, the leaders of the LSM recognized that the territory taken possession of by Jews would have to be limited.

Under this territorial moderation the vigilant protection of the exclusive Jewish employment sector never wavered. The historian Dan Giladi has noted that "this issue left its imprint on all social relations in the Yishuv, and excited the passions more than any other single question" (Giladi 1969: 95). In consequence of the struggle for "Hebrew labor," the LSM "won a most important propaganda, moral, and political victory, which it knew how to exploit to the full, both politically and educationally." At

---

[3] The common English rendering of the Histadrut's full name, Federation of Jewish Laborers in Palestine, is inaccurate, because the Histadrut was in fact a centralized body. The term *histadrut* in Hebrew does not mean "federation," but rather "association" or "organization."

[4] Part of the appeal the Peel Commission's partition plan of 1937 had for Ben-Gurion was that it proposed the transfer of about 200,000–300,000 Palestinians from the projected Jewish state to the Arab state (Morris 2000: 43).

the same time, the moral damage to the cause of the planters (called, at the time, *ikarim* – farmers), and indirectly to the Jewish right wing in Palestine, was immeasurable (Giladi 1969: 98). Thus, in 1932–6, in view of the rising political strength of the Revisionists and the citrus growers, which threatened its control over its own membership, the Histadrut staged "a demonstrative and often violent 'principled' struggle . . . against the employment of Arab labor by Jewish employers." This struggle, which was conducted in the face of a decline in unemployment and general economic prosperity, served to brand the Histadrut's opponents as anti-Zionist "and cement the popular identification of the [LSM] as the vanguard of the Jewish national struggle" (Shapira 1977: 252–7; see also Shalev 1990; 1996).

The Jewish agricultural workers in Palestine developed a militant nationalist approach to the Palestinians as a consequence of their failed struggle to displace them and take their jobs in the Jewish plantations. In addition, they carried over from that failure an emphasis on demographic colonization, a strategy of exclusion, and an enfeebled internationalism. In yet another lesson from this struggle, the Jewish workers transferred their hopes from capitalist processes that operate through the market to political solutions that circumvent it. They thus sought for themselves a role as foot-soldiers of a national public institution, such as the WZO or one of its organs, that would act as a quasi-state and would subsidize or, in their terms, provide them with "national protection." In this new conception, whereas private capital was hostile to Zionism, as shown by the preference of the planters for Arab over Jewish labor, "national capital" was the key to Zionism's success. The preference of the LSM for extra-market solutions originated from this predicament. Thus the Labor economy and, subsequently the Israeli economy of which it was to become a key element, remained dependent on "national" subsidies and were directed by political and national considerations.

Ironically, then, the corollary of colonization by a labor settlement movement was its dependence on subsidies provided by middle-class Zionists who did not wish to settle in Palestine themselves. This incongruity was well captured in the popular cynical definition of a Zionist, as "one who donates money to another to arrange for the immigration of a third person to Palestine."

Yosef Gorni, one of the main historians of the LSM, has expressed annoyance at the occasional application of the term *chaluka* – a form of charity in which funds raised from Jews in Europe served to sustain the small traditional communities of Orthodox Jews (*charedim*) in Palestine – to the subsidies received by the Zionist settlers from the WZO. The former used the monies only to preserve their way of life, he argued, whereas the latter used them to expand their settlement (Gorni 1983: 21). Indeed, the goals and methods of these two groups were different. After all, the Zionist settlers, as Gorni indicated, "nationalized" what we would today term "fund-raising." Nevertheless, the pioneers were no more able to live by the sweat of their brows than the *charedim* had been willing to do so.

The predominance of the LSM within the Zionist movement could seem surprising – and, indeed, was slow in coming – since its members were without resources of their own and, consequently, in need of public support. But the dependence on the public purse and the pursuit of nationalist aims by the LSM were not unrelated. Giladi's comparison of the worker-settlers with middle-class Zionists puts this in nice perspective:

The economy of the bourgeois circles was not dependent on public budgets, hence they did not place themselves as individuals or organizations at the disposal of the Zionist movement's leadership. It was precisely the dependence of the workers and their need for national financial support . . . that turned them into a "national army" that conquers targets set by commands from above. (Giladi 1969: 97)

In contemporary and historical interpretations of the period, the allegedly intrinsic single- and high-minded dedication to pioneering among the LSM immigrants appears firm, fixed, and unrelated to actual conditions in Palestine. But the immigrants' idealism did not exist apart from the narrowly constraining social and economic conditions of the country, and their turning and twisting preferences reflected the changing conditions there. After all, 90 percent of the immigrants of the Second Aliya, considered most idealistic of all, eventually emigrated from Palestine, whereas most of those who came in the second most idealistic wave – the Third Aliya – stayed in the country. The crucial difference between these two *aliyot* was not their levels of ideological dedication but the fact that during the interval between them the WZO–LSM "alliance" had developed effective absorption institutions. Thus, in need of national protection, the settler-immigrants of the LSM came to identify themselves with the nation and offer themselves as the anvil on which to hammer out the national project. Those most dependent on national largesse thus became entitled to it as the nation's vanguard (Shafir 1989: 46–7).

The foundation of the LSM's identification with the national–colonial state-building enterprise was the ethos of "pioneering" – *chalutziyut* – which allowed the movement to station itself securely as the core of the Zionist project. The "first and foremost" element of pioneering, on Eisenstadt's list, was "social and personal sacrifice" (Eisenstadt 1968: 17). Self-imposed asceticism and deprivation for the sake of performing the common tasks of the community served as the basis of the LSM's appeal for the Zionist movement. The redemptive activities of the pioneers consisted of physical labor, agricultural settlement, and military defense, undertaken voluntarily as service for the collective they led by personal example. The LSM leadership thought of itself, and was viewed by its following, according to Horowitz and Lissak, as a "service elite" (Horowitz and Lissak 1978: 109). This orientation resembled the Greek notion of the citizen's transcendence of the instrumental sphere of necessity, where one toils to satisfy material wants, into the sphere of freedom, where the practice of freedom is its own reward (Pocock 1998). While the Jewish "citizens" of the LSM performed their pioneering in the instrumental realm, and not in collective deliberation of their political affairs, the pioneer, again in Eisenstadt's words, exhibited "lack of interest in direct, immediate rewards of position, wages, material comforts, or even political power" (Eisenstadt 1968: 18). The pioneer was lauded because s/he toiled for the collective good and frequently lived in collective communities whose structure embodied their members' preference for the common good over individual "goods." Since these ideals were expressed in their fullness in the kibbutz, pioneering was most clearly bound up with that institution. The kibbutz was the *polis* of the Yishuv: a close-knit, intimate, communitarian body. "Idealistic and deeply dedicated," as anthropologist Alex Weingrod put it, "the pioneers formed an elite group – they were the most esteemed members of the colonist society" (Weingrod 1965: 8).

In the LSM's world-view, the strongest commitment to the national goals was expressed in the practice of *hagshama atzmit*, a term seemingly easily translatable as "self-fulfillment" or "self-realization." In fact, the individualist bent the term carries in English is totally lacking in Hebrew. (The equivalent term in Hebrew, much in use in the 1980s and 1990s, would be *mimush atzmi*.) *Hagshama atzmit* was not an individual's act but the self-realization of the virtuous citizen, namely, the carrying out of the movement's pioneering goal by the individual member as his/her duty *qua* citizen. *Hagshama atzmit* meant personal participation in the collective endeavor of transforming Palestine into a Jewish homeland. The LSM's younger generation, as well as later immigrant waves, were asked to measure up to, and measure themselves against, the pioneers who were engaged in putting into effect these ideals. *Hagshama atzmit* first gave the pioneers their vanguard status; later they sought to assimilate others into their ranks with the promise of raising their citizenship status as well. With the passage of time, the early pioneers were satisfied to delegate to others the arduous pioneering activities, while retaining for themselves the role of leadership and the rhetoric of pioneering.

The pioneers were indeed an elite, the vanguard of the colonial–national effort. But the material benefits they gave up individually they received collectively, and what they renounced directly was returned to them indirectly. The pioneers were placed at the head of the queue for national funds, public rewards, and access to institutions, and were thus their privileged recipients in comparison with other Jewish immigrants to Palestine. "The organized workers' movement in Palestine [i.e. the LSM] is not the movement of the 'proletariat,'" argued Chaim Arlosoroff, one of its foremost leaders. "The Histadrut is a settlement aristocracy. If a proletariat, which views itself as lacking public influence, is to be found here, then it is among Middle Eastern and North African Jews" (Arlosoroff 1969: 68).

The LSM's reliance on the WZO and the middle class for subsidies and on other immigrants to create a Jewish majority in Palestine, and its primary devotion to its own members' welfare, rendered it incapable of installing the pioneering ethos in the community as a whole. The criteria for membership in the Yishuv thus remained fragmented, and individuals and groups often found common ground with one another outside the LSM's republican virtue discourse. Among the Jewish non-pioneering groups were the middle class, Mizrachim, and the Orthodox, whose Jewishness secured their place in a common ethno-nationalist framework of citizenship with the LSM (which continued to target individuals belonging to these groups for recruitment into pioneering projects). Thus the foundation was laid for distinguishing between the civic virtue (or "desert") of different groupings within the Jewish community, based on their presumed contributions to the project of Zionist redemption. In contrast, Palestinian Arabs were excluded from all Zionist discourses, not only in practice but in principle as well. The LSM's institutions systematically excluded Arabs since their very *raison d'être* was this exclusion. Tellingly, on the few occasions when feeble attempts were made to incorporate some of them – those who did not compete directly with Jews, such as employees in parts of the Mandatory economy – they were not invited into Jewish bodies but into separate joint institutions specifically devised for this purpose (Shapira 1977: 64–85; Bernstein 2000).

In its effort to accommodate non-pioneering Jewish parties and groups, and ensure their continuing support, the LSM accepted formal criteria of democracy within the voluntary institutions of the movement itself and participated in democratic competition within the WZO and the Yishuv. The Histadrut itself was created with a democratic structure due to internal divisions in the LSM. The limited availability of tools of coercion, which usually are at the disposal of sovereign states, made any other choice unlikely. And yet, the democratic rights of the members of the Yishuv, as of Israel's citizens later on, were seriously constrained and fell far short of liberal democratic citizenship.

Of the two main principles of democracy – majority rule and the limitation of that rule – in both the Yishuv and Israel the former overwhelmed the latter. The weakness of the protection accorded minority rights was connected with the frailty of the legal system. The British common law tradition did apply in Mandatory Palestine, but in the truncated form adopted for the colonies. When, following statehood, the legal personnel of mostly German Jews invoked that tradition, they did so with extreme caution in the face of competing pioneering and nationalist claims. This situation would begin to change only in the 1990s (see chap. 10, below).

The central role played by the LSM in the colonial project and in the creation of the nation-state and the rights associated with national citizenship, as well as its control of public resources, anchored its place at once at the heart of the ethno-nationalist, the liberal democratic, and the republican citizenship frameworks. As long as the LSM could plausibly insist on the overlap between these three discourses, there was no platform from which it could be successfully assailed, and its hegemony was ensured. Social groups that did not accept or share in the pioneering endeavor were coopted into the LSM-based incorporation regime, where their relative ranking was determined by their contribution to the state-building project. Even among Ashkenazim, immigrants from Poland and Russia, where the Zionist movement originated, were placed above immigrants from countries with weak Zionist credentials, such as Hungary and Romania.

As long as subsidies remained central to the project of colonization, and were therefore centrally controlled, the LSM's success also depended on its organization or institutionalization in a political party (or parties). Such institutionalization had important consequences, in that it resulted in the predominance not of the actual pioneers but of *apparatchiks* and party hacks, and in politically motivated developmentalism in the Yishuv and later on in Israel as well. This topic will be explored in some length in the next section of this chapter, devoted to power and democracy and to the state-centered economy.

The WZO's "national capital" allowed the LSM elite to create an elaborate, centralized, coherent, and bureaucratized network of social institutions, as well as an ideological apparatus, and this institutional regime enabled it to co-opt, shape, and label large cross-segments of subsequent waves of immigration. This institutional regime extended to Europe as well, and was used to train and indoctrinate newcomers by preparing them for life in the LSM institutions. Similarly to social democratic parties elsewhere and to the New Deal in the USA, the LSM institutional regime also provided social citizenship rights, closely coupled, in this case, with the colonization project.

The prestige of colonization, the promise of national citizenship in the new state, and the social rights ensured by this citizenship, were the key to the growing and sustained influence of the LSM in the Yishuv and in Israel, as we shall see in the third section. The formation of the LSM's hegemony over the Yishuv at large will be discussed in the concluding section of this chapter.

The institutional regime

The material resources provided by the WZO and the human resources mobilized by the LSM combined to produce, through trial and error, a coherent institutional regime for the colonization of Palestine, namely for the possession and cultivation of land and for the employment and settlement of immigrants. As this method and the institutional regime supporting it evolved in response to multiple challenges – from roughly 1908 until the mid-1930s – the balance of power within the LSM–WZO "alliance" shifted, with the former gradually enhancing its power at the expense of the latter.

The alliance between the LSM and the WZO commenced during their joint establishment in 1908 of the first communal settlement – kibbutz Degania – in Um-Djuni, on the shores of Lake Tiberias. Arthur Ruppin, head of the WZO's Jaffa office, successfully identified the three elements necessary for such an alliance – publicly owned land, cooperative settlement, and financial subsidies. These elements were derived from a blueprint formulated by Franz Oppenheimer for implementation in eastern Germany, to establish cooperative settlements on publicly owned land; from the Prussian government's nationally inspired and state-subsidized "internal colonization" project of replacing Polish with German peasants on its eastern marches; and, finally, from the Jewish agricultural workers' own early cooperative experiments with the small-scale *kvutza* as a cost-saving measure (Shafir 1989). "Cooperative organization" thus became for the WZO and the workers the accepted formula for national colonization. Protection from competition with Arab workers in the labor market provided the kibbutz with a guaranteed, if low, European standard of living. In addition, the self-selection of the members ensured a high level of solidarity; the commonly owned resources promoted economic rationalism and efficiency under conditions of a relatively undeveloped economy; the settlement on nationalized land encouraged dedication to the national cause; and the fact that kibbutzim often originated in "conquest groups," which settled on land freshly transferred from Arab to Jewish hands, disciplined the members. Established on JNF land, which could be leased only to Jews and on which non-Jews could not be employed, the kibbutz was as closed a "shop" as there ever was – it was here that the foundations were first laid for a separate Jewish community and nation-state in Palestine.

National ownership of land was even more important than exclusive Jewish employment in accounting for the significance of the kibbutz for Israeli state formation, as comparing kibbutzim with Jewish towns would demonstrate. Since urban land was more expensive and, therefore, easily given to speculation, the WZO could not overturn the market principle in the towns. As a result, Jewish towns, which frequently developed in partial or complete separation from the Palestinian Arab population, but mostly on private land, were never mobilized as thoroughly for national causes as was the kibbutz. The kibbutz also became the most ethnically homogenous body in Israeli society: it was founded on the exclusion of Palestinian Arabs, included almost exclusively Eastern European Jews, and was unwilling to embrace even Mizrachi Jews.[5]

The economic circumstances of middle-class Jews in Palestine did not require national organization on their part. The development of industry was retarded by the virtual lack of comparative advantages and by investors' preference for the handsome profits that could accrue to land speculators. Different bourgeois sectors had opposing labor market interests, and could not coalesce in a political body (Giladi 1969: 97). Small-scale manufacturing produced mostly for the domestic market and hence was more open to pressures to employ Jewish workers. Some companies, like the Dead Sea Works, required financial support from the WZO and presented their own industrial undertaking as a "pioneering" project but, being oriented toward Middle Eastern export markets, employed a combined Arab and Jewish labor force. Citrus was the major export branch and also the largest employer of Arab workers. Thus labor market interests continued, albeit not exclusively, to provide the rationale for, and circumscribe the parameters of, political organization in the Yishuv (see Shafir 1989: 46–7; Frenkel et al. 2000).

During the Mandatory period, out of the kibbutz and moshav (semi-cooperative farming settlement) evolved a comprehensive cooperative economic sector based on the principle of national separation. At its peak, this economic sector encompassed agricultural, industrial, construction, marketing, transportation, and financial concerns, as well as a

---

[5] Ironically, the kibbutz came to be known as the institution whose members were "content with little," a term applied earlier to Yemenite Jews (Shafir 1989).

whole network of social service organizations. This included, for example: an agricultural marketing company, Tnuva; a general marketing organization, Hamashbir Hamerkazi; a road and housing construction company, Solel Bone; a workers' bank, Bank Hapoalim; an insurance company, Hasneh; a sick fund (HMO), Kupat Cholim; an industrial concern, Koor; a public bus company, Egged; and many more. Most of these institutions, although privatized in the 1990s, are still among the giants of the Israeli economy.

The economic bodies of the LSM were owned and administered by the Histadrut's holding company, Chevrat Haovdim (the Workers' Society), set up in 1924 as the owner of all the financial and cooperative institutions of the Histadrut. Chevrat Haovdim was expected "to see to it that all Histadrut institutions and enterprises serve the national goal," and "safeguard the cooperative nature and structure of all Histadrut institutions" (Kurland 1947: 172–4). Central ownership, then, was meant to obviate the danger that befell successful economic cooperatives elsewhere, namely, a return to hired labor. Like the kibbutz, Chevrat Haovdim cooperatives were protected from outside competition and enjoyed the advantage of shared resources and an internal market. Thus, in developing rural settlements and urban employment opportunities, and in setting up its own economic enterprises, required for the absorption of immigrants, the Histadrut in effect created a new and separate national society and acted as its state-in-the-making. Each member of the Histadrut now became a citizen of that state-in-the-making.

Power and democracy

The key to the flourishing of the LSM was its simultaneous organizational control of the loyalty of its members and the resources of the WZO. The resources allowed it to discipline its members, and punish those who were not loyal to its institutions, and the loyalty of its members was the guarantee that the WZO could not bypass the LSM and approach its members directly. By disciplining its members the movement sought to prevent the privatization of the "national capital" they used, because, as its experience with the planters of the First Aliya had demonstrated, private capital favored individual and not Zionist interests. More socialist or communist bodies, which could have also weakened the Zionist aims of the movement, such as the Third Aliya's Gdud Haavoda (Labor Brigade), were also reined in. Consequently, the individual members and the corporate bodies of the movement were always embedded in larger networks and, somewhat incongruously for a "revolutionary" movement, bound by elaborate legal edifices. Finally, the self-organization of the LSM membership in cooperative cells and horizontal and vertical umbrella organizations allowed their mobilization on behalf of both the colonial project and the protection and augmentation of the LSM's own power and authority.

The single-minded coherence of the Histadrut's institutional structure resulted from the fact that its different constituent bodies were engaged in parallel efforts to solve all manner of problems posed by the colonization of a less-developed land in competition with its indigenous inhabitants. As we have seen, capitalist colonization, self-interested and market driven, ran counter to the Zionist, and especially to the workers', interests. The national goal was consequently built into the Histadrut's institutions from its genesis and was enshrined in its constitution. Elkana Margalit has referred to this as the Histadrut's unique "primeval (*bereshiti*) partisan-political structure" which survived, he added, to the present (i.e. to 1994, when he wrote his analytic account of Israeli labor unions). The "secret of the Histadrut's power," according to Margalit, was its all-encompassing character – indicating not separate institutions but a comprehensive and coherent institutional regime – and the "practical management of the everyday professional, economic, social, educational, and cultural needs" of its members in a single organization, politically directed by the dominant party or coalition of parties. The influence of the political factor flowed through a "single integrative and authoritative route from the Histadrut's central legislative and executive institutions to the local cell" (Margalit 1994: 18–19).

The authority of the LSM's pioneering ideal, so frequently hailed as its trademark, was, as demonstrated by Yonathan Shapiro, tempered, reshaped, and corrupted by its political apparatus, or machine (the Hebrew term *manganon* has connotations of both). This double-headed machine, which was present in both a political party, Achdut Haavoda, and in the Histadrut, was formed in the second half of the 1920s in an effort to maintain the authority of the LSM in the face of several economic challenges: the collapse of Histadrut enterprises (including Solel Bone, its flagship construction company); severe criticism of the Labor economy's inefficiency by a more market-oriented group of American Zionists; and growing competition with owners of private capital who were arriving in Palestine, for the first time, during the Fourth Aliya. This machine turned out to be very long lived indeed. In its latest incarnation, as the Tel Aviv Block ("*gush*"), it was active well into the 1960s (Shapiro 1976; 1977; 1996a).

Atop its "closed shop" economy then, the LSM now fashioned a machine-run political order. Political machines were common in immigrant societies, especially in large immigrant cities in the USA. But in the Yishuv the political machine took on all the characteristics of the LSM which it served. A machine party, as Shapiro indicated, operates by dispensing material rewards to gain the loyalty of its followers. It "buys," so to speak, supporters. In our terms, it replaces citizenship rights with patronage. The existence of a population in need of such resources, and their availability for recruitment, both conditions which obviously prevailed in the Yishuv and later on in Israel, encouraged such mutual dependence (Shapiro 1977: 103). The very key to the predominance of the LSM, and especially of its central political party, Achdut Haavoda (later Mapai and the Labor Party), was its elite's adeptness at locating itself in the "narrow bottleneck" linking the financial resources of the WZO and the man- and woman-power of the Yishuv. As a result, a great share of the resources that flowed from the former to the latter were piped and distributed through the movement (see Ram 1995: 77).

Shapiro made it clear that the LSM machine put its imprint not only on the political sphere but also on the "social structure in its entirety" (Shapiro 1977: 104). The main effect he emphasized was the subordination of the efficiency and profitability of Histadrut-owned enterprises to the needs of the machine. For this purpose, a whole elite stratum of party *apparatchiks* or administrators (*askanim*) was formed within the LSM. Their accomplishments were evaluated not by their ability to lead successful enterprises but by their expertise in mobilizing support for the Histadrut and the LSM in general. The LSM produced as well an elite of economic managers responsible to the party rather than to the market. These two elite groups reaped the benefits of the LSM's social standing and were shielded by its pioneering prestige. Proximity to the collective subsidy bowl provided a leg-up for them. The leaders of the movement became those who in fact, or for all practical purposes, left the collective colonies and moved into the cities, where they assumed the leadership of the new institutions. In their political jargon, prosaic management activities were imbued with the glory of pioneering, but their salaries and way of life were much above that of regular party members. The "idolized self-sacrificing and future-oriented pioneers" described by Eisenstadt were portrayed by Shapiro "as rank-climbers and status-seekers nesting in their movement's bureaucracy and later in the Zionist movement's and the state's" (Ram 1995: 83; Sussman 1974).

In Shapiro's view, the establishment of the state of Israel in 1948 marked not so much the replacement of pioneering voluntarism in a stateless society with state sovereignty, but rather the extension of Mapai, the LSM's dominant party, from a pressure group holding a social bottleneck position in the 1920s ... into a state apparatus domineering all areas of the Israeli polity [by the 1950s]: the Zionist movement, the source of finance and [immigrant] manpower; the state itself, a depository of legal authority and coercive means; and the [LSM] (especially the Histadrut), the backbone of its organizational infrastructure. (Ram 1995: 83)

This institutional regime and the patronage networks it spawned were counterproductive not only for the prospects of liberal democracy, as Shapiro lamented, but also for the kind of voluntary participation that republican pioneering was supposed to have been all about. On the Yishuv's late frontier, as pointed out in a recent work by Sofer, "in vain would one seek to find ... the free association de Tocqueville found in American democracy." Here the single voluntary act was the joining of "a closed framework which demanded absolute loyalty and discipline." Consequently, "voluntary association ... was an exceptional phenomenon" and "each organization and movement was controlled centrally." This was a collectivist regime in which "the individual was required to identify completely with the common aim, divesting himself of all individualism, not deviating from existing norms" (Sofer 1998: 13).

This characterization of the Jewish community in Palestine by Sofer (in fact an unwarranted projection on the author's part from the LSM to the entire Yishuv) is the very obverse of the functionalist perspective of Eisenstadt, Lissak, and Horowitz. In their view the Yishuv's democracy was voluntaristic, the leadership only coordinating and regulating the realization of communal wishes. In fact, the authority of the LSM was due precisely to the fact that its members were not simply members, but rather the movement's citizens. Thus, voluntarism within the LSM was hardly as spontaneous as functionalist sociology made it out to be, but neither was its leaders' control as total as Sofer's description would have us believe.

The LSM's notion of citizenship was most accurately captured by Uri Ben-Eliezer as a "community of civic republican virtue." In Ben-Eliezer's complex portrait of what he called "political participation in a non-liberal democracy," or in a "collectivist democracy," the democratic element always appeared eclipsed. Rights and duties, voluntarism and mobilization, commitment and indoctrination, were lopsidedly expected and enforced. In the LSM's youth movements and paramilitary organizations in the 1930s and 1940s, a great deal of emphasis was placed on eliciting the compliance of the younger generation with the leaders' views. An obsessive devotion by the leaders to marathonic discussions with the younger members gave the latter the opportunity to be outspoken, to air their views and raise their objections, but all the while accept their elders' lead. Thus an oxymoronic pattern of critical compliance and active conformism was established, a form of participation in which "the training experienced by the members of the collective movements had the effect of maximizing the idea of participation while minimizing the importance of influence." In this community of republican virtue, participation and influence were institutionally separated (Ben-Eliezer 1993: 402–4; see also Shapiro 1984).

This dynamic was most clearly evident in the military sphere, in the Yishuv's main paramilitary bodies, which were recruited by and from the LSM. Anita Shapira and Baruch Kimmerling presented Israeli militarism as an anomaly – as, respectively, an intrusion of an alien ideological element into a morally superior world-view, or a temporary break in the normalcy of everyday life caused by a military emergency (Shapira 1992; Kimmerling 1985a). Ben-Eliezer, in contrast, has demonstrated that these contradictory elements were integrated into the political *modus vivendi* between the LSM's older and younger generations and articulated in the ethos of its military and paramilitary institutions.

Israelis were always proud of the fact that, in spite of repeated wars fought by their country and the centrality of the military in their society, the Israeli military remained under civilian control. Ben-Eliezer demonstrated, however, that civilian–military relations in Israel were far from simple or benign. His argument challenges the traditional distinction between civilian control over the military, on the one hand, and praetorianism and militarism, on the other. In "nations-in-arms," such as France for a long period of its history and Israel, Ben Eliezer has argued, a more useful distinction would be between praetorianism – *coup d'états* carried out by soldiers – and militarism – the predominance of military thinking and military images and the priority of military over other means of solving social problems. Military coups by "praetorian guards," Ben-Eliezer reminded us, have never taken place in militaristic societies, since the desires of the military and their world-view are already hegemonic in these societies (Ben-Eliezer 1998b).

The military service of the Greek citizen in defense of his *polis* and of the French citizens during the revolutionary wars served as a foundation of civic republicanism. A similar bond of virtuous citizenship was forged at the core of the Jewish paramilitary bodies in Palestine, especially in their elite units, which were an integral part of the LSM. Here the identity of the settler and the soldier was established. This identity is one key to understanding the absence of recourse to military coups in Israel, since those who wielded military power already had a privileged citizenship status and, consequently, favored access to institutions.

According to Ben-Eliezer, the foreign-born leadership of the LSM adopted the militarism that sprang up in the first native-born (sabra) generation of Israelis during the Arab Revolt (1936–9) and in the years leading up to the war of 1948, in return for the younger generation's willingness to give up its praetorian tendencies and accept the older generation's leadership. One of the darker consequences of this *modus vivendi* was that the leadership never had to order unsavory actions which, nevertheless, were carried out because they were implicit in the militaristic world-view. Within the Israeli military, the extension of warfare to non-combatants, both before and during the war of 1948, as well as the massive expulsion of Palestinians, were condoned, if not encouraged. A more ambiguous legacy was the maintenance of freedom of criticism within the military which, however, never impeded its loyalty and obedience, creating what is known in Israel as the "shooting and crying" syndrome (Ben-Eliezer 1998a; 1998b; Morris 1987; 2000; Pappe 1992).

In sum, Israeli democracy was limited by the indoctrination of the LSM's own members and the movement's ability to co-opt and, if necessary, disregard its opponents. When citizenship rights were granted, they were not conferred on individuals but on members of social sectors, and thus were not rights but corporate privileges. Massive patronage networks rendered citizens dependent. Democracy never appeared in its liberal version, based on the recognition of individual rights and the value of political participation, and on the protection of those rights and participation from government arbitrariness. On the contrary, the LSM's "non-liberal democracy" embodied mechanisms that impeded liberal democracy from coming into being.

State-centered economy

Zionist attempts to colonize the economically unattractive Palestine by private initiative usually ended in failure. Capitalist profit calculations which, as we have seen, condoned the employment of low-paid Arab workers on Jewish-owned land, were at odds with the nationalist goal of creating a Jewish majority. The predominant Zionist method of colonization – developed by the LSM – came, consequently, to be based on the imposition of extra-market mechanisms on land acquisition and allocation and on labor market regulation. The circumvention of the land and labor markets was the task of two institutions: the JNF and the Histadrut, respectively. Their colonization method also made possible the provision of "civilized wages" to Jewish workers, who otherwise might have emigrated to more highly developed countries. The demographic goal of Zionism favored the socialist approach and co-operative institutions of the LSM because these were conducive to massive Jewish immigration, as well as to the disciplining of the immigrants in the service of national goals such as the "conquest of land" and "conquest of labor."

In the terminology used by economist Ephraim Kleiman, the socialist or etatist features of the Yishuv's politico-economic system were the result of the need to compensate for "market failures" in the capital, land, and labor markets, which jeopardized the nationalist goals of the Zionist movement. A free-enterprise system failed to attract sufficient capital to develop the country; land prices had to be kept low by restricting competition among the buyers through the services of a monopsonistic buyer; and immigrants were uneasy undergoing proletarianization and needed ideological comfort. All in all, the way things were set up initially "represented an attempt to deal with real or perceived failures of the market to create the conditions for the attainment of national or social goals" (Kleiman 1997: 148). Kleiman holds that the model that won out, namely the LSM's institutional complex, did so through the "survival of the fittest" and "the convergence of needs and ideologies" (Kleiman 1997: 154–5).

Without accepting his deterministic analogy – of course, it is only possible to tell with hindsight who was the "fittest," and the "fittest" in the short term frequently pays a price in the long term for its precociousness – we agree with Kleiman's characterization of the problems faced by Zionist immigrants. Kleiman, however, is at his best when explaining what may be termed the "survival of the unfit": why the LSM's political–economic system long outlived its usefulness. In Kleiman's words, "the main explanation of the prevalence and persistence of interventionism seems to lie in the opportunities it offers for political manipulation," namely for enriching rent-seekers (Kleiman 1997: 159). The instruments of intervention were particularly effective, he observes, because they combined discretionary freedom for their operators with low public visibility. The consequence of such etatism was the privatization of profits and the nationalization of losses (Kleiman 1997: 162). Two other well-respected economists, Lerner and Ben-Shahar, also concluded that in Israel where the "government lends money to many groups in the society . . . the rich [have] a share in these loans greater than their proportion in society" (Lerner and Ben-Shahar 1975: 148).

This economic system and the institutional regime that buttressed it persisted, and their reach was extended after the establishment of Israel in 1948. Emma Murphy has summed up this approach: "The high living standards required to attract immigrants were achieved through the subsidization of the economy by foreign aid, Diaspora revenues and international loans rather than through high productivity" (Murphy 1993: 241). The twin goals of immigration and colonization led to the identification of state building with economic development by the LSM's elite. This accounts for the designation "revolutionary" frequently applied to Zionism, a designation that bestowed on the movement and its institutions, and later on on the Israeli state as well, the legitimacy, both domestic and international, for imposing a tutelary regime on the society. Israel was not "exceptional" in approaching the task of economic development with statist tools. It shared this approach with many of the new states formed after the Second World War and, indeed, with late-developing states that fashioned themselves into self-conscious "developmentalist states." But in contrast with many other new states, Israel was already on its inception a "strong state" in Joel Migdal's terms, with a long and successful practice of developmentalism (Migdal 1988). The confluence of nationalist and colonial goals and the disciplinary means of socialist and military practices endowed the institutions of the Israeli state-in-the-making with a generous measure of autonomy. This developmental model fulfilled the expectations attached to it for about two-and-a-half decades after Israel's establishment.

Many of the observers who associated the LSM with its explicit socialist ideology were puzzled by its lukewarm and opportunistic commitment to socialism when it finally came to hold governmental power. We suggest, however, that socialism was no more than the handmaiden of the LSM's national–colonial aims. The LSM, in contradistinction to its Eastern European sisters, was not bent on the nationalization of the means of production, except for land – the main resource over which the colonial struggle was waged. Nor was the LSM opposed to private enterprise, provided that it was geared towards creating employment and willing to maintain a policy of "closed shop," that is, employ "Hebrew labor" only. After the achievement of statehood, Israeli Labor governments were supportive of private, public, and Histadrut investments, using the criteria of job creation as their main yardstick. Moreover, even after the imposition of a military administration over Israel's Palestinian citizens eliminated their labor market competition with Jews, Labor party-led governments did not seek to do away with the sectoral divisions of the economy that were typical of the pre-statehood years. In the assessment of economists Assaf Razin and Efraim Sadka, in addition to encouraging state- and Histadrut-owned enterprises, "the government aggressively searched for private entrepreneurs and investors and heavily subsidized them. In this respect, the economic system was far from a socialist command economy. Indeed, Israel has always had a flourishing private sector" (Razin and Sadka 1993: 1–2; see also Sternhell 1998; Khenin 2000).

One of the main reasons for the LSM's unusual willingness to pursue its aims within a plural economy was its ability to exert considerable control not only over the land and labor markets, but also over flows of capital into the Israeli economy. Whereas before 1948 only "national capital" was available for state-building purposes, after 1948 the state became the greatest importer of capital (in the form of untaxed US savings bonds, German reparations and personal compensations to Holocaust survivors, etc.). As Razin and Sadka emphasized, "the government was the major intermediary in the capital market," and, consequently, the major force behind the developmental path chosen for the economy (Razin and Sadka 1993: 2, 6).

Together with Taiwan and South Korea, Israel, as Michael Barnett has pointed out, was the major beneficiary of unilateral capital transfers. This was due to the three countries' ideological and geo-strategic positions in the Western camp during the Cold War. All three had few direct ties with private foreign capital and received only scanty foreign investment. Nor did they possess indigenous capitalist strata or landed aristocracies, and, consequently, were able to assert a relatively high level of domestic autonomy (Barnett 1996: 122–4; Shalev 1992). The ability to concentrate so many resources in their own hands put these three states in the limited category of developmental states. But unlike most other states in this category, which encompasses many late developers, these three were successful in their industrialization drives.

In addition to being in control of parceling out land and labor in its own sector and influencing it in the private Jewish sector, this third prop – effective control over the distribution of capital – was added to the LSM's institutional regime after 1948. This change signaled an important socio-economic and institutional transition: whereas in the Yishuv partial de-commodification of land and labor, the institutional arenas in which the Jewish–Palestinian conflict was played out, was the key to the Zionist aims, after statehood the third component – capital imports and dis-bursement – played the central role in further state building.

In no other area was the combination of state-centered economic de-velopment with the institutions of pioneering so evident as in the capital market or, actually, in its practical absence. In Ephraim Kleiman's calcu-lation, approximately three-quarters of all capital imports were received by the public sector, which, in turn, financed nearly two-thirds of all capi-tal formation (Kleiman 1967: 233). The distribution of foreign funds and the control over foreign currency served as key elements in buttressing the state's economic weight, but domestic capital formation also enhanced and reproduced both the state's and the Histadrut's economic influence.

The major sources of domestic investment capital in Israel were per-sonal savings deposited in pension or provident funds (*kupot gemel*).[6]

---

[6] *Kupot gemel* are saving plans based on monthly deposits, paid out in lump or monthly sums until exhausted. They are administered by commercial banks mostly for the self-employed or organized groups of employees. Pension funds provide regular payments after retirement.

These could have served as a basis for sizable stock and bond markets, but an elaborate institutional and financial arrangement kept them under state control. Their operation provides a fascinating window into the Israeli developmentalist state and its institutions. As with so much of Israel's economic infrastructure, the major provident funds were also sectoral: they were initiated and administered during the Mandatory period by the Histadrut. In 1950, the provident funds and the Histadrut's own Bank Hapoalim jointly established a special financial enterprise, "Gmul," to invest the accumulated funds. This allowed Bank Hapoalim to predominate in the provident fund market, which included a few private pension funds as well. In the late 1980s, 95 percent of the members in provident funds belonged to the seven funds owned by the Histadrut (Aharoni 1991: 203).

On embarking upon a policy of industrialization in 1957, the Israeli government and the Histadrut agreed that 65 percent of the amount accumulated in the latter's provident funds were to be invested in government "approved investments," a portion that increased steadily until it reached 92 percent by 1977 (Aharoni 1991: 118; Grinberg 1991: 91).The Histadrut was required to use 50 percent of that sum to purchase non-tradable government bonds, the returns for which were invested by the government in its own companies, or in private firms, or otherwise used at its discretion. In return, the state consented to the Histadrut's continued investment of the remaining 50 percent in Gmul's fixed-yield bonds, thus developing further the enterprises of Chevrat Haovdim, the holding company of all Histadrut-linked economic entities. This agreement served as the basis for Chevrat Haovdim's yearly "financial plan." The exposure of the Histadrut-generated funds to market risks was limited in 1962 when the Ministry of Finance consented to tie the value of the bonds' yield to the standard of living index, thus, in effect, equalizing them with government-issued non-tradable bonds (*igrot chov meyuadot*) that were guaranteeing a real annual yield of about 5 percent (Grinberg 1991: 91–2; Aharoni 1991: 20, 117–19). Under pressure, the government also authorized the Industrial Development Bank and the Manufacturers' Association to issue bonds under similarly favorable conditions. Simultaneously, the government required all other long-term institutional savers, such as pension funds and life-insurance companies, to participate in its bond program (Reiner interview). In sum, capital formation in Israel was a circular affair which made available to the government the Histadrut's pension and provident funds for loans to public and private investors for investments approved by the government itself.

This ingenious method of maintaining state control over capital formation and, to a large extent, over capital allocation as well, not only had the effect of preventing the formation of a free internal capital market, but also had a number of far-reaching consequences for the structure of the economy and the relationship between the spheres of "politics" and "economics." First, it was difficult to tell where the Histadrut "ended" and the government "began," since they pooled their resources and both operated under the same sheltered conditions. Second, in the view of Efraim Reiner, a past director general of Bank Hapoalim and secretary of Chevrat Haovdim, this arrangement ensured sturdy ties between the political and economic elites of the LSM and reduced the possibility of conflict between them. Among the second generation of the LSM elite, the majority of whom were recruited from the movement's kibbutzim, were many who specialized, by their own personal preferences, in managing the economic enterprises of the Histadrut–state conglomerate. Though the "economic wing" of the LSM elite sought on occasion to invoke an economic rationale, in order to gain a measure of autonomy, whereas the political wing was afraid of such autonomy and sought to curtail it, the two always remained tied to each other within the given set of institutional arrangements (Reiner interview; for the future development of this relationship see part 3, below).

By importing foreign capital itself, the government was in a position to favor those sectors of the economy that provided maximum employment, a goal Israel shared with other developing countries (although in Israel's case the target population was exclusively Jewish, and was not rural but immigrant). In the early 1950s the task of providing employment for new immigrants became even more pressing. Priority was therefore assigned to labor-intensive industries, most prominently agriculture. Only with the exhaustion of agricultural assets, most of which were the expropriated lands of Palestinian refugees, was the first industrial policy adopted, aiming, as in many other new industrializing countries, to substitute local production for imports, in order to ease foreign currency shortages. The main tools of the new industrial policy were exchange-rate controls, multiple exchange rates, direct administrative allocation of foreign currency, investment subsidies, and tariff barriers to protect infant industries. In 1962 new efforts were undertaken to enhance exports, side by side with import substitution. This was done by subsidizing exporting companies and by selectively encouraging industries, such as textiles, which were expected to perform in the international market. For the first time, a policy of trade liberalization was adopted, promising to replace administrative controls over imports with tariffs. But the gradual reduction of the latter, the second part of the program, remained very partial (Bar 1990: 29–31). Throughout the whole period, government ministries treated various industrial branches selectively, eager to pick winners. The 1955–65 period witnessed a rapid growth in the Israeli economy: an average of 12 percent per annum growth of industrial production, accompanied by an 5.5 percent growth in employment, 10 percent in capital reserves, and 20 percent in exports (Bar 1990: 29).

The formative impact of the Jewish–Palestinian and later the Israeli–Arab conflict on the Israeli economy and society accounts for the Yishuv's and Israel's heavy investment in war-making capacities, which further contributed to the construction of powerful mobilizing institutions. After the 1967 war and the consequent escalation of the conflict, Israel set out to develop a military–industrial complex, proportionately very large for the size of its economy. While military production was also shielded to a significant extent from the market, as most of its product was purchased by the IDF, its higher level of technology called for institutional modernization, since large-scale production required the development of export markets as well. The capital market and the military–industrial complex contributed in decisive ways to further strengthening the old institutional regime, after 1948, and will therefore occupy an important place in any analysis of the Israeli economy. Whereas capital markets remained under tight political control until the mid-1980s, however, the military–industrial complex served to pry open and, ultimately, break the mold of the Israeli economy, in the process forcing the liberalization of the capital market as well (see chap. 9, below).

The creation of a state-owned military–industrial complex began as yet another facet of the "import-substitution industrialization" (ISI) policy – its extension, as it were, to a new economic arena. The political impetus was the imposition of an embargo on military supplies by the French government in the wake of the 1967 war and the ensuing resolve of the Israeli government to develop in Israel the production capacity for supplying the Israeli military with its main weapon systems. But the formative impact of the military–industrial complex on the Israeli economy went much farther than import substitution. Military production became the engine of growth and the focus of knowledge dissemination for advanced high-technology industries and the primary influence in the modernization of industry and large segments of the economy (Lifshitz 1995: 5). The military metal and electronic industries employed a higher level of mechanization than until then had been customary in Israeli enterprises, utilized newer and more sophisticated equipment in its production processes, established higher quality standards, and required a similar level of quality control from their non-military subcontractors. The new industries trained and recruited technological and managerial manpower, a portion of which subsequently moved to private and/or civilian industry as employees and entrepreneurs. Military production led to spinoffs of civilian uses and at the end of the 1970s high-tech civilian companies began to expand rapidly.

Starting in the late 1970s, the complex of military industries also became the main source of growth for exports, sometimes even establishing partnerships with foreign companies (Ministry of Industry and Commerce 1990: 7, 10–11) and, in general, moving Israeli industry from ISI to genuine export orientation. Defense contractors included three of Israel's top five corporations, and they became major earners of foreign currency. While domestic purchases for the Israeli military remained at a fixed level of 7–8 percent of GNP in the 1976–85 decade, the share of military exports grew from 17 to 25 percent of all industrial exports (excluding polished diamonds), and the share of exports out of the military industries' own production rose to 60–80 percent by the end of the decade. Not only did military production produce relatively high added value but it also helped open doors for Israeli civilian products. The crisis of the military–industrial complex in the late 1980s began the process of the transformation of Israeli developmentalism. Whereas capital controls persisted into the early 1980s under the control of the political elites, the growing export orientation of the military–industrial complex began to sever the strong bond between politics and economics. It led to the questioning of the role played by the *apparatchik*s in running the economy, and saw the replacement of developmental economics, which strengthened the state even as it developed the economy, with market-driven development. Ultimately, the pressure of export orientation under conditions of domestic economic stagnation in the 1980s led to the liberalization of the capital market as well, thus bringing down the institutional regime of the LSM and ushering in a new period, which is the focus of part 3 of this book.

The origins of social citizenship rights

The LSM's institutional structure was geared towards directly subsidizing colonization by providing the pioneers and their dependents with the social resources needed to maintain their European standard of living in Palestine. During the Yishuv period the LSM preferred this approach to both the traditional philanthropic approach, adopted for example by the ultra-Orthodox Agudat Yisrael party, and modern social welfare programs, even though some of the American representatives in the Jewish Agency were well-known experts in this area. The Mandatory government, a unit of the British Colonial Office, also "did not generally involve itself in the welfare problems of the Jewish community" (Neipris 1966: 72–3).

In his study of the origins of the Israeli welfare state, Neipris argued that since the LSM leadership "saw little place for social work or philanthropy in their scheme"; when relief actions became necessary, they habitually assigned the responsibility to outsiders (Neipris 1966: 72–3). What later became Israel's Ministry of Welfare began, therefore, in 1931, as a department of the Vaad Leumi (National Council), first headed by the then seventy-year-old Henrietta Szold from Baltimore, founder of the Hadassah organization of Zionist women. Upon arriving in Palestine she found that no services had been deemed necessary for the aged and, even more significantly, that there were no Jewish welfare organizations in Palestine "concerned with the family as the object of service" (Neipris 1966: 81). Between 1948 and 1953, the LSM handed the Ministry of Welfare to Agudat Yisrael, the political party farthest removed from pioneering. Neipris's study demonstrates that there was a fundamental clash between the conceptions of social citizenship, sought by the Histadrut for its members, and social welfare. The LSM's institutions rejected social welfare, since they viewed it as a form of dependence, and favored mutual self-help (*ezra hadadit*) programs and self-management by the insured members. The Histadrut

> concerned itself with broad welfare [i.e. social citizenship] programs for its members ... It offered total medical coverage and afforded up to two years of free hospitalization for all chronic medical conditions. The Histadrut developed unemployment and strike-benefit funds. It did little, however, during the pre-state period to develop an old age and survivors' benefit program. By 1948, a few trade unions of the federation had developed broad coverage for their workers. That year approximately 25% of the Histadrut membership was included in an insurance program covering survivors benefits and pensions. (Neipris 1966: 85–6)

For the LSM, real social service stood for "a process of mutual self-help within the union structure" and as "the antithesis of the 'philanthropic methods' that outside relief agencies and social workers might seek to develop and apply in the country" (Neipris 1966: 106). Ben-Gurion expected the participation of the Jewish worker in the program of national renaissance to ensure not only the realization of Zionism but concurrently the social aims of the worker as well. In his words: "The first and foremost of the builders and fighters for the Hebrew renaissance is the Hebrew worker, and everything that brings about his entrenchment, development, the extension of his social and political rights, the increase of his material and mental strength – simultaneously benefits the nation in general" (quoted in Gorni 1974: 103–4). Since by ensuring the workers a "European" standard of living through the application of "national capital" the workers themselves were made available to carry out national tasks; social rights served as a particularly important lever and cement of Zionism. This "identity" of socialism and nationalism ruled out the need for class struggle.

Just as the Jewish LSM was dissimilar to other labor parties and trade unions, the rights it provided to Jewish worker-immigrants were atypical in many ways. The rights of the Histadrut's citizens included housing, access to (sometimes subsidized) employment or unemployment benefits, and health benefits, i.e. what was necessary for an immigrant to sink roots in a low-wage country. Among Israeli sociologists, Zeev Rosenhek has done the most to make visible this connection between particular social rights and colonization. In the conclusion to his study of labor exchanges and public housing he found that "the emergence of an embryonic welfare state during the pre-state era [was] intimately connected with the Zionist–Palestinian conflict and the process of Zionist state-formation." Labor exchanges were set up by the Jewish workers' parties to ensure their members access to the sparse employment opportunities available. With the founding of the Histadrut in 1920, the exchanges were placed under its aegis, and in 1943 they were transformed into general exchanges (Rosenhek 1996; Greenberg 1980). In 1930 Berl Katznelson, the renowned leader of Labor Zionism, articulated explicitly the colonizing and national purpose of this institution. He asked rhetorically: "What do we want from the labor exchanges?" and answered: "That they will help us in the 'conquest of labor' ... The problem is the expansion of the labor market for the Hebrew worker: in Arab workplaces by replacing Arab workers, but there are also reasons for struggling to expand the Hebrew labor market in Hebrew workplaces" (Rosenhek 1996). The Histadrut also initiated the construction of public housing for its members, starting with the Borochov Quarter near Tel Aviv in 1920, mostly on land supplied by the JNF. Housing served both to subsidize the higher-paid Jewish workers and to further national territorial goals (Rosenhek 1996). In negotiating with the Farmers' Association, David Remez, secretary general of the Histadrut, required part of the workers' housing costs to be paid by the farmers, and promised that another part would be donated by the Jewish Agency through the construction of houses in the colonies. "I am not saying," he added, "give cash supplements to the worker or to the farmer, but housing – yes" (Rosenhek 1996). Similar strategies were employed in the towns, with the aim of tying the settler-immigrants to Palestine by giving them a home in the new land and, thus, a stake in the new society.

In contrast to the meager welfare rights given all members of the Yishuv as a last resort by marginal institutions, the social citizenship of the Histadrut was defined broadly and placed at the heart of the colonial state-building institutions. Social citizenship rights, in contrast to welfare services, were not means based and did not single out vulnerable individuals as needing protection. Rather, they were "universal" and attained as a right by virtue of citizenship in the LSM community of republican virtue.

Social citizenship rights in Israel bear the imprint of the colonial project in many other unusual ways. The Histadrut, after all, was not only a trade union and a provider of social services but also an employer. For example, in the 1960–8 period, Histadrut-owned enterprises employed, on average, 24 percent of the labor force and produced 22 percent of the domestic product, with the state sector producing another 25 percent. Employment at a Histadrut-owned plant or service may itself be seen, and was presented as a new, socialist, social right: a citizen of the Histadrut and co-owner of its Chevrat Haovdim was removed from the vagaries of the market, hence his or her labor was decommodified. Thus, in the Yishuv, employment became a collective right, rather than an individual burden.

The social rights granted by the Histadrut were originally associated with the just desert of the colonizing pioneer. The allotment of these rights, however, also served as a controlling mechanism which operated through institutions of incorporation. In Shalev's words, "far more than in other countries, the Histadrut traditionally relied on its social and economic functions, not only its trade union role as the workers' representative, in order to attract and retain rank-and-file members." Most famously "the Histadrut's health care system was effectively utilized to draw citizens into the labor organization and its political sphere of influence" (Shalev 1992: 28).

The control over economic resources provided by the WZO made possible the institutionalization of social citizenship rights for members and sympathizers of the national–colonial project. Since the criteria for allocation were political and not civic, and the portioning out was carried out by the LSM's and the WZO's own institutions, and transferred later to state institutions only partially and haltingly, political criteria of citizenship remained crucial. As in the *polis*, the definition of the community was political. Social and political rights remained primary, and civil rights secondary, under the incorporation regime of the LSM. In the state of Israel social citizenship rights, especially the wage structure and health insurance, continued to be tied to the Histadrut and through it to the pioneering colonial project. The LSM's hegemonic position in the Yishuv thus derived not from values or organizational capacity alone, but from the effective combination of its ideal of state building with an ability to furnish employment and a plethora of social services to those "building the state." Only by becoming a source of attraction and inspiration to new immigrants and whole social groups, and by simultaneously rendering them dependent on its growing economic resources, was the LSM able to co-opt them.

As Shapiro (1977) has pointed out, the great gap between the ideology and reality of Israeli society, a subject extensively commented on by historians and sociologists, resulted in part from the reliance by the LSM institutions on social citizenship rights to extend their influence, even where pioneering was not at stake. Furthermore, the ability to provide or withhold access to institutions which dispensed essential rights that could not be acquired in other ways in Mandatory Palestine created a vast network of patronage. Dependence on the patronage of party *apparatchiks* undermined the active participation republican citizenship presumes.

Nor were the Histadrut's own *apparatchiks* able to resist the corrupting proximity to the public bowl. The very division between the private and public spheres, so central to the liberal discourse, was slow to emerge. Even when caught lining their private pockets from public funds, the "pioneering" *apparatchiks* were forgiven, in view of all that they had done for the virtuous community. The willingness to live with the deep-seated contradiction between public-minded republican ideology and privatizing behavior, in Shapiro's words, was "attached to a whole stratum of managers and administrators in the public sector who occupy a central position in the stratification structure of Israeli society" (Shapiro 1977: 33).

Although the Histadrut prided itself on paying its own workers equal wages, based on family size, in fact it was common knowledge that its bureaucrats' incomes were many times over the officially sanctioned level (Sussman 1974). In addition, the bureaucrats enjoyed special benefits such as housing loans, loans to defray the cost of helping relatives come into Palestine, etc. When an internal investigation of the Histadrut revealed this state of affairs in 1927, Ben-Gurion responded with the unforgettable words: "I believe in the hegemony of the Workers' Movement, but it will be founded not on us being more competent or more honest, but on us being more Zionist than others" (*Davar*, July 20, 1928). In 1950, when employees of his department at the Jewish Agency were caught embezzling funds, Levi Eshkol invoked the biblical principle of "thou shalt not muzzle the ox when he treadeth out the corn" (Deuteronomy 25:4, cited in Shapiro 1977: 33). A particularly egregious misappropriation of the pioneer's status was its inflationary extension beyond the actual pioneers to every member of the Histadrut apparatus. The pioneering ethos of the LSM was unduly inflated to include the mundane operations of the Histadrut's economic and political-cum-economic enterprises, allowing their exploitation for private gain.

All of this having been said, viewing them as political patronage only would seriously misrepresent the nature of social citizenship rights in the Yishuv and in Israel (as did Amitai Etzioni: see 1959: 203–4). While clientelist relations, as well as a considerable amount of patronage and corruption, did certainly exist, many of the resources were awarded not as "gifts" for individual loyalty but as "rights" earmarked for occupants of positions in the process of state building. These rights were built into the fabric of the social order and reflected its priorities.

In the Yishuv rights were conferred in accordance with the republican citizenship discourse, and the two remained closely tied to each other after statehood, despite Israeli society's evolving commitment to liberal democracy. The tug-of-war between the republican-virtue and liberal citizenship discourses after 1948 shaped the debates over immigrant absorption and national insurance. The National Insurance Law – establishing a social security administration and framework – adopted in November 1953 and put into effect on April 1, 1954, was based on a "power equilibrium" between the two positions (Neipris 1966: 103). The NI Law was developed by Kanev, who headed the Histadrut's research center and "reflected the . . . labor orientation that social insurance is to be seen as one of the rights of the working man" (Neipris 1966: 107), that is, of the member of the Histadrut, which marked the broadest parameter of the collective republican community. The national insurance did not do away with the Histadrut's social programs; most importantly, the Histadrut retained its powerful Kupat Cholim. In fact, "the National Insurance Law . . . could only strengthen the Histadrut by freeing it to pursue other activities" (Neipris 1966: 87–8), since it made the state responsible for only three categories of welfare payments: old-age retirement pensions, maternity benefits, and work accident insurance (Neipris 1966: 113). When relief actions became necessary, such as during the massive immigration waves of the late 1940s and early 1950s, the state turned the responsibility for the handicapped, chronically ill, and welfare case immigrants – "until the latter are absorbed in the working community" – to outside organizations, such as the Joint Distribution Committee and the Jewish Agency (Neipris 1966: 109, 151).

The duality of republican pioneering and "universalist" democracy was frequently overlooked by observers of Israeli society. For example, Amitai Etzioni, in a seminal article in 1959, designated Israel a democracy, since government policy reflected changing public opinion and the "vital harmony between state and society . . . [was] maintained" (Etzioni 1959: 197). Liberal democracy, however, was but one of the discourses of Israeli political culture and it remained severely constrained by the pioneering and national discourses. Civil rights remained weak. Social rights were not universal, but remained based on involvement with various aspects of colonial state building and, therefore, contingent and differentially allocated. Israel was not a liberal democracy when Etzioni wrote his article, nor is it today. However, in various spheres, and supported by segments of the new middle class and professional elites, there are strong indications that a liberal democratic possibility is gaining strength at the expense of the pioneering, if not yet of the ethno-nationalist, citizenship discourse. The rights of Israeli citizens are affected by these changes, as we shall see in later chapters.

Conclusion: the formation of hegemony

The leadership achieved by the LSM over the Yishuv and over the Zionist movement's state-building venture can be most usefully analyzed as a form of hegemony. According to Antonio Gramsci, hegemony may be attained when an emancipatory movement, justifying its goals in universalistic terms, secures the leadership of a broad coalition of parties and social strata. These parties and social strata are motivated to follow the hegemonic leader's broadly conceived moral and intellectual leadership by its promise to assimilate them into its own ranks, and thus create a more equitable social order and higher level of civilization. To the extent that the emancipatory aspiration achieves the status of common sense, the alliance formed around it becomes a stable historical bloc, rather than merely a shifting electoral coalition. In different theoretical terms, we could say that a successful hegemonic project represents a well-institutionalized social order; that it not only constrains the political agenda, but becomes this agenda itself; and that it allows for effective and sustained social mobilization and thus reduces the drag of free riders. As such, hegemony stands apart from both the more narrowly conceived corporate mentality of trade unions and domination based on coercion (Gramsci 1971: 12, 180–5). The universalist ambition of the hegemonic project, the comprehensiveness of its inclusionary perspective, and the political and moral leadership required for such an undertaking make successful hegemonic projects a rare phenomenon.

In the original Leninist perspective only the proletariat was seen as capable of providing hegemonic leadership and cementing a class alliance. Gramsci, however, superseded the Leninist approach to hegemony as a proletarian-centered class alliance in three ways. First, Gramsci applied the same perspective to the bourgeoisie by comparing cases, such as England and France, where bourgeois hegemony and rule existed through consensus, with Italy, where the bourgeoisie had a narrow vision of its historical task and its rule relied in large measure on coercion. The latter was a case of "passive revolution": far-reaching political changes were introduced but garnered only limited popular support and had only limited social impact (Gramsci 1971: 106–14). Second, by adopting as his own Machiavelli's early modern concern with the problem of founding a new state, Gramsci broadened the application of the concept of hegemony even further. He replaced Machiavelli's individual prince with the "modern prince": the revolutionary political party which undertakes and fuels the hegemonic venture (Gramsci 1971: 129). Third, whereas Lenin's and Machiavelli's approaches were essentially political, Gramsci's Hegelian and Crocean approach saw hegemony rooted in the voluntary institutional network of civil society, parties, trade unions, schools, etc. Gramsci's Hegelian and Machiavellian twists gives hegemony broad applicability to the analysis of universalist emancipatory projects.

One fruitful application of hegemonic analysis, and perhaps an extension of its purview, is an examination of the effects of granting new citizenship rights to a group or large cross-section of the population. Such a social reform is usually associated with modern political parties that aim at incorporating new social groups for the first time, or more deeply, into the body politic. Like other political parties that were associated with the granting of new generations of citizenship rights – the Republican Party in the USA to freed African-American slaves, the British Labour Party which instituted universal suffrage, or the Scandinavian socialist parties and the Democratic Party in the USA which granted social rights (the latter in the "New Deal") – the Israeli LSM (and the Histadrut) gained the lifelong, and even intergenerational loyalty of its following. It thus became hegemonic and identified with an epoch.

The LSM's goal – founding a socialist Jewish nation-state in Palestine – was habitually described as revolutionary, as were the all-encompassing party and trade unions that were its central tools in this undertaking. The LSM's project, as the functionalist school keeps reminding us, was also universalistic: the promise of the "core," i.e. the LSM, was to assimilate the peripheries of Jewish immigrants into its pioneering institutional network and create an entire new society in its own image. This was, without doubt, a hegemonic venture.

Having seen in this chapter the main stages of the evolution of the LSM's state-building strategy, from the methodical bypassing of the market in order to provide its following with the means of livelihood in Palestine, to the building up of a bureaucratic machine party in order to better control them, we will now look at the critical phase of its ever-expanding political and cultural mobilization, the phase that led to the achievement of cultural and moral hegemony over the Yishuv and the Zionist movement in general. The LSM clinched its hegemonic status in the decade that lasted from 1927 to 1937, when it was able successfully to measure up to twin challenges: internal, from within the WZO, and external, from the Palestinian Arab population.

The LSM–WZO alliance found itself severely challenged at the time of the most significant institutional transformation in the Yishuv. In 1929 the Jewish Agency, which had been provided for in the League of Nations' Mandate as a world Jewish representative to facilitate Jewish development in Palestine, was officially set up. The agency was based on parity between the WZO and non-Zionist Jewish organizations, some of which were led by wealthy Jews, such as British industrialist Lord Melchett and American banker Felix Warburg, who challenged the extra-market strategy that guided Palestinian colonization. In 1927, the executive of the Zionist Congress turned against fundamental aspects of the WZO–LSM "alliance": unemployment benefits were curtailed, public work projects were scaled back, and, most significantly, subsidies to Jewish workers employed by the Mandatory authorities at wages equal to those of Arab employees were discontinued. In 1928 harsh criticism of the "alliance" policies was contained in the report of a committee of experts appointed in anticipation of the establishment of the Jewish Agency. The committee's report expressed the most hostile opinions heard until then towards the current colonization policies. The institutions and policies of the Histadrut came in for the severest rebuke: they were viewed as wasteful and the political intervention in them was depicted as counterproductive. Instead of financing the settlement of penniless immigrants, the experts recommended, support should be redirected towards wealthier settlers who could establish profitable enterprises (Shapiro 1976: 185–6).

The broad-based rejection of the experts' recommendations clearly illustrated the support and moral authority enjoyed by the LSM outside its own circles by the late 1920s. The middle-class elements of the Yishuv stood shoulder to shoulder with the workers. Shlomo Kaplansky, an LSM representative who headed one of the WZO's departments, and Meir Dizengoff, the General Zionist mayor of Tel Aviv, submitted a joint proposal in which they demanded that investment in agriculture be enhanced and that investment and subsidies in Palestine be allocated on the basis of nationalist rather than market-based criteria. The WZO executive came around and reaffirmed its commitment to "Hebrew labor" and to nationally rather than privately owned land. The editor of *Haolam*, the official publication of the WZO, summed up the predominant sentiment in the organization: "even someone who is not a socialist must support the wishes of the worker, and even concede him a lot, since he is at the moment the most loyal stay of our future in this land and since he is the symbol of our national energy and dedication here" (cited in Shapiro 1976: 187).

In 1930, the badly scarred LSM underwent an internal consolidation. Achdut Haavoda (which in 1930 united with Hapoel Hatzair to form Mapai, the key political party of the LSM) built up a powerful party machine to receive, administer, control, and distribute to its members and supporters the resources placed at its disposal. Some of these resources were deployed to co-opt other sectors of the Jewish immigrant community, gaining for the LSM undertakings at least partial legitimacy from religious and middle-class Jewry. After Mapai's formation, the religious Mizrachi Party and the petty bourgeois General Zionists split between factions that supported the LSM and joined some its institutions (e.g. Hapoel Hamizrachi which joined the Histadrut's Kupat Cholim), and those that sought to preserve their autonomy. The split in these rival political parties along lines reflective of the central place of the LSM fully illustrates its appeal. Its draw was now based not only on its pioneering role but also on the social services the comprehensive institutional framework of the LSM extended to its citizens. In 1934 Ben-Gurion attempted to reach an agreement with Jabotinsky's Revisionists, which would have allowed the latter to enjoy the services of the Histadrut's labor exchanges while remaining organizationally independent of it, but his plan was scuttled by the LSM apparatus.

The electoral weight of the LSM in the WZO now grew rapidly. Whereas before 1927 it was a pressure group with 22 percent of the vote, in 1933 Mapai, the united party of labor, attained 44 percent. As a result, by 1933 Mapai controlled not only the Histadrut, but also the political department of the Jewish Agency, and the Vaad Leumi (National Council) of the Yishuv. It became the largest party in the WZO, and instead of a single member in the WZO executive, Mapai now constituted it, with Ben-Gurion joining this body and in 1935 becoming its president.

It was not until the second challenge, however, this time not to the LSM alone, but to the whole Zionist enterprise, that the Yishuv's majority coalesced around the hard core of the LSM and confirmed its hegemonic position in leading the state-building effort. The Arab Revolt of 1936–9, the most intense conflict prior to the 1948 war, played the major role in placing the capstone on the institutional structure of the LSM's hegemony. The strike by Palestinian Arab producers and workers paralyzed public services and sections of the Jewish private economy and led to a quick replacement of the strikers with Jewish hands, following the model established by the LSM. The monopoly of the Histadrut in supplying labor-power quickly convinced unorganized workers of its might. In Yoav

Gelber's conclusion "the Arab Revolt transformed the character of the Yishuv's economic development by strengthening the standing of its central institutions." The import of private capital declined and construction, which had been financed largely by private capital, declined rapidly as well, and came to rely on "national capital." Private agriculture and industry also turned to national capital for support (Gelber 1994: 377–80).

Simultaneously, the movement's military wing, the Hagana militia, evolved into a national body in charge of ensuring the safety of the entire Jewish population. In 1937 the first attempt to establish a standing Jewish military force took place. Security now came to be viewed, for the first time, as weightier than economic considerations. With the outbreak of the Arab Revolt in 1936, military discipline was superimposed on organizational discipline, while organization itself became a code word for membership in the Yishuv. The LSM defined itself and its supporters as the "organized Yishuv" (*hayishuv hameurgan*), whereas the independent, Revisionist paramilitary organizations, the Lehi (named by the British at the time the Stern Gang) and the Etzel (or *irgun*), were the "separatists" (*porshim*).

Most adept at handling and weathering the Jewish–Palestinian conflict through its separatist approach, the LSM proved the superiority of its nationalist strategy over opposing approaches when the national conflict reached its first zenith. The LSM's demonstrated ability to further the general Zionist interest by expanding colonization even under the adverse conditions of a civil war, combined with the imprimatur of the WZO and the prestige gained in large sections of the Mizrachi and General Zionist parties, sealed the LSM's hegemony. It became identified in the public mind with the nation-state-building project, and this led to its consequent continuous and long-term domination of Israeli society, which lasted until 1977. But, if the LSM gained hegemony over most of the Yishuv, why did its republican citizenship not prevail over alternative and competing citizenship discourses? There is no escape from the conclusion that the LSM's hegemony was fraught with contradictions due, we believe, to its elitist, sectoral, and nationalist limitations.

The LSM's hegemony was elitist. In spite of its pretense to represent the entire Yishuv, it could not accommodate the masses of Jewish immigrants. The pioneers, like rising and self-conscious elites elsewhere, sought to remodel the Yishuv in their image. But it is in the nature of vanguards that only as long as very few follow in their footsteps can they protect their high status. Quality, to so remain, needed quantity as its counter-principle. As an elite movement the LSM was not capable of shouldering the burden of state building and achieving demographic majority in Palestine all by itself. The kibbutzim and moshavim were suitable for laying claim to territory, but the Jewish towns and cities of Palestine attracted more immigrants. Accepting the pluralism of the Yishuv would have undermined the LSM's pioneering status and would have led to questioning its proximity to the public purse. By elevating its own contribution to the state-building effort to the status of "pioneering," the LSM created a hierarchy that, in fact, required the existence of other citizenship discourses, subordinate to its own.

The LSM's main efforts went into building up and fortifying its own socio-economic "sector": the companies of Chevrat Haovdim, the Histadrut's institutions, and the co-operative network. Though it also sought to extend its institutional framework, and attract or co-opt new immigrants, as well as members of the middle class and Orthodox Jews, its very dependence on WZO subsidies to support its members, and on non-members to increase the Jewish population in Palestine, meant that the LSM could not impose its will and had to cooperate with others with different convictions, traditions, and interests.

If the LSM's hegemony was based on its effective, and ultimately successful, revolutionary strategy for creating a modern sovereign Jewish nation-state, that revolution remained in many respects a "passive revolution." It resembled the unification of Italy, in that a profound political change was effected, but only partially transformed the social order, because many groups were left out. The LSM failed to assimilate the masses of Mizrachim, the Orthodox, and certainly Palestinian Arabs, and assimilated women only in a limited fashion into its institutional domain. It failed to provide universal access to the rights ensured by its institutions, since its universalism was limited to gaining and providing national citizenship. Thus the hegemony of the LSM's colonial state-building approach was at once inclusionary and exclusionary. It was built on maintaining, rather than suppressing or alleviating, the social differences that necessitated its construction in the first place, and for many years it granted social rights only to those who participated in its own particular method of state building.

Thus Israeli state building was neither fully pluralistic or consociational, because the various social groups were arranged in a rigid hierarchy within the LSM's citizenship framework, nor was it fully hegemonic, because the LSM was unable and unwilling to assimilate all groups into its institutional framework. What did keep the LSM's historical bloc together, in spite of its elitist and sectoral tendencies, was the realization of nationalist aspirations. This was the ultimate promise of Zionism, and the LSM shared it with competing Zionist parties. Many have pointed to the crucial significance of the nation-state as a vehicle for winning rights in the modern world, but Hannah Arendt has probably done so most forcefully. The aspiration for a nation-state of one's own was based on the authoritative illustration by the French Revolution of the far-reaching success of "combin[ing] the declaration of the Rights of Man with national sovereignty." The tight interdependence of sovereignty and rights was manifested with special clarity after the First World War, when the Minority Treaties at once placed non-sovereign peoples under the governments of the national majorities, while charging the League of Nations with the duty of safeguarding their rights. This, in effect, was an admission that the majority nations could not be trusted to uphold minority rights. In Arendt's words:

> The worst factor in this situation was not even that it became a matter of course for the nationalities to be disloyal to their imposed government and for the governments to oppress their nationalities as efficiently as possible, but that the nationally frustrated population was firmly convinced – as was everybody else – that true freedom, true emancipation, and true popular sovereignty could be attained only with full national emancipation, that people without their own national government were deprived of human rights. (Arendt 1973: 272)

Arendt highlighted the fundamental paradox of modern citizenship: since the sovereign nation-state was the primary enforcer of the "inalienable" and, therefore, universal human rights, individuals did not enjoy rights by virtue of their humanity, but by virtue of their membership in the major political institution of the day – a particular, territorially based nation-state. "Because the sovereign state had become the vehicle for claiming rights, members of nations who had not achieved sovereignty had no effective rights" (Klusmeyer 1996: 71). A homogenous Jewish state was to be, as it was for other ethno-nationalist movements in the nineteenth and most of the twentieth century, the broad framework of the institutions of national citizenship which enable citizens to exercise their rights. This goal was shared by all Zionist parties. What singled the LSM out, and conferred on it moral and political leadership, was its ability to effectively implement this aspiration. The "pure," or homogeneous, settlement colony, assembled piecemeal from socialist, co-operative, and quasi-militarized colonies, was its distinct contribution to Zionism and for it the LSM claimed and assumed hegemonic influence. The appeal of the LSM was that it seemed to be alone in being able to carry out the widely shared national program of Zionism, to create a Jewish nation-state in Palestine. The key to the LSM's hegemony, then, was not its socialism, but its nationalism.

Nationalism was a double-edged sword, however: it acted as the cement of the LSM's hegemony because it provided the institutional framework of national citizenship, but it did not require the equalization of social conditions, the assimilation of lower-status groups into the LSM. In fact, the LSM's own communal republican, namely elitist, definition of citizenship as voluntary participation in and contribution toward the "common good," and its attendant institutions, served as a hindrance to the realization of even common ethno-national citizenship. It led to the creation of a multilayered citizenship framework with second-class ethno-national citizenship for Mizrachim and women, whose contribution was viewed as quantitative, and third-class citizenship to Palestinian Arabs, whose national aspirations were denied and who were admitted to citizenship as individuals only. Instead of creating a single standard of membership by assimilating all groups into its institutional network, the LSM stratified membership in the new society and, as the rest of this study will show, created a multi-tiered incorporation regime within which each group found its place according to alternative citizenship discourses. But until the nation-state was attained and secured, the LSM's promise of effective national citizenship was able to mediate these competing citizenship discourses.

3 Mizrachim and women: between quality and quantity

Mizrachim

If they give back the territories, the Arabs will stop coming to work, and then and there you'll put us back into the dead-end jobs, like before. If for no other reason, we won't let you give back those territories...Look at my daughter: she works in a bank now, and every evening an Arab comes to clean the building. All you want is to dump her from the bank into some textile factory, or have her wash the floors instead of the Arab. The way my mother used to clean for you. That's why we hate you here. As long as Begin's in power, my daughter's secure at the bank. If you guys come back, you'll pull her down first thing. (A (fictional?) Mizrachi resident of Beit-Shemesh, a development town, to novelist Amos Oz (Oz 1984: 36)

The dominant status of Ashkenazim in Israeli society is commonly explained by reference to their having been the pioneers, the earlier Jewish settlers in the country. Massive Mizrachi[1] immigration took place only after 1948, so the argument goes, and by then the old-timer Ashkenazim, especially those belonging to the LSM, had laid the foundations for a new institutional edifice in which they occupied the commanding heights. On this interpretation, chronology, without regard to social interests and conflicts, was directly transposed into history.

In actual fact, however, Mizrachi Jews had been immigrating to Palestine throughout the period of the Yishuv, and their share among the immigrants – roughly 10 percent – was proportionate to their share of the world-wide Jewish population at the time (Smooha 1978: 57; Eisenstadt et al. 1993: 4). But the Mizrachi presence in Palestine did not register in Zionist collective memory. The Zionist movement was a European movement in its goals and orientation and its target population was Ashkenazi Jews who constituted, in 1895, 90 percent of the 10.5 million Jews then

---

[1] Mizrachi (also known as Oriental or Sephardic) Jews are those whose origins are in the Muslim countries of the Middle East and North Africa. Those who hail from Europe or America are called Ashkenazi (pl. Ashkenazim). In the data collected by the Central Bureau of Statistics a person's continent of origin is determined by their father's birthplace. For the origins of the names of the two groups, and a historical overview of their relations, see Swirski 1984; Ben-Rafael and Sharot 1991: 24–5.

living in the world (Smooha 1978: 51). Until the Second World War, the Zionist movement "was not active among Orientals [i.e. Mizrachim]. It did not set up chapters in lands where Orientals lived, and, with minor exceptions, did not send any emissaries among them . . . It did not recruit and train Oriental immigrants for Aliyot" (Smooha 1978: 53; see also Chetrit 2001: 59–60).

One important reason for this neglect was that the Zionist movement shared the Orientalist outlook of Europe and the European colonial movements, and considered its project an outpost of European civilization in the barbaric East (Smooha 1978: 55). According to Herzl, "we should there [in the Middle East] form a portion of a rampart of Europe against Asia, an outpost of civilization as opposed to barbarism" (Herzl 1946: 96, cited in Chetrit n.d.: 3). And Max Nordau, Herzl's chief lieutenant, declared at the Eighth Zionist congress (1907): "We shall seek to do in western Asia what the English did in India – I mean the cultural work, not rulership and domination. We aim to come to *Eretz Yisrael* as messengers of culture and we aim to extend the moral boundaries of Europe all the way to the Eupharates" (Nordau 1929: 123–4). Thus, when Herzl tried to persuade the Ottoman sultan to allow Jews to settle in Palestine, he was referring to European Jews, who would have been foreign immigrants in the Ottoman Empire, and not to Mizrachi Jews, whose settlement in Palestine would not have required the crossing of any international border (Chetrit n.d.: 24).

This Orientalist attitude was reflected in the way Mizrachi immigrants were treated by the Zionist organizations operating in Palestine. The most revealing case was that of the Yemenite Jews (Shafir 1989: 91–122). Jewish immigrants from Yemen arrived in Palestine during both the First and Second Aliyot (1881 and 1907), but are never counted among the pioneering heroes of the Yishuv. During the "conquest of labor" stage of the Second Aliya, Yemenite Jewish workers, believed to be capable of subsisting on "Arab" wages, were recruited by the Palestine office of the WZO to replace Palestinian agricultural laborers in the Jewish-owned plantation colonies. These Yemenite Jewish workers not only received lower wages than European Jews, but were also given smaller and cheaper houses and supplementary plots of land. And while both groups of Jewish workers failed to displace the more experienced Palestinian laborers, the Ashkenazim of the LSM, having been allotted land by the JNF, went on to establish kibbutzim and moshavim and become the pioneering founding fathers of the country. The Yemenite Jews, no less pioneering in actual fact, were left to fend for themselves, and were excluded from both the collective settlements and Zionist collective memory. About 30 percent of the Yemenite Jews were eventually settled in separate quarters near the larger plantation colonies of the First Aliya, where they were expected to provide part-time, unskilled labor. This prefigured the settlement of future Mizrachi immigrants by the state of Israel in development towns, where they would provide cheap, unskilled labor to veteran kibbutzim and moshavim (Smooha 1978: 54–5; Druyan 1981; Shohat 1988; Shafir 1989: 105–6; 1990; Nini 1996; Eraqi-Klorman 1997).

The different historical trajectories of the two communities reflected the superior organizational ability of the LSM's Ashkenazi workers, which placed them in a better position to procure resources from the WZO (as discussed in chap. 2, above). The Ashkenazim legitimated their demands, however, by invoking the discourse of republican virtue, in terms of which they described themselves as "idealistic" and "civilized," and the Yemenites as "natural" workers. "Idealistic workers" were those who acted virtuously by forfeiting the comforts of European urban life and the opportunity of immigrating to America and joining the project of Zionist redemption instead. "Natural workers," on the other hand, were neither idealistic nor civilized. They were "natural" in a dual sense: their participation in the Zionist project stemmed naturally from their ethno-national identity as Jews, rather than from ideological conviction; and, being non-modern, they were naturally suited for hard work, harsh discipline, and scanty material rewards (Druyan 1981: 134; Shafir 1990). "Idealistic workers," the bearers of republican virtue, were the stuff pioneers were made of, blazing the trail and setting moral standards for the nation. "Natural workers," on the other hand, were to be foot-soldiers in the Zionist campaign, adding "quantity" to the pioneers' "qualitative" efforts.

The distinction between "quality" and "quantity" was meant to convey the difference between those who were members of the virtuous republican community and those whose membership in the Yishuv was based on ethno-national ties only. Its aim was to bridge the gap between the pioneers' claim to be a dedicated, exclusive vanguard, deserving of special privileges, and the need to draw the Jewish masses to Palestine. Mainstream Israeli sociology uncritically adopted this distinction and elevated it to a theory of the cultural superiority of Ashkenazim. In seeking to explain the failure of Mizrachi immigrants to be successfully integrated into Israeli society, S. N. Eisenstadt distinguished between "*chalutzim*" (pioneers), "*olim*" (literally "pilgrims"), and "*mehagrim*" (immigrants). *Chalutzim* were the trailblazers while *olim*, Eisenstadt argued, were ideologically motivated settlers, whose physical migration was preceded by a cultural and spiritual transformation, a conscious break with traditional Jewish values. This enabled them to embrace more easily the pioneering values of the Yishuv and join its core republican community. "Immigrants," on the other hand, were refugees fleeing their home countries without any cultural or spiritual preparation. They were, therefore, less able to adopt the values of Zionist civic virtue and, as a result, had greater difficulty integrating into its institutions. Before 1948, Eisenstadt argued, most Jews who had come to Palestine were *olim*; after 1948 they were immigrants. Mizrachi Jews, however, were mostly immigrants, whether they migrated before or after 1948. This conceptual distinction, although not necessarily expressed in these precise terms, was followed by an entire generation of Israeli sociologists (Eisenstadt 1947; 1948; 1950: 200–3; 1954: 90–103; 1969; 1985: 124, 297–300; 1986; Cohen 1983; Zameret 1997: 143; Lissak 1999).[2]

This analysis proved to be of crucial importance in the 1950s and 1960s, when the pioneers, now occupying all dominant positions in the society, addressed the massive wave of Mizrachi immigrants. This influx was by no means a spontaneous movement. It was initiated, orchestrated, and carried out by the newly established state of Israel which, in the wake of the Holocaust and the barring of emigration from communist Eastern Europe, resorted to the hardly tapped demographic (quantitative) potential of Middle Eastern and North African Jews. And while relations between these Jews and the states in which they were residing were indeed becoming tense, due to the Jewish–Palestinian conflict, Israel's motivation in evacuating them was not, in the words of a leading Israeli politician, "the need to rescue [them], but the need to create a Hebrew majority in *Eretz Yisrael*" (cited in Swirski 1995: 35, see also 9–70).

The decision to transplant the Jewish communities of the Middle East to Israel did not involve a change of heart with respect to their cultural qualities and was not taken without misgivings (Tsur 1997).[3] No less a figure than David Ben-Gurion is reported as saying, in the mid-1960s:

–The Moroccan Jew took a lot from the Moroccan Arabs. The culture of Morocco I would not like to have here. And I don't see what contribution present Persians have to make.
–We do not want Israelis to become Arabs. We are in duty bound to fight against the spirit of the Levant, which corrupts individuals and societies, and preserve the authentic Jewish values as they crystallized in the [evidently European] Diaspora.

---

[2] For previous critiques of this approach, see Smooha 1978; Bernstein and Swirski 1982. In this context, Smooha's remark that "Zionism failed to serve as a modernizing agent for non-Ashkenazi Jews and to make them equal partners in the enterprise of nation-building" is very pertinent (Smooha 1978: 53).

[3] This transplantation, it is important to note, resulted in the disintegration of these communities in Israel, rather than in their continuing existence as coherent social bodies. This, paradoxically, was an important reason for the Mizrachim's "failure" to integrate in Israeli society (Swirski 1990; 1995).

And indirectly:

> In the midst of the operation of *Kibbutz Galuyot* (Ingathering of Exiles) [that is, in the early 1950s] Prime Minister Ben-Gurion cried out that the country was in danger of Levantinization because the flood of primitive panicky Oriental Jews was not matched by [a] comparable flow of volunteer Jews from the trained West. But the Arabs were beaten precisely because they are Levantinized, and if there was no prospect of compensating contribution from the West, the tide of Eastern immigration into Israel should have been controlled . . . and not whipped up artificially. (Smooha 1978: 88, 372–3)

Apart from expressing the kind of Orientalist prejudices that have spread far and wide in the West, the association made in these statements (and countless others could have been quoted) between Middle Eastern Jews and Arabs shows the imprint the colonial state-building project had on the incorporation of Jewish immigrants and explains the ambivalent attitude with which Mizrachi immigrants were greeted in Israel. As Jews immigrating under the Law of Return, the prime institutional expression of the ethno-national discourse, Mizrachi immigrants were granted all civil and individual political citizenship rights. At the same time, since their inclusion was based *only* on their ethno-national qualities, they were economically and socially marginalized from the core republican institutions and discouraged from expressing their collective voice in the formulation of the common good of society (see Chetrit 2001: 73–82).

The widely used Ashkenazi–Mizrachi distinction is an Israeli social construct that reflects that ambivalent attitude and disguises important differences among the Mizrachim themselves. Mizrachim have originated in two distinct geographical and cultural areas: the Middle East, primarily Iraq and Yemen, and North Africa, primarily Morocco. Middle Eastern Jews arrived in Israel mostly in the early 1950s and were settled primarily in central areas of the country, in many cases in towns, villages, or neighborhoods deserted by Palestinians. North African Jews arrived mostly in the late 1950s and early 1960s and many of them were settled in "development towns" located in outlying areas. Thus Middle Eastern Jews became the owners of, or at least protected tenants in, high-value real estate located in prime areas of the country, which they could bequeath to their children. North African Jews, on the other hand, acquired housing mostly in public housing projects in areas of low demand and little real estate value (Benski 1993; Lewin-Epstein, Elmelech, and Semyonov 1997; Lewin-Epstein and Semyonov 2000). These differences can partially account for the emerging class differentiation within the Mizrachi group itself. About one-third of Mizrachim can now be classified as belonging to the middle class, and they have been more or less integrated into the Ashkenazi mainstream of society. Middle Eastern immigrants and their descendants are overrepresented in this group, as compared to North African ones (Ben-Rafael and Sharot 1991; Benski 1993).

In spite of these internal differences, the significant social reality is that both groups have been viewed as a uniform Mizrachi population, and by and large excluded from the LSM's virtuous pioneering project, institutions, and citizenship. As common "quantity" their "qualitative" differences could not be recognized, and they tended to be identified with the lowest common denominator among Jews – ethno-nationality. Thus they were assigned "quantitative" tasks, such as populating remote or vacant areas of the country, beefing up the lower ranks of the military, and providing cheap, unskilled labor for the country's agriculture and emergent industry (Smooha 1978; Hasson 1981; Bernstein and Swirski 1982; Swirski 1984; Levy 1997: 29–34). The effects of this form of incorporation are visible in the "ethnic gap" between Ashkenazim and Mizrachim in the educational and occupational spheres, to be related in some detail below. One result of this gap is that even when they attain individual social mobility Mizrachim have to struggle against exclusionary stereotypes. Thus, notwithstanding the socio-economic differentiation among Mizrachim, it is still appropriate to view their citizenship status as an issue that unifies rather than divides them.

The marginalization of Mizrachim was expressed primarily through limited access to the institutions of the new state and diminished social rights. In the first section of this chapter we focus on two of these social rights: housing and education. Housing, as we saw in the previous chapter, was a key resource used to tie the pioneers to their new country. The Israeli state extended housing rights to all immigrants, but the implementation of these rights was often used to achieve colonial state ends, such as "population dispersion" (Rosenhek and Shalev 2000). This resulted in a spatial, hence also social, economic, and political peripheralization of many Mizrachi immigrants. By the same token, since education is the main tool of individual social mobility, the Mizrachim's lower educational attainments left them less capable of taking advantage of Israel's economic liberalization and more reliant on the state, even as the role of the state has been shrinking in recent years. The Mizrachim's attitudes towards the state, and their political reaction to their second-class citizenship experience in general, will be examined in the second section of this chapter.

Second-class social citizenship

Development towns. Unlike most Middle Eastern immigrants, who were settled primarily in central areas of the country, many North African immigrants were settled in "development towns" and in newly established moshavim located in its peripheral regions. This was done in order to impose the authority of the state over border regions of the country, many of them previously populated by Palestinians, and provide cheap labor to the kibbutzim and veteran moshavim located in these areas.

Development towns (DTs) are small urban settlements that were established mostly in the 1950s. Until the massive immigration of Soviet Jews in the early 1990s (see chap. 12, below), between 15 and 20 percent of Israel's population lived in DTs (DTs are defined differently for different official purposes), where the population was, on the average, 75 percent Mizrachi. This made DTs home to between one-quarter and one-third of the country's Mizrachi Jews. Since the early 1990s the demographic composition of DTs has changed, their population having been augmented by between 25 and 50 percent due to the influx of immigrants from the former Soviet Union (Berler 1970: 58–185; Goldberg 1984: 1–12; Swirski and Shoushan 1986; Efrat 1987; Ben-Zadok 1993; Carmon and Yiftachel 1994; CBS 1994; Yiftachel and Meir 1998; Lissak 1999).[4]

Socially, as well as geographically, DTs form a peripheral "spatial sector" within Jewish Israeli society (Ben-Zadok 1993; Yiftachel and Meir 1998). Being remote from the larger urban centers and commercial hubs makes them less desirable residential locations and reduces the range of employment opportunities. In 1987 the Central Bureau of Statistics (CBS), a government agency, computed the socio-economic status (SES) of every urban locality in the country (not including the OT), based on data from the 1983 national census. On a scale of standardized scores combining sixteen different socio-economic variables and running from −2 (lowest SES) to +2 (highest SES) (with only a few Palestinian communities scoring below −2), the average score for all development towns was −0.40. This score placed development towns between the fifth and sixth SES clusters, out of twenty, or below 70 percent of the entire population (CBS 1987; cf. Heimberg [Shitrit] and Dor 1994; CBS 1995a; Yiftachel and Tzfadia 1999; 2000).[5]

In 1983, 53 percent of the DT workforce was employed in "traditional," low-paying industries, compared to 43 percent in the country as a whole (including both Jewish and Arab workers) (Borukhov 1988: 9–10). Over 27 percent of the DT labor force was employed in the textile industry, the

---

[4] These newly arriving immigrants, the vast majority of them Ashkenazim, joined the society close to the bottom of the socio-economic ladder. Since the early 1990s, therefore, the only comparison that is relevant for understanding the relative position of Mizrachim is that between second-generation members of the two groups.

[5] The relative placing of development towns would have been much lower had the calculation been made for the Jewish population only (Khalidi 1988: 133–8). The 1983 census is more suitable for our purposes than the subsequent one, conducted in 1995, because the latter reflects the effects of the large-scale settling of formerly Soviet Jews in DTs.

lowest paying of all, compared to only 15 percent of the entire Jewish labor force. Educationally, in 1999 the rate of college graduates in DTs was 10 percent, compared to a national average of 14 percent, while the rate of people without a high-school diploma (*teudat bagrut*) was 63 percent, compared to 56.4 percent nationally. These educational figures would have been even lower without the presence of immigrants from the former Soviet Union in DTs.

Widespread unemployment has been endemic in DTs since the early 1970s, with rates sometimes as high as twice the national average. While only about 17 percent of Israel's population resided in DTs in 1987, they housed 40 percent of the country's unemployed. In December 1989, when the national unemployment rate was about 10 percent, unemployment in several DTs reached the 20 percent mark. In July 1998, about half of the sixteen localities with a rate of unemployment of over 10 percent were DTs (and the rest were mostly Palestinian communities). Moreover, many more people in DTs than in the rest of the country leave the labor force permanently, so that they are no longer counted among the unemployed. These unemployment figures naturally affect income levels as well. Thus, in 1998 average disposable income in DTs (after direct taxes and transfer payments) was only 83.4 percent of the national average (Lavy 1988: 4, 20; Peled 1990; Ben-Zadok 1993; CBS 1996a; 1999a; 1999b; National Insurance Institute 2000: 58–9).

The occupational and income gap. The differential geographic and institutional incorporation epitomized by DTs characterizes the working-class Mizrachi population as a whole. A social mobility study conducted in 1974 found that:

Almost 70 percent of [Mizrachi males are] concentrated in the areas of skilled, semiskilled, and unskilled labor, as well as in service occupations and in agriculture. By . . . comparison, only about 45 percent of European-American Jewish males are engaged in these occupational areas. Nearly one-third of the European-Americans are found in the upper nonmanual occupations . . . whereas only one-tenth of Asian-African [i.e. Mizrachi] Jewish males hold positions of this kind. . . . These basic differences between the two ethnic groups are replicated in each of the age cohorts. The greatest dissimilarity in occupational distribution is found among the *youngest* cohort. (Kraus and Hodge 1990: 66; emphasis added)

Generally, the authors of this study found that

although Asian-African Jews raised their educational levels, the average educational gap between this group and Jews of European-American origin decreased only very slightly. In fact, the difference between ethnic groups with regard to postsecondary schooling actually increased steeply. At the same time, the occupational prestige gap between the two ethnic groups widened, attended by growing disparities between the groups in regard to their concentrations in particular occupational categories. (Kraus and Hodge 1990: 68; cf. 172)

Changes that have taken place in the following decade-and-a-half (until the onset of massive immigration from the Soviet Union in the late 1980s) have not changed significantly the relative standing of the two Jewish ethnic groups (Wolffsohn 1987: 138–55; Shavit 1990; Schmelz et al. 1991: 109–12; Smooha 1993a; Nahon 1993a; 1993b; Cohen and Haberfeld 1998; Cohen 1998). Most of the gains made by Mizrachim in this period have been either outstripped by the gains made by Ashkenazim, such as in the areas of education, occupational status or income, or else have been in fields that have declined in their social significance.

In only two social fields – self-employment/small-business ownership and politics – can the Mizrachim be said to have improved their standing in relation to Ashkenazim. The rate of the self-employed (including employers of others) in the two groups was equalized by 1983, at about 17 percent. Ashkenazim, however, still predominated among large-business owners, and the income gap between the two groups, while smaller than among wage earners, was still meaningful and was larger among members of the second than of the first generation (Nahon 1993c: 80–1; see also Yaar 1986; Shavit and Yuchtman-Yaar 2000). Even more significantly, perhaps, in spite of the great strides Mizrachim have made in politics (see below) they constituted, in 1985–6, only 19 percent of the upper echelons of the civil service. This was a marked improvement, however, over 1967, when only two Mizrachim were counted among the forty-two most senior members of the service (Schecter 1972; Ben-Rafael and Sharot 1991: 35; Nachmias 1991: 415; Grinberg 1993a; 1993b; Kashti 1997d).

Table 3.1 presents a few characteristic indicators of the relative socio-economic standing of Ashkenazim and Mizrachim at the present time. Housing density of less than one person per room was enjoyed in 1988 by 60 percent of the foreign-born Ashkenazim and only 32 percent of Mizrachim, while the figures for the Israel born were 40 percent and 23 percent, respectively (reflecting, obviously, the older age, rather than the greater affluence, of the foreign born) (Smooha 1993a: 317; for comparable figures for 1991 see Smooha 1993b). In 1988 close to 40 percent of the foreign-born Ashkenazim were in the three top occupational categories (professionals, managers, and technicians) compared to 20 percent of the foreign-born Mizrachim. The gap between the Israel-born members of the two groups was even wider: 50 percent to 21 percent. In 1995 72 percent of second-generation Ashkenazim worked in white-collar occupations, and 28 percent were blue-collar workers;

Table 3.1 *Selected socio-economic characteristics by ethnic origin, different years*

		Ashkenazim	Mizrachim
Occupational status (3 top categories), 1988			
foreign born		40%	20%
Israel born (IB)		50	21
income	1988	100	80
income per capita	1988	100	64
employee income (IB ages 25–24)			
	1975	100	79
	1982	100	70
	1992	100	68
	1995	100	69
college graduates			
	1975	100	100
	1982	100	83
	1992	100	88
	1995	100	78
housing (<1 p/r) 1988			
foreign born		60	32
IB		40	23
education (IB employees ages 25–54)			
years of schooling			
	1975	12.8	9.9
	1982	13.8	10.5
	1992	14.2	11.6
	1995	14.4	12.0
% college graduates			
	1975	25.0	6.0
	1982	25.5	8.7
	1992	38.0	10.3
	1995	36.6	10.3

Sources: Smooha 1993b; Cohen and Haberfeld 1998; Cohen 1998.

among second-generation Mizrachim the figures were 46 percent and 54 percent, respectively. Unemployment among second-generation Ashkenazim in 1993 was 4.9 percent, and among Mizrachim 13.2 percent (last two sets of figures not shown). In 1988 the average Mizrachi head of household earned 80 percent of the income of an Ashkenazi one, but only 64 percent per capita. And at least among wage-earners the income gap has been widening: an Israel-born Mizrachi wage-earner earned

79 percent of the income of an Ashkenazi wage-earner in 1975, 70 percent in 1982, and 69 percent in 1995 (Smooha 1993a: 317; Adva Center 1995; CBS 1997: 44; Kashti 1997b; 1997f; 1997g: 25; Cohen and Haberfeld 1998; Cohen 1998). Most revealingly, perhaps, whereas in 1975 the income of an Israel-born Mizrachi employee with a college degree was equal to that of a similarly qualified Ashkenazi, in 1995 the former's income was only 78 percent of the latter's.

Tracking and discrimination in the education system. This continuing social gap between Ashkenazim and Mizrachim, a gap that persists, and in some respects even widens, in the second generation, attests to the failure of "absorption through modernization," the battle cry of both mainstream sociology and the political establishment in their dealing with the Mizrachi immigration of the 1950s and 1960s (Ram 1995: 38–43). Underlying this slogan was the unwarranted assumption, so basic to modernization theories, that all Mizrachim were more "traditional" and less "modern" than Ashkenazi Israeli Jews. As a matter of fact, however, many Mizrachi youngsters – 50,000 in Morocco, 36,000 in Iraq – had been attending "modern" schools in their countries of origin prior to their immigration to Israel. In many cases the academic level of those schools was higher than that of the schools in which they were to be enrolled in Israel. For these youngsters, the encounter with the Israeli educational system, the primary vehicle of "absorption through modernization," meant a retreat from better to lesser education (Swirski 1990: 28–31; cf. Shavit 1997: 20; Ben-Ami 1998: 23).

Probably the best indicator of educational achievement in Israel over the years has been the ability to gain the state matriculation certificate (*teudat bagrut*), a high-school diploma that is necessary (although no longer sufficient) for admission to institutions of higher education. Comparing the numbers of students of different ethnic backgrounds eligible for this certificate is thus a good place to start a discussion of the educational aspect of Israel's incorporation regime. The ratio of Mizrachi eighteen-year-olds holding the certificate in 1995 was 28 percent, up from 17 percent in 1987, while among Ashkenazi eighteen-year-olds it was 38.7 percent in 1995, up from 31.6 percent in 1987. But the rising rates of eligibility reflect not only higher educational attainments but the lowering of the requirements for matriculation as well. As a result, the value of the diploma for admission to universities has been eroding. Thus, in 1999 only 87 percent of those gaining the diploma could thereby meet the minimum requirement for admission. Of the 1986–7 cohort of matriculation certificate earners, 45 percent of Ashkenazim but only 30 percent of Mizrachim had gone on to post-secondary education by 1995

(Adler and Balas 1997: 136–7, 153 n.11; Kashti 1997e; Adva Center 2000a).[6]

These figures, of course, refer to students who are second-generation, in some cases third-generation, Mizrachim. They reflect, therefore, the workings of the Israeli educational system, or rather systems. For as Swirski (1990) has shown, Israel in reality has four different state education systems, designed for four different populations: secular Ashkenazim, religious Zionist Ashkenazim, Mizrachim, and citizen Palestinians. (In addition, a number of parochial systems cater to the needs of various *charedi* groups: see chap. 5, below.)

Within the framework of the Yishuv, there existed three different (mostly elementary) school systems: General Zionist, Labor Zionist, and Religious Zionist. In addition, the *charedi* Agudat Yisrael, which was not part of the organized Yishuv, had its own independent school system. In 1948 about 50 percent of the students enrolled in the official Yishuv systems attended General Zionist schools, about 27 percent attended the Labor schools, and about 22 percent attended the Religious Zionist ones. The independent Agudat Yisrael schools were attended by roughly the same number of students as the Labor and Religious Zionist schools (Eliav 1988: 218–19; Swirski 1990: 41; Zameret 1997: 21). The three Zionist systems competed fiercely for the enrollment of immigrant children, and as a result of being in power, the share of the Labor Zionist system increased by 1953 to 43 percent of all Jewish students, while the General Zionist's declined to only 27 percent, the Religious Zionist's to 19 percent, and Agudat Yisrael's to 11 percent (Swirski 1990: 41–2; cf. Zameret 1997: 191–4).

In 1953 the State Education Law did away with the official sectoral school systems of the Yishuv period. In their stead, two state systems were established, one secular and one religious, the latter under the *de facto* control of the National Religious Party (NRP). In addition, a separate state system was established for Arab students, and the independent system of Agudat Yisrael was brought under state financing, without real state supervision. Ironically, then, the only school system effectively abolished by the Mapai-led government was the Labor Zionist system (Zucker 1973: 134–8; Liebman and Don-Yehiya 1983: 84, 126; Zameret 1997: 190–252; cf. Swirski 1990: 41, for a different interpretation).

The nationalization of the school systems brought to an end the competition over immigrant children, with the majority of Mizrachi immigrant children being assigned now to national religious schools. As a result,

---

[6] Due to the military service required of Israeli Jews, of three years for men and two years for women, there is normally a gap of a few years between graduating from high school and starting post-secondary education.

the national religious system's share of Jewish elementary-school pupils grew, between 1953 and 1968, from 19 to 29 percent. In 1970 84 percent of the students in the national religious system were of Mizrachi origin, compared to 51 percent in the secular state system (Swirski 1990: 41–2). In 1965 21 percent of the teachers in the secular state system, but fully 40.5 percent in the religious system, lacked proper teaching credentials (Swirski 1990: 53).

This first phase in the evolution of the educational system is conventionally referred to as "the stage of formal equality." Formal equality meant absorption of the immigrant children into the existing school systems, teaching them the same curriculum and judging them by the same standards. It did not mean either integrating them into the veteran student population or assigning to their education an equal share of the educational resources of the state (Swirski 1990: 59; 1995: 76–86).

Until 1957 the state did not concern itself with the educational fortunes of its youngsters beyond the elementary level. Post-elementary education was limited to a narrow elite stratum and was privately paid for. As a result, in 1957 82 percent of the students in all high schools – academic, agricultural, and vocational – were Ashkenazim, with their share among academic school seniors reaching 92 percent. In order to redress this imbalance, a system of tuition subsidies was introduced by the state in 1957, based on both merit and need. Merit was determined by a psychometric test known as the *seker* (survey). This test was used not only for the purpose of subsidizing high-school tuition but for screening applicants to the better high schools as well. In the first year it was administered, 81 percent of Ashkenazi children passed the test, most of them receiving grades in the upper portion of the scale. Among Mizrachi children only 46 percent passed, most of them in the lower portion of the scale (Swirski 1990: 79).

The introduction of the *seker* was the first step in the construction of an elaborate tracking system that directs the "good," mostly Ashkenazi, students to academic high schools leading to matriculation and higher education, and the "weak," mostly Mizrachi, students to vocational schools. This development corresponded with the early phase of rapid industrialization that began with the onset of German reparations in the mid-1950s. The new, industry-based economic policy required a significant increase in the supply of skilled and semi-skilled industrial workers. Vocational schools were to be the vehicles for training large numbers of Mizrachi youth for these jobs, while Ashkenazim were to be trained in the academic schools and, increasingly, at universities, for professional and managerial careers. As part of this move, a special "compensatory" track was introduced in 1963 in the elementary schools, where mostly

Mizrachi students have been receiving more limited education, consistent with their "aptitudes, needs and goals" (Swirski 1990: 94) and preparing them for vocational secondary schools. Not surprisingly, at this stage the "formal equality" of the first phase was abandoned, together with the egalitarian educational ideology that went with it, in favor of a new, achievement-oriented ideology of "excellence" (Swirski 1990: 11, 87–137; Shavit 1990).

Two additional elements of the reform, which were implemented only in 1968, were the introduction of junior high schools (that is, a shift from a system of 8+4 to a system of 6+3+3 years of schooling) and a plan for the (intra-Jewish) ethnic integration of high schools. Junior high schools were introduced in order to provide the upper-track, middle-class (and mostly Ashkenazi) students with longer and better preparation for the matriculation examinations, while the integration plan was meant to camouflage the ethnic character of the newly elaborated tracking system. Not surprisingly, the former aspect of the reform proved to be quite successful, while the latter was subverted in many different ways and is universally considered to have been a failure (Swirski 1999: 190–7). The sustained differences in the educational attainments of Ashkenazim and Mizrachim attest to this failure. In fact, educational sociologist Yossi Shavit has argued that the higher rates of post-secondary education among citizen Palestinians, as compared with Mizrachi Jews, despite the much smaller share of resources allocated to Palestinian education, stem from the fact that the Palestinians have their own, segregated system and do not have to compete against the privileged social group – Ashkenazim – in either education or the labor market (Shavit 1990; see chap. 4, below).

The Mizrachi search for political expression and rights

In terms of both the liberal and the ethno-nationalist citizenship discourses, Mizrachi immigrants were entitled to full political citizenship rights. In fact, however, the exercise of their rights was curtailed and their use to promote distinct Mizrachi interests and identities was delegitimized. The story of Mizrachim in Israeli politics, therefore, is one of struggle to possess and master the rights they formally hold. Even so, the political expression of Mizrachim has rarely been a Mizrachi political expression; more commonly it was channeled into the left–right division and, increasingly, into the secular–religious one. As a result, the Mizrachi vote has become a swing vote, but rarely a distinct voice.

The second-class citizenship occupied by Mizrachim in Israel's incorporation regime is reflected in their designation in the public discourse as "*edot*."[7] The Ashkenazim, by implication, constitute normative Israeli society. This distinction marks the boundary between the virtuous republican and the merely ethno-national modes of incorporation in the society. Thus, regardless of the numerical ratio between the two groups (roughly 50: 50), social movements and political parties initiated by Mizrachim have been consistently stigmatized as "ethnic," hence separatist, while no such designation has ever been applied to organizations dominated by Ashkenazim (Herzog 1985: 51, 58; 1986: 290). This has been an important factor in shaping the political expression of Mizrachi interests and aspirations.

Generally speaking, Mizrachim have not reacted to their marginalization in the society by trying to engage in political mobilization on the basis of shared cultural markers. As a semi-peripheral group, "sandwiched" between the Ashkenazim and the Palestinians, they have sought to ally themselves with the Jewish state and with the Ashkenazim who control it, rather than with the subordinate Palestinians, with whom they share many socio-economic and cultural attributes. As a result, Mizrachi protest has usually not contested the existence of multiple discourses of citizenship, but has sought rather to enhance the status of the ethno-national discourse at the expense of the republican and liberal ones (cf. Yiftachel, forthcoming; for a review of Mizrachi resistance movements see Chetrit 2001).

As early as the Ottoman period, Yemenite workers were complaining bitterly about being treated by their Ashkenazi employers and co-workers as if they were Arabs. Their solution, however, was not to organize themselves separately (let alone together with the Arabs), but to demand equality and integration with the Ashkenazim (Shafir 1989: 118–22). During the British Mandate several Sephardi and Mizrachi political parties participated in elections to the institutions of the Yishuv, with some success. This was tolerated, even encouraged, by the Zionist leadership, because under Mandatory law membership in the Yishuv was voluntary, and disgruntled groups could simply opt out. The Zionist leadership had an obvious interest in having the Yishuv encompass all Jews in Palestine, for demographic and legitimational reasons, and they were willing to make concessions not only to Mizrachi groups but to anti-Zionist *charedi* groups as well (unsuccessfully in the latter case; see chap. 5, below). Furthermore, since Mizrachim constituted a relatively small and *declining* portion

---

[7] "Ethnic groups" would be the closest English equivalent: cf. Krausz 1986. It is instructive that the designation is "*edot*," in the plural, while the social reality has been for all Mizrachim to crystallize into one group, in socio-economic terms as well as in the public consciousness, both their own and the Ashkenazim's. See Nahon 1993a: 34–7; Eisenstadt 1969: 11–12; Swirski 1995: 60.

of Jews in Palestine (from 40 to 20 percent in 1918–48) (Horowitz and Lissak 1989: 69), ethnically based political parties were not seen by the dominant Labor Zionist movement as a political threat (Herzog 1984).

Things changed dramatically, however, with the arrival of massive waves of Mizrachi immigration in the 1950s. With the Mizrachi portion of the population reaching and then exceeding 50 percent, the specter of their coming to influence the existing social order, either politically or culturally, became a matter of serious concern (Smooha 1978: 86–94; Lewis 1985). Major efforts at delegitimizing "ethnic" political organizations were undertaken by the dominant Ashkenazi institutions, and indeed, political parties catering specifically to Mizrachi voters almost disappeared from Israel's political scene. The few "ethnic" political parties that did participate in elections failed to draw significant electoral support (Herzog 1985; 1986: 288). Rather, until 1973 over 50 percent of Mizrachi voters had been voting for the Labor Party, in its various manifestations. This reflected both their desire to identify with the dominant political force in the society and the virtual stranglehold the LSM had, through its various social and economic institutions, on employment opportunities and the provision of social services to the immigrants (Shapiro 1989: 178–9; Shalev 1990).

Between 1973 and 1996, however, over 50 percent of Mizrachi voters voted Likud (Shapiro 1989: 178). This shift, which was largely responsible for Likud's victory in 1977 and its return to power in 1996, was caused by a combination of structural and ideological factors:

(1) Structural changes in the economy, which preceded the 1967 war but were greatly accelerated by the occupation of the West Bank and Gaza, reduced the dependence of many Mizrachi immigrants on LSM institutions for employment and social services (Farjoun 1983; Goldberg and Ben-Zadok 1988; Shalev 1992).

(2) The appearance of a new generation of Mizrachi voters, resentful of their secondary status in society and more politically assertive than their immigrant parents (Abramson 1990).

(3) The *mitun*, a government-induced recession launched in 1965 in order to curb growing labor militancy, caused high levels of unemployment and decline of real wages, especially among Mizrachi workers (Schwartz Greenwald 1972; Shalev 1984; Shapiro and Grinberg 1988; chap. 9, below).

(4) The military administration imposed on Israel's Palestinian citizens in 1948 and used, among other things, to prevent their entry into the Jewish labor market, began to be relaxed in the late 1950s and was finally abolished in 1966 (chap. 4, below). In 1967, following

the occupation of the West Bank and Gaza, non-citizen Palestinians began to enter the Israeli labor market in ever-increasing numbers. Thus, for the first time since 1948, (mostly Mizrachi) Jews and Palestinians were again competing with each other in the secondary sector of the Israeli labor market (Farjoun 1983; Semyonov and Lewin-Epstein 1987).

(5) The 1967 war and its consequences confronted the colonization strategy of the LSM with a challenge it was not equipped to deal with: military control over territories densely populated with Palestinians and completely devoid of Jewish settlers. The different strands of Labor Zionist ideology now dictated contradictory strategies of action: the territorial and military aspects required settlement and continued control of these territories; the demographic and civic aspects called for relinquishing them. As a result, for the first time in its history, the LSM lost the strategic initiative and fell into disunity and inaction. This was clearly demonstrated in the poor performance of the government and the IDF in the war of 1973.

Likud was perfectly poised to take advantage of the new situation. Traditionally the party of opposition, it had always appeared as the champion of those (Jews) excluded from the virtuous republican community. Disdainful of the "constructive" pioneering activities, it had always advocated military conquest over settlement as a method of territorial acquisition. Strongly committed to ethno-nationalism, it had no problem justifying the continuing military occupation of a large Palestinian population deprived of all rights (Shapiro 1989).

But while Likud has succeeded, between 1973 and 1996, in mobilizing a majority among Mizrachi voters, towards the end of the 1980s it began to feel the effects of having been in power for several years. Despite some highly publicized anti-poverty programs, during the time in which Likud was the main governing party, the (mostly Ashkenazi) rich in Israel grew richer and the (mostly Mizrachi) poor grew poorer. (This trend continued during Labor's tenure in 1992–6; see chap. 9, below). And while the unemployment rates had been fluctuating, their overall tendency, until the early 1990s (and again since 1997), was upwards. Furthermore, labor-market friction between low-paid Palestinian and Jewish workers had not subsided under Likud governments, until well into the first intifada. And Mizrachi workers, especially in DTs, felt seriously threatened by Palestinian competition (Peled 1990).

Most importantly, perhaps, the mid-1980s witnessed the beginning of a profound restructuring process in the Israeli economy. When Likud came to power in 1977 it embarked on a program of economic liberalization that was designed to do away with the political–economic edifice constructed by the LSM. In the face of opposition from the Histadrut, however, Likud finance ministers were hesitant in implementing that program. Thus, the only tangible result of these efforts, by the mid-1980s, was an annual inflation rate that reached 445 percent in 1984 (Shalev 1992: 240). In 1985 the national unity government, in which Likud and Labor shared power, instituted a harsh anti-inflationary program known as the Emergency Economic Stabilization Plan (EESP). The plan not only brought inflation to a halt, at the price of economic slowdown, lower wages, and increased unemployment, but prepared the ground for the liberalization process that has since reshaped the Israeli economy (chap. 9, below).

Beyond the immediate goal of stopping inflation, the EESP began to smooth the way for Israel's integration into the process of economic globalization. As Peter Beyer has argued, globalization can have adverse economic and cultural effects on the weaker sectors of society, who often react by reasserting their particularistic socio-cultural identities through nationalist or sub-nationalist movements. Furthermore,

> In some circumstances, religion has been, and continues to be, an important resource for such movements, yielding religio-political movements in places as diverse as Ireland, Israel, Iran, India, and Japan. Because of their emphasis on socio-cultural particularisms, such religious movements often display the conservative option [of opposing globalization] with its typical stress on the relativizing forces of globalization as prime manifestations of evil in the world. (Beyer 1994: 108)[8]

The earliest appearance of such religio-political movements in Israel, catering specifically to poor Mizrachim and enjoying meaningful support in DTs, was in 1984. In that year both Shas, a Mizrachi–*charedi* political party, and Meir Kahane's racist Kach movement made their debut on the national political scene. Shas won four Knesset seats in the general elections of 1984, the best showing of a Mizrachi political party since 1948. Kahane's 1.2 percent of the national vote entitled him to one seat only. In DTs, however, Shas and Kahane had an almost equal share of the vote, around 3.5 percent each (Shafir and Peled 1986). In 1988, based on Peled's pre-election survey, 8.5 percent of the voters in DTs were planning to vote for Kahane (making his party the third-largest party there, after Likud and Labor), while Shas was expected only to retain its 3 percent of the vote (Peled 1990).

---

[8] The movement Beyer chose to focus on in Israel, Gush Emunim, is not really the case that illustrates his point. One indication of this is that Gush Emunim, and the political parties that express its agenda, do not enjoy much support among the poorer strata of Israeli society. The Israeli religio-political movement that fits Beyer's analysis is Shas.

Kahane's appeal for his voters, almost universally Mizrachim of low socio-economic status, was based on his calling for the "transfer" of all Palestinians, citizens and non-citizens alike, out of *Eretz Yisrael*. The idea of total transfer was attractive to Kahane's potential voters for two reasons. First, if carried out, it would have removed Palestinian workers as competitors in the labor market (Peled 1990). Second, and more importantly perhaps, by calling for the transfer of all Palestinians, citizens and non-citizens alike, Kahane rejected both the republican and the liberal discourses of citizenship and embraced the ethno-nationalist discourse in its most extreme form. In articulating a notion of Palestinian (or "Arab") identity that transcended the question of citizenship, he also articulated, as in a mirror image, a notion of *Jewish* identity that transcended the question of citizenship as defined by the dominant discourse (cf. Roediger 1991).

As Erik Cohen has argued, the Mizrachim had always claimed, as against official Zionist ideology, that "mere Jewishness, rather than the internalization of any particular Zionist or 'Israeli' values, attitudes and patterns of behavior, [should be] sufficient for participation [in the center of Israeli society]" (Cohen 1983: 121). This assertion of the primacy of the ethno-national discourse, as against the pioneering aspects of the dominant, republican one, found its echo in Kahane's rhetoric.

In the actual elections of 1988, from which Kahane had been barred (Peled 1992), the *charedi* parties, primarily Shas and the Ashkenazi Agudat Yisrael, had more than tripled their strength in DTs, from 5 percent in 1984 to 18 percent in 1988, as against a doubling of their strength nationally. Shas itself received 8.7 percent of the vote in DTs, while both Likud and Labor lost support there and the extreme right-wing parties espousing the territorially expansionist ideology of Gush Emunim retained their relatively low levels of support. Unlike Kahane, the *charedi* parties were not calling for "transfer"; but, like him, the ethno-national discourse of citizenship was central to their world-view. Thus, although the vast majority of the DT population is not *charedi* but rather "traditional" in its religious outlook, it was the *charedi* parties, rather than the territorial right-wing parties, with their own version of the republican discourse, that were able to benefit from Kahane's removal from the race (Shokeid 1984; Don-Yehiya 1990; 1997b; Ben-Zadok 1993; Deshen 1994; Peled 1998; the figures for election results, here and elsewhere, may vary slightly due to the different definitions of DTs used by different authors).

By 1992, as we have mentioned, the demographic composition of DTs had undergone drastic change by the settlement of immigrants from the former USSR. Support for religious parties was virtually non-existent among these new voters (Fein 1995), and indeed the religious parties' share of the vote declined in DTs by close to 30 percent (from 21 percent in 1988 to 15 percent in 1992) (CBS 1993). This would seem to indicate, however, that the level of support for religious parties among *veteran* voters in DTs remained more or less constant. Unlike 1988, however, of the *charedi* parties only Shas had a significant showing in DTs and among Mizrachim in general in 1992.

Several reasons have been adduced for the virtual disappearance of support for Agudat Yisrael among poor and working-class Mizrachim in 1992, but the argument that it was caused by Agudat Yisrael's neglect of its Mizrachi voters' ethnic concerns was not among them (in this respect these voters should be distinguished from the *charedi*–Mizrachi core of Shas activists, who had seceded from Agudat Yisrael in 1984 precisely for this reason) (Don-Yehiya 1990; Heilman 1990: 149–50; Horkin 1993; Deshen 1994; Willis 1995: 130–1). Be that as it may, the significant point is that non-*charedi* Mizrachi voters in DTs were willing to support a strictly Ashkenazi *charedi* political party. This would seem to indicate that the appeal Shas has had for this type of voter is based on something it shares with other *charedi* parties, rather than on something that distinguishes it from them.

What Shas shares with other *charedi* parties is its commitment to the ethno-nationalist discourse, a commitment expressed in its concern for the enhancement of the role of Jewish religion in the public and private lives of Jews in Israel. The concrete meaning of its main slogan, "*lehachazir atara leyoshna*" ("restore the crown to its old glory") is "synagogues, ritual baths, keeping the Sabbath, yeshivot, torah schools, and the Wellspring" (*maayan hachinuch hatorani*, Shas's independent school system) (Willis 1995: 123; Horkin 1993). The goals of El-ha-maayan, Shas's adult education network, are stated in its incorporation by-laws: "to promote the traditional and Jewish values of religious Jewry in Israel . . .; . . . to promote religious Jewish education in the educational system in Israel . . .; . . . to improve religious services . . .; to help improve the quality of religious life . . .; . . . to supply the religious needs of *charedi* religious Jewry . . ." (Horkin 1993: 82–3). It would be very difficult to find, in Shas's official pronouncements, political demands that refer specifically to Mizrachi culture. Students of Shas have even compared its political goals to those of the pre-1967 (mostly Ashkenazi) NRP, before the latter had turned into an ultra-nationalist party (Willis 1995: 134; Levy 1995: 129; Heilman 1990: 146–7).

In making this point we are not trying to suggest that Shas, the only successful Mizrachi political party in the history of Israel, does not have its own unique characteristics or that it is not concerned with the plight of its Mizrachi constituency. Our argument, rather, is that Shas was able to define the concerns of its constituency in terms of the ethno-nationalist discourse of citizenship, and in this way organize its constituency around an integrative, rather than a separatist, message with respect to the broader (Jewish) society (cf. Herzog 1990: 108–11; 1995: 88). Ezra Nissani, an important Shas operative, has described Shas as a movement that articulates the interests of the "popular strata." These strata have been excluded from the center of Israeli society and seek to transform that society, in order to take their rightful place in it. They include "Mizrachim, *charedim* and national minorities" (i.e. citizen Palestinians) and the values of the Jews among them are "traditional-religious Jewish" values. Thus, restoration of these values, rather than specifically Mizrachi values, however defined, is presented as a remedy for both the cultural and the socio-economic plight of Mizrachim (Nissani 1996).[9]

In the general elections of 1996 Mizrachim of low socio-economic status responded to the Shas formula in unprecedented numbers.[10] In most DTs Shas became the second-largest party, after Likud, with between 10 and 20 percent of the vote. In one DT, Ofakim, it received the largest share, 24 percent, compared with 23.7 percent for Likud. Not surprisingly, perhaps, in 1995 Ofakim had the lowest SES ranking and the highest unemployment rate of all Jewish localities in Israel. In 1999 Shas became the largest political party in DTs, with 22 percent of the vote. In moshavim populated by Mizrachim (where the population is ethnically more homogeneous than in DTs) Shas received 29 percent of the vote. In the general electorate, Likud lost to Shas the status it had enjoyed since 1977, that of the largest Mizrachi political party (CBS 1995a; Kashti 1997f; 1997h; Yiftachel forthcoming; Shalev with Kis 2001).

Conclusion

Segregated from the Ashkenazi mainstream of Israeli society spatially, economically, culturally, and educationally, most Mizrachim have been alienated from the LSM and disaffected with its discourse of republican civic virtue, which has been used to legitimize their exclusion. Their

[9] The investigation, trial, conviction, and imprisonment of Shas's political leader, Arie Deri, for corruption charges, a process that took ten years (1990–2000) and was accompanied by accusations of anti-Mizrachi discrimination, may result in an amplification of the ethnic content of Shas's ideology and political action; see Peled 2001.

[10] The 1996 elections were the first in which the prime minister was elected directly by the electorate, so that voters could split their vote between their Knesset and prime minister ballots. This caused the major parties to decline and the parties representing minority sectors to grow significantly. Therefore, the results of the 1996 elections are not strictly comparable to the results of previous elections; see chap. 10, below.

opposition to this discourse of citizenship, and to the LSM that espoused it, has not led them, however, to adopt either a class-based or a culture-based oppositional discourse. To emphasize their connection to the dominant Ashkenazi majority, they have clung, rather, to the ethno-nationalist discourse, the discourse that defined, and limited, their membership in the society in the first place. This took the form, first, of supporting the secular right-wing version of ethno-nationalism espoused by Likud, and then increasingly the religious version of Shas. Ironically, in the language of mainstream Israeli sociology the Mizrachim are seen, therefore, as having "failed ... to become satisfactorily 'absorbed'" or to embrace the "universalistic component of the Zionist ideology" (Cohen 1983: 117, 120). It would be more accurate to say, however, that the limited space accorded such universalism by the elitist republicanism of the LSM left the Mizrachim no choice but to identify with another constraining form of citizenship – ethno-nationalism.

Shas has invested a great deal of effort in building a base in poor Mizrachi communities. Much of the abundant subsidies provided it by the state as a result of its growing political power (Horkin 1993; Tessler 2001) have gone to establish a whole array of educational institutions, from day-care centers and up, in DTs and in poor city neighborhoods. In this way Shas (like other *charedi* parties in their own communities, and like the Islamic Movement among citizen Palestinians) has stepped in to fulfill the role, largely abandoned by the state, of providing essential social rights to the poor (Adva Center 1998b). However, neither Shas nor Likud nor, indeed, any political movement that espouses the ethno-nationalist discourse is likely to work towards a transformation of Israel's incorporation regime in a way that would allow the Mizrachim to be integrated in the society on an equal footing. The objective socio-economic conditions of poor Mizrachim have always worsened under Likud governments, and it was Shas that blocked the efforts to pass a constitutional basic law that would guarantee social rights (see chap. 10, below). Most significantly, the traditional Jewish education provided in Shas's institutions is unlikely to prepare its students for secular higher education and for employment in the upper echelons of the occupational ladder.[11]

Women: Golda notwithstanding[12]

Of all the social groups surveyed in this volume, Jewish women probably possess the most fragmented citizenship status. They partake of all

---

[11] For a more comprehensive treatment of Shas, see Peled 2001.
[12] "Golda not withstanding" is the title of the section dealing with women in politics in Swirski and Safir 1991.

three citizenship discourses, and for them the contradictory effects of this multiplicity are transparent as for no other group. This is because in the case of women each citizenship discourse applies to a distinct sphere of their lives: republican to the public-political sphere, liberal to the occupational sphere, and ethno-nationalist to the private sphere.

In addition to the well-known general factors that make for women's subjugation in liberal democratic societies, and that are legitimated (or at least condoned) by the liberal discourse of citizenship, Israeli Jewish women have suffered from specific burdens imposed by Israel's character as a colonial frontier society and legitimated by its two other citizenship discourses, the republican and the ethno-nationalist.

The pioneering activities that constituted civic virtue in the Zionist version of the republican discourse – physical labor, agricultural settlement, and military service – were all conceived of as essentially masculine. While women have shared in these activities, in different ways and to different extents at different times, historical analyses concur that their role has always been secondary and supportive, and their participation did not impart to them, but only to the men, the aura of republican virtue. As a result, Israeli citizenship discourse has always been gendered and intertwined with values, experiences, rituals, and practices that both explicitly and implicitly privilege men. As Kathleen Jones has pointed out with respect to military virtue:

Within any discourse that defines citizenship as the armed struggle to defend one's way of life, women's bodies are problematic. Since this discourse defines women as weak and as needing (men's) protection, women cannot become active in their own defense without either calling into question their identity as women or threatening the sexual iconography upon which the discourse is based. (Jones 1990: 786)

This value orientation heightens the significance of women's role as nurturers and caretakers, of both the present and future generations of soldiers (and settlers). This not only reinforces the assignment of women to a supportive, secondary position, it also stifles their efforts to organize themselves politically.

The familist orientation that is part and parcel of the republican discourse (Sarvasy 1997: 70) has been further enhanced in Israel by the intense frontier conflict and by the demographic anxiety caused by the numerical inferiority of Jews in the Middle East. Due to this anxiety, not only has *aliya* always been a major national concern, but "internal *aliya*," that is, Jewish fertility, has been, and remains, a matter of national policy. As a result, in the private sphere Jewish women have been relegated to the role of mothers and caregivers (at least as their primary responsibility) and are expected to excel in the "battle of the cribs" against Palestinian women. To enhance this natalist orientation, maternity has been defined as women's primary contribution to the common good (Berkovitch 1997). This conception of women's citizenship, which views their contribution as quantitative rather than qualitative, has had a pronounced negative effect on their struggle for equality, even in the most egalitarian sector of Jewish society – the kibbutz (Safir 1991b; Palgi 1991; Fogiel-Bijaoui 1992a).

Jewish Israeli women have not only been marginalized by the republican discourse, however. The ethno-nationalist discourse, which claims the unity of all Jews as its highest value, has curtailed women's citizenship rights even more significantly. In order to ensure the inter-marriageability of all Jews, Orthodox Jews demanded, and received, exclusive authority to determine who, among Jews, could marry whom, and a monopoly over the performance of marriage and divorce ceremonies conducted in Israel (chap. 5, below). This monopoly, which originated in the Ottoman *millet* system and was continued during the Mandatory period, has remained in force with respect to the religious authorities of the other religious communities as well. As Jewish (and Muslim) religious law treats women as a subordinate class of persons, the result is that Israeli family law has a pronounced pro-male bias. This is manifested in marriage and divorce laws that discriminate against women, in an intrusive (though not prohibitive) abortion law, and in an unquestioned acceptance of the traditional patriarchal model of the family as normative (Hecht and Yuval-Davis 1978; Safir 1991a; Azmon and Izraeli 1993a; Jerby 1996; Yishai 1997; Berkovitch 1997). At the same time, the traditional privileges of such gendered division of labor within the family are also upheld: shared custody is rare and Jewish women almost invariably gain sole custody of their children in case of divorce.

And yet, in other areas Israel has followed the practices of liberal citizenship and accumulated an impressive record in legislating for women's rights and gender equality. A Women's Equal Rights Law was enacted as early as 1951, guaranteeing women equal legal standing with men in judicial proceedings and inheritance, and disallowing polygamy (a common practice among Muslims and some Jewish groups). Since then a whole plethora of statutes have been enacted relating to equal employment opportunity, equal pay for equal work, equal retirement age, etc., as well as statutes relating to the protection of women on the job, maternity benefits and leave, alimony, family violence, sexual crimes and harassment, and so on (Raday et al. 1995; Yishai 1997: 19–22, 70, 160–7; Berkovitch 1997; Swirski 2000). However, this impressive body of legislation has not touched on the most fundamental aspect of women's inequality – the assignment of family law jurisdiction to religious institutions – and therefore has had only a marginal effect on women's civil rights. Moreover, in other spheres of social life as well, "while women's equality has received adequate attention, this has been confined to the institutional level rather than converted into action" (Yishai 1997: 22).

This peculiar combination of a declaratory commitment to equality and continuing discrimination in practice has been analyzed by Nitza Berkovitch as resulting from the interplay between liberal and republican elements in Zionist ideology. (Berkovitch has incorporated what we call the ethno-nationalist discourse into the republican one.) While liberalism stresses the equality of rights between abstractly conceived individuals, republicanism stresses the different contributions made by concretely situated individuals and groups to the common good of society, and views individual rights as secondary to that common good. Moreover, while both discourses distinguish between the private and public spheres, they also consider the family to be the cornerstone of society and therefore as lying legitimately within the sphere of state regulation (Berkovitch 1997).

The conjunction of these diverse ideological elements has resulted in what Berkovitch has called "the dialectic of similarity and difference": a public conception of (Jewish) women as being both equal to men and different from them. The equality of women lies in the fact that their contribution to society must be recognized and rewarded as much as the men's; their difference lies in the unique nature of their contribution: motherhood. Thus, the equality of women not only coexists with their difference, it is dependent on it. Difference posits the boundary that equality cannot transgress. Both equality and difference, moreover, are subject to the overarching value of Jewish unity and national survival, hence to religious regulation of the construction and dissolution of family units (Berkovitch 1997).

In this chapter we examine, primarily, the citizenship rights of the most privileged group of women, Ashkenazi Jewish women, who have been at the center of most public discussion of gender issues in Israel (Berkovitch 1997). As a rule, all other groups of women are as disadvantaged in relation to this group as their male counterparts are in relation to Ashkenazi Jewish males (for discussions of other groups of women see, e.g., Lewin-Epstein and Semyonov 1993: 87–113; Hassan 1991; Shokeid 1993; Nahon 1993d; Swirski 2000). We will analyze the citizenship of Ashkenazi Jewish women in accordance with the three kinds of rights we have been discussing all along: civil, political, and social, but not in the order stipulated by Marshall. Marshall had English*men* in mind when he constructed his historical account of the evolution of citizenship, and his account does not fit the history of women, not even in England. For example, as far as women were concerned, in many cases some social rights preceded the two other kinds (Sarvasy 1997: 61). Our presentation of women's citizenship in Israel will proceed, then, in the reverse order to Marshall's: We shall begin with social rights, where we will discuss women's economic positions; under political rights we will consider the role played by women in electoral politics and in the military; and under civil rights we will discuss family law, reproductive rights, and violence against women. We will conclude the chapter with a discussion of women's political organization and struggle, that is, of the Israeli women's and feminist movements.

Social rights

Gender equality was an important element in the ideology of Labor Zionism at the time of the Yishuv, but in reality no serious effort was made to implement it. Even in the *kvutza* (early forerunner of the kibbutz),

while social and sex equality were stated goals, formal planning to create the necessary conditions for sex equality did not occur ... What was viewed as sex equality was in fact only the limited movement of women into jobs that were traditionally masculine, along with rejection by women of a feminine or female appearance. They cut off their flowing locks, threw away their cosmetics and put their dresses, skirts and jewelry away. At the same time, both men and women accepted age-old ideas about their own and each other's biological nature and abilities. (Safir 1991b: 251)

As in other societies, since the time of the Yishuv women have constituted a reserve army of labor, moving in and out of "men's" jobs, and the labor market in general, in accordance with the fluctuations of the economy. Since, overall, the Israeli economy has been growing, women's share in the employed population has increased from 25.6 percent in 1960 to 42.5 percent in 1995 (in 1995 their share among the unemployed was 54.4 percent) (CBS 1996a: 7; IWN 1997: 19). Not surprisingly, however, women's participation in the economy has been characterized by both horizontal and vertical segregation. Thus, in 1992, 72 percent of all female employees, as compared with 28.5 percent of male employees, were concentrated in three typically feminine occupational categories: teaching and nursing, clerical work, and services (Yishai 1997: 153, 174; Jerby 1996: 32–6; Bernstein 1993; Maor 1997).

In all sectors of employment, even the most "feminine" ones, such as teaching, women are disproportionately concentrated in the lower echelons of the hierarchy. Iris Jerby has calculated an index of inequality that measures the relation between the ratio of women to men in senior as compared to junior positions in different sectors of employment: education, banking, industry, the civil service, the judicial system, and politics. Where a value of 1 would indicate equal representation of women in the upper and lower echelons, in 1991 the average index of inequality was 0.17, ranging from 0.07 in the civil service to 0.36 in the state prosecutorial system (the standard deviation was 0.09). The very low representation of women in the upper echelons of the civil service, where anti-discrimination legislation might have been expected to have a greater effect than in the private sector, stems from the fact that the upper ranks of the civil service are made up largely of political appointees and retired military officers. These methods of recruitment cannot be used in the judicial system, because of the professional qualifications required for entry into it, and therefore women fare better in that system. Women fare best in the state prosecutorial system because similarly qualified men prefer to go into private legal practice (Jerby 1996: 37–60; Yishai 1997: 48–9; Bernstein 1993; Maor 1997; *Haaretz*, November 16, 1999; for the sad situation of women in academe, see Hershkovitz 2000).

This hierarchical segmentation is reflected, of course, in income levels as well. Two-thirds of working women, compared to less than one-half of all employees, do not earn enough to be liable for income tax. In 1995 female employees earned an average of NIS 3,411 a month, while male employees earned NIS 6,015, for hours actually worked. Women's average wage, then, was close to 60 percent of that of men overall, but the difference between them was growing as wage levels were rising. Thus, for every 10 percent of increase in men's wages, women's wages increased only 7.1 percent. As a result, in the poorest localities in the country women's average wage was 70–90 percent of that of men, while in the wealthiest localities it was less than 40 percent. The differential is expected to grow by an additional 5 percent every two or three years, as wage levels continue to rise (Adva Center 1998c: 4, 6; IWN 1997: 27; Adva Center 2000b: 9).

One important reason for these wage differentials is the fact that many more women than men work only part time. While women's hourly wage is, on the average, about 80 percent of that of men (NIS 23.4 to NIS 29.2 in 1996) (CBS 1997: 51; Adva Center 2000b: 9), in 1995 the number of average weekly hours actually worked was 42.8 for men and 30.6 for women (CBS 1996a: 7). Overall, in 1995 37.8 percent of working women worked part time, compared to 14.9 percent of working men (IWN 1997: 21). Israeli labor legislation has encouraged part-time labor by providing many measures of employment and social security to part-time and full-time workers equally. This, together with generous maternity benefits and a relatively well-developed system of child-care institutions, has helped women to enter the labor market, while making it easier for them to be confined to their own, part-time, "mommy track." In the words of Yael Yishai: "Torn between her duty to the nation, substantiated as familial responsibility and the raising of children, and her desire to carve herself a place in the professional 'masculine' world, the Israeli woman has sought employment outside her home, but equivocally: She has remained content with part-time jobs, often low-paid" (Yishai 1997: 157).

Political rights

The greatest, and so far unequalled, political achievement of Jewish women in Israel took place in 1925. After a six-year struggle, during which women voted on the basis of an interim arrangement, they succeeded in securing for themselves an unqualified right to vote and be elected to the representative institutions of the Yishuv. This success resulted from the efforts of women's organizations, over the opposition of the religious, Sephardi, and right-wing sectors of the Yishuv, and with the lukewarm support of the LSM and some liberal political groups. Gaining the right to participate in elections to the national institutions of the Yishuv did not mean, however, that women had similar rights in local elections as well. Those rights depended on local decisions, and the process through which women were enfranchised on the local level extended from the early years of the twentieth century to 1940 (Swirski 1991a: 293).

The highest point in the representation of women in elected national institutions came shortly *before* women had officially gained the franchise. In the elections to the second elected assembly of the Yishuv, in 1925, women's parties elected thirteen delegates, and twelve other women were elected as representatives of other parties. The twenty-five women constituted about 15 percent of the delegates, a high point that has never been matched since. After 1948, women's representation in the Knesset has only once reached 12.5 percent, in the fifteenth Knesset elected in 1999. This placed Israel forty-ninth in the world in terms of women's representation in parliament, right behind the USA, with 12.9 percent. Only one woman was ever elected to the Knesset as representative of a women's party, in 1949 (Fogiel-Bijaoui 1992b; Yishai 1997: 28; *Haaretz*, November 1, 2000). Only about ten women have served as cabinet ministers in the history of Israel, including Golda Meir, who served as prime minister from 1969 to 1974. Only two women have so far been elected mayors of major Israeli cities (in 1998) (IWN 1997: 15–18).

One reason for the gross underrepresentation of women in elected political positions is that an important avenue of advancement in politics, as in other areas of social life – the military – is not available to them.

Retired generals have played a very prominent role in Israeli politics, reaching their political positions not by rising through the ranks in political parties but by "parachuting" from their senior military posts to senior political ones. Since very few women have military careers, and even those who do do not become part of the "old boys' network," this shortcut to success in politics is blocked to them.

Like many other issues relating to gender equality in Israel, the issue of military service for women is also replete with paradoxes. Israel is the only country in the world where women are subject to mandatory military service. The rationale behind this has to do with the personnel needs of the military as well as with the principle of gender equality, in both its liberal and republican varieties. (Jewish) women, so the argument goes, should be equal in their duties to men, just as they are equal to them in their rights; they should also not be deprived of the right to contribute to their country's defense (Jerby 1996). The way these principles are implemented in practice, however, does everything but enhance the equal standing of women in the society.

In its application to the issue of female military service, the equality principle comes up against the ethno-nationalist Jewish discourse, as well as against contradictory principles within the liberal and republican discourses themselves. As a result, here too equality is subsumed under difference. This is manifested both in the process through which women are selected for service and in the way they are treated after their enlistment.

The first line of division that applies in this case, as in many others, is that between Jewish and Palestinian citizens. Like most Palestinian men, Palestinian women are not called up for military service. Next comes the conception that women's supreme contribution to the common Zionist good is their ability to bear children. Therefore, women who are married, pregnant, or mothers are exempt from service, as are those women who declare that military service would violate their religious beliefs (and, although this is not stated publicly, harm their marriage prospects). No parallel exemptions are granted to men (with the partial exception of yeshiva students; see chap. 5, below). The same principle determines that women would serve a shorter term than men (less than two years for women and three years for men, at the time of writing) and would not be called up for reserve duty once they are married, have children, or reach the age of twenty-four. Again, no similar provisions apply to men, who generally serve in the reserves until their late forties (Bloom 1991: 133–4; Berkovitch 1997: 609–11).

Since the length of service for women is much shorter than it is for men, especially if reserve duty is taken into account, the military is much more selective in its choice of female recruits than it is of male recruits. This means that fewer women of low socio-economic status (and Mizrachi origin) are being drafted (Azmon and Izraeli 1993b: 12; Sharoni 1995: 47). In addition, the military is reluctant to invest too many resources in training women for highly skilled (and prestigious) jobs, because the returns on this investment are short lived. As a rule, women are also barred from combat duty, for the same reasons that apply in most other countries – fear of mistreatment if they become prisoners of war, interference with the male bonding that is deemed essential for the morale of combat troops, etc. And even though the prohibition on women in combat is slowly being eroded under the pressure of the equality principle, by and large women in the Israeli military serve in their own secondary and supportive female niche (Bloom 1991; Jerby 1996; Almog 1996; Izraeli 1997). Thus, not only are the avenues of advancement within the military blocked to them, but

the IDF has adopted a binary social construction [of gender] that makes a categorical distinction between men and women and attributes to them greater or lesser capabilities, based on their sex, while under-valuing personal potentialities and motivations. [Thus] the military system preserves the logic of the civilian one, strengthens [gender] stereotypes and deepens the status differences between the sexes in the society as a whole. (Jerby 1996: 121; see also Bloom 1991: 137)

Civil rights and the private sphere

As we have indicated, the most serious impairment of women's citizenship rights in Israel occurs in the area of civil rights, and results from the fact the matters of family law, in particular marriage and divorce, have been given over to the jurisdiction of religious courts. Since the two most important religions in Israel, Judaism and Islam, consider women to be lesser human beings than men, women find themselves at a great disadvantage when they come before these courts. Thus, as mentioned already, matters of family law have been explicitly excluded from the purview of the Women's Equal Rights Law of 1951 (Raday 1996: 211 n. 60). As we have done all along in this chapter, we will consider the effects of this situation on Jewish women only, with the acknowledgment that the situation of Muslim (and Druze) women is much worse (see Swirski 2000).

At the most immediate level, women are in an inferior position in Jewish religious courts because the judges in these courts (*dayanim*) are exclusively men, and only the testimony of men is admissible in them, officially at least. (In recent years, however, women have been authorized to function as *toanot* in rabbinical courts, a role equivalent to that of lawyers in civil courts.) Moreover, these rabbinical courts operate, in cases of marriage and divorce, by the rules of Orthodox Judaism (*halacha*) and are not bound by the principle of equality or by other precepts of Israeli civil law. Thus, the only marriage and divorce ceremonies recognized by these courts are the Orthodox ones, in which the woman plays a completely passive role. In fact, one of the major objections of the Rabbinate to Reform rabbis conducting marriage ceremonies is the fear that these rabbis may allow the bride to make commitments to her bridegroom, and not only the other way around (C. Shalev 1993; Raday 1996: 226–7; see also chap. 5, below).

Another key difference in the treatment of men and women in Jewish family law has to do with the question of consent in cases of divorce. The consent of both parties is required for divorce, and the court cannot force either side to give its consent. However, the consequences of the other party's refusal or inability (due to incapacitation, disappearance, etc.) to give (men) or receive (women) divorce are very different for women and for men. If a man refuses or is unable to divorce his wife she is legally forbidden to have a relationship with another man. If she does "have a sexual relationship with another man, she is considered a rebellious wife and . . . may lose her rights to child custody and spousal maintenance payments . . .; she will also be prohibited from marrying her lover" in the event she is eventually released from her original marriage. Should this woman have a child with another man, that child and her/his descendants would be considered bastards and prohibited from marrying any Jew except other bastards or converts to Judaism. None of these prohibitions apply to men who are refused a divorce by their wives, and, moreover, such men may be granted permission to legally marry another woman while still married to their original wife (Raday 1996: 230–1).

One area of family law that lies outside the jurisdiction of religious courts is abortion. There is a question under what conditions abortion is permitted by the *halacha* (Yishai 1997: 219), but it is clearly not practiced as a form of birth control by Orthodox Jewish women. As for non-Orthodox Jewish women, there is a clash between the liberal discourse, which grants women exclusive authority over their bodies, and both the republican and ethno-nationalist discourses with their obsession with the question of demography. As a result of this clash, the state has pursued a clearly natalist policy without, however, forbidding abortion as a form of birth control.

Until 1977 abortion was formally a criminal offense, although it was practiced widely in both public hospitals and private clinics, with the government turning a blind eye. In 1977 two legislative proposals to decriminalize abortion were put before the Knesset. One was a private member's bill submitted by a feminist legislator, Marcia Freedman, which would allow every woman to terminate her pregnancy within the first twelve weeks. The other was a government-sponsored bill that stipulated that abortion would remain illegal unless:

a. The woman was under the legal age of marriage (17) or over 40; [or]
b. The pregnancy resulted from a non-marital relationship or an illicit act; [or]
c. The fetus was suspected to be malformed; [or]
d. Continuing the pregnancy may endanger the woman's life or health; [or]
e. Family or social conditions . . . dictated an abortion; [and]
f. A [hospital] committee consisting of . . . [two doctors] and a social worker (in December 1979 it was decided that at least one member of . . . [the] committee must be a woman), approved the request for abortion; [and]
g. The abortion would be performed in a recognized, state authorized medical institution. (Yishai 1997: 211; Amir and Navon 1989: 88–9)

The government's version of the bill was approved by a two-thirds majority, over the fierce opposition of the religious members and with the support of most women members and most women's organizations. The latter preferred the government's intrusive bill to Freedman's liberal one for demographic reasons, even though "an overwhelming majority of Israelis, men and women, favor granting women the right to decide" whether or not to terminate her pregnancy (Yishai 1997: 205, 208–17).

The abortion law was enacted under a Labor government, and when Likud came to power a short time afterwards, it and its religious coalition partners set out to overturn it. (The presence in the government coalition of the liberal Democratic Movement for Change, which with fifteen Knesset seats, was the third largest party in the house, made little difference in this regard; see chap. 8, below.) These efforts met with strenuous opposition on the part of women's organizations, and at the end only clause 5, the "social clause," was removed as one of the conditions to be considered by the abortion committees (Amir and Navon 1989: 90–1; Yishai 1997: 217–20). Further efforts to legally restrict abortions were all defeated under the influence of women's organizations, and the removal of the "social clause" has not resulted in a decline in the number of abortions, but rather in more frequent resort by abortion committees to the medical clause. In 1991, out of about 18,000 requests for abortion, 15,000 were approved by the committees (Yishai 1997: 221–30; see also Amir 1995).

According to the Israel Women's Network, a feminist lobbying organization, 10 percent of all married women in Israel have been beaten by their spouses, and 7 percent of these women are beaten consistently and systematically. In 1995, 200,000 women were beaten. Every year the police receive 9,000 complaints of beating by spouses, and 40,000 women are brought to hospital emergency wards because of beatings (*Jerusalem Post* 1996; IWN 1997: 37–49). Still, until the late 1980s the issue of domestic violence did not attract serious political consideration. On the one hand, relations between "him and her" were considered to lie in the private sphere, outside the jurisdiction of the state, and were supposed to be regulated by traditional mores. On the other hand, the common belief was that Jewish men do not beat their wives (Swirski 1991b; Yishai 1997: 198–203), and the fate of Palestinian women did not cause too much concern among Jewish lawmakers and public officials.

The issue of domestic violence was raised in the Knesset for the first time by a female MK, Beba Idelson, in 1962, but was basically ignored. The next time it was raised, in 1976, by Marcia Freedman, it was met with ridicule and denial but could not be struck from the Knesset agenda as the government proposed to do (Swirski 1991b: 321; Dayan 2000a). Since then the issue has remained on the public agenda, both inside and outside the Knesset, and in 1991 a law criminalizing family violence was enacted (Makayes 1995). In a similar vein, in the penal code adopted in 1977 rape was defined as a serious criminal offense carrying with it a maximum sentence of sixteen years imprisonment, or twenty years if the rape was carried out under aggravated circumstances. In 1981 the Supreme Court determined that marital rape was a form of rape for the purposes of this law. Since the penalties imposed by judges in rape cases continued to be lenient, in 1998 the Knesset adopted a law imposing mandatory sentences of 25 percent of the maximum penalty provided for in the law for sexual offenders (i.e. four or five years in cases of rape). In 1998 a law banning sexual harassment of all kinds in all areas of social life was also adopted (Shachar 1993: 179, 198–9; Swirski 2000; *Yediot Achronot Weekend Supplement,* July 10, 1998; *Haaretz,* July 15, 1998).

Women's political expression

The history of political organizing by women in Palestine/Israel goes back to 1911, when the Women Workers' Movement (WWM) was established in order to struggle for the equal participation of women in pioneering activities. Like their male counterparts, the women of the Second Aliya sought not only to transform the land and the people, but to transform themselves in the process as well. The ideology of self-transformation, rather than the transformation of traditional gender relations, helped the women emphasize their commitment to the Zionist cause and assuage their fear of being dubbed separatist by their male colleagues (Izraeli 1992: 187–8).

When the Histadrut was established in 1920, the WWM was co-opted into it, and a special branch for women was created in the Histadrut's organizational structure, under the title Women Workers' Council (WWC). Soon a struggle ensued within this new organization between the "radicals" of the Second Aliya, who were more ardent feminists, and the "loyalists" of the Third Aliya, who believed the male leadership of the Histadrut could be trusted to look after the interests of women workers as well. Interestingly, the radical women were supported by the non-socialist and moderately nationalist party within Labor Zionism at the time, Hapoel Hatzair, while the loyalists were supported by the larger, more socially and nationally "activist" Achdut Haavoda. (These two parties merged in 1930 to become Mapai.) The final defeat of the radicals came in 1927, when their leader, the militant feminist Ada Maymon, was replaced as secretary general of the WWC by Golda Meirson (Meir), the future prime minister. In 1930 Meirson was replaced by Beba Idelson, who was to hold the position of secretary general for forty years (!). At that time the name of the WWM was changed to the Organization of Working Mothers (OWM), and in 1976 the OWM and the WWC merged into a new organization titled Working and Volunteer Women (Naamat) (Izraeli 1992: 193–205; Yishai 1997: 62, 256 n. 5).

Since 1930 the OWM and Naamat, like their General Zionist counterpart, WIZO (Women's International Zionist Organization), have functioned as family-oriented service organizations for women and children, providing day-care centers, vocational training, women's clubs, and so on, without articulating any feminist demands. Because of their familist orientation, these organizations failed to play a leading part in the legislative battles for gender equality at the workplace and have contributed to the persistence of the definition of women's citizenship as motherhood (Pope 1991; Yishai 1997: 166–78).

Feminism as a social, political, and academic concern was revived in Israel only in the 1970s, as a result of the immigration of feminist women from the West. One of these immigrants, Marcia Freedman, probably the most prominent feminist activist in Israel so far, was elected to the Knesset on the Ratz (Civil Rights Movement; see chap. 8, below) ticket in 1973. Freedman's feminist views were not welcome in the party, however, and she eventually defected from it and was not reelected in 1977. Several attempts to run women's parties in Knesset elections since then have not been successful.

The work of this new generation of feminists – shelters and crisis centers for battered women and rape victims, pro-choice agitation, writing, publication and teaching of feminist works, etc. – has resulted in a wider acceptance of feminism among Israeli women. In a survey conducted in 1998, 45 percent of them (compared to only 35 percent of women in the

USA) identified themselves as feminists (*Haaretz*, July 13, 1998). As a result, women's issues have become a legitimate part of the political agenda and the traditional women's organizations have shifted their orientation somewhat from the national flag to the feminist banner, to use Yishai's words (1997: 234–5; Swirski 1991a: 294–301; Ram 1993). These developments, together with the general liberalization of the society, are responsible for the spate of progressive legislation and judicial decisions relating to women's issues that have taken place since the mid-1980s (Raday 1996: 234–5; Yishai 1997: 234–40).

Overall, however, the record of feminism in Israel has been disappointing. In spite of the progressive legislation and the fact that, overall, women in the Israeli workforce are better educated than men (CBS 1998: 5), none of the major problems affecting women's incorporation in the society have been alleviated to any significant degree. Israeli feminism has been hampered by a number of powerful forces, many of them stemming from the colonial frontier context in which it operates. As a frontier society involved in a protracted conflict with all of its neighbors, (Jewish) Israeli society must uphold the traditional family as both a source of "internal *aliya*" and a place where male warriors can find care and comfort. Any criticism of gender roles within the traditional family thus appears unpatriotic. Moreover, the unity of the Jewish people, essential for mobilizing its resources for the conflict, seems to dictate that Orthodox Jewish religion play a role in the public life of the country, especially in matters of marriage and divorce. The acceptance of Jewish unity as the supreme value also prevents Jewish women from allying themselves with Palestinian ones. On top of that, class divisions, which correspond both to the Jewish–Palestinian divide and to the ethnic divide within the Jewish community, also impede the capability of Israeli women to unite around feminist issues. As a result,

Israeli feminism is more often than not reduced to a list of reforms, especially, but not only, by "feminism from above." This type of enterprise, concerned with adding "the women's component" to existing institutions, has no vision of a society or world in which the relations between women and men are basically different and in which women participate in history, but rather is devoted to improving things so that women have a little more of this and a little more of that. (Swirski 1991a: 300; see also Kazin 1998)

Conclusion

The "contribution" of both Mizrachim and women to the common Zionist cause has been defined by the republican discourse as quantitative rather than qualitative. This definition has placed both groups in a secondary citizenship status, with the similarities between them evident particularly in the field of political rights. (We are here treating women and Mizrachim as somewhat abstract categories, of course, since in real life there is a 50 percent overlap between them.) Unlike groups whose contribution is considered to be qualitative, such as Orthodox Jews, political organizing by women and Mizrachim has been frowned upon as separatist, and both groups had fared better, in terms of political representation, in the Yishuv than in the period of statehood. (That is, until Shas succeeded in legitimizing Mizrachi political organizing by draping it in an Orthodox garb.)

Aside from the attitude of the dominant groups in society, groups defined by their difference and granted second- and third-class citizenship, such as women, Mizrachim and citizen Palestinians face an inherent difficulty when coming to organize politically on the basis of their distinctive features. The aim of their organizing is, ultimately, to achieve equality; and this aim comes into conflict with the basis of their organizing efforts, namely their difference and lack of equality. As stated succinctly by Brigadier-General Orit Adato, commander of the IDF's Women's Corps: "I see myself as heading an organization whose goal is its own demise" (IWN 1998: 24).[13] On August 1, 2001 the IDF Women's Corps was indeed abolished.

This inconsistency between the principle of political organizing and its aim is probably one of the major causes for the difficulties faced by women and other similar groups in affecting fundamental change in the society. Thus, in spite of occasionally significant protest activities by these groups, the transformation of Israeli society that is the subject matter of this book was triggered, among inferior-class citizenship groups, by the one group whose political goal was not equal incorporation in the society, but rather separation from it: non-citizen Palestinians.

---

[13] Adato has recently been appointed commissioner of the Prison Service, so it should be hoped that she has the same view of her current command.

4   The frontier within: Palestinians as third-class citizens

> The idea of autonomy for the Palestinians within the State of Israel simmers under the skin of the entire problem, hidden but present, threatening and suspicious like a false bottom that contains no one knows what, and gives a special resonance to every pronouncement heard as between the two peoples. (Grossman 1992: 137)

In 1948 the nature of the Jewish–Palestinian frontier struggle was radically transformed. The intercommunal conflict, which had taken place within the framework of British Mandatory rule, had now split into two: on the one hand, an international conflict between a number of hostile sovereign states and, on the other, an internal frontier struggle between the state of Israel and the Palestinians who had remained within its territory at the end of the 1948 war (Pappe 1992). These, the "1948 Palestinians," and their offspring now count just under one million, constituting about 17 percent of the total population of Israel. (These figures do not include the approximately 170,000 Palestinians living in east Jerusalem, virtually all of whom are legal residents but not citizens of Israel.)

Oren Yiftachel has defined an internal frontier as "a region within a state where an ethnic minority forms a majority, and where the state attempts to expand its control over territory and inhabitants" (Yiftachel 1996: 496). In Israel the Palestinians are indeed concentrated in three geographical regions – the Galilee in the north, the "Triangle" in the east, and the Negev in the south – and, depending on how regional boundaries are drawn, they can be said to constitute a majority in at least the first two of these regions (see map in Yiftachel 1992: 64). Moreover, there is no question that the Israeli state has consistently sought, since 1948, to "expand its control" over its Palestinian citizens and, especially, over their land.

Of the 150,000 Palestinians who had remained in the territory of the state of Israel at the conclusion of the 1948 war, about 60,000 were granted immediate Israeli citizenship, and the rest were entitled to it if they met certain conditions stipulated in the Nationality Law of 1952. These conditions prevented many Palestinians from becoming citizens until the Nationality Law was amended in 1980 (Kretzmer 1990: 36–40). But the very fact of granting citizenship to Palestinians – as opposed to instituting an apartheid-like *Herrenvolk* democracy for Jews only – was in accord with the liberal discourse of citizenship, and mitigated somewhat the exclusionary effects of the republican and ethno-national ones.

The liberal imperative was reinforced by more practical considerations, however. The Palestinian population of Israel had been reduced by the war from a 2:1 majority (in the area of Mandatory Palestine) to a small minority of about 12.5 percent (of the population of the state of Israel) (Lustick 1980: 48–9; Morris 1987; Kamen 1987/88; Pappe 1992, chap. 3). More importantly, "the Jewish leadership . . . [believed] that the minority problem had been all but eliminated by the mass Arab exodus – that the number of Arabs left in the state was insignificant" (Lustick 1980: 53). This made it easier for them to include the remaining Arabs in the body politic of the state.

In addition, the international situation had to be considered as well. In the deliberations leading to the United Nations Partition Resolution of 1947, Moshe Shertok (Sharet), Israel's future foreign minister, declared: "When we speak of a Jewish State we do not have in mind any racial state or any theocratic state, but one which will be based upon full equality and rights for all inhabitants without distinction of religion or race, and without domination or subjugation" (Robinson 1947: 208). The resolution itself, which had legitimated Israel's founding in international law, required that elections to the legislative organs of both states (Jewish and Arab) be conducted on the basis of "universal suffrage" and that they guarantee all persons equal and non-discriminatory rights in civil, political, economic, and religious matters and the enjoyment of human rights and fundamental freedoms, including freedom of religion, language, speech and publication, education, assembly, and association (Medding 1990: 11–12).

Arab delegations at the United Nations complained about the treatment of the Palestinians in Israel, and Israel's first application for membership in that body was denied in December 1948 (Lustick 1980: 61). Furthermore, the government sought to avoid the possibility that the remaining Palestinians, concentrated in clearly demarcated geographical areas that had been assigned by the Partition Resolution to the Arab state, would demand secession from Israel on the basis of their right of national self-determination (as has indeed happened in the territories occupied in 1967, whose residents have not been granted Israeli citizenship) (Lustick 1980: 61–3).

Until 1966, however, the Palestinian citizens' rights were largely suspended in practice, and they were ruled through a military administration "which imposed severe restrictions on their freedom of movement and economic opportunities, and placed them under surveillance and military law" (Medding 1990: 25; Jiryis 1976: 31–55; Lustick 1980; Benziman and Mansour 1992: 103–14; Hofnung 1991: 150–72). The military administration was justified, in the face of mounting criticism at home and abroad, as a security measure, an instrument of control over a potentially hostile population. However, Shmuel Toledano, who served in senior positions in several of Israel's security services and was for ten years (1966–76) the prime minister's adviser on Arab affairs (the key official responsible for conducting government policy towards the citizen Palestinians), has recently disputed this claim: "After the first few years of the state the [military] Administration's contribution to security was a total zero" (Shalit 1996: 48).

The military administration's real task had to do with the two issues that were most crucial for the success of the colonial project: labor and land. It controlled the entry of Palestinian workers into the Jewish labor market, which was characterized, through the 1950s, by an oversupply of labor due to the massive Mizrachi immigration (Shalev 1992: 48), and it enabled the state to effect a massive transfer of land from Palestinian to national Jewish ownership.[1] A further important function was to ensure that the votes of the Palestinian citizens in Knesset elections would be secured for Mapai and its Arab affiliates. And indeed, from the second Knesset elections in 1951 to the seventh elections in 1969 (inclusive), these parties received over 50 percent of the Palestinian vote (Rouhana 1986:136; al-Haj 1995: 32–3).

Social and economic conditions: the proletarianization of an agrarian community

The struggle for land has been at the heart of the frontier conflict in Palestine/Israel, as elsewhere, and continues to be the most hotly disputed issue in the relations between Israel and the Palestinians, both citizens and non-citizens, to this day. As we have shown, the redemptive

---

[1] In a document prepared by the operations branch of the military administration in 1963 or 1964, and obtained by Ian Lustick, one of the three major tasks of the military administration is described as "Helping to solve land problems (preventing the seizure of vacant land intended for settlement and preventing the habitation, or reestablishment of abandoned villages by those uprooted and evacuated)." The other two tasks mentioned are preventing external and internal security threats. (By that time the control of labor was no longer an issue, as it was a period of labor shortages in the Jewish economy.) The document was translated by Lustick and we are grateful to him for allowing us to consult it.

activities that were the crux of pioneering civic virtue were all related to the struggle over land: working it, settling it, defending it. In 1948 the task of "redeeming" the land was shifted from the virtuous pioneering vanguard of the LSM to the state. *Mamlachtiyut* was the ideological banner under which the state was to continue the frontier struggle with its own Palestinian citizens. And it conducted the struggle with the thoroughness and efficiency characteristic of the modern state.

The exact amount of land that has been expropriated from Palestinians and turned into national (Jewish) land is hard to determine, due to the maze of legal instruments created and/or utilized for that purpose and due to the fact that the process has not ended yet (Oded 1964; Zureik 1979: 115–21; Lustick 1980: 170–82; Kimmerling 1983: 134–46; Kretzmer 1990: 49–76; Hofnung 1991: 159–72; Benziman and Mansour 1992: 157–71; Lewin-Epstein and Semyonov 1993: 46; Haidar 1995; Yiftachel 1992; 1996; Kedar 1998). According to Aziz Haidar, in 1945 Palestinian localities that would become part of the state of Israel had controlled 1,441,146 dunams of land, not including the land at the disposal of Bedouins in the Negev. In 1981 Palestinian citizens owned 397,080 dunams, excluding the Negev. By these figures, aside from the Negev Bedouins, the Palestinians in Israel lost about 70 percent of the land they had owned, an estimate with which most knowledgeable observers would tend to agree (Kimmerling 1983: 140; Sa'di 1996: 395; cf. Kedar 1998, esp. 684–6). (Some of this loss, however, resulted from the fact that a certain amount of land owned by Palestinians who became Israeli residents was not included in the territory of the state of Israel.) The bulk of the loss, two-thirds of the land originally held by Palestinians, occurred as a result of the flight and expulsion of the majority of Palestinians during the 1948 war and the declaration of their land as state land (Morris 1987). The losses per capita give an even clearer picture of the magnitude of the change: from 19 dunam per capita in 1945 to 0.84 in 1981 (while in the country as a whole the decline during the same period was from 19 dunams p/c to 3.8) (Haidar 1995: 44).

While the overall picture of land loss can be described only in general terms (see Yiftachel 1992: 86–7, 190; Kedar 1998), several scholars have studied the losses in specific villages in greater detail. Thus Lustick provided a list of eighteen villages, drawn from a variety of sources and representing, presumably, the situation in several different years. Losses in these eighteen villages ranged between 25 and 80 percent, for an average of 70 percent of the original land possessed by the villagers (Lustick 1980: 179). The figures provided by Lustick for one village, Majd al-Krum – a loss of 13,000 of its 20,000 dunams – have been corroborated by a much later study (Yiftachel 1996: 501–2; but cf. Haidar 1995: 161, who cites an even greater loss). According to Haidar, in 1980 the village (now city) of Taibe had 19,000 dunams left of the 32,750 dunams it had in 1945, by the lowest estimate available. According to Lustick, Taibe had originally possessed 45,000 dunams, of which it lost 32,000. In the mostly Druze village of Maghar in the Galilee, the land area owned by the villagers has decreased from 54,000 dunams to 13,000 (Haidar 1995: 170; on the expropriation of Druze-owned land in general see Atashe 1995: 174–84; Yiftachel and Segal 1998).

Haidar's description of the way in which Taibe lost much of its land is worth citing at some length, because it reveals the dynamics that have operated throughout the country:

All the areas west of the [Israeli–Jordanian] cease-fire line before the village was transferred to Israeli jurisdiction [in 1949][2] were immediately expropriated by the [Israeli] government. All land belonging to refugees was also confiscated, even when their relatives had remained in the village. Also expropriated were all lands not previously listed under the names of their owners and other lands ... which were closed off for military purposes or annexed to nearby Jewish settlements. In addition to loss by expropriation, the village forfeited all its eastern and northern lands and some of the southern areas which remained across the border [as] determined by the 1949 Rhodes Agreements. Taibe's land area was again diminished with the expropriation of [an] additional 1,080 dunams between 1974 and 1978. Under pressure from the inhabitants which expressed itself in an accelerated burst of building on the newly confiscated lands, about 700 dunams were returned to the villagers. (Haidar 1995: 140)

Although under some of the laws enacted to facilitate the expropriation of land the original owners were entitled to compensation in cash or in kind, it should be quite clear that adequate compensation would have defeated the purpose of expropriation. Anything like equitable compensation in alternative land, or the true value of the expropriated land in cash, would have enabled the Palestinians to maintain their land holdings or else invest significant amounts of capital in other productive enterprises. Neither of the two outcomes would have served the purposes of Zionism, the aim of which was to transfer resources from Palestinians to Jews. So while some Palestinian landowners have been compensated over the years, "the government's compensation program has been of little consequence" (Lustick 1980: 179; Oded 1964). As a result, "the mass expropriation of Arab land has been the heaviest single blow which

[2] In the "Triangle" region, where Taibe is located, the Israel–Jordan cease-fire line was shifted eastward in the armistice agreement signed in Rhodes in 1949, adding some 6,000 square kilometers and 31,000 Palestinians residents to the state of Israel (Lustick 1980: 41, 283 n. 26; Jiryis 1976: 289; Stendel 1996: 3).

government policy has dealt to the economic integrity of the Arab sector" (Lustick 1980: 182).

In 1976 the Palestinians' anger and frustration over the continuing expropriation of their land finally erupted in violence. The National Committee for the Defense of Arab Lands, formed by the Israeli Communist party in 1975, declared March 30, 1976 to be Land Day and called for a general strike and demonstrations against the expropriation of land, to be held on that day. The government, then headed by Yitzhak Rabin, responded with force and imposed a curfew on a number of villages in central Galilee, some of whose land was about to be expropriated. In skirmishes that ensued between demonstrators who defied the curfew and the security forces six Palestinians were killed in three villages, many more were wounded, and hundreds were arrested (Lustick 1980: 246; Sa'di 1996: 404).

Since Land Day large-scale expropriations of land have subsided, except in the Negev, but the "Judaization" of the land has continued in more subtle forms. The most important of the new methods have been the exchange of land between Palestinian landowners and the Israel Land Administration (ILA), at rates highly unfavorable to the Palestinians, and the inclusion of Palestinian-owned land under the jurisdiction of Jewish municipal and planning authorities, many of them created especially for this purpose. At present, Palestinian local government bodies have authority over only 2.5 percent of the country's local government area (Yiftachel 1992; 1996; 1997: 12; for the paradigmatic case of "Judaization," that of Upper Nazareth, see Rabinowitz 1997).

In general, local and regional planning authorities have been very slow in approving outline plans for Palestinian localities, making all physical development impossible, or else illegal (Yiftachel 1992; 1996; Haidar 1995: 33). In Majd al-Krum, for example, it took twenty-seven years for the outline plan to be approved, from 1964 to 1991 (Yiftachel 1992: 501). In the meantime all kinds of *ad hoc* legal arrangements were improvised, largely in response to unauthorized building by the inhabitants, who could not be issued building permits without an approved outline plan. The resulting hardships for the villagers, as described by Yiftachel, have been replicated in every Palestinian locality in Israel:

Quite often, demolition orders would be issued for unauthorized dwellings, fines for illegal construction imposed, and in some (rare) cases the houses would be demolished. Coupled with the associated hardship of living without basic infrastructure (which would not be provided by the state without a building permit), the constant existence of unauthorized dwellings in the village has allowed the district (mainly Jewish) planning authorities to exert a continuous level of control over the village's residents. The very basic function of constructing family homes on private land had become a risky and uncertain venture, due to the constant fear of demolition and lack of services. (Yiftachel 1992: 504)

As far as non-residential land is concerned, over 90 percent of it is owned by the state or by the JNF and administered by the ILA. The JNF-owned land, most of it acquired through the sale to the JNF of "abandoned" Palestinian land, amounts to about 20 percent of the total and is prohibited by law from being leased to non-Jews. State-owned land may be legally leased to non-Jews, but in practice such leases are rare, outside the Negev, and are limited to short-term, one- to three-year leases. Long-term leases, of forty-nine years, are made exclusively to Jews, mostly to kibbutzim or moshavim, and sub-leasing them to non-Jews is prohibited by the terms of the lease, as well as by law (Kretzmer 1990: 60–9; Haidar 1995: 8, 45).

Palestinian farmers are discriminated against in the allocation of water for irrigation as well. Thus, while in 1988 they worked about 19 percent of the land in Israel, they received only 2.7 percent of the water. Correspondingly, "the average income per dunam in the Arab sector [in 1979–80] was only 27.7 percent of the average income per dunam in the Jewish sector" (Haidar 1995: 48, 66). Under these conditions, agricultural employment among Palestinian citizens has declined rapidly: Whereas as late as 1972 28 percent of the jobs in the Palestinian sector were still in agriculture, by 1983 this ratio declined to only 7.2 percent, a loss of about 60 percent in the course of eleven years (Lewin-Epstein and Semyonov 1993: 50). As Haidar has noted, "the persistence of farming in the Arab sector does not depend on economic viability as much as on the utilization of cheap [i.e. family] manpower [sic] in cultivating the labour-intensive crops that Israeli agriculture has left to the Arab farmers" (Haidar 1995: 70).

In Lustick's view,

the expropriations, the inadequacy of compensation programs, and discrimination against Arabs in regard to the leasing of land are even more significant as aspects of a general pattern of economic discrimination against Arabs in all matters pertaining to development – a pattern that corresponds to government policy and that contributes to the continued underdevelopment of the Arab sector. (Lustick 1980: 182)

Underlying this policy, he argues, is not only an economic logic, but a political logic as well – to contribute to the ability of the state to control its Palestinian citizens.[3] From a broader perspective, as we have noted,

---

[3] In the document cited in note 1 above the Palestinians' dependence on the Jewish economy is mentioned specifically as one of the factors preventing the Palestinian citizens from aiding the Arab cause against Israel by fighting the state from within.

the prevention of economic development among the native population, by the transfer of its resources to the settlers, is an essential characteristic of the colonial strategy of "pure settlement colony."

Thus, while Palestinian agriculture in Israel has been all but destroyed by the state's land and water policies, the Palestinians have had access neither to private capital nor to the government aid and encouragement that would have been necessary for the development of alternative productive bases. As a result, self-employment among the Palestinians has declined significantly, from almost one-half of all jobs in the Arab sector in 1972 to slightly more than one-quarter in 1983 (Lewin-Epstein and Semyonov 1993: 33, 50–2). As summarized by Lewin-Epstein and Semyonov:

The most striking feature of [the change in the Arab economy between 1972 and 1983] was the shift ... from agriculture to an economy based on services, mostly public services. Although manufacturing expanded, it still played a small role in the Arab sector, and most blue-collar workers were employed in the Jewish sector. The change in the Arab economy entailed a substantial decline in self-employment and ownership of means of production. Most of those employed in the Arab sector were either paid by the national or local government, or by large firms, some of which were owned by Jewish companies. (Lewin-Epstein and Semyonov 1993: 58–9)

Due to the dearth of economic opportunities in the Palestinian sector, about two-thirds of the citizen Palestinian workforce are presently employed in the Jewish sector of the economy, mostly as commuters from their places of residence to Jewish localities (the remainder are residents of mixed-population cities or are employed by Jewish employers in their home towns) (Shavit 1992; Lewin-Epstein and Semyonov 1993: 33, 48; Smooha 1999: 66). Needless to say, the position of Palestinian workers in the Jewish sector is a subordinate one: "The integration of Arabs into the Israeli (Jewish) economy has entailed social and economic disadvantages in that Arab workers have generally been accepted into the lower level occupations only ... They tend to be relegated to the end of the job queue and are viewed [by employers] primarily as a source of cheap unskilled and semi-skilled labor" (Lewin-Epstein and Semyonov 1993: 59, 68).

This reality is reflected in the occupational distribution of Jewish and Palestinian workers. As we see in table 4.1, in 1990 32 percent of employed Jews, but only 13.5 percent of employed Palestinians, worked in the top three occupational categories of scientific/academic, professional, and managerial. In 1975 the figures were 24 percent and 9 percent, respectively, indicating only a slight narrowing of the gap, due primarily to the expansion of academic and professional opportunities

Table 4.1 *Selected socio-economic characteristics, Jewish and Palestinian citizens, selected years*

	Palestinians	Jews
Occupational status (3 top categories)		
1975	9%	24%
1990	13.5	32
Occupational status (skilled and unskilled workers)		
1975	54.4	32
1990	52	23.4
Occupational of university gradates, 1983		
teachers	38.7	15.3
MDs	13	
professional and semi-professional	6.6	16
managers and administrators in public		
sector	0.5	15
architects and engineers	5	14.5
blue collar	11	2.8
Average family income, gross (Jewish = 100)		
Per standard adult		
1980	77	54
1985	70	56
1993	72	56
Average family income, after taxes (Jewish = 100)		
1980	86	58
1985	77	60
1993	78	60
Incidence of poverty, % of families, gross		
1980	38.7	12.8
1985	49.2	29.9
1996	46.3	28.2
Incidence of poverty, % of families,		
after taxes and transfer payments		
1980	47.66	14.8
1985	35.55	9.43
1996	28.3	12.4
Infant mortality (ratio)	2	1

Sources: Lewin-Epstein and Semyonov 1993; Ghanem 1996; NII 1998.

in the Palestinian sector of the economy, mostly in public service. (Public service employment among Palestinians rose at exactly the same rate – 4.5 percent of the total – between 1975 and 1990.) At the other end of the scale, in 1990 only 23.4 percent of employed Jews, but fully 52 percent of employed Palestinians, worked as skilled or unskilled workers. In 1975 the figures were 32 percent for Jews and 54.4 percent for Palestinians, indicating a significant decline in this type of employment among Jews, but not among Palestinians (Lewin-Epstein and Semyonov 1993: 25, 55–6). It should be noted that the wages of Palestinian blue-collar workers tend to be lower than those of their Jewish counterparts, even in the same occupation and when working for the same firm (Lewin-Epstein and Semyonov 1993: 79).

This occupational disparity and income discrimination against Palestinians are naturally reflected in the income levels of the two groups. The average gross income of a Palestinian family was 77 percent of that of a Jewish family in 1980, 70 percent in 1985, and 72 percent in 1993. The respective after-taxes figures were 86 percent, 77 percent, and 78 percent. Looking at income per standard adult, which takes into account the larger size of Palestinian families, we find that gross Palestinian income was 54 percent of Jewish income in 1980, and around 56 percent in both 1985 and 1990, while net income was 58 percent and 60 percent, respectively (Ghanem 1996: 12; cf. Lustick 1980: 6–7; J. Landau 1993: 13).

In the words of Lewin-Epstein and Semyonov, "the economic disadvantage of Arabs is nowhere more evident than in the official figures on poverty." In 1986/7 57.2 percent of Palestinian families, as against 24.3 percent of Jewish families, reported income that was below the poverty line. After transfer payments, 37.5 percent of Palestinian families, but only 7.3 percent of Jewish families, remained officially poor (Lewin-Epstein and Semyonov 1993: 27–8). The equivalent figures for 1993 (after transfer payments) were 15.6 percent for Jews and 35.3 percent for Palestinians, reflecting the high rates of poverty among recent Jewish immigrants from the former Soviet Union. Among children, 44 percent of Palestinian children were below the poverty line in 1993, a decrease from 66 percent in 1980 and 50 percent in 1985, while 19.4 percent of Jewish children were in that category in 1993, an *increase* from 16.5 percent in 1980 and 11.7 percent in 1985 (Ghanem 1996: 12; Sa'di 1997; cf. NII 2000).[4] This disparity in the poverty levels, and in the levels of social services (Haidar 1991; Rosenhek and Shalev 2000), is reflected in the different rates of infant mortality among Jews and Palestinians. Although the absolute numbers have declined significantly over the years in both sectors, the ratio between them has held more or less steady at

[4] Until 1995 the annual income surveys of the CBS, from which the data on poverty was derived, included, in the Palestinian sector, only localities with 10,000 inhabitants or more. Since one-third of the Palestinian population live in localities smaller than 10,000 inhabitants (Lewin-Epstein and Semyonov 1993: 31), and this tends to be the poorer sector among them, until 1995 the figures probably understated the size of the economic gap between Jews and Palestinians. Since 1995 the surveys have covered both Jewish and Palestinian localities of 2,000 inhabitants and up, or 85 percent of the population in both sectors (NII 1998: 41, 70–1).

2:1 since 1955 (Lewin-Epstein and Semyonov 1993: 17–18; Ghanem 1996: 3; Swirski et al. 1999: 17; Adva Center 2000c).[5]

An important issue in discussions of labor market inequality is the rate of return on "human capital" among different groups of workers. Occupational and income inequalities that correspond to differences in human capital cannot be attributed to discrimination in the labor market (although they can be attributed to discrimination in access to resources that create human capital, primarily education). In this respect the situation of citizen Palestinians in Israel has gone through a drastic change between the census years of 1972 and 1983:

Whereas in 1972 there appears to have been no "market discrimination" against Arabs in that their occupational status, on average, was not lower than expected based on their human capital characteristics (age and education), by 1983 Arabs of all age groups experienced "labor market discrimination" and their actual occupational status was lower than what one would predict based on their market-relevant attributes. (Lewin-Epstein and Semyonov 1993: 58)

This change reflected the combined effects of the proletarianization of the Palestinian population, on the one hand, and the educational advances they had made, on the other. In 1983 "nearly 40 percent of the income gap between [Jews and Arabs] can be attributed to differential returns on human resources and group membership." And the gap between the Palestinians' educational training and occupational attainment seems to be increasing (Lewin-Epstein and Semyonov 1993: 119, 57, 24).

As can be seen in table 4.2, the rise in the Palestinians' educational levels has been one of the more pronounced changes that this community has gone through since its incorporation in the state of Israel. In 1948 80 percent of the Palestinians in Israel were illiterate; in 1988 only 15 percent. Median years of schooling for Palestinians aged fifteen and over increased by a factor of 8 between 1961 and 1993, from 1.2 to 9.7, while for Jews it increased by only 50 percent, from 8.4 to 12, over the same period. In 1961 only 1.5 percent of the Palestinians had any post-secondary education, compared with 10 percent of the Jews; in 1993 11 percent of the Palestinians and 32.3 percent of the Jews had at least some post-secondary education (al-Haj 1995: 20–3; Ghanem 1996: 6; Rouhana 1997: 85–90).

But the two systems educating Jews and Palestinians in Israel have been, and remain, separate and unequal, except at the post-secondary level: "There is total separation in formal education between Jews and Arabs

---

[5] For the argument that the higher rates of genetic diseases and infant mortality among Palestinian citizens is caused by higher rates of endogamous marriages within families: see Chayot 1998; Nir 2001.

Table 4.2 *Selected indicators of educational attainment,*
Jewish and Palestinian citizens, selected years

		Palestinians	Jews
Illiteracy	1948	80%	
	1988	15%	
Median years of schooling (age 15+)	1961	1.2	8.4
	1993	9.7	12
Some post-secondary education	1961	1.5%	10%
	1993	11%	32.3%
School attendance, 14–17	1993/94	70%	93%
In twelfth grade (% of age group)	1993/94	44%	
Gained matriculation certificate (% of age group)	1994	14.4%	39.5%
% of students in universities	1994/95	5.3%	

Sources: J. Landau 1993; al-Haj 1995; Ghanem 1996; Rinawi 1996; Rouhana 1997.

from kindergarten through secondary school, in all forms and grades"
(J. Landau 1993: 59; Swirski 1990). This separation is manifested in
the educational goals of the two systems, in their curricula, in their budgets and facilities, in the rates of success of their students, and in the
occupational opportunities open to their graduates.

Education policy is a major mechanism for dispensing social rights.
As such, the evolution and internal contradictions of Israel's education
policy in the citizen Palestinian sector is very revealing of the nature of
its incorporation regime. The liberal aspect of this regime precluded the
possibility of excluding non-Jews from the purview of the State Education
Law of 1953. However, the way in which this law has been applied
in the Arab sector points to the limited role the liberal discourse has
been allowed to play in the society.

In the early years of sovereignty there was a debate between two
schools of thought regarding the proper way of educating Palestinian
children. The more liberal school advocated assimilating them into the
same education system as Jewish children, while the ethno-nationalist
school advocated what Majid al-Haj has termed "controlled segregation."
Advocates of the liberal approach believed that blending Palestinian and
Jewish children in the same institutions would de-nationalize the former
and defuse their subversive potential. The advocates of segregation realized that such an approach would be futile unless it was part and parcel
of a general liberal, integrationist policy towards the citizen Palestinians.

Given the nature of the society, it should come as no surprise that the segregationists won the day (al-Haj 1995: 121–4).

Controlled segregation meant that Palestinian children would be educated in their own separate system, where the language of instruction would be Arabic, and that this system would be tightly controlled by the state (for the exclusionary effects of this policy, see Kook 2000). So while the Palestinian education system is separate, it can in no way be described as autonomous (Smooha 1999). Until 1987 it was headed by a Jewish official of the Ministry of Education, and the appointment of a Palestinian as its head coincided with a significant reduction in the authority of this position (al-Haj 1995: 71). Still, al-Haj has discerned two different periods in the implementation of controlled segregation, before and since the mid-1970s. The primary difference between the two periods has had to do with the extent to which the liberal discourse has been allowed to mitigate the influence of (Jewish) ethno-nationalism on Arab education (al-Haj 1995, chap. 6).

In curricular terms the segregation of Jewish and Palestinian education is reflected in an imbalance between the different requirements in the two systems relating to nationally specific subjects such as language, culture, and history. In the words of Jacob Landau, a generally sympathetic observer of Israel's treatment of its Palestinian citizens:

While in Jewish schools a minimum of Arab history and literature is studied, and only a limited amount of Arabic is compulsory, pupils in Arab schools learn Hebrew, certain chapters of Hebrew literature (including chapters from the Bible), and Jewish history (including the basics of Zionist history) ... [In sum] the Arab minority is supposed to learn more Hebrew and Judaism than the Jewish majority Arabic and Arab culture. (J. Landau 1993: 64–5)

More specifically, as al-Haj has pointed out, until the mid-1970s Palestinian high schools devoted an equal amount of time to Arab and Jewish history (about 20 percent of instructional time) while Jewish schools devoted only 1.4 percent of their time to Arab history, and 38.8 percent to Jewish history. The reforms of the mid-1970s have not changed the Palestinian curriculum in any fundamental way, but have added the Arab–Israeli conflict as a subject of instruction, taking up 22.2 percent of the time, in the Jewish schools (al-Haj 1995: 124–52).

The most important asymmetry between the two history programs, after the reforms, according to al-Haj, lies in their stated goals. The goal in the Jewish schools is the ethno-nationalist goal of fostering identification with the aims of Jewish nationalism, while in the Palestinian schools the aim is the liberal Zionist one of achieving a more balanced view of the Arab–Israeli conflict (al-Haj 1995: 146–7). Summarizing the general goals of the Palestinian education system before and after the reforms, al-Haj argues that, originally, Palestinian education was intended to create submissive human beings, ready to accept their inferiority vis-à-vis the Jews and deny their Palestinian identity. Since, with the passage of time, this policy was perceived to be counter-productive (cf. J. Landau 1993: 65), a more liberal policy was adopted. The new policy, formulated in the mid-1970s, was designed to portray Zionism and the state of Israel in the best possible light, to minimize hostility towards the state, and to take note of Arab nationalism without, however, encouraging the nationalist tendencies of the Palestinian students themselves (al-Haj 1995: 127–8, 143).

In terms of both physical facilities and educational services the Palestinian school system has been seriously underbudgeted compared to the Jewish one. In the first ten years of sovereignty the state allocated only 5 percent of the funds required for the construction of classrooms in the Palestinian sector. In 1972 the Ministry of Education determined that the Palestinian school system was short 1,200 classrooms, and that 900 of the existing classrooms were sub-standard. According to al-Haj, in 1989 the system was still short 1,200 classrooms, which amounted to 20 percent of the total, while 100–15 new classrooms were needed each year to keep up with demand (al-Haj 1995: 103–8). In 1992 the state comptroller determined that "funding for the Palestinian educational system per pupil did not exceed one third of the amount allocated to its Jewish counterpart" (Sa'di 1996: 396).

The Palestinian school system lacks completely, or is seriously under-provided with, related education services such as psychological counseling, truancy officers, health-care services, computers, extra-curricular activities, and so on. In 1985 an inter-ministerial committee estimated that Palestinian education was lagging behind the Jewish one by twenty to twenty-five years (al-Haj 1995, chap. 5). This reality is reflected in the dropout rates of Palestinian students, in their success in acquiring the matriculation certificate, and in their rate of attendance at institutions of higher education.

In the 1993–4 school year, 93 percent of Jewish fourteen-to-seventeen-year-olds but only 70 percent of Palestinians of the same age group were attending school. Only 44 percent of the relevant age group among Palestinians reached the twelfth grade in that year, and of those only 33 percent gained a matriculation certificate (constituting 40 percent of those who actually took the matriculation examinations). Of the total age group, 14.4 percent of Palestinians and 39.5 percent of Jews gained the matriculation certificate in 1994. By the end of the century the figures rose to 20 percent among Palestinians and over 50 percent among Jews. Among the Palestinians, students of private Christian schools, which educate about 30 percent of all Palestinian high-school students, have been highly overrepresented among those who succeed in gaining matriculation certificates (Rinawi 1996: 2–3; cf. Ghanem 1996: 7; al-Haj 1995: 94–101; J. Landau 1993:70–1; Adva Center 2000a; Eshet 2001).

Many of the matriculating Palestinian students earn matriculation certificates that are not good enough to gain them entry into universities. Thus in 1998 90 percent of Jewish high-school graduates, but only 70 percent of Arab ones (not including Druze and Negev Bedouin graduates, whose rates were even lower) gained matriculation certificates that met the universities' admission requirements. As a result, in the 1994–5 academic year Palestinian students constituted only 5.3 percent of the students in Israeli universities (Rinawi 1996: 3; cf. Ghanem 1996: 7; al-Haj 1995: 195; Adva Center 2000a). This was a slight decline from the rates achieved in the late 1980s, due, in all probability, to the difficulties facing Palestinian university graduates in finding employment commensurate with their educational qualifications (al-Haj 1995: 194).

As we saw in table 4.1, by far the largest group among Palestinian university graduates work as teachers – 38.7 percent in 1983, compared with 15.3 percent of Jewish university graduates. The second-largest group are medical doctors (13 percent in 1983), followed closely by blue-collar workers (11 percent). Among Jews, the three largest occupational categories among university graduates, aside from teachers, are professional and semi-professional employees (16 percent), managers and administrators in the public sector (15 percent), and architects and engineers (14.5 percent). Among Palestinians these three groups comprise 6.6 percent, 0.5 percent (!) and 5 percent of university graduates, respectively. Only 2.8 percent of Jewish university graduates worked as blue-collar workers in 1983 (their numbers have undoubtedly increased since the onset of massive immigration of Jews from the former Soviet Union). These figures clearly illustrate the different labor-market opportunities facing Jews and Palestinians possessing similar "human capital" (al-Haj 1995: 205, chap. 8; cf. Shavit 1990: 124).

Almost invariably, high-status occupations are available to Palestinians only in their own labor market, especially in the public sector (Shavit 1992; Lewin-Epstein and Semyonov 1993). In 1983, however, "almost 50 percent more highly educated persons resided in Arab communities than there were high status jobs in the Arab labor market" (Lewin-Epstein and Semyonov 1993: 56). Those educated persons who could not find employment in the Palestinian labor market had to settle for jobs for which they were overqualified in the Jewish market.

The "educational–occupational mismatch" suffered by highly educated Palestinians is a clear expression of some of the internal contradictions that beset the incorporation regime due to the multiple, partially contradictory, discourses of citizenship it embodies. While the liberal discourse mandates that Palestinian citizens be given the opportunity to be educated at the level and in the fields for which they may be personally qualified (although this opportunity is also mitigated by the ethno-national discourse), this principle works much less effectively in the labor market. Israel's law against employment discrimination allows employers wide discretion in refusing to hire workers for security reasons. Since every Palestinian is considered a security risk, and since much of Israel's sophisticated industries and public utilities are, by definition, security related, national discrimination is rampant in the higher segments of the labor market. Ironically, the security argument is used not only against Muslim and Christian Palestinians, who normally do not serve in the military, but also against the Druze who do (Lewin-Epstein and Semyonov 1993: 80–2; Atashe 1995: 116–33; Hajar 1995). Moreover, anti-Palestinian discrimination is not limited to the private sector. In the public sector as well, including the state civil service and the higher education system, Palestinians are notoriously underrepresented, except as teachers in the Arab school system. Their exclusion is especially noticeable in positions of high status, authority, and income (Nachmias 1991: 414–15; J. Landau 1993: 15–17).

Civil and political status

Since the abolition of the military administration in 1966, Palestinian citizens have formally enjoyed civil and political rights on an individual, liberal basis.[6] They have been excluded, however, from political citizenship in the republican sense – that is, from participation in attending to the common good of society. This exclusion is normalized by the dominance of the ethno-republican discourse of citizenship: Jewish ethnicity is a necessary condition for membership in the political community, and the contribution to the process of Zionist redemption is a measure of one's civic virtue. This conception necessarily excludes the Palestinians: As non-Jews they cannot belong to the ethnically defined community; as those from whom the land is to be redeemed they cannot partake of Zionist civic virtue. Starting with this a priori exclusion, however, under the liberal discourse Israel's Palestinian citizens are more or less secure in the exercise of their individual rights, as long as these rights do not conflict with the national goals of the Jewish majority. As we

[6] The year 1966, when the military administration was formally abolished, is a convenient symbolic marker rather than a real drastic turning point. Many of the constraints placed on citizen Palestinians had eroded even before 1966, and in many ways control of the Palestinian population continued afterwards, albeit in more subtle forms.

have seen above, this caveat has had momentous consequences especially for the Palestinians' ability to enjoy the right of private property in land.

One important *obligation* that is denied to most Palestinian citizens is military service, which is mandatory for most Jewish citizens. This exemption is not a matter of law but of administrative practice, and is probably unavoidable as long as the primary task of the Israeli military is to fight other Arabs (Hofnung 1991: 237–8). Still, many social rights in Israel have been tied to the performance of military service, so that most Palestinian citizens either do not enjoy them or are entitled to smaller benefits (Kretzmer 1990: 98–107). This is one reason for the socio-economic inferiority of the citizen Palestinians, described above. The vacuity of the rationale tying this discrimination to the Palestinians' exemption from military service is evidenced by the fact that it affects the Druze, who do serve, practically as much as it affects all other Palestinian citizens (Lewin-Epstein and Semyonov, 1993: 81–2; Atashe 1995: 116–33; Hajar 1995).

Moreover, the possibility of instituting some form of alternative national service for Palestinians (which has been done in the case of religious Jewish women) has not been seriously considered by either the state or the Palestinians themselves. This is despite the fact that in 1993–4 54 percent of Palestinian citizens favored some form of national service, with 42 percent favoring non-military service and 12 percent favoring military service (interestingly, 57 percent of the Jewish citizens *objected* to the institution of any form of national service for Palestinian citizens) (Levinsohn et al. 1995: 17). Since any notion of citizenship entails the equality of rights *and* obligations, and especially in view of the extraordinary importance accorded national service in the republican view of citizenship (Oldfield 1990: 166–7), this omission is highly emblematic of the Palestinians' exclusion from attending to the common good. It has also become a major issue in the debate over their citizenship rights. Thus, for example, in the general elections of 1988 three right-wing Jewish political parties demanded that national service for Palestinian citizens become a condition for their enjoyment of full citizenship (Nakdimon et al. 1988: 75, 133, 142; Smooha 1989: 96, 224; Horowitz and Lissak 1989: 39–40).

The exclusion of Palestinian citizens from attending to the common good was formalized for the first time in 1985, in an amendment to the law governing elections to the Knesset. The statute, an amendment to *Basic Law: The Knesset*, reads:

A list of candidates shall not participate in elections to the Knesset if its goals, explicitly or implicitly, or its actions include one of the following:

(1) Negation of the existence of the State of Israel as the state of the Jewish people;
(2) Negation of the democratic character of the State;
(3) Incitement of racism. (Knesset 1985: 3951)

It should be noted that this amendment states the particularistic norm of Israel being the state of the Jewish people explicitly, while the universal norm of equality before the law appears only implicitly, under the more general category of "democracy." During the debate leading to the adoption of the amendment, two changes proposed by representatives of the Democratic Front and the Progressive List for Peace (PLP), both predominantly Palestinian parties, were voted down. Their proposals would have removed or mitigated the particularistic content of article (1) by having it conclude with either "the State of Israel" or with "the State of Israel as the state of the Jewish people and its Arab citizens" (Kretzmer 1990: 29; Gavison 1986: 198).

The purpose of the 1985 amendment was to create the legal means for disqualifying political parties on the basis of their ideology, which had previously been impossible under the law. (Regardless of this legal situation, a Palestinian party, the Socialist List, had been disqualified in 1965 for ideological reasons.) Its immediate targets were Rabbi Meir Kahane's Kach party, which called for the "transfer" of all Palestinians, citizens and non-citizens alike, out of the Land of Israel, and the PLP, which was viewed by the state as overly nationalistic. After a series of administrative and legal maneuvers, Kahane's party was indeed disqualified in 1988 and the PLP was not (Peled 1992).

In the deliberations leading to this outcome it became clear, however, according to legal scholar David Kretzmer, that participation in Knesset elections could be legally denied to a list of candidates "that rejects the particularistic definition of Israel as the state of the Jewish people, even if the list is committed to achieving a change in this constitutional fundamental through the parliamentary process alone." Moreover, in Kretzmer's view, the decision also implied that

on the decidedly fundamental level of identification and belonging there cannot be total equality between Arab and Jew in Israel. The state is the state of the Jews, both those presently resident in the country as well as those resident abroad. Even if the Arabs have equal rights on all other levels the implication is abundantly clear: Israel is not *their* state. (Kretzmer 1990: 31; original emphasis)

This view was shared by Smooha: "From the Israeli-Arabs' viewpoint, the provision that Israel is the land of Jews all over the world, but not necessarily of its citizens, degrades them to a status of invisible outsiders, as if Israel were not their own state" (Smooha 1990: 402).

Political rights and political mobilization

Israel's Palestinian citizens are by no means satisfied with the place
accorded them in the incorporation regime (Smooha 1990; 1997; 1999).
However, the limited, liberal citizenship status they enjoy has endowed
them with sufficient political rights both to enable and induce them to
conduct their struggle within the constitutional framework of the state,
rather than against it. This has been a key factor in allowing Israel to maintain a stable democratic regime in the context of an acute ethnic conflict.

The commitment of the Palestinian citizens to abide by the law of the
land was strained, however, by the two intifadas (uprisings) launched by
their brethren in the occupied territories since 1967, and by the brutal
methods utilized by Israel in trying to suppress them. The first intifada
(1987–93) greatly increased the momentum of Palestinian protest activity
inside Israel – strikes, rallies, demonstrations, petitions to the government – that had been on the rise anyway since the mid-1970s. Unlike
the uprising in the occupied territories, however, and unlike the second,
al-Aksa intifada (2000), these activities, with only marginal exceptions,
remained non-violent and were carried out within the framework of the
law. The state also reacted with relative restraint, so that the first intifada
did not result in major confrontations within Israel's pre-1967 borders.
(On the second intifada, see below.)

The reasons for the restraint exercised by citizen Palestinian were articulated by their leaders. As Nadim Rouhana has put it, "the Arab leadership made clear that the Arabs in Israel would act only within the law.
It was argued that their status is different from that of other Palestinians
and therefore, that their efforts would be expressed differently" (Rouhana
1989: 47; 1997: 73–5). Furthermore, the citizen Palestinians' increasing
political confidence was fed, according to Rouhana, "by the sense of security that their status as Israeli citizens provides, as well as their formal
equality before the Israeli law" (Rouhana 1989: 54; cf. Cohen 1989a).

Paradoxically, their "Israeliness" is an important component of the
citizen Palestinians' sense of collective identity, in spite of their growing
self-identification as Palestinians. (This attests, perhaps, to the success of
the educational policies outlined above.) As Smooha has argued,

the acquisition of various Palestinian identifications is manifested mostly in feelings of solidarity but not in a desire to dissociate oneself from Israel and to join
any Palestinian entity. The overwhelming majority of the Arabs would be relieved
by a settlement of the Palestinian problem, and in particular, 80 percent would
feel better as Israeli citizens if a Palestinian state were to be established in the
West Bank and Gaza Strip. Yet, only 8 percent of them . . . are willing to consider
a move to such a state. (Smooha 1989: 92–3)

More recently Smooha has stated this thesis in an even stronger form:

The Palestinian citizens of Israel are going through an historical process of the Israelization of their identity and politics. This process has a double significance: growing integration into Israeli identity and politics on the one hand, and a growing distance from Palestinian identity and politics on the other ... [This despite the fact that] the Palestinianness of the Arabs in Israel is solid ... They are a special and distinct population that is inevitably Israeli-Palestinian in its identity and political behavior. (Smooha 1998b: 41–2; see also 1997)

From the perspective of the state, and of the Jewish majority, however, there is a limit beyond which the Palestinians' exercise of their Israeliness and of their citizenship rights will not be allowed to proceed. This limit is located at the transition point between struggling to have their liberal rights respected, even expanded, in the conduct of official policy, and attempting to challenge the prevailing notion of the common good of society. Smooha's own studies have shown that in 1995 72.6 percent of Israeli Jews agreed with the current definition of Israel as the state of the Jewish people; 58 percent would have preferred to live in a Jewish non-democratic state rather than in a democratic non-Jewish state; 31 percent supported the abrogation of the Palestinian citizens' right to vote in Knesset elections ; and 31.5 percent supported the "transfer" of the Palestinian citizens altogether (Smooha 1998b: 51–2).

The Palestinian citizens, then, desire civil and political, albeit not cultural, integration with the Jewish majority, whereas the Jewish citizens oppose such integration, in order to maintain the Jewish character of the state. This clash, according to Ghanem and Smooha's latest findings, has finally brought the "Israelization" process to a halt. Surveys undertaken in 1999 and 2001, that is, both before and after the outbreak of the al-Aksa intifada, show that citizen Palestinian opinion has reverted to where it was in 1976. Thus, in 1999 only 32.8 percent of the Palestinian respondents described their identity as "Israeli," compared to 63.2 percent in 1995. The percentage of those rejecting Israel's right to exist as a state rose from 6.5 percent in 1995 to 15.6 percent in 2001 (it was 20.5 percent in 1976), and of those rejecting Israel's right to exist as a Jewish-Zionist state rose from 35.3 percent in 1995 to 46.1 percent in 2001 (it was 62.1 percent in 1985). Significantly, in 2001 about one-third of the Palestinian respondents agreed to the transfer of Palestinian-populated areas near the Green Line to the future Palestinian state (Ghanem and Smooha 2001).

During the 1970s, following the abolition of the military administration in 1966 and the war of 1967, Palestinian citizens were becoming increasingly assertive of their rights and had shown growing willingness to use the political system for promoting those rights. A number of countrywide representative organizations had emerged in that period, such as the Committee of Heads of Arab Local Councils and the Committee to Defend the Lands. These organizations have gained the grudging *de facto*, if not *de jure*, recognition of state authorities (Lustick 1980: 246–9; Smooha 1989: 211–12; al-Haj and Rosenfeld 1989; 1990).

In terms of electoral politics, until 1965 the only Palestinian political parties that participated in national elections were *hamula*- (extended family) based lists affiliated with Zionist parties, primarily with Mapai. The only exception was the Israeli Communist party, which had been taking on more and more the character of a Palestinian party. In 1965 the Socialist List, organized by the Palestinian nationalist group al-Ard (the land), sought to participate in the Knesset elections held in that year, but was disqualified for ideological reasons (Zureik 1979: 172–5; Peled 1992; Kaufman 1997).

Between 1965 and 1984 no Palestinian party had attempted to field a list of candidates in Knesset elections. (In 1980 a public meeting called by Palestinian organizations to discuss the possibility of forming a unified Palestinian political party was banned by the government: Smooha 1997: 217.) Instead, Palestinian voters had been shifting their votes from Mapai and the Labor Party, and their Palestinian affiliates, to the Communist Party, whose following has become overwhelmingly Palestinian. Thus, the Communist Party gained about 50 percent of the Palestinian vote in 1977 and 1981, and has been receiving about one-third of that vote since then, with the exception of the 1992 and 1999 elections, when it received 25 percent and 22 percent, respectively (Ozacky-Lazar and Ghanem 1996: 38; Ghanem and Ozacky-Lazar 1999: 20).

A major reason for the decline in the Communists' share of the vote after 1981 was the appearance of new Palestinian parties – avowedly nationalist and Muslim. Together, the Communists and the all-Palestinian parties were receiving about half of the Palestinian vote since 1984, and in 1996 they reached the two-thirds mark for the first time. In the 1996 elections the Palestinian vote was divided almost equally between three blocs – the secular and moderately nationalist Democratic Front (Communists and their affiliates), the Muslim-nationalist United Arab List (made up primarily of the Arab Democratic Party and a section of the Islamic Movement), and liberal ("left" in Israeli political parlance) Zionist parties that espouse a relatively integrationist stance towards citizen Palestinians. In the 1999 elections the Muslim-nationalist list received 31 percent of the vote, the Democratic Front received 22 percent, and a secular nationalist list received 17 percent (Ghanem and Ozacky-Lazar 1999: 20–1; Kaufman and Israeli 1999). In the fourteenth and fifteenth

Knessets, elected in 1996 and 1999, the number of Palestinian deputies, elected by both Palestinian and Zionist parties, was proportionate, for the first time, to the share of Palestinian voters in the electorate – 10 percent (Ozacky-Lazar and Ghanem 1996; Smooha 1997: 215).

This shift in Palestinian voting behavior and, as a result, the growth of the Palestinians' parliamentary power, coupled with the growing political polarization among Jews over the future of the occupied territories, have led Lustick to predict that if the political deadlock between the Jewish political blocs continues, Palestinian parties may be included in governing coalitions in the not-too-distant future. This, he argued, would be one more step towards making Israel a binational state *de jure*, not only *de facto* (Lustick 1989; 1990). The closest this prediction has come to being borne out was in 1992, when the Rabin government had to rely on six "Arab" delegates (one was actually Jewish), representing the Democratic Front and the Arab Democratic Party, to maintain its Knesset majority. These two parties were not included in the governing coalition, nor did they receive ministerial posts. But in return for their support, crucial, among other things, for passing the Oslo Accords in the Knesset, the citizen Palestinians received much better treatment from that government (1992–6) than they had from any other government, before or since (Hareven and Ghanem 1996).

In evaluating this episode one could consider the glass half-full or half-empty. It could be argued that for the first time Palestinians had real influence at cabinet level, albeit from the outside, and that they used this influence to promote both the peace process and the material interests of their community. On the other hand, it could be pointed out that the Labor government was attacked viciously for its dependence on Arab votes and that both Rabin and Shimon Peres (who succeeded him as premier after Rabin was assassinated in November 1995) made frantic efforts to enlarge their coalitions, so they would not have to depend on these votes. According to Smooha's findings, in 1995 "even among leftist [i.e. liberal] Jewish voters, there was no majority to unconditionally support the inclusion of Arab parties in government coalitions (only 38.8 percent agreed unconditionally)" (Smooha 1997: 226). Moreover, Benjamin Netanyahu's trump card, thrown in at the very last minutes of the 1996 election campaign, was the slogan "Bibi is good for the Jews" (see Smooha 1990; 1995; Sa'di 1996: 406).

Their confidence having been bolstered by their experience in the 1992–6 Knesset, since the 1996 elections all major Palestinian parties have been calling for a fundamental transformation in the formal definition of the Israeli state, from an ethno-national Jewish state to a liberal-democratic state of all of its citizens, where Palestinians will be recognized as a *national* minority. One party, the Democratic National Alliance, which ran as part of the Democratic Front in 1996 and independently in 1999, winning one Knesset seat in each race, went so far as to demand national-cultural, non-territorial autonomy for the Palestinian national minority. In June 1997 its representative, Azmi Bishara, introduced a series of legislative proposals aimed at instituting several measures of cultural autonomy for citizen Palestinians. These proposals were unanimously supported by all Palestinian MKs (Ozacky-Lazar and Ghanem 1996; Smooha 1997: 224; 1999: 80–3).

The Palestinians' demand to liberalize their citizenship status as individuals received important encouragement from the High Court of Justice when it finally ruled on the long-pending Qaadan case in March 2000 (Bagatz 6698/95, *Qaadan vs. ILA, Katzir, and others*, reprinted in Mautner 2000: 427–48; see also Barzilai 2001; for the history of the case, see Ziv and Shamir 2000). The Qaadans, a citizen Palestinian couple, petitioned the court in 1995 to intercede on their behalf with the ILA and five other governmental and quasi-governmental bodies that had refused to lease them land in Katzir, a "community settlement" being established by the Jewish Agency in the "Triangle" area, not far from Israel's 1967 border with Jordan. In a path-breaking decision, president of the Supreme Court Aharon Barak determined that it was illegal for the state to discriminate between its Jewish and Arab citizens in the allocation of land, even when that discrimination was effected indirectly, through Jewish "national institutions" (the Jewish Agency in this case). The ethno-national Zionist interest in "Judaizing" various regions of the country, Barak ruled, could not overcome the liberal principle of equality.

Furthermore, to counter the argument that the equality principle was compatible with a "separate but equal" allocation of land, Barak asserted that "a policy of 'separate but equal' is by its very nature unequal ... [because] separation denigrates the excluded minority group, sharpens the difference between it and the others, and embeds feelings of social inferiority" (Bagatz 6698/95, par. 30). Significantly, Barak based this assertion on the US Supreme Court's decision in *Brown vs. Board of Education*, and determined that "any differential treatment on the basis of religion or nationality is suspect and prima facie discriminatory" (Kedar 2000: 6).

Predictably, the court wished to protect itself against the allegation that its decision undermined Israel's character as the state of the Jewish people. For, as many commentators were quick to point out, if the state cannot give preference to Jews in the allocation of land, what was the practical import of its being a Jewish state (Steinberg 2000)? In anticipation of this argument, Barak repeated his long-held position that the Jewish values of the state were not in contradiction with its liberal-democratic values, and that the equality principle was rooted equally in both sets of values (see chap. 10, below). He also stressed that the decision applied in the particular case before the court only, and that its implications were future-oriented and should not be seen as raising any question about past practices. Moreover, in certain cases, he argued, discrimination on the basis of national affiliation could be warranted, so the court did not decree that the state lease the Qaadans the property in question, only that it reconsider its previous decision not to lease it to them.[7]

With all these disclaimers, Barak was cognizant of the fact that the *Qaadan* decision was "a first step in a difficult and sensitive road" (Bagatz 6698/95, par. 37). How difficult and sensitive the road ahead was would become evident with the outbreak of the second intifada, the al-Aqsa intifada, in October 2000 (see chap. 7, below).

For the citizen Palestinians the second uprising in the occupied territories came after a five-year period of increasing frustration with Israeli government policies. The assassination of Yitzhak Rabin in November 1995 was a serious blow to their hopes for peace between Israel and the Palestinians and for more equal citizenship within Israel itself. Despite that, they were largely excluded from the rituals of national mourning and remembrance that followed the assassination. Rabin's successor, Shimon Peres, who had played a major role in the peace process, decided, on the eve of the 1996 elections, to launch a very aggressive military operation in Lebanon. During this operation, named by Israel "Grapes of Wrath," one hundred Lebanese civilians were killed in one village by Israeli artillery bombardment. Nevertheless, in the elections for prime minister held in the following month, 95 percent of the Palestinian voters (who cast valid ballots) voted for Peres, compared to 44 percent of Jewish voters (Ozacky-Lazar and Ghanem 1996).

Peres's loss to Benjamin Netanyahu of Likud in 1996 inaugurated a period of alienation between the government and its Palestinian citizens. Not only was the peace process stalled, but friction was renewed around the issues of budgetary allocations, land expropriation, and demolition of houses. This alienation broke out in violent clashes with police in the Palestinian town of Um-el-Fahem, in September 1998, during which police for the first time fired rubber-coated steel bullets at Israeli demonstrators, resulting in a number of them being seriously wounded (Yiftachel 2000: 78).

---

[7] By December 2000 no action had been taken by the respondents in the case, and the Qaadans appealed to the High Court again, asking for a ruling of contempt of court against them (*Haaretz*, December 18, 2000).

In the next election for prime minister, in 1999, again 95 percent of the Palestinian voters voted for the Labor Party candidate, Ehud Barak, although he had practically ignored them during the election campaign (Ghanem and Ozacky-Lazar 1999). Barak's snubbing of the citizen Palestinians continued after his election victory, and was expressed both in his refusal to include their representatives in the government coalition, in any form, and in the policies pursued by his government after it was formed.

When the al-Aksa intifada erupted in October 2000, demonstrations of solidarity by citizen Palestinians assumed a more violent character than before, and resulted in a number of major highways being temporarily blocked (for an analysis of the broader context of this reaction see Rabinowitz et al. 2000). Although the police and the demonstrators have different versions of the events that ensued, it seems highly unlikely that any lives were endangered by the demonstrations. Still, throughout the Northern police district, where the majority of citizen Palestinians live (and only in that district), the police fired live ammunition at the demonstrators, killing between ten and fifteen of them and wounding many more.[8] In some areas Jewish demonstrators also attacked Palestinians, resulting in major property losses, injuries, and perhaps even deaths.

This series of confrontations, which lasted almost two weeks, resulted in the heaviest death toll among citizen Palestinians since the Kafr Kassem massacre of 1956, when forty-nine villagers were murdered by police for breaking a curfew of which they were unaware (Benziman and Mansour 1992: 106; Rosental 2000). Still, it took six weeks of strong pressure from the Palestinian political leadership and from some Jewish public figures for the government to appoint a state commission of inquiry, headed by a Supreme Court justice, to investigate the clashes. At the time of writing the commission of inquiry has not concluded its hearings yet.

The confluence of the *Qaadan* decision and the murderous reaction by police to demonstrations of unarmed Palestinian citizens may seem paradoxical. But as Meir Amor has shown in a wide-ranging study of the subject, the removal of legal disabilities and granting of equal rights in many cases portend much greater physical danger to oppressed minorities than what they experienced in the period of official discrimination (Amor 1999). Suffice it to think of African-Americans in the post-bellum South and of European Jews in the twentieth century to be impressed with the power of this observation. It could very well be that the growing political confidence of the citizen Palestinians, and especially their demand that Israel give up its formal definition as a Jewish state – a demand that

---

[8] It may be significant that the commander of the Northern police district, Alik Ron, was previously chief of police in the West Bank.

was greatly bolstered by *Qaadan* – made them threatening enough in the eyes of sufficient numbers of Jews to warrant their treatment as enemies of the state. This hypothesis is strengthened by the fact that the Jewish majority reacted to the events of October 2000 by instituting an unofficial economic boycott of the citizen Palestinians, a boycott that still continues at the time of writing and that resulted in a 50 percent decline in the volume of Palestinian business within Israel.

Conclusion: the question of autonomy

The events of October 2000 demonstrated, if such demonstration was needed, that even the granting of truly equal liberal rights to Israel's Palestinian citizens – a prospect that is still far off in the future – would not amount to their admission to full membership in the society. As Azmi Bishara, the most prominent advocate of the idea of national-cultural autonomy for citizen Palestinians, has argued: "The individual integration offered [citizen Palestinians in Israel] is false integration, that involves giving up [their] collective identity ... Israelization as a collective-cultural option is not being offered, and cannot be offered ... because we live [under] the worst kind of ethnic republicanism" (Bishara 1993: 16). Therefore, only true liberal equality can be the basis for national-cultural autonomy for the citizen Palestinians.

Smooha has summarized the positions of the two sides on the issue of autonomy this way:

The Arabs demand non-territorial institutional autonomy: control over their educational system, state recognition of Arab national organizations ... the freedom to form nationalist Arab parties, the right to establish an Arab university, and a proportional share of the national resources. Israel rejects this drive for autonomous institutions because it appears as impinging on its Jewish-Zionist character and engendering secessionist sentiments. It grants Arabs an ethnic (religious, cultural, linguistic) minority status while they pursue a Palestinian national minority status. (Smooha 1992: 266)

The status being pursued could be interpreted as the extension of the ethno-republican principle to the Palestinian citizens as well. Thus, rather than a core Jewish republican community surrounded by peripheral individual non-Jewish citizens, the state of Israel would be reconstituted as two republican communities – Jewish and Palestinian – each conducting its own affairs by itself, and cooperating in matters of common concern.

In 1988 Smooha found that 47.5 percent of his Palestinian respondents supported the option he defined as "consociationalism" ("allowing Arabs to organize independently and become partners in state institutions" and "granting Arabs separate legal status, like the autonomy offered to the

Arabs in the West Bank and Gaza Strip"). In 1976 only 36 percent of Palestinian respondents had supported that option. More significantly, perhaps, support for this option among Jewish respondents increased from 5 percent in 1980 to 17 percent in 1988. Among Palestinian respondents, about an equal number (48.3 percent) supported the liberal-democratic option ("achievement of equality and integration with Jews"), while among Jewish respondents this option was supported, for the first time, by fewer people (15.3 percent) than the consociational one (Smooha 1992: 113).

Support for autonomy had increased significantly among Palestinians by 1995, when it was the arrangement favored by the largest number of respondents – 81.5 percent. The second largest number – 66 percent – supported what Smooha defined as "improved ethnic democracy" – a more limited version of autonomy, maintaining Israel's character as a Jewish–Zionist state (respondents, evidently, were not limited to one choice only). Of three possible "liberal democratic" arrangements, the most popular was supported by 40.5 percent. Unfortunately, the consociational option was not presented to Smooha's Jewish respondents in 1995, but by far the largest number among them – 71.5 percent – supported the "improved ethnic democracy" option. Only 4.5 percent supported the one "liberal democratic" option Jewish respondents were asked about (Smooha 1997: 231).

The only arrangement on which majorities among both Palestinians and Jews could agree, based on these findings, is "improved ethnic democracy," which seems to be Smooha's own preferred model as well (Smooha 1997: 230, 235–6). The improvement in this model, over the current situation, which Smooha has termed "ethnic democracy," is a strengthening of the liberal element at the expense of the ethno-national one. This would be manifested primarily in more genuine respect for the Palestinian citizens' individual rights and obligations and in making their separate educational, cultural, and religious institutions genuinely autonomous. The overall character of the state would remain, however, "Jewish–Zionist" (Smooha 1997: 231).

The advantage of "improved ethnic democracy" is that it could be instituted gradually, through the normal political process, without incurring too much resistance from the Jewish majority. Under the best of circumstances – peace between Israel and an independent Palestinian state and regional economic prosperity – it may also prove to be a stable political arrangement (Smooha 1994a). In the mid-1990s this may indeed have been the best practicable solution. Its practicality, however, may be questioned now, in view of the shift in Palestinian opinion cited above.

5   The wages of legitimation: Zionist and non-Zionist Orthodox Jews

> And we must have faith that neither the coming of the Messiah nor even the advent of Redemption will originate via channels which neither approach nor relate to the Torah of Israel; redemption cannot be linked with Sabbath violation and the uprooting of [religious] precepts ... Redemption of the body must not override redemption of the spirit. (Rabbi Eliezer Schach, shortly after the 1967 war: in Friedman 1989a: 165)

Students of Zionist and Israeli politics have been puzzled, over the years, by the accommodating, even subservient, attitude displayed by the Zionist movement and by the Israeli state towards Orthodox Jews, many of them non- and even anti-Zionist. Zionism, after all, has always proclaimed itself a secular national movement in the tradition of the Enlightenment, intending, in Herzl's famous words, to keep the rabbis in their synagogues and the soldiers in their barracks. Furthermore, Orthodox Jews have constituted a relatively small minority in the Yishuv and in Israel, and their political influence has been vastly disproportionate to their electoral strength.

In terms of the reckoning of rights and obligations implied by the concept of citizenship, Orthodox Jews, most of whom have traditionally shunned the pioneering activities of physical labor, agricultural settlement, and military service,[1] have not only been awarded the full range of citizenship rights and, in addition, autonomy in education, but have also been given control of other people's rights, as in the areas of family and dietary laws and in regard to the observance of the Sabbath in the public sphere. The privileged status accorded Orthodox Jews, we argue, has resulted from their symbolizing the ethno-national principle of Jewish historical continuity and Jewish claim to *Eretz Yisrael* and from the crucial importance this principle has had for the legitimacy of the Zionist colonial project.

---

[1] The two notable exceptions have been the small Hapoel Hamizrachi (religious Zionist) and Poalei Agudat Yisrael (*charedi*) kibbutz and moshav movements and, since 1967, the National Religious Party and, especially, Gush Emunim (see chap. 6, below).

In this chapter we present the various Orthodox reactions to the emergence of Zionism, the privileges granted Orthodox Jews in a number of important areas of social life, and our explanation of these "wages of legitimation" in terms of the conceptual framework we have developed in this book.

Orthodox reactions to Zionism

The emergence of Zionism as a secular political movement actively seeking to return the Holy Land to Jewish sovereignty constituted a formidable theological dilemma for Orthodox Jews, a dilemma which has been aggravated by the Holocaust and by every Zionist success. While the return to Zion had been at the core of Jewish hopes for redemption for two millennia, it was never expected to materialize through the this-worldly efforts of heretics who had strayed from the fold. Even more inconceivable was that the return to Zion would result in a secular society where Jewish religious laws would be openly and publicly violated as a matter of course.

The different ways in which various Orthodox groups and rabbinical authorities have responded to this dilemma can be classified, with some simplification, under four headings (Marmorstein 1969; Zucker 1973; Abramov 1976; Biale 1983; Don-Yehiya 1984; Friedman 1986; 1987; 1988a; 1989; Liebman 1983; 1987; 1993; Luz 1985; Ravitzki 1993; Ross 1996; Schwartz 1996).

Pragmatic accommodationism

This response characterized the Mizrachi movement (established in 1902 as an Orthodox faction within Zionism) in its early period. The ideological position of this group, formulated originally by Rabbi I. J. Reines (1835–1915), viewed the Zionist enterprise as a project of physical survival, essentially indifferent in terms of religious values. Setting up a secular Jewish society in *Eretz Yisrael* (or anywhere else for that matter), where Jews could be safe and prosperous, was a worthwhile undertaking, although it had no bearing on the hoped-for messianic redemption. Orthodox Jews, according to this view, should actively participate in this undertaking both because of its intrinsic value and because their participation could mitigate its secular character. This position has been associated with "modern Orthodoxy," the tendency that in general has sought limited accommodation to modern secular society.

Principled accommodationism

This position was formulated by the ultra-Orthodox rabbi A. I. Kook (1865–1935), chief Ashkenazi rabbi of Palestine from 1921 until his death. According to Kook's famous "synthesis" Zionist settlement in Palestine was the "advent of redemption" (*atchalta degeula*), a preliminary but essential stage in the holy process of redemption. Secular Zionists, while indeed sinners, were unknowingly carrying out God's will in setting up the physical prerequisites for the final spiritual redemption. Although final redemption required that all Jews repent and return to religion, the preparatory work done by secular Zionists was potentially and partially sacred, and so were its perpetrators.[2]

Kook's position was adopted by the Mizrachi movement and by its successor, the NRP, precisely because it endowed the Zionist project with religious significance. After the 1967 war most religious Zionists adopted a much more radical version of the Kookist ideology. Kook had attributed sanctity to an abstract, post-redemption, ideal Jewish society in Israel. From that he derived the potential and partial sanctity of the secular Zionist efforts. In the new version, worked out by his son, Rabbi Z. Y. Kook (1891–1982), sanctity was attributed to the existing state and especially to its efforts to liberate the Holy Land by force. The younger Kook's formulation then became the ideological cornerstone of a militant, messianic, territorially expansionist brand of religious Zionism (see chap. 6, below).

Pragmatic rejectionism

This is the most common *charedi* (non-Zionist ultra-Orthodox) position, distinguished by its rejection of ideological, though not necessarily of practical, Zionism. Most groups that adhere to this position, organized in 1912 as Agudat Yisrael (AY), have been grudgingly willing to take part in the Zionist enterprise on a limited basis and without endowing it with any theological legitimacy. Their co-operation with Zionism has been motivated by two sets of considerations. One had to do with defense of their own material interests in a society where all material resources were controlled by Zionist organs. In that sense co-operating with the Israeli state (or the pre-state Zionist institutions) was similar to co-operating with non-Jewish governments in the *galut* (exile), although the former is viewed by some *charedim* as a greater abomination than the latter. The

---

[2] We realize that this is a highly simplified rendering of Kook's very complicated and sophisticated body of thought on this issue.

other consideration was similar to that of the religious Zionists, namely, an effort to minimize as much as possible the violation of Jewish religious codes in the society as presently constituted.

Principled rejectionism

This position is held by the extreme, most religiously Orthodox fringes of the *charedi* community, which view Zionism and the state of Israel as demonic enterprises and refuse to have anything to do with them.

In recent times the two tendencies described here as "principled accommodationism" and "pragmatic rejectionism" have increasingly been showing signs of convergence, with religious Zionists becoming more Orthodox in their religious behavior and *charedim* (with the exception of the "principled rejectionists") becoming more nationalist in their political outlook. This phenomenon was very obvious in the elections campaign of 1996, when the *chassidic* Chabad movement campaigned aggressively for Benjamin Netanyahu under the slogan "Bibi is good for the Jews" (Liebman 1993: 138–9; Peres 1995: 95; Shamir and Arian 1999; Cohen 1997a: 102–4; Herman and Yuchtman-Yaar 1998; Ilan 2000a: 35).

A fifth type of response – accepting Zionism but seeking to redefine it in an exclusively ethno-religious way – has been developed since the mid-1980s by the Mizrachi *charedi* party, Shas. We consider the emergence of Shas as primarily a reaction to the differential incorporation of Mizrachim in the society, and we discussed it in chapter 3, above.

Orthodox privileges

The basic document outlining the place of Jewish religion in Israeli public life was a letter sent in June 1947 by David Ben-Gurion, then chairman of the Jewish Agency executive, to the executive committee of AY. The letter was designed to win the support of AY (who had seceded from the Yishuv when women were enfranchised in 1925)[3] for the founding of the state. Commonly referred to as the "status quo letter," it stipulated that the future state would continue to observe the religious arrangements that had prevailed in the Yishuv in four specific areas: Saturday would become the national day of rest; *kashrut* (Jewish dietary laws) would be observed in all government kitchens; religious courts would maintain exclusive jurisdiction over marriage and divorce; and the autonomy of the

---

[3] The Mandatory government allowed Jews in Palestine to exclude themselves from membership in the Yishuv. This was done with the agreement of the Zionist authorities, in order to accommodate the non-Zionist Orthodox: Friedman 1988a: 195–6.

existing religious education systems would be preserved (Marmorstein 1969: 86–8; Liebman and Don-Yehiya 1984: 32; Varhaftig 1988: 35–6; Friedman 1988b; Don-Yehiya 1997a).

These stipulations, by and large, have been maintained in the fifty years since the writing of the "status quo letter," but the Orthodox's privileges have been augmented in two important areas not mentioned in the letter: Orthodox women and Orthodox yeshiva students have been exempted, fully or in part, from mandatory military service, and the Orthodox conception of "who is a Jew" has become increasingly influential in defining the boundaries of the Jewish Israeli collectivity (Liebman 1993: 154–5). Thus, Orthodox Jews are blatantly privileged in a number of significant areas pertaining to their own citizenship rights and duties, as well as those of others.

Education

Under the British Mandate, the Yishuv enjoyed complete autonomy in educational matters. In addition to the three official school systems of the Yishuv, one of them religious Zionist (Mizrachi), AY had its own independent school system. In 1953 the State Education Law ostensibly abolished the independent school systems and established two state systems instead, one secular and one religious, the latter under the *de facto* control of the NRP. The independent system of AY was brought under state financing, without real state supervision (Zucker 1973: 134–8; Liebman and Don-Yehiya 1984: 35; Zameret 1997).

Effectively then, the only school system abolished by the Mapai-led government was the Labor Zionist system (see chap. 3, above). The reason for this move was that, in the view of Mapai, the Labor education system had become excessively influenced by Mapai's left-leaning Labor Zionist rival, Mapam. Thus the Labor movement deprived itself of the major agent that had been socializing its youth into the pioneering ethos, and gave state sanction to institutions propagating the ethno-national discourse of citizenship (Shapiro 1984; Liebman and Don-Yehiya 1983: 84, 126; see also Zucker 1973: 123–43; Schiff 1977: 170–94; Zameret 1997: 190–210).

Family Law

During the Ottoman and Mandatory periods jurisdiction over family law (primarily marriage and divorce) was the purview of the various officially recognized religious communities of Palestine (*millet*s). This situation was written into the Israeli legal system in the Rabbinical Courts

Jurisdiction (Marriage and Divorce) Law of 1953. This statute granted rabbinical courts exclusive jurisdiction over marriage and divorce of Jews in Israel. (Similar laws were enacted with respect to the religious courts of non-Jewish communities.) The most important practical consequence of this law has been that, officially, non-religious civil marriage and the possibility of interreligious marriage is not available in Israel (Abramov 1976: 179–8; Zucker 1973: 100–21; Liebman and Don-Yehiya 1984: 25; Shifman 1995).[4]

The rationale underlying the surrender of jurisdiction in this crucially important area to parochial courts and religious laws was the need to preserve Jewish national unity. Had the choice of non-religious marriage been available to Jews in Israel, Orthodox Jews would have refrained from marrying non-Orthodox ones because of their concern that religiously illegitimate unions, sanctioned by civil courts, may have occurred in the candidates' families in the past. Thus, it was argued, two separate, en-dogamous Jewish communities would have developed in Israel (Zucker 1973: 100–21; Shifman 1995). In reality, however, marriages between Orthodox and non-Orthodox Jews rarely occur anyway, except in cases where one of the partners adopts the religious convictions of the other.

Other problematic cases from the perspective of Jewish law, such as when one of the partners is non-Jewish or doubtfully Jewish, or when a *cohen* and a divorced woman wish to be married, have been settled in practice by the expansion of legally recognized non-marriage forms of cohabitation, such as common-law marriages, and by civil marriages conducted in other countries. As a result, the increase in the number of Jews in Israel has not been reflected in a similar increase in the number of official, that is, religious marriages. Thus, while in 1975, with close to 3 million Jewish citizens, the number of officially sanctioned Jewish marriages was 28,583, in 1994, when the number of Jewish citizens had increased to almost 4.5 million, the number of officially sanctioned marriages had declined to 26,149. Between 1948 and 1995 the number of (officially sanctioned) marriages per thousand people in the Jewish population of Israel has declined by 46 percent, compared to an average decline of 27 percent in the developed countries (Shifman 1995; Hemdat 1996: 46; Etner-Levkovitch 1997: 45–50). In addition, since the mid-1990s the establishment of civil family courts has eroded the role played by rabbinical courts in family matters other than the performance of marriage and divorce.

---

[4] The conventional way of describing Israeli family law is to say that the option of civil marriage in not available in Israel. A more accurate description, however, would be that there is a legal identity between religious and civil marriage, so that neither one of them is available without the other (Shifman 1995).

Military service

A major factor in the institutional growth of the *charedi* communities in recent years has been the exemption from military service granted to yeshiva students. Mandatory military service of three years for men and about two years for women is required by law of all citizens of Israel, with the exception of women who are married, pregnant, or mothers. As a matter of policy Palestinian men, with the exception of those belonging to the Druze and Ciracessian minorities, and all Palestinian women, are administratively exempted by not being called up. Jewish women can be exempted if they declare that military service violates their religious beliefs, and have the option of doing an alternative, civilian service (an option that very few have chosen to take). *Charedi* and some national-religious yeshiva students, and students in Druze religious schools, are granted deferments to the end of their studies, as are a very small number of college students each year. Unlike the college students, and students in national-religious yeshivot (see below), the vast majority of *charedi* yeshiva students in effect do not serve even after they graduate (Hofnung 1991; Ilan 2000a: 113–48).

In the fifty years between 1948 and 1998 70,000 deferments of military service, most of them *de facto* exemptions, had been granted, mostly to *charedi* yeshiva students. In 1999 they were held by 30,400 people. The rate at which deferments have been granted has been accelerating rapidly in recent years: 2.5 percent of the male draft-eligible cohort were granted deferments in 1968, 5.3 percent in 1988, and 9.2 percent, or about 3,900 men, in 1999 (Horovitz 1989: 10, 68–9; Hoffman 1989: 233; Hofnung 1991: 245; Israel Religious Action Center 1992: 166; Ilan 2000a: 114, 126; Gonen 2000: 4).[5] Since only full-time yeshiva students (*shetoratam umnutam*) are eligible for deferments, and since deferments become exemptions once their holder reaches the age of forty-one (thirty-five if he has four children or more), most of these students continue to study, or at least be registered in yeshivot, and do not enter the labor market for many years, if at all. Thus while the average age of leaving a *charedi* yeshiva in Israel is forty-two, in the US, where no special privileges accrue to yeshiva students, the average leaving age is twenty-five (Ilan 2000a: 259–63; Gonen 2000: 16).

State subsidies for yeshivot are based on enrollment, so yeshivot have no interest in terminating their students, bona fide or otherwise. Thus in 1993 the number of full-time adult male yeshiva students reported by the Ministry of Religious Affairs was 50,000 and in 1997 it was

---

[5] Since the size of draft-eligible cohorts is considered a military secret, these figures should be taken as approximations only.

71,000. These numbers, the accuracy of which is notoriously doubtful, represent the entire cohort of draft-eligible men in the *charedi* communities. Both the numbers and the phenomenon of entire age cohorts that go on to advanced religious studies in yeshivot are without parallel in Jewish history (Berman and Klinov 1997: 10 n. 15; Cohen 1997a: 96; Adva center 1998a, esp. 21–2; Gonen 2000; Ilan 2000a: 126). Needless to say, this situation could not have been sustained without massive state subsidization.

Charedi young men, who are prevented from joining the labor force or seeking secular education at least until the age of thirty-five, for fear of being drafted, have come to depend on state subsidies and on their wives' earnings for their livelihood. In 1993 these non-earning *charedim* constituted 2.3 percent of all working age Israeli males, and 67 percent of all men who had ever been in a yeshiva were not working for a living, officially at least. This has caused the rate of civilian non-participation in the labor force of prime-aged males (between twenty-five and fifty-four) in Israel to be 12.2 percent, the highest in the developed world (Berman and Klinov 1997). It has been calculated that their absence from the labor market costs the Israeli economy NIS3.5 billion (US$1 billion) a year in lost production. In 1998 the Ministry of Religious Affairs, the primary source of funds for yeshivot, budgeted NIS684,000,000 (about $170,000,000) in subsidies for adult yeshivot and *kollelim* (yeshivot for married students). Total state expenditure for religious purposes in 1997 was estimated by the Israel Religious Action Center (an arm of the Reform movement in Israel) at NIS5.25 billion, or almost equal to the combined budgets of twelve government ministries (Israel Religious Action Center 1996: 6; Rubinstein 1996; 1997a; 1997b; Plotzker 1997; Elboim 1997; Adva center 1998a: 14; Ilan 2000a: 185–202, 259–63).[6]

Unlike the *charedim*, religious Zionist young men do serve in the military. Students of certain religious Zionist yeshivot (*yeshivot hesder*) also receive deferments, but they perform a shortened military service, in their own separate units, combined with their studies. As the motivation to serve in the military, especially as a career, has declined with liberalization among secular Ashkenazim, the role of national religious youngsters (and of Mizrachim) in the military has steadily become more pronounced (Hofnung 1991: 232–48; Levy 1997: 178; Inbar 1996; Cohen 1997b). This has caused concern that under certain circumstances nationalist-religious soldiers may obey their rabbis and defy military orders, to dismantle West Bank settlements, for example. This fear has not come to

---

[6] See also the very interesting interview given to Yehuda Koren of the daily *Yediot Achronot* by Professor Yehuda Friedlander, rector of the religious Zionist university, Bar-Ilan (Koren 1997).

the test yet, but *yeshivot hesder* have been hotbeds of radical Jewish nationalism and major recruiting grounds for Gush Emunim. Yitzhak Rabin's assassin, Yigal Amir, is a graduate of one of these yeshivot (Cohen 1997a: 105–39).

"Who is a Jew?"

This is a crucially important political question in Israel, in view of the role played by the ethno-national discourse in defining the Jewish Israeli collectivity and the privileged status of Jews in the society. Thus, a person's nationality is officially defined by his or her ascriptive religious affiliation, rather than by citizenship. This is expressed most clearly in the Law of Return, the Nationality Law and the Law of Population Registry. Over the years the official definition of "Jew" for the purposes of these laws has become progressively restricted and more closely aligned with Orthodox thinking.

In 1958 the Minister of Interior belonging to Achdut Haavoda (a left-leaning Labor Zionist party) issued a directive to the offices of the Population Registry that "any person declaring in good faith that he is a Jew, shall be registered as a Jew and no additional proof shall be required" (Zucker 1973: 173). This directive expressed the liberal, rather than ethno-national, conception of nationality, in that it made entry into the Jewish national collectivity a voluntary matter, distinct from belonging to Judaism as a religion. Precisely for this reason that directive was very short lived. Through a series of government crises, coalition agreements, and judicial rulings too tedious to be related here, the definition has been changed until today a Jew is defined in the Law of Return as "a person born of a Jewish mother, or who converted to Judaism, and is not a member of another religion" (Zucker 1973: 206, slightly altered translation; see also 172–207; Abramov 1976: 270–320; Schiff 1977: 195–207; Eilam 2000).

This religious definition is too restrictive, however, in view of the demographic aim of Zionism, to maintain and increase the Jewish majority in Israel. As a result, the Law of Return was amended, in 1970, so that only one Jewish grandparent is now required in order to entitle a person and her/his spouse and minor children to the privileges provided by the law. Thus, it is estimated that up to 25 percent of the immigrants from the former Soviet Union are not Jews by the Orthodox definition (see chap. 12, below). As marriage, divorce, and burials are all under the exclusive jurisdiction of religious authorities (whether Jewish or non-Jewish), these non- and doubtful Jews run into problems when they come to need these services, unless they convert to Judaism. One paradoxical result of the amended Law of Return, reflecting a contradiction between the demographic and legitimational imperatives of Zionism, is thus the development of a diverse non-Jewish, non-Palestinian citizenship group in Israel (see chap. 12, below).

The Orthodox parties are still struggling to restrict the definition of a Jew in the Law of Return even further, by having the law read, following the word "converted," "in accordance with *halacha*." This because, as it now stands, the definition covers people who may have converted to Judaism according to non-Orthodox procedures. In 1989 an attempt to institute this change was narrowly defeated in the Knesset, after the Reform and Conservative Jewish establishments in the US had threatened to cut their contributions to Israel. In this case, then, when Orthodox political power came up against a basic Zionist interest, it could not prevail (Landau 1996; cf. Hoffman 1989: 215–40). In 1997–8 another, more moderate attempt to deprive non-Orthodox conversions to Judaism of official recognition, if performed in Israel, has also been shelved (*Haaretz*, April 1, 1997; *New York Times*, April 17, 1997; Friedman 1997; Don-Yehiya 1997a).

Privileged Citizenship Explanation

The usual explanation for the privileges enjoyed by Orthodox Jews has been that Israel's system of proportional representation has enabled Orthodox political parties to hold the balance needed for forming coalition governments. As "one-issue" movements, so the argument goes, these political parties can be satisfied with budgetary allocations and with concessions regarding the role of religion in the public sphere. Thus, gaining their parliamentary support does not require (or, at least, did not in the past require) the major political parties to pay any price in more important policy areas: social, economic, military, etc. (Landau 1996: 7; Zameret 1997: 228, 246; Cohen 1997a: 86–7; cf. Don-Yehiya 1997a: 12).

While this explanation may be able to account for tactical decisions made by the major parties, primarily Mapai, at particular historical junctions, it cannot account for the depth and breadth of the role Judaism as a religion has been able to play in Israeli public life. Yonathan Shapiro examined, and rejected, both the coalition-based explanation and the argument that the "concessions" made to the Orthodox were necessitated by the religiosity of Mizrachi immigrants who were arriving in the country *en masse* during the first decade of statehood. He presented the embrace of religion by the secular Israeli political leadership in the early years of the state as a *deliberate choice of one discourse of legitimation over another*. While not using the specific conceptual framework developed in this study, Shapiro has argued, in effect, that the liberal discourse of citizenship was considered, and consciously rejected, when Mapai decided not to adopt a written constitution in 1950 (see chap. 10, below). Instead, faced with the decline of the republican discourse with the founding of the state, the leadership turned to the ethno-national discourse in order to enhance its legitimacy. This was reflected in the adoption of two of Israel's most important early pieces of legislation, the Law of Return (1950) and the Nationality Law (1952), and in a whole series of measures designed to enhance the saliency of Jewish religious laws and rituals in the country's public life (Shapiro 1996a: 27–69; cf. Liebman and Don-Yehiya 1983).

In accordance with his elitist theoretical framework, Shapiro explained the rejection of the liberal discourse as motivated by the desire of leading politicians in Mapai, primarily Ben-Gurion, to avoid the limitations that a written constitution and bill of rights would have imposed on their freedom of action. But he also mentioned, almost in passing, two other considerations related to the frontier struggle which, in our analysis, has played a major role in shaping the Israeli incorporation regime: the desire to limit the citizenship rights of Israel's Palestinian citizens and a reluctance to accept the 1949 armistice lines as the country's final borders (Shapiro 1996a: 33). In our analysis the frontier situation would bear a much larger portion of the explanatory burden than the power interests of politicians.

Another, related, point on which we would differ with Shapiro is his emphasis on the founding of the state as a crucial turning point from the republican to the ethno-national discourse and hence in the public role played by religion in the society. In our view, while the institutionalization of religion in the constitutional framework of a sovereign state is certainly a very significant move, strong ethno-national or ethno-religious elements were present within the Zionist republican discourse all along (Susser and Don-Yehiya 1994).

Of all the political movements spawned by the crisis of Eastern European Jewry in the second half of the nineteenth century, Zionism alone claimed to speak on behalf of a world-wide Jewish nation. The only cultural attribute common to this Jewish nation, however, was Jewish religion, to which the vast majority of Jews still held. (AY was, until the Second World War, one of the largest political parties in the Jewish world.) Claiming to speak in the name of world Jewry, both internally and externally, Zionism needed at least the tacit approval of those universally recognized as the Jewish spokesmen – the Orthodox rabbis. But, with the exception of the small Mizrachi movement, the rabbis were not rushing to give their approval. On the contrary, they became increasingly anti-Zionist as the secular aims of the movement were becoming clearer to them.

The threat that could be posed to Zionism by Orthodox Jewry, and the length to which the Zionists were willing to go in fighting it, were tragically illustrated by the story of Dr. I. J. De Haan (Friedman 1988a: 230–52). De Haan (1881–1924) was a Dutch Jewish socialist jurist, writer, journalist, and poet. A brilliant man of unstable personality, De Haan, who had married a non-Jewish woman, became a *baal teshuva* (returnee to the Orthodox fold) and in 1920 joined AY in Jerusalem. Having come from the outside, and possessed of great communicative skills, De Haan rapidly became a prominent member of the community and its major contact person with the outside world. A somewhat similar contemporary personality is Uri Zohar, Israel's most prominent entertainer, film director, and bohemian character of the 1970s, who has since embraced ultra-Orthodoxy and become a major *charedi* spokesman (Beit-Hallahmi 1991: 159–61; on the phenomenon of *teshuva* in general see also Aviad 1983; Ilan 2000a: 203–36).

The Zionist establishment in Palestine found in De Haan a powerful opponent, a representative of "authentic" Judaism who was at the same time completely at home in the modern world. The Zionists could have tolerated De Haan's spirited advocacy of *charedi* interests, but for one thing: his attempts to forge an anti-Zionist alliance with the Arabs. De Haan established contacts with the Hashemite brothers, Fasial and Abdallah, then in the process of being installed by the British as kings in Iraq and Transjordan, respectively. He drafted a joint Arab–*charedi* statement calling on the Zionists to give up their efforts to establish a Jewish national home in Palestine or face endless war with the Arabs. He also tried to lobby for his plans with the British government and on Fleet Street. Had it succeeded, De Haan's Arab policy "could have greatly strengthened the arguments of the Arab national movement and seriously undermined the Zionist movement's claim to be the only legitimate representative of the Jewish legacy and its affinity to Eretz Yisrael" (Friedman 1988a: 237). On June 30, 1924 De Haan was assassinated by the Hagana, the semi-clandestine military arm of the Histadrut. His activities and the way they ended helped the Zionist leadership and AY establish mutually acceptable rules of engagement for their ongoing relationships from that time onward (Friedman 1988a: 252).

Zionism, of course, was not unique among national movements in its efforts to co-opt the bearers and symbols of tradition. All national movements have had to rely on primordial cultural elements in order to mobilize their target populations for essentially modernizing aims (Tom Nairn has therefore termed nationalism a "Janus-faced" ideology)

(Nairn 1977; Avineri 1994). For Zionism, however, the need to rely on primordial factors for legitimation and mobilization was particularly acute, since there was no modern culture common to all Jews. This dictated, firstly, the choice of the movement's target territory (in dispute until Herzl's death in 1904) (Vital 1982, chaps. 9–10) and then the use of a whole array of Jewish religious symbols and other cultural constructs. From the dubbing of immigration to Palestine *aliya* (pilgrimage), through the choice of the star of David and the seven-branch candelabrum (*menora*) as the official emblems of the state, to the celebration of Jewish religious holidays as national holidays, traditional Jewish themes abound in Zionist lore.

The arrangements discussed in the "status quo" letter had deep roots in Zionist practice as well. The educational autonomy of the Zionist religious movement inside the bounds of the Yishuv (unlike that of AY which was outside it) dated back to 1920. In 1898 the Second Zionist Congress resolved that "Zionism will not act in any way to infringe upon the Jewish religion." In the Nineteenth Congress, in 1935, an agreement was reached between Mapai and Mizrachi according to which "no public desecration of the Sabbath was to occur, and dietary laws were to be maintained in public institutions." This was the foundation of a "historic partnership" between the two movements, which lasted until 1977 (Liebman and Don-Yehiya 1984: 33; Kolatt 1994b).

While different tendencies in Zionism have tried, in varying degrees, to endow the traditional religious themes with secular national meanings (Liebman and Don-Yehiya 1983), they could never be purged of their original religious content. Nor did even the Labor Zionist movement really seek to completely secularize the traditional meaning system. As Norman Zucker has put it: "Mapai and the Mapai-led Israel Labor Party have surrendered to some of the demands of the religious parties because they do not totally reject religious values, nor do they desire a totally secular state" (Zucker 1973: 3, 58; see also Shapira 1991). In 1957, in response to "widely felt … anxiety about Israeli youth's possible estrangement from their Jewish heritage" (Herman 1970: 35), the Mapai-headed government launched an intensive program of "Jewish consciousness" instruction in the secular state school system. The rationale for adopting the program, in the revealing words of education minister Zalman Aranne, was that knowledge of the Jewish tradition was essential "for the *national* education of the Hebrew nation" (emphasis added). The program, described by Aranne as "Jewish inoculation," has been intensified considerably since then (Liebman and Don-Yehiya 1983: 173; see also 170–7; Zucker 1973: 139–42; Shapiro 1996a: 48–50, 56–60).

In the conventional language of Israeli politics, the institutionalization of the public role of religion, and the privileges granted Orthodox Jews, are referred to as "concessions." This designation is in line with the view that these decisions resulted from narrow instrumental calculations of coalition politics. Many of theses "concessions," however, enjoy wide support among the Jewish population in Israel, even among those who consider themselves "secular."

In 1991 the Guttman Institute for Applied Social Research conducted a wide-ranging survey of attitudes towards religion among Hebrew-speaking Jews in Israel. As shown in table 5.1, this survey found that 67 percent of Israeli Jews were in favor of maintaining or increasing the religious content of public life, while only 36 percent defined themselves as either "observant" or "largely observant" (40 percent defined themselves as "somewhat observant," and only 20 percent as "non-observant") (Levy et al. 1993 [English summary in Levy et al. 1997]; cf. Peres 1995; Shamir and Arian 1999; see Herman and Yuchtman-Yaar 1998 for a different breakdown, indicating a much higher incidence of non-observance).

When asked about actual religious practices, however, 93 percent of the Guttman respondents were found to observe at least one of ten religious precepts in the areas of the Sabbath, *kashrut*, or Jewish holidays. In other words, only 7 percent of the respondents were found in fact not to observe any religious precept, as against 20 percent who described themselves as completely non-observant. Moreover, of the self-described non-observant, 92 percent were found to have a *mezuza* on their front door, 10 percent indicated they would have liked to be more observant, and fully 50 percent indicated they would like their children to be more observant than themselves (Levy et al. 1993: 2–4, 16). Forty percent of the respondents indicated that they observed the rules of *kashrut* in their entirety, while fully 90 percent indicated they observed some of them, at least occasionally. As to the public sphere, 94 percent supported the maintenance of *kashrut* in military kitchens, and 89 percent supported its maintenance in civilian public kitchens (Levy et al. 1993: 35, 92).

In view of these figures it might seem surprising that 54 percent in the Guttman Institute survey were found either to support or be willing to entertain the idea of the separation of state and religion, while 51 percent either supported or were willing to consider the idea of instituting civil marriage in Israel (Levy et al. 1993: 89). The solution to this riddle lies in the observation that attitudes towards religion are not identical in Israel to attitudes towards the role played by the state in religious affairs. Thus, while 67 percent of the Guttman respondents were in favor of maintaining or increasing the religiosity of public life, only 44 percent of them supported the suggestion that the government should see to that,

Table 5.1 *Selected indicators of religiosity among Jews in Israel, 1991*

Self-definition		
"Observant" and "largely observant"	36%	
"Somewhat observant"	40	
"Non-observant"	20	
Do not observe any religious precept	7	
Favor maintaining or increasing religious character of public life	67	
Government should act to achieve that	44	
Of the "non-observant":		
Have a *mezuza* on front door	92	
Would like to observe more	10	
Would like children to observe more	50	
Kashrut		
Observe fully	40	
Observe some	90	
Should be kept in military kitchens	94	
Should be kept in civilian public kitchens	89	
Favor, or will consider, separation of state and religion	54	
Favor, or will consider, institution of civil marriage	51	
Of these, self or family member will choose civil marriage	36	
Object to children marrying non-Jews	84	
Observance motivated by "identification with Jewish people"	69	
"Important" or "very important" values		
Feeling part of Jewish people	94	(81)
Living in Israel	93	(85)
Serving in IDF	91	
Observing Jewish holidays	89	(67)
(parentheses: % of "non-observant")		

Source: Levy et al. 1993.

and 56 percent opposed it (Levy et al. 1993: A–9, B–11; cf. Liebman 1997a: 92). Similarly, while about half of the respondents either supported or were willing to consider the institution of civil marriage, over half indicated they themselves or their family members would not avail themselves of this option, if it existed. Even among the supporters of civil marriage only 36 percent indicated they themselves or their family members would choose to marry in a civil ceremony (Levy et al. 1993: 89). The rationale behind this reluctance reveals itself when we consider that 84 percent (of respondents who answered this question) objected to their children marrying non-Jews (Levy et al. 1993: 77).

A majority (69 percent) of the respondents indicated that their religious observance was motivated by "identification with the Jewish people" (Levy et al. 1993: 2–4, A–6). This was corroborated by the values they considered to be "important" or "very important" in their lives: "feeling a part of the Jewish people" was so considered by 94 percent of the respondents, living in Israel by 93 percent, and serving in the IDF by 91 percent. Even among the completely non-observant (by self-definition), living in Israel was considered important or very important by 85 percent, and feeling a part of the Jewish people by 81 percent. Ninety-two percent of the non-observant considered themselves part of a world-wide Jewish people, compared to 96 percent of the general population. Similarly, observing the Jewish holidays in some form, not necessarily the traditional ones, was considered important or very important by 67 percent of the completely non-observant, as compared to 89 percent of the general population (Levy et al. 1993: 108–13, 117, 121–5).

Secularization

For fifty years the need for religious legitimation precluded the possibility of Israel adopting one of the fundamental attributes of a liberal state – the separation of state and religion. Thus, a central dilemma of liberal Israelis was how to address the conflict between their concern for individual rights and their commitment to the ethno-national definition of the state. Their preferred strategy was based on a dual approach: gradually eroding the religious "status quo" through liberal legislation and judicial action, on the one hand, and finding practical ways of circumventing the religious constraints on individual rights, on the other.

But in the late 1990s this strategy was transformed into a much more aggressive effort to reshape the nature of state–religion relations. Not surprisingly, the exemption from military service enjoyed by *charedi* yeshiva students served as a fulcrum for this effort. This exemption violates both the liberal equality principle and the republican notion of civic virtue, and is thus an effective target around which to mobilize popular opinion. In 1997, as part of his (successful) drive to be elected prime minister, Labor Party leader Ehud Barak introduced a bill in the Knesset to limit the number of deferments granted yeshiva students to 700 a year, and allow these 700 deferees greater freedom of employment during their period of study at the yeshiva. The bill, however, was defeated in the Knesset.

After his election as prime minister, Barak, egged on by a Supreme Court ruling that questioned the legality of the deferments, appointed a committee to propose legislation to regulate the military service of yeshiva students. The committee, headed by a religious Zionist retired Supreme

Court Justice, Zvi Tal, wisely addressed its recommendations not to the issue of drafting the students, a political impossibility, but rather to that of allowing them to join the labor force. Its key proposal was to lower the age when the deferment officially becomes an exemption to twenty-four, at which age the deferee would be able to choose between basic military training of four months and civilian national service of one year. After that he would be free to pursue whatever course of life he chooses (Ilan 2000a: 122–4).

If implemented, the Tal Committee recommendations would enable tens of thousands of young *charedi* men to enter the labor force, and would deplete the yeshivot of much of their student body. Both of these results would save the state a great deal of expenditure. The recommendations would also weaken the hold the rabbinic establishment now has over its own community, clearly a desirable outcome from the point of view of secular Israelis. Nevertheless, secular Israelis reacted with hostility to the committee report, on the grounds that it failed to enforce the principle of equality. This reaction indicates that what the liberal public in Israel is interested in is not pragmatic accommodation with the *charedi* sector, but rather a head-on confrontation. This was the political logic behind another of Barak's initiatives in this area, his declaration of a "civil revolution." While falling short of a separation of state and religion, that "revolution," if carried out, would have significantly reduced the role of religion in public life (*Yediot Achronot*, September 12, 2000).

At the time of writing (December 2000), which coincides with the twilight of Barak's government, the fate of his "civil revolution" and of the Tal Committee report is unclear. But the social realities behind these political moves are more stable than any particular government, and no matter what the outcome of the upcoming elections, the drive towards the secularization of the society and the state is bound to continue. This drive is propelled by two facets of the evolution of Israeli society in the 1990s: the decline of the republican discourse of citizenship and the large-scale immigration from the former USSR.

One consequence of the decline of the republican discourse is that political arguments based on the collective needs of Zionism carry much less weight than they used to. Thus, liberal Israelis have become much less tolerant than they were even ten years ago of the infringement of their individual rights that stems from the privileged status accorded Jewish religion in the public sphere. This is manifested, among other things, in the strong resentment liberals feel now about the exemption of *charedi* yeshiva students from military service. Paradoxically, for a long period of time, during which the manpower needs of the military were much greater and the republican discourse of civic virtue was much stronger, liberal

Israelis did tolerate that exemption. What has changed now is that they are no longer willing to pay in the coin of privilege for the legitimation provided by the *charedim* to the Zionist project.

The decline of the republican discourse enhanced the status not only of the liberal discourse, but of the ethno-national discourse as well. One indication of that is the continuing electoral success of Shas, the *charedi* Mizrachi political party (see chap. 3, above). Unlike the traditional, Ashkenazi *charedi* parties, which were small in numbers and seemed to occupy their own social enclave, Shas is a large party that challenges many of the republican and liberal foundations of the prevailing incorporation regime. It has therefore generated a great deal of anxiety among the Ashkenazi middle class, which reacted, among other ways, by forming Israel's first militant anti-clerical political party, Shinuy. In the 1999 elections, which took place a short time after Shinuy was founded, the party gained six seats in the Knesset. (Ten more seats were gained by the older, more moderately secularist Meretz.) At the time of writing, public opinion polls predict that it could as much as double its strength in the next elections.

Israeli secularism was buttressed in the 1990s by the arrival of close to one million immigrants from the former Soviet Union, many of whom are non-Jewish or doubtfully Jewish from the point of view of *halacha*. The vast majority of these immigrants would like to see religion taken out of the public sphere and their electoral weight has drastically changed the relations of power between the two sides on this issue (see chap. 12, below).

Conclusion

As Kimmerling has noted, "when the vast majority of Israeli Jews refer to their collective identity, that identity is defined for the most part by concepts, values, symbols and collective memory that are anchored primarily in the Jewish religion" (Kimmerling 1994: 129, cited in Liebman 1997b: 105; see also Liebman and Katz 1997). What accounts for the forthcoming attitude displayed by the state and by non-observant Israeli Jews towards Jewish religion, then, is primarily the need for religious affirmation of their collective, ethno-national identity. Because their culture symbolizes Jewish unity and the continuity of Jewish history, the *charedim*, and to a lesser extent the religious Zionists as well, can provide the Zionist project with the ideological resources it requires for legitimating its claim to act on behalf of a world-wide Jewish nation that possesses a historically substantiated right to the Land of Israel. Thus, even Shinuy has refrained from calling for the separation of state and religion, because of the implications this would have for Israel's character as a Jewish state (*Shinuy Barosh*, 2, 1999).

Still, the decline of the republican discourse, and the intensifying clash between the liberal and ethno-national ones, have moved some liberal Israelis to take up the option of separating the state from religion. Significantly, the prominent liberal daily *Haaretz* has already called for the separation of state and religion, in the wake of a massive demonstration held by *charedim* against the Supreme Court in February 1999. The same paper also called for the institution of civil marriage, citing the hardships caused to the immigrants from the former USSR who cannot be married in the rabbinical courts (*Haaretz*, editorials, February 15, 1999, December 1, 1999).

As the process of liberalization continues, and as more and more of the formerly Soviet immigrants, or their children, reach the age of marriage, the pressure for the separation of state and religion is certain to increase. If peace with the Palestinians is achieved, and ethno-national anxieties subside, the momentum towards separation will become that much stronger. As many still fear, the relegation of religion to the private sphere will indeed be a major step towards the liberalization of the Israeli state, its redefinition as a state of its citizens. As we related in chapter 4 above, this will have profound implications for the relations between Israel's Jewish and Palestinian citizens as well.

Part 2

The frontier reopens

6   New day on the frontier

The major barricade in [*Eretz Yisrael* today] is the one that divides
Jews from Israelis. The Jews are those who want to live, to one degree
or another, in accordance with the Bible. The Israelis pay lip service,
maybe, to the heritage, but in essence they aspire to be a completely
new people here, a satellite of Western culture ... I think that the positions of Gush Emunim really do constitute an irritating and alarming
threat to the legitimacy of this secular, hedonistic, "Israelism." The existence of Gush Emunim disturbs your experience of modern Western
existence, including permissiveness and pacifism and internationalism.
(Yisrael Harel, a leader of Gush Emunim, to novelist Amos Oz: Oz 1984:
115–16)

The 1967 war was followed by a process of colonization, first halting,
then swift, in the occupied territories (OT). Its purpose, as before 1948,
was to establish a permanent presence in the designated areas, alter their
demographic constitution, and eventually annex them to Israel. But the
location, significance, and justification of colonization, as well as the citizenship discourse used to legitimate it and the rights granted the settlers,
show clear though partial signs of Israel's burgeoning transformation. For
the first time, the republican discourse encountered serious competition
in the sphere of colonization, its home turf so to speak. This took the
form, first, of a religiously redefined nationalist discourse and, later on,
of a liberal discourse as well. Each of the three discourses was used to
legitimate a particular phase of renewed colonization: military, religious,
and economic. At the same time, the fact that all three discourses could
be, and have been, used to justify the colonial project shows their interdependence as constituent elements of the Israeli hierarchical citizenship
and incorporation regime. Significantly, the new contending discourses
emerged as products of alternative institutional frameworks as well: the
religious one of the cross between the autonomous educational institutions of the NRP and the military; the liberal one of the harnessing of
private initiative to national goals.

Military colonization

Israel's borders were determined, by and large, by the boundaries of Jewish settlement and by its fortunes in the 1947–8 Jewish–Palestinian and Israeli–Arab wars (Morris 1987; Pappe 1992). The settlement of Jews in sparsely populated border areas and the expropriation of Palestinian-owned land continued unabated during the 1948–67 period and were considered important national priorities (Yiftachel 1992; 1996). Still, the debate over desirable borders not only lost its saliency but altogether vanished from the public eye in this period of Zionist normalcy. Even the Herut party showed "little inclination to challenge in public either the territorial status quo or the strategic doctrine that took it as its point of departure" (Horowitz 1975: 5).

Only the 1967 war demonstrated that the colonial frontier had not been "closed." Indeed, the colonial dimension of Jewish–Arab relations, which had been confined, for nearly twenty years, to the territory of the sovereign state of Israel, was bound to burst out, as long as no single authority or agreed-upon division were established in the territory of post-Mandatory Palestine. The immediate incentive for renewing settlement activities outside the Green Line (i.e. the 1949 armistice line) was the lingering memory of the high status, the status of virtuous republican citizens, that had been accorded the early colonizers. At the end of the 1967 war settlement in the newly occupied territories commenced spontaneously, mainly by members of kibbutz movements, with support from the existing settlement bodies and the military, prior to official government approval. In fact, some of these early settlements were established in direct contravention of government decisions, such as the decision to return the territories conquered from Syria in return for peace, or in spite of the government's inability to decide, on the fate of the West Bank, for example. Subsequently, individual cabinet members became sponsors of settlement activities in various regions, with or without government approval. Thus Yigal Allon sponsored settlement activity on the Golan Heights and Moshe Dayan in the Gaza Strip (as Shimon Peres would do, after the 1973 war, in the West Bank). In the first year after the war, settlements had been granted government approval only *ex post facto*. The first formal decision to settle anywhere in the OT came in January 1969, when the government adopted that part of the Allon Plan that called for settling Jews in the Jordan rift (Pedatzur 1992: 253–75).

Historically, the LSM's pioneering activity, as a movement of colonization and the absorption of immigrants, had been the main source of its legitimacy. Thus, when Dayan was asked, in 1968, what was Labor to do in regard to the OT, he found it easy to answer: "The first step is the traditional one in the realm of action in the State of Israel – settlement" (Dayan 1969: 164). Israel Galili, a leader of the Kibbutz Hameuchad movement, a minister without portfolio in Golda Meir's cabinet and her closest confidant, explained in the 1971 congress of the Labor Party that "the trust accorded the Labor Party by the public" stemmed, first and foremost, from "its settlement pathos." By continuing and expanding the old-timers' calling after 1967, the younger generation was legitimizing it, and in so doing also found justification for its own life project. In Galili's words, expansion, whether to Tel Aviv or to the Jordan river, originated from the same pure source (Galili 1971: 5). When colonization was resumed, Allon reiterated its purpose in unmistakable terms: "We accustomed ourselves and the entire world to treat [our settlement] activity as facts with particularly weighty significance. This turned into one of the weapons of our revival movement. It can be assumed, therefore, that no one will misunderstand the importance of this activity" (Pedatzur 1992: 258).

The guiding principles of Labor's position on the issue of West Bank settlement were laid down in the Allon Plan. Although never officially adopted by the party, that plan was largely followed in practice, as long as Labor remained in power. Allon's intention was "to shape [the] borders with the view, first and foremost, of turning them into security borders" (Tsur 1982: 94). The main elements of the blueprint were: (1) setting up the Jordan river as Israel's security border, by constructing in its rift a chain of settlements, 6–10 miles in width; (2) retaining the Jordan rift under Israeli sovereignty; (3) refraining from colonization in the mountainous region of the West Bank, heavily populated by Palestinians; and (4) offering to negotiate peace with Jordan in return for the non-colonized areas of the West Bank. This security-minded policy towards settlement and the Palestinian population was continued after the 1973 war by the first Rabin–Peres government, in which Allon served as foreign minister (Rabin 1979: 549; Golan 1982: 179).

The settlement planks of the Allon Plan were implemented only half-heartedly by Labor governments, indicating the lessening commitment of the LSM to its pioneering ethos. All in all, at the end of the Labor era in 1977 there were fifteen settlements in the Jordan rift, one or two established per year. The area, once planned for a population of 20,000, was inhabited in 1986 by about 3,500 settlers (Markovski 1977: 638; Benvenisti and Khayat 1988: 33, table 3).

Evidently, the native-born Labor leaders' colonial ambitions were more limited than those of their parents. In their view, the period of massive frontier expansion had, by and large, come to an end in 1948. Consequently, they evinced a readiness to search for diplomatic solutions in order to close the frontier in a mutually agreed-upon fashion. The result was a middle-of-the road position: expansion, but under severe limitations; continued frontier settlement, but its definition as a problem of secure borders. This vague, mixed, and undeclared policy made it difficult to endow the settlers with the mantle of "new pioneers." The republican discourse of pioneering, constructed to accompany settlement during the classic colonial period, and to legitimate the privileges due those championing and realizing it, was rarely invoked by Labor to justify the new project of colonization. This contradiction between the diluted colonial discourse and its renewed practice opened up a yawning gap that would be filled, after 1973, by a messianic version of a new, synthetic, religious–republican discourse promoted by Orthodox youth organizations.

Even Labor itself, however, could not abide by its own self-imposed territorial restrictions. In the decade of its rule following 1967, there were three significant deviations from the stated aims of the Allon Plan:

(1) Two settlements outside the Jordan rift, hence not clearly part of the Allon Plan, were established through grassroots pressure, only to be incorporated *ex post facto* into the settlement map. Kfar Etzion, halfway between Jerusalem and Hebron, and the Jewish quarter of Hebron itself (one a pioneer settlement, the other an ancient urban quarter) had been violently uprooted prior to 1948. Occupying a special place in Israel's frontier memory, they could easily be described as being "resettled." In reality, however, their settlement in 1967 and 1968, respectively, constituted significant steps towards opening the frontier anew. This embarrassed the policy makers, who were anxious to appear as if their hands had been forced. Thus the settlement of Kfar Etzion was consented to only at the last minute, under the pressure of the original settlers' children, who threatened to move there even in defiance of the government. Tellingly, the government demanded that the event be celebrated in secret (*Maariv*, September 28, 1967; Ben-Yaakov 1978: 327–9; Gvati 1981: 222). Later, a whole additional settlement cluster, known as Gush Etzion, was built around Kfar Etzion.

The Eshkol government's lack of resolve to uphold its authority on the issue of West Bank settlement is even more clearly evident with regard to Hebron, one of the most populous Palestinian cities in the West Bank. A group under the leadership of Rabbi Moshe Levinger negotiated unsuccessfully with the government for six months to obtain permission to move into Hebron, the city of Abraham. While the government was well aware of the group's long-range intentions, it permitted its members to enter Hebron in 1968, presumably for celebrating the Passover (*Maariv*, June 8, 1973). When the festive party refused to move out, the government agreed to build housing for it in Kiryat Arba, on the outskirts of Hebron, thus violating the principle of avoiding settlement amidst dense Palestinian population. Gush Etzion and Kiryat Arba, which by the end of 1999 had 9,200 and 5,900 residents, respectively (*Report on Israeli Settlement in the OT*, May/June 2000), had become hothouses for the formation of the leadership cadre of the religious settlers' movement – Gush Emunim – when it was first formed, in the spring of 1974.

(2) In September 1973, on the eve of the planned 1973 general elections and, unknowingly, of a new Arab–Israeli war, a plan formulated by Galili was adopted into the electoral platform of the Labor Party. The Galili Protocol called for increasing the Jewish population of the OT and enhancing the services and economic opportunities provided for the settlers. It approved the construction of the city of Yamit in northern Sinai, the city of Katzrin on the Golan Heights, the regional urban center of Maale Efraim in the Jordan rift, and settlement in the triangle of western Samaria, where the city of Ariel was constructed. In addition, the Galili Protocol not only instructed the ILA to acquire land through every effective means available to it, but for the first time authorized colonization by the private sector as well, by consenting to the private purchase of land, though under the control and within the framework of government settlement policy (Peretz 1986: 47–8; Aronson 1987: 31; Benvenisti interview).

By giving in to the pressure of religiously minded settlers, and by resolving the "long debate over private acquisition of Arab lands and property in the occupied areas" (Peretz 1986: 48) in favor of private initiative, these two deviations from the Allon Plan opened up cracks in the conception of military frontier which, with time, turned into major conduits for colonization. Each of these additions to the Allon Plan, as we shall see later in this chapter, inaugurated new stages, and produced new types of settlement, in the colonization of the West Bank.

(3) The third deviation concerned the preference of settlement over a potential diplomatic solution. When the possibility of finally closing one frontier by mutual agreement presented itself, through the United Nations-sponsored Jarring peace mission, directed at the Egyptian front, Israel failed to take advantage of it (Shafir 1999). In February 1971 Anwar Sadat, Egypt's new president, declared his willingness "to enter into a peace agreement" with Israel, demanding, in return, Israel's full withdrawal to the pre-1967 borders, as well as a

number of lesser concessions. Sadat also promised "to give Israel all the guarantees she had asked for," and the Jarring Plan included various security measures as substitutes for border corrections. The Meir government's reply specified that it was ready to withdraw to "secure, recognized, and agreed upon borders to be established in the peace agreement," but added that "Israel will not withdraw to the pre-June 5, 1967 line" (Shafir 1984; 1999).

A second plan, originally raised by Dayan and then taken up by Sadat, based on the principle of land for peace, was to begin with an Israeli withdrawal from the Suez Canal, in return for its opening by Egypt to international shipping. This was, in Sadat's words, "the only alternative to a military [solution]." In fact, Sadat claimed that "if the United States or Israel had shown enough interest in that initiative, the October [1973] War would not have taken place" (Sadat 1977: 221–2, 279–80; *Arab Report and Record, March 1–15,* 1971: 158–9; see also Touval 1982: 157–9). But if the Israeli government vacillated, at the end of the 1967 war, as to the wisdom of settling in the OT, Sadat's offer found an Israeli government that had already invoked its ingrained legacy of colonization as the means for achieving security, and was therefore committed to its "military frontier."

The 1973 war raised serious questions as to the ability of military colonization to achieve its declared aim of achieving security. Moreover, by the mid-1970s peace agreements, which would put an end to the recurring cycle of frontier wars, could have replaced the tactical necessity of settlement. This conclusion, however, was problematic for the military–settler generational nucleus, one of whose key members, Yitzhak Rabin, assumed the position of prime minister in 1974. As a generation that had developed no independent world-view of its own, the native-born leadership had no alternative vision to fall back on (Shapiro 1984; Ben-Eliezer 1998a; 1998b). Therefore, after a short lull, "the final two years of Labor rule saw the official settlement system expand more rapidly than at any other time since 1967" (Harris 1980: 27). Housing minister Abraham Ofer undertook a plan to thicken Jewish settlements around Jerusalem, and in 1976 Galili, continuing the line of thinking behind his 1973 Protocol, approved the construction of a number of settlements, among them the city of Ariel across the Green Line from Kfar Saba, which would serve as "capital" of Samaria.

Thus, while the idea of "territorial compromise" remained the basis of the Labor Party's peace plan, the party's native-born military leaders, who were influential in opening the West Bank for Jewish settlement, were unable to abide by the restrictions they sought to place on the process.[1] They were in the position of the sorcerer's apprentice who set a potentially deadly process on course only to learn that he has forgotten the magic word, which alone could put an end to it. Since the possibility of peacefully closing the frontier detached the means of the military frontier from the goal of security, continued settlement became an end in itself, searching for a new justification. Other interests and groups were waiting in the wings to justify settlement in new terms, in order to continue and expand the venture begun in the Labor era.

Religious patrimony

A new stage in the process of colonization opened up at Kfar Etzion in February 1974, with the foundation of Gush Emunim (Bloc of the Faithful), which demanded the removal of the restrictions imposed on the settlement process by the policy of "military frontier." Gush Emunim was dedicated to unbridled settlement on all fronts – with special emphasis on Samaria, the northern half of the West Bank. In line with this view, it vehemently opposed any Israeli withdrawal as part of the disengagement agreements on the Egyptian and Syrian fronts after the 1973 war. These far-reaching goals were accompanied by new and militant methods. Yearly marches across the West Bank of thirty to forty thousand participants, frequent street demonstrations, and, most significantly, repeated attempts to settle forcefully at chosen sites, in spite of evacuations by the military, were the methods that placed Gush Emunim on the margins of Israeli democracy but at the heart of Israeli politics. While its successes during the era of the first Rabin government were scant, Gush Emunim displayed a vitality and persistence not previously encountered in Israeli social movements.

The cradle of Gush Emunim was the NRP with its network of autonomous educational institutions, built up with the support of Labor governments. The NRP's "well-integrated network" of separatist institutions can be described as forming a series of concentric circles, within which national religious youth move from elementary to higher education. It includes the state religious education system, encompassing kindergartens to high schools, the Bnei Akiva youth movement, the *yeshiva tichonit* high-school network, where high-level traditional religious

---

[1] Galili had been chief of staff of the Hagana, and Allon had been commander of the Palmach, its elite strike force, until they were both ousted by Ben-Gurion at the beginning and the end of the 1948 war, respectively. Dayan and Rabin were both high-ranking officers in 1948 who stayed on to become chiefs of staff of the IDF before going into politics.

studies are coupled with secular education, the *yeshivot hesder*, in which, through special arrangement with the military, the students alternate periods of religious study and military service, usually in their own separate units, and topped by the national religious university, Bar Ilan (see chapter 5, above). These autonomous national-religious institutions, funded out of the state budget, were cross-pollinated with the military to eventually produce the dedicated man- and womanpower of the militant social movement, Gush Emunim.

Until 1967 the religiously and nationally moderate old-timer leadership of the NRP successfully maintained its hold over the party by preventing intra-party elections and substituting for them power-sharing arrangements. Following the 1967 war, however, Zevulon Hammer, Yehuda Ben-Meir, and other leaders of the party's youth faction moved to assume the political representation of the Hebron and Gush Etzion settlers and urged the NRP to take the lead in forcing the settlement of the West Bank. This militant expansionist stance provided a primary element in the crystallization of an independent national-religious world-view that came to vie for primacy with security-mindedness as the central component of Israeli nationalism. This world-view served the NRP young guard well in their intra-party generational conflict, as it was a source of influence within the national-religious community, beyond the ranks of their age group. They were thus able to force democratic elections on the foreign-born leadership, from which they emerged greatly strengthened (support for the youth faction within the party rose in late 1968 from 9 percent to 22.5 percent) (Don-Yehiya 1979; *Maariv*, September 11 and November 30, 1968).

The powerful impact the young guard was able to have on the NRP did not stem solely from their elaboration of a religious justification for expanding Israel's border into the West Bank, the biblical Judea and Samaria, nor from the different connotations the traditional term *Eretz Yisrael* had for Orthodox Jews, as compared to the modern and secular concept of the state of Israel (Kimmerling 1985b). Frontier expansion appealed to younger Orthodox Jews, students and graduates of the NRP's institutional network, because it released them from the procrustean bed of their elders who, having abandoned the ultra-Orthodoxy of Agudat Yisrael, became only a pale imitation of the Labor movement and were criticized and humiliated by both camps. Shmuel Sandler, among others, has pointed out that:

By turning the issue [of settling the West Bank] into both a national and a religious cause the *Mizrachi* camp emerged as a leading force in both areas, for in taking the lead on settlement in the territories, it could demonstrate its loyalty to the sacred ideals of settling the land and security, while at the same time criticizing the *Agudah* circles for their disloyalty to the Land of Israel. Thus, while the old leadership continued to play second fiddle to Labor, an issue had arisen in which the NRP camp could potentially provide leadership in both the national and the religious areas. (Sandler 1981: 164; see also Don-Yehiya 1979: 37–8; the classic depiction of this transformation from a personal standpoint is Michael 1984)

The republican discourse of citizenship, which had been diluted by the LSM, was now available for religious redefinition, and its new champions were well placed to demand elite status within both secular Israeli society and the religious community. To materialize, their ambition required, however, that the flickering flame of colonial expansion be relit and for that aim a new, synthetic religio-republican citizenship discourse was generated.

While the dynamic of generational shift was at the base of both the Labor and the NRP sabra elites' political theory and practice, the relationships each group had with its respective elders were mirror images of each other. The foreign-born leaders of the Labor movement had stamped a very powerful imprint on Israeli society, an imprint that the younger generation of the movement was unable to match (Shapiro 1984). The old NRP leadership, on the other hand, had remained a junior partner in the performance of national tasks, at most a religious lobby representing sectoral interests. The NRP youth, not dwarfed by a generation of giants, was able to exploit the conquests of the 1967 war in full in order to make its own impact on Israeli history.

A second jolt produced by the young national-religious youth, after taking over the leadership of the NRP, was the formation of Gush Emunim and breaking out of the confines of the NRP into the national arena. Most leaders of Gush Emunim had grown up in the same national-religious educational institutions as the other members of their peer group in the NRP, but were, in addition, graduates of the higher Merkaz Harav Yeshiva and settlers living in Gush Etzion or Kiryat Arba. The dominant spirit in the Merkaz Harav was Rabbi Zvi Yehuda Kook, son of its founder, Rabbi Abraham Isaac Kook. The younger Rabbi Kook expressed, more explicitly than any other rabbinical authority, the view that the movement of return to Zion was the first step in the providential fulfillment of the process of redemption (*atchalta degeula*). That view had originated with his father but remained only latent in the Mizrachi camp until 1967. The secular Zionists, in the Kooks' view, were the unwitting tools of this messianic design, "whose beginnings were slow but [its] forward direction was certain" (O'Dea 1976: 40–1; chap. 5, above). No wonder that the occupation of the Old City of Jerusalem and the other holy sites of the West Bank were seen by students and graduates of Merkaz Harav as the vindication of their faith, and as a decisive step towards complete redemption. Israel's partial withdrawals from the Sinai and the Golan Heights, in the wake of the 1973 war, seemed to them setbacks in the process of redemption and called forth the defensive reaction of Gush Emunim (O'Dea 1976; Raanan 1980; Biale 1983; Lustick 1988).

Gush Emunim had its debut in 1974, in a series of protest activities aimed at halting Israeli withdrawals on the Egyptian and Syrian fronts. But soon its Eilon Moreh group turned to what made Gush Emunim famous – repeated attempts to settle near the Palestinian city of Nablus, without government authorization. The Gush considered the settlement project a national project that required individual sacrifice, and took great pride in presenting itself, in the words of Rabbi Levinger, as "the direct and legitimate offspring of the pioneers of Zionism" (*Yediot Achronot*, June 18, 1976; Avruch 1978/9: 26).

Gush Emunim activists self-consciously adopted the language, demeanor, and even casual dress style and bearing of kibbutz members, and demanded the same prestige that in the past had been accorded the vanguard of Zionism in the colonial struggle to inherit the land. They grafted their own messianic religious discourse onto the old discourse of republican virtue, and claimed the mantle of the moral community attending to the common good by settling the Land of Israel. Not satisfied with that, they also sought to elbow aside the LSM itself, by asserting that the movement was replacing its own tradition of republican citizenship with a new, liberal orientation. In this comparison the liberal discourse, with its emphasis on individual subjectivity and individual rights, was denigrated as hedonistic. In one of its first publications, the Gush ridiculed the "phenomena of decadence and retreat, indifference and ignorance . . . pursuit of easy and comfortable life, luxuries, and an atmosphere which brings in its wake unwillingness for self-realization" (D. Rubinstein 1982: 129). For the LSM, *hagshama atzmit*, or self-realization, as explained in chapter 2, was not an individual undertaking but the participation of the virtuous citizen in the collective endeavor of transforming Palestine into a Jewish homeland. It was the virtuous act of the republican citizen in realizing the pioneering goal of Zionism as his or her duty *qua* citizen. Hanan Porath, a Gush leader from Kfar Etzion, rudely told opponents from the Labor movement: "You finished your role, just don't interfere with our attempt to continue it" (D. Rubinstein 1982: 126–30; see also A. Rubinstein, 1980: 115). In short, to gain national legitimation Gush Emunim adopted as its own the great legacy of colonization and reasserted, even as it reinterpreted it in religious vein, the active participation of the republican citizen who has the will and capacity to participate in the determination, protection, and promotion of the common good.

As heir to the colonial settlement project, Gush Emunim indeed succeeded in mobilizing support from non-religious groups and individuals as well. The Movement for Greater Israel and the Ein-Vered circle, and later on the Tzomet party, all rooted in the Labor movement, as well as the Techiya party, where secular activists joined with religious settlers, all played a crucial role in transferring the torch of pioneering to Gush Emunim. Efraim Ben-Chaim, a member of Kibbutz Beit-Oren and secretary general of Techiya, saw the value of Ein-Vered and the other bodies precisely in the symbolic act of conferring on Gush Emunim the validation of the old pioneering movement. The new movement replaced the old and, in the process, he argued, "synthesized" Rabbi Kook's faith "with the best values of the Second Aliyah" (Raanan 1980: 213, 218–19). These Labor veterans supported the Gush precisely because it followed the traditional course of settlement, which carried with it an inherent aura of legitimacy, in a society where pioneering had been a core element of nationalism and a major source of prestige and influence. Even Prime Minister Rabin who (in his first term as PM) ordered the dismantling of several early Gush Emunim settlements, found it useful to express his admiration for their "pioneering zeal" (Sachar 1987: 17). Without Allon, Rabin, and Peres, the settlements of Kiryat Arba, Ofra, and Kadum would not have been established (A. Rubinstein 1980: 126).

Ehud Sprinzak, grandson of one of the founding fathers of the Second Aliya, who studied Gush Emunim in the context of the ascendance of Israel's radical right, also could not but recognize the value the endorsement by Labor veterans had for the new settlement movement. He highlighted the fact that Techiya and Tzomet were "devoid of any original thinking" and as time went by resorted to "draw[ing] upon the past, upon the pre-1948 Zionist thinking." The "ideological connection between the past and present" in the radical right, he argued, was manifested in their reliance on the "old paradigm" of pioneering. At the same time, however, supporters of Gush Emunim among the Labor veterans were not typical of their own movement, and failed to bring with them its younger generation. The man- and womanpower of the settlement movement was provided by national religious youth (Sprinzak 1991: 142, 170–1, 176–7, 296–7).

Though Gush Emunim claimed the mantle of republican citizenship, its definition of pioneering was narrower than that of the LSM. The West Bank settlers abandoned the agrarian settlement based on manual labor, such as kibbutz and moshav, and replaced it with *yishuv kehilati* (community settlement), a "semiurban, commuting, half-open" community which was likely to evolve into "an urban settlement and [even] become a dormitory suburb" (Benvenisti 1984: 53). In this, as we shall see in detail in the next section, Gush Emunim conformed to the emerging new middle-class life style, though not to its individualistic ethos. In the OT the bare act of settlement became coterminous with pioneering, preempting its social attributes and discarding its socialist justification. Colonialism pure and simple became the civic virtue of this new vanguard of nationalism, now justified through religiously accented terms of republican virtue. Not surprisingly, the WZO recognized the *yishuv kehilati* as a "pioneering settlement" in 1977, making it eligible for financial support from the Zionist movement (Benvenisti 1984: 52–3).

The most innovative dimension of Gush Emunim, and the political consequences of its messianic orientation, were to be found in the attitude of its leaders towards the principles that lay behind the Allon Plan. In 1974–6, during the many-phased "duel" between the Eilon Moreh group and the Rabin government, the line that separated their respective frontier conceptions was sharply drawn. Gush Emunim opposed the self-imposed refusal to settle next to populous Palestinian towns and in densely populated areas, which constituted the basis of Allon's settlement views. After a conversation with Gush Emunim representatives in July 1974, Peres concluded that "we are living in two separate countries. You live in a country that needs to be settled, while I in a country that needs to be defended" (Golan 1982: 181). Hanan Porath wrote in March 1975 that

the struggle results from different worldviews regarding the correct dimensions of Zionism. Does Zionism constitute a safe haven for Jews and we have to exert efforts for providing the certain number of Jews who are found here with a life of security, so they can succeed in holding their own and exist? Or maybe the process of redemption in its concrete sense – the redemption of the people, and the redemption of the land – and in its divine sense – the redemption of the godhead, the redemption of the world – is taking place. (*Ptachim*, March 1975: 8 (Hebrew); see also deposition by Gush Emunim members to the High Court of Justice, Bagatz 390/79)

If the native-born Labor leaders had only to emulate and protect the national pioneering legacy in order to claim it, Gush Emunim had to transform the existing sentiment by going all the way. Where the large LSM allocated a few settlers, they had to settle in person; whenever Labor could afford to be moderate, they had to be militant; and messianic extremism served their determination to revitalize Zionist settlement. Just how far Gush Emunim's position had come from that of the "military frontier" may be seen from its rejection not only of the principle of security, which was accepted in 1967 even by the Movement for Greater Israel, but also of striving for peace. "A secular peace," said a founder of Gush Emunim, "is not our goal." The starting point in regard to peace was religious and messianic, and therefore peace was seen as attainable only in the End of Days (Friedman 1979: 28; see also Raanan 1980: 125).

These religious frontiersmen, viewing the West Bank as a sacred patrimony, adhering to the "promised borders" over secure and recognized ones, and acting in opposition to the central institutions of the society, ushered in a new phase of Israeli nationalism. In contrast to the curiosity about the Palestinians raised among many Jews in the aftermath of the 1967 war, as the opening of new frontiers usually does, "Gush Emunim cultivates the image of the Arab above all as the enemy" (D. Rubinstein 1982: 92). Furthermore, "the fostering of feelings of hatred [by Gush Emunim] toward Arabs ... arouses deep-seated emotions and sympathy among fairly large and diverse sectors of the Israeli public" (D. Rubinstein 1982: 95). For many Gush Emunim settlers this hatred is more than a form of consciousness; it in many cases directs their actions. The Gush has had a history of violent confrontations with the Palestinian Arabs. The press almost daily testifies to the friction and active hostility between Gush Emunim settlers and residents of Palestinian towns and villages in their vicinity. Typically of frontier regions, there emerged a vicious cycle of violence: land expropriation, road construction, and rumors of impending settlement propel Palestinian youths to stone Israeli vehicles, which in turn leads to settler vigilantism in the form of vandalism, beatings, and the use of firearms.

The sluice-gate to the overflowing energies of Gush Emunim was thrown open with the end of the Labor era and the formation of the Likud government of Menachem Begin. During Rabin's first tenure as prime minister (1974–7) only three Gush Emunim settlements – Mishor Adumim, Ofra, and Kedumim – were set up, and even these were designated "temporary"; in the course of 1977 alone Gush Emunim established seven settlements in the West Bank. In spite of the apparent slowdown of settlement during the Israeli–Egyptian peace negotiations, eight Gush Emunim colonies went up in 1978–80, and it was busy with the expansion (*ibuy*) of the existing ones. In consequence, the Jewish population of the West Bank rose from 4,400 to 12,500. In a second drive, Gush Emunim added six new locations in 1981. Over half the Jewish settlement in the West Bank between 1977 and 1981 was affiliated with Gush Emunim. The Likud, not having an independent settlement policy and only an insignificant settlement movement of its own, used Gush Emunim during this period as its major settlement arm.

Gush Emunim, however, never succeeded in creating a mass movement of settlers. Religio-republicanism was a hybrid which could not multiply the drawing powers of the two types of citizenship by combining them. Republicanism was in ebb in a society that had already had its day on the frontier, and the messianic appeal remained limited to the national Orthodox segment of the Jewish population. The man- and woman-power reserves of Gush Emunim were quickly exhausted, without having significantly changed the demographic balance between the Jewish and Palestinian populations on the West Bank. At the same time, the process of radicalization that gave rise to Gush Emunim did not come to an end with the achievement of its aim: the settlement of its cadre. More militant members, such as Rabbi Meir Kahane's supporters, and more far-reaching goals, such as expulsion of the entire Palestinian population, have continued to surface (Sprinzak 1991). In the context of the partial Israeli withdrawals, agreed to as part of the Oslo Accords, this process of radicalization reached an even more dangerous plane. After the evacuation of Gaza and Jericho, a settler from Kiryat Arba, Baruch Goldstein, massacred close to thirty Palestinian worshipers at the Patriarch's Cave in Hebron. With the commencement of Israeli withdrawal from the Palestinian cities of the West Bank, Yigal Amir, a graduate of a *hesder yeshiva*, a student at Bar Ilan University, and an ardent supporter of religious settlement in the West Bank, though not himself a settler, assassinated Yitzhak Rabin.

Suburban sprawl on the frontier

Generational change produced the social motivations for the opening of the frontier and the influx of the first two waves of settlers. Both the military and the religious phases of frontier settlement, however, were inherently circumscribed: the former by self-imposed security considerations; the latter by the limited availability of ideologically motivated settlers. These weak drives were superseded in 1981, with the second term of the Begin government. The Likud, in line with its right-wing conception venerating the eternal and inalienable right of the Jewish people to the territories of Greater Israel, resolved to embark on a campaign that would alter, in its view once and for all, the demographic balance between the Palestinian and Jewish populations on the West Bank.

A new, second, settlement division was formed within the Jewish Agency especially for this project, while the old division was instructed to continue expanding settlement in the Allon Plan areas. The new drive, formulated by Mattityahu Drobless, head of the new settlement division, projected in October 1981 the presence of 1.3 million Jews alongside 1.8 million Arabs in the West Bank by the year 2010, that is, within thirty years. The operative part of this drive, entitled "The One-Hundred-Thousand Plan," laid the planning groundwork for settling an additional 80,000 Jews on the West Bank by the end of 1985, thus bringing the number of settlers, together with the 16,200 already there in 1981, to close to 100,000 (Drobless 1978; 1981; *One-Hundred-Thousand Plan* 1981: 7). This settlement campaign, ambitious beyond everything that had been tried before, adopted radically new methods for the fulfillment of its aims.

A rising standard of living in Israel, and the accompanying embourgeoisement of large segments of the society, gave rise in the 1970s to urban sprawl, that is, to the movement of people from the aging Tel Aviv metropolitan area to smaller townships, and from two- or three-room condominium apartments to private homes with gardens. It was this process of urban sprawl and suburbanization that was redirected by the grand settlement plan of the Likud government towards the West Bank. To encourage this process Drobless, with the active support of Ariel Sharon as chair of the ministerial settlement committee, turned settlement, for the first time in Zionist history, into a capitalist venture, encouraging the employment of private funds and private initiative in the construction of settlements (*One-Hundred-Thousand Plan* 1981: 15). "The dominant incentives for migration" to the West Bank, according to the planners, were to be found in the possibility of "purchasing high standard housing with land attached, at lower costs" (*One-Hundred-Thousand Plan* 1981: 14).

The major reason for the lower housing prices in the West Bank was the absurdly low land prices: the government charged construction companies only 5 percent of the value of the land, while in nearby areas on the Israeli side of the border they were obliged to pay 80 percent. Consequently, apartments in some of the larger urban centers of the West Bank cost half as much as similar-sized apartments in Tel Aviv or Jerusalem, and for the price of the latter the potential settler could afford a private home in the West Bank. In addition, entitlements and subsidies were conferred on the settlers by the Likud and national unity governments, and, following a reduction by the second Rabin government, restored by Netanyahu in 1997. Under these plans most settlements are classified "Area of National Priority – A," which entitles them to the most generous benefits, or as "Area of National Priority – B," which confers lesser, but still significant, benefits. Among these are an $8,600 grant for the purchase of a new apartment in Area A (or $5,700 for Area B) plus a soft loan of an equal amount, and coverage of most development costs. Government-backed mortgages are being utilized at a higher rate in the settlements than in Israel proper, because of their lower cost. Certain categories of desired occupations receive additional incentives: Social workers and teachers receive three to four years of seniority upon relocation to a West Bank settlement (*Report on Israeli Settlement* 1997).

The settlement plan, though inspired and justified by a lofty ideology, relied in fact on powerful economic incentives to attract settlers. Since material interests dominated the actual settlement process, setting its pace and selecting its locations, this phase of colonization could be designated the "economic frontier."

Social services are provided to the settlers by their local and regional councils, which receive a large share of their operating budget, as within Israel proper, from the Ministry of the Interior's general grant-in-aid program. We have two sets of reports, from 1983/4, on the size of these grants per capita, and on their share in the per capita expenditures of select local and regional councils (Benvenisti 1986a; Dehter 1987). Although the reports diverge significantly, they paint the same picture. The reason for the similarity of conclusion, in spite of the different figures, is that 1983/4 was a year of rapid inflation, and as a result the exchange rate between the NIS and the US dollar varied over the year, thus affecting the numbers, though less significantly their consistency. Of the two sets of data, Dehter's is likely to be more carefully chosen: while Benvenisti provided only a few numbers as part of a more general study, and without citing his sources, Dehter undertook a study using data collected from the budgets of the councils he studied, provided by the Ministry of the Interior and by the councils themselves (Dehter 1987: 3–4, 31). His express purpose was to find out, as his title indicates, *How Expensive are West Bank Settlements?* We calculated, using the Ministry of the Interior's data, the numbers for 1992.

As seen in table 6.1, with the exception of some special cases, the size of Ministry of Interior grants, per capita, was much larger in West Bank regional councils than it was in the state of Israel itself. In 1992, although the size of the grants grew in all districts, they remained considerably lower outside the West Bank, whether in adjacent or in remote regions of the country. In some regions within Israel the grants even decreased (Ministry of Interior).

Table 6.2 shows a comparison of the general Ministry of Interior grants as a percentage of the total expenditure per capita in local councils in 1983/4 and 1992, while table 6.3 shows the same thing for regional councils, for 1992 only. What the three tables together indicate is that, with few exceptions, local and regional councils in the West Bank have been allocated more funds in relative terms (on average twice as high), as well as in absolute terms (on average 1.25–3 times as high). They can, therefore, spend more on services, such as education, culture, religion, or public health (not including ordinary medical care, which is not part of their responsibilities). This is despite the fact that self-generated income

Table 6.1 *Ministry of Interior grants per capita, selected regional councils, 1983/4 and 1992*

West Bank		Israel	
Benvenisti figures (1983/4)			
Gush Etzion	$230	Mateh Yehuda	$86
Benjamin	245	Shaar Hanegev	126
Shomron	357	Upper Galilee	97
Jordan Valley	408		
Dehter figures (1983/4)			
Gush Etzion	$488	Mateh Yehuda	$151
Benjamin	497	Southern Sharon	133
Shomron	659	Modiin	129
Jordan Valley	305	Arava[1]	612
		Misgav[2]	924
1992 figures			
Gush Etzion	$599	Mateh Yehuda	$219
Benjamin	447	Shaar Hanegev	220
Shomron	760	Upper Galilee	245
Jordan Valley	1,326	Southern Sharon	117
Har Hebron	1,425	Modiin	234

Sources: Benvenisti 1986a; Dehter 1987; Ministry of Interior.

[1] A long stretch of desert along Israel's southern border with Jordan, sparsely populated with kibbutzim and moshavim.

[2] A region of newly established exurban Jewish settlements (*mitzpim*) in the midst of a heavily populated citizen Palestinian area in the Upper Galilee. The functional equivalent of settlements, inside Israel (Yiftachel 1992).

is higher in West Bank localities than it is in the Israeli comparison cases. Significantly, only in the area of welfare was the expenditure higher within Israel (Dehter 1987: 6, table 3). The 1992 data show that the share of the Interior Ministry's general grants fell in the general expenditures of both local and regional councils, although less so in the latter, and that its share in the West bank, especially in regional councils, remained higher than within Israel. Within the West Bank, the grants to the Allon Plan (Jordan Valley) and Gush Emunim settlements, which enjoy the status of pioneering settlements, were higher than those granted suburban settlements.

Three additional comparisons are instructive. In 1983/4, the Allon Plan settlements, located in a relatively remote area with small population per settlement, were the only ones in which the general grant of the

Table 6.2 *Ministry of Interior grants as percentage of municipal expenditures per person in selected local councils, 1983/4 and 1992*

West Bank		Israel	
Benvenisti figures (1983/4)			
Elkana	52.8%	Rosh Haayin[1]	44%
Ariel	52.8	Or Yehuda	36.8
Maale Adumim	60.8	Or Akiva	28.9
Kiryat Arba	68.8	Ramat Hasharon	11.6
Dehter figures (1983/4)			
Elkana	69%	Kfar Yona	38%
Ariel	64	Kadima	45
Maale Adumim	47	Shlomi	51
Kiryat Arba	64	Rosh Pina	64
1992 figures			
Maale Adumim	23.5%	Rosh Haayin	33.3%
Ariel	37.5	Or Yehuda	21.2
Givat Zeev	39.4	Or Akiva	32.5
Kiryat Arba	46.6	Kfar Yona	32

Sources: Benvenisti 1986a; Dehter 1987; Ministry of Interior.
[1] First three local councils are development towns.

Ministry of the Interior represented less than half of the total expenditure (Dehter 1987: 26). This was no longer the case in 1992, when the figure for the Jordan Valley was 59.1 percent. The second comparison, often considered irrelevant, is that between expenditures on public services, as measured by total municipal outlay, in overlapping but ethnically segregated regions. Benvenisti paired the local councils of Kiryat Arba, where the relevant sum in 1983/4 was $260, with neighboring Hebron, where it was $54; the regional council of Samaria – $568, with the Jenin subdistrict – $12; and Mateh Benjamin – $406, with the Ramallah subdistrict – $8.5 (Benvenisti 1986a: 56). These figures clearly demonstrate, if a demonstration is needed, the sharp gap in the West Bank between those (Jews) who enjoy the benefits of every kind of citizenship and those (Palestinians) dispossessed of any citizenship rights.

The third comparison, for 1996 (last year of the second Rabin–Peres government, which vowed to change national priorities), is between total government grants per capita and municipal expenditure per capita in three categories of localities: OT settlements, development towns within

Table 6.3 *Ministry of Interior grants as percentage of municipal expenditures per person in selected regional councils, 1992*

West Bank		Israel	
Gush Etzion	43.3%	Mateh Yehuda	23.4%
Har Hebron	47.7	Shaar Hanegev	12.5
Benjamin	42.2	Upper Galilee	19.3
Shomron	44.3	Southern Sharon	12.5
Jordan Valley	59.1	Modiin	34.1

Source: Ministry of Interior.

Israel, and citizen Palestinian localities. Total government grants were $831, $600, and $440 per capita in the three categories, respectively, while municipal expenditure per capita was $1205, $954, and $605 (*Haaretz*, February 11, 1998).

In the educational sphere we encounter a similar phenomenon of privileging the West Bank settlements, especially the smaller Gush Emunim ones. A special department of the Ministry of Education attends to the educational needs in, and teacher training for, the settlements. Given the small size and dispersal of the Gush Emunim colonies the expenditure on schooling, whether pre-school, elementary school, junior high or high school, is magnified by low teacher–student ratios in pre- and elementary schools, and by the cost of transporting children to regional junior and high schools (Benvenisti 1986b: 70–1). In 1983, for example, 10 percent of the gainfully employed in Mateh Benjamin were educational staff. Since the Ministry of Education covers teachers' salaries and transportation costs, this is an added subsidy for these settlements. In addition, the ministry financed in those Gush Emunim settlements that requested them the establishment of higher yeshivot for boys and *ulpanot* for girls, in addition to the regular state religious schools. As a consequence, publicly funded education, especially in its religious form, serves as a main source of employment for many settlers in the smaller settlements, who have failed to find independent forms of income. In general, public agencies, including Jewish local government, employed 51 percent of the West Bank settlers in 1995, compared to 33 percent of the gainfully employed in Israel proper (*Haaretz Weekly Magazine*, December 15, 1995).

The Likud's settlement policy, which freed the powers and potentials that were latent in the Galili Protocol of the limitations imposed by the notion of military frontier, transformed Israeli colonization for the third time, by harnessing individual self-interest to the colonial project. Privately undertaken colonization had nothing to do with the old, Labor, or the new, national-religious forms of republican citizenship. Its motivation was the exact opposite: whereas pioneering was hailed as dedication to the common good that overrode individual interests, the new settlement drive was undertaken by individuals for their own benefit. There was no need to share in the collective purpose that led the Likud governments to subsidize the settlements and authorize private companies to build them, in order to take advantage of them. In fact, many Israelis moved to these newly constructed "quality of life" settlements because of their affordability, in some cases luxury, in spite of their stated moderate political opinions. Some of these settlements even boast branches of the Labor Party. Individual interest, which played such a crucial role in other movements of colonization, became, after 1981, the main justification for colonization in Palestine too. Ironically, the use of this justification, and its acceptance as legitimate, was part and parcel of the rise of a new spirit of individualism and, indeed, of a liberal citizenship discourse in other spheres of Israeli society as well (see part 3, below).

The "One-Hundred-Thousand Plan" transformed the settlement movement in accordance with the emerging economic liberalism of Israeli society and the new balance of power between Jews and Palestinians. In the process, all traditional patterns of settlement were turned on their heads: urban instead of agricultural settlement; capitalist venture instead of co-operative pioneering; disjointed areas of settlement amidst the Palestinian population, in order to divide it, instead of settlement in contiguous zones apart from the Palestinians, in order to create a Jewish majority; and as a result, settlements dependent on regular IDF troops for their defense, instead of serving as military outposts themselves. The most dramatic ideological change was the abandonment of the Revisionists' historical opposition to settlement as a means of staking out political claims. The Revisionists' preferred method, never tried in practice, had been reliance on military, political, and diplomatic means to accomplish this goal (Avineri 1980: 189; Isaac 1981: 139). Once in power, however, both Gush Emunim, which grew up under the wings of Labor's junior partner, the NRP, and Likud followed the traditional LSM practice: colonization in order to gain territorial control. Israeli colonialism, albeit in a weakened form, and the repeatedly transformed types of citizenship that sustained it, continued throughout the 1980s and the post-Oslo period of the 1990s. Indeed, it seems that colonization had remained the "constant" in a changing state of Israel; when in doubt, one is tempted

Table 6.4 *Israeli settler population in the West Bank and the Gaza Strip by year*

	Gaza Strip	West Bank
1972	700	800
1983	900	22,800
1985	1,900	44,100
1989	3,000	69,800
1990	3,300	78,600
1991	3,800	90,300
1992	4,300	101,100
1993	4,800	111,600
1994	5,100	122,700
1995	5,300	133,200
1996	5,600	142,700
1997	5,700	154,400
1998	6,100	163,300
2000	6,500	188,500

Sources: Report on Israeli Settlements in the OT, July/August 2000. These numbers are drawn from the Statistical Abstracts of Israel. The numbers published by Yesha Council are consistently higher by 10–15 percent, putting them at 193,680 at the end of 1999. Data for December 2000 is from Peace Now (*The Economist*, December 16, 2000: 52).

to conclude, Israeli governments, one and all, were sure of one thing – it was time to settle!

The most dramatic, and unexpected, instance of continuity in settlement policy is that between Shamir's Likud-led government and the Rabin–Peres Labor-led government that took power in 1992 vowing to "change national priorities." Though Rabin attacked the settlers' ideology, in Geoffrey Aronson's cogent assessment

his enduring commitment to remain in overall strategic control of the West Bank and Gaza Strip, combined with the legitimate demands of a growing settler community of 150,000, set the stage for Labor's unwillingness to strike at the sustainability of a government-directed enterprise which continues to attract new settlers and which further entrenches itself with every passing day. (*Report on Israeli Settlement in the OT*, July 1996: 7)

The Oslo peace process, which was expected to lead to the partitioning of Palestine, was in fact carried on in parallel with continued Jewish colonization in the West Bank. As part of this policy, the Labor government allowed 11,000 housing units begun under the last Shamir government to be completed. Nor did Labor suspend the granting of building permits for private home construction in settlements throughout the West Bank, of which in early 1993 there were 1,100 under construction. The expansion of the network of roads bypassing Palestinian localities, such as the Jerusalem–Efrat road, tied settlements more closely to Israel and thus further encouraged the expansion of the settler population. Mortgage subsidies, lower land prices and infrastructural costs, combined with lower construction code standards than in Israel, reduced the price of single family homes sometimes by as much as 40 percent (*Report on Israeli Settlement in the OT*, January 1993).

The Rabin government also selectively expanded settlements in the West Bank, lamely distinguishing between "security settlements" (the Allon Plan and suburban settlements) and the "political settlements" of Gush Emunim. The settler population grew between 1992 and 1996 by over 40 percent, from 101,100 to 142,700, consistent with projections made by the Rabin government in 1992, which envisaged a settler population of 140,000 in the West Bank and Gaza Strip by 1995 (see table 6.4). The Jewish population of East Jerusalem grew by about 50,000, to close to 200,000, during the same period. Significantly, the Rabin–Peres government's decisions not to relocate settlements – including the most isolated ones, such as Netzarim in the Gaza Strip, and the most murderously anti-Palestinian one, namely the Jewish Quarter in Hebron, after Goldstein's massacre of Muslim worshipers at the Cave of the Patriarchs – indicated that it envisioned their permanency. In sum, the Rabin–Peres years witnessed a "deliberate continuation of the expansion and consolidation of settlements, according to government plans and aided by government subsidy and direct allocation" (*Report on Israeli Settlement in the OT*, July 1996: 7).

The Barak government, which replaced Netanyahu's in 1999, also continued settlement, though at a somewhat slower pace. Nevertheless, in the second half of 1999 it issued tenders for the construction of close to 3,200 housing units in the West Bank and the Gaza Strip (*Report on Israeli Settlement in the OT*, January/February 2000: 10), and by December 4, 2000 had built 2,830 new units in the West Bank and the Gaza Strip. In December 1999 two Jewish municipal jurisdictions in the West Bank – the Benjamin regional council and the city of Maale Adumim – passed the 25,000-resident mark. Five additional jurisdictions (Ariel, Betar Ilit, Givat Zeev, Kiryat Sefer, and Shomron) had over 10,000 inhabitants. According to the Yesha Council's usually inflated reports, the number of West Bank settlers went up to 193,680 by late 1999.[2] According to

---

[2] Yesha (acronym for Judea, Samaria and Gaza) Council is the coordinating body of Jewish local governments in the OT.

Peace Now, by December 2000, that is, in Barak's first eighteen months in office, the population grew by 13,000, to 195,000 (not including, of course, the 180,000 Jewish residents of East Jerusalem and the adjacent areas of the West Bank annexed to Israel, who are not considered settlers in the official statistics). Amiram Goldblum of Peace Now concluded that "in such matters as issuing building tenders, or bestowing economic privileges on settlers, there has been no difference in Mr. Barak's and Mr. Netanyahu's policies" (*Report on Israeli Settlement in the OT,* May–June 2000: 9; *The Economist,* December 16, 2000: 52; see also *Haaretz,* 21 February 2000; 5 December 2000).

The same pattern of continuity, expansion of construction, and settlement, regardless of the political party in power, has been evident in Jerusalem. On June 27, 1967, on the heels of the 1967 war, Israeli jurisdiction was extended to all of East Jerusalem and about 11 percent of the surrounding West Bank. In 1981 the Knesset passed the "Jerusalem Law," formally annexing this area to Israel. The goal of Israel's settlement policy is to surround the Palestinian population of East Jerusalem by a ring of ten major Israeli settlement neighborhoods (e.g. Ramot Allon, Neve Yaacov, Pisgat Zeev, Gilo), and thus, while creating a Jewish majority in East Jerusalem, to separate the Palestinian population from the rest of the West Bank. While Israeli governments "enforced a strict quota on Arab construction in East Jerusalem," with the aim of ensuring that the percentage of Palestinians in all of Jerusalem remain around 26 percent, they were engaged in massive construction for Jewish newcomers. Over the past thirty years 42,000 housing units were built and the Jewish inhabitants of East Jerusalem "comprise a startling 80 percent of the total increase in the city's Jewish population since 1967." The Jewish population of East Jerusalem rose from 9,200 in 1972 to 103,900 by 1986, when it roughly equaled the Palestinian population. Unlicensed construction since 1992, fueled by Palestinian movement into the city, recovered and maintained a small Palestinian majority since then. At the same time, not all Palestinians carrying Israeli-issued Jerusalem identity documents (as few as 86,000, according to the Palestinian census and other estimates) actually reside in the city. On the other hand, most Jewish neighborhoods are built to capacity, with the exception of the most recent, Har Choma (Jebel Abu Ghneim), currently under construction, which would plug one of the last remaining holes in the Jewish settlement ring (*Report on Israeli Settlement in the OT,* May–June 1999: 7–8). While the initiative for the construction of Har Choma was born during the Rabin government, it was unable to implement it, and the Palestinians succeeded in blocking the Netanyahu government's efforts to do so. The construction finally began under the Barak government; of the 6,500 housing units planned, about 1,600 were already put up for sale in February 2000, and the first residents were expected to move in by the end of 2001 (*Haaretz*, February 6, 2000). The planners expect that with the completion of these units, "the expansion of Jerusalem's Palestinian neighborhoods throughout East Jerusalem will be constrained by a ring of settlement communities housing more than 200,000 Israelis connected by a modern transportation and communication infrastructure with both Israel's coastal plain and West Bank settlements in metropolitan Jerusalem" (*Report on Israeli Settlement in the OT,* May–June 1999: 9).

Conclusion

The pattern of colonial settlement that served as the basis of state building in the Yishuv has never been discarded. Settlement constituted the "heroic" aspect of Israeli citizenship, a major route for the acquisition of hegemonic influence, elite position, and social prestige. The compelling character of the formative national experience was still alive in 1967 and provided the initial impetus for the renewed settlement drive. The dispute between the major political camps, both of which were involved in different phases of settlement in the OT, concerned the extent and goals of expansion, not its desirability. Whether colonization was necessary under conditions of national sovereignty remained an unasked question.

At the same time, the forces and interests favoring the expansion of settlement had been weakened by 1967. Israeli society had become considerably more urban and individualistic than the Yishuv. Not surprisingly, no spontaneous mass movement of colonizers, similar to the Stockade and Watchtower settlers of the 1940s, had emerged from within the LSM. For some fifteen years, only insubstantial settlement, motivated by the relatively weak momentum of intergenerational change, had taken place. By the end of 1983 less than 1 percent of Israeli Jews had moved to the West Bank. Only in late 1981 did government policy, by turning construction and settlement into profit-making ventures, create the potential for making a dent in the solid Palestinian demographic majority on the West Bank.

Colonization drives could no more be justified by appeals to the virtue of pure republican citizenship. Gush Emunim, while claiming the mantle of republicanism, created a weak synthesis with its own messianic religious convictions. Private enterprise, or a form of liberal-colonialism (in fact, still heavily subsidized), was then adopted as the preferred method of settlement. Ultimately, however, liberalism was used to criticize not to enhance colonization. Though settlement to improve individual lifestyle and living conditions was more effective than religious settlement, what it gained in numbers it lost in intensity: most dormitory settlements were constructed near the old Green Line.

In adopting the "religious" and then the "economic" frontier strategies, Israel undermined the logic of the security considerations that had supposedly underlain the "military" frontier. Palestinian opposition to each additional phase of settlement was more intense than to the earlier, more modest, phase. Each additional stage of expansion intensified the frontier conflict, raised the stakes involved, and made it less likely that either side would back down from its position. Similarly, while the military frontier may have had a chance of becoming hegemonic in Jewish Israeli political culture, the sabotaging of its "rational" and collective argumentation by zealous messianism and pecuniary individual interest ensured the failure of renewed colonization as a hegemonic project (Lustick 1993a). When, in December 1987, the conflict finally erupted in a mass popular rising – the first intifada, this asymmetry was manifested in Israel's failure to curb it through military means, and consequent turn to diplomacy. During the al-Aksa intifada, which broke out in September 2000, an even more thorough decolonization option began to be pondered.

The occupation of the West Bank and Gaza Strip brought under Israeli rule a large part of the Palestinian people.[1] If for a brief moment after the war innovative policy options were entertained – such as the Israeli government's secret decision, on June 19, 1967, to consent to withdraw to the Egyptian and Syrian international borders in return for a peace treaty; or Allon's suggestion, on August 19, 1967, to establish in the West Bank a miniature sovereign Palestinian state tied to Israel by a treaty of mutual defense and a common market, a plan supported by the high military command as well – these passed away rather rapidly. In their stead, the old colonial logic gradually reasserted itself, as we saw in the previous chapter.

The place of the Palestinian population of the occupied territories (OT) in Israel's incorporation regime was determined by the contradiction inherent in the desire to annex some or all of these territories without making their residents citizens of Israel. The slowly evolving solution to this dilemma became "creeping annexation" through Jewish settlement and the partial extension of Israeli institutions into the OT.

Unlike the Palestinians within Israel's 1948 borders, who had been granted civil and political rights as individuals, those on the West Bank and Gaza were left in legal limbo. They were not integrated into the state of Israel, but remained under a military government that, on its part, accepted only partially the international legal framework that is supposed to guide belligerent occupation. When that framework clashed with the desire to settle Jews in the OT, the Palestinian residents were marginalized in favor of the settlers, who enjoyed, not to say flouted, their rights as Israeli citizens, in spite of the fact that Israeli law had not been extended to these territories.

Kimmerling has described the political formation created by the occupation as a "control system": "a territorial entity comprising several

---

[1] We will not be able to discuss the fate of the 15,000 Druze living on the Golan Heights, which was officially annexed to Israel in 1982, or of the sparse Bedouin population of the Sinai Peninsula, which was returned to Egypt in the early 1980s.

sub-collectivities, held together by purely military and police forces and their civil extensions." What characterizes a control system, as distinguished from almost all other political formations, is "the ruling sector's virtually total lack of interest and ability [to create] a common identity or basic value system to legitimize its use of violence to maintain the system." All the rulers are interested in is acquiescence, in return for which they are willing to grant their subjects "minimal human rights and guarantee 'law and order,' so long as these privileges are not perceived as contradicting the interests of the ... ruling sector" (Kimmerling 1989b: 266–7).

Within this control system there was no citizenship category that the Palestinian residents of the OT could fill: as a collectivity they had no national rights, and as individuals they were deprived of all political and most civil rights. In a manner typical of authoritarian regimes, it was only in the area of social citizenship that they received a modicum of rights, in direct correspondence with their economic integration into Israel. But as that integration was of a colonial character, these rights remained severely limited. Social rights and economic development, nevertheless, did produce a period of acquiescence. But as the trajectory of economic development tapered off, the significance of the limited social rights wore off as well. By December 1987 the Palestinians, their civil rights circumscribed by military rule and colonization, devoid of political rights, and with declining social rights, rose up against Israel and shook its control of the OT.

Social rights and economic incorporation

The only explicit policy decision made by the Israeli government with respect to the West Bank and Gaza Strip immediately after the 1967 war was to integrate their economies with that of Israel. This was meant to accomplish through economics what was thought not to be feasible in the realm of politics: the piecemeal, but nevertheless permanent, incorporation of the West Bank and Gaza into the Israeli control system.

The report of the Economic Advisory Team for the Political Negotiations (1993) with the Palestinians, comprising distinguished professors of economics, representatives of the Ministry of Finance and Bank of Israel, a prominent industrialist, and chaired by Professor Haim Ben-Shahar, provided the conventional wisdom of the Israeli side on its relationship with the Palestinian economy:

Following the Six Day War, in effect, a common market comprising Israel and the territories was formed ... The integration (*shiluv*) of the Territories' economies into the Israeli economy led to an unprecedented economic prosperity in them and, in spite of the slowing down of the rapid growth with the exhaustion of this process, the standard of living attained in its wake was preserved and even continued to rise until the intifada's outbreak.

The foremost reason for this prosperity was the opportunity provided to the Territories' population to work in Israel. In effect, until the onset of the intifada Israel supplied employment to nearly all the addition to the labor force produced by population growth ... But economic growth did not skip over the economies of the Territories either. Agricultural production grew extensively, in the process terminating the hidden unemployment that had characterized this industry in the past; and in spite the uncertainty that made investors fret, and a policy that rejected the establishment of enterprises that would compete with Israeli producers, industrial production, albeit mostly on a small-scale, developed as well. (Economic Advisory Team 1995: 138–9)

The gap between the Israeli and the OT economies indeed narrowed somewhat under the occupation: the per capita GNP of the OT rose from 13.8 percent of Israeli GNP in 1970 to 22.7 percent in 1986 (Kleiman 1993: 309). But a survey of the relations between the Israeli and Palestinian economies leads to the conclusion that the Economic Advisory Team's assessment is as optimistic as it is partial, and in many respects blind to the debilities caused by the dependency of the OT on Israel.

An extensive study by the World Bank demonstrates that the development of the OT's economy was only partially the result of its integration with the Israeli economy. The WB's report breaks down the economic trajectory of the OT into four distinct stages, each associated not only with its integration with the Israeli economy but also with the economies of the Gulf states where hundreds of thousands of Palestinians were also employed:

(1) The years 1967–75 indeed witnessed the rapid growth that Israeli authorities proudly proclaimed, but it was driven both by the Gulf boom and by higher wages (compared to the pre-1967 period) paid in Israel to the Palestinian laborers employed there.

(2) Between 1975 and the early 1980s economic growth continued due to the remittances of Palestinians employed in the oil-rich Gulf states. These helped offset the adverse impact of the slower growth of the oil-dependent Israeli economy.

(3) The early 1980s to 1987 were a period of economic stagnation in the OT due to the collapse of the oil-driven boom in the Gulf. This was cushioned to some extent by employment in the Israeli labor market but the significant once-off gains of the integration could not be reached again with employment opportunities in Israel peaking out.

(4) Following the outbreak of the intifada, labor and commercial strikes, and the barring of entry of laborers during the Gulf war

and cyclically during the intifada, and the expulsion of Palestinian workers from Kuwait, all led to massive economic decline (World Bank 1993: 10–16).

Economic stagnation, in short, began before the intifada and, as we shall see, helped precipitate it, in tandem with the intensifying assault on other Palestinian rights.

Yet another, comparative, perspective shows that the economy of the OT did not fare as well under Israeli domination as many of the accounts, including Ben-Shahar's, indicate. A significant measure is the average rate of growth in comparison with the Arab economies. For example, in 1987, when it stood at $1, 717, the West Bank and Gaza had "marginally ... higher per capita GNP than...Syria ($1,640) or Jordan (1,560)." In general, the growth rate in the West Bank and Gaza was "not higher than the comparably endowed Jordan" (Hamed and Shaban 1993: 121, 124, 145 n. 5). The WB study pointed out that the per capita growth rate of the OT in the booming 1970s was only 0.8 percent higher than in the rest of the region (7.1 percent versus 6.3 percent), a gap that was also maintained in the slump of the 1980s (1.1 percent versus 0.3 percent). The OT's rate of growth, in fact, correlated more closely with the regional rate than with Israel's. The latter was below the OT's in the 1970s (2.8 percent) and above it in the 1980s (1.9 percent) (World Bank 1993: 17, fig. 4). If we add the fact that the estimates of the OT's economic performance are affected by the size of its population, and that Israeli calculations underestimated that number, the picture becomes even less rosy. Since the population census taken immediately after the 1967 war no additional censi were taken, and, consequently, the growth of the Palestinian population under Israeli rule was not known. According to the first census conducted by the Palestinian National Authority in December 1997 there were 2.9 million Palestinians in the OT, including 210,000 in annexed East Jerusalem (*Haaretz*, February 2, 1998).

The main argument of the Ben-Shahar Commission and the few Israeli economists who paid any attention to the economy of the OT was that the amalgamation of the OT's economy with that of Israel, i.e. the integration of a low-wage with a high-wage economy, should lead to an upward pressure on wages and, consequently, to their rise in the Palestinian economy (Kleiman 1993: 310). But according to the Histadrut's Economic and Social Research Institute, as late as 1992 the average wage of Palestinians working in Israel was only 38 percent of Israeli wages (Histadrut 1993: 9). The explanation provided for the persistence of such a wide gap, that "the distribution of occupations among the workers from the Territories shows concentration in occupations characterized by low wages" (Histadrut 1993: 9), is nothing but tautological. The reason for this lopsided concentration is hardly the absence of a stratum of educated Palestinians. While 30 percent of the West Bank labor force was employed in white-collar occupations (Kleiman 1993: 313), only 5 percent of the Palestinians employed in Israel were so employed, and most of them, probably, were working in East Jerusalem. The Ben-Shahar report explicitly admits that "the employees in Israel represent a lower cross-section of the educational and skill continuum than those residents of the Territories that in the past were employed in the Gulf states" (Economic Advisory Team 1995: 140). The real reason for the wage gap is that under Israeli rule a rigidly stratified ethnic labor market was established, pushing educated Palestinians to leave (Semyonov and Lewin-Epstein 1987; Lewin-Epstein and Semyonov 1993).

A related question is: Why has the flow of the factors of production, under conditions of economic integration, been unidirectional? Why were the workers transported to the machinery but the machines were not delivered to the workers? In short, why was Israeli – and, by extension, foreign or Palestinian – capital not invested in the OT? Kleiman's explanation, that political uncertainty prevented investors from doing so, rings true for Israeli and foreign investors, but we still need to account for the paucity of Palestinian investment. It is, in fact, agreed that attempts by Palestinian entrepreneurs to establish factories or financial institutions were thwarted by the refusal of the Israeli authorities to grant permits for enterprises that could compete with their Israeli counterparts. A Harvard University report concluded that development and capital investment in the OT were "particularly low" (Institute for Social and Economic Policy 1993: 26). The report of the Israeli Coordinating Bureau of Economic Organizations pointed out that "there is almost a complete lack of physical infrastructure in the Territories" (Coordinating Bureau 1993: 7). Most of the $60 million invested in infrastructure in the OT were financed by contributions from the Gulf states and only a small part came from the Israeli civil administration. The latter (like the British Mandatory authorities in Palestine) used a balanced budget approach, investing in the OT only tax revenues generated from the Palestinian residents themselves (Kleiman 1993: 316).

Instead of Israeli capital flows into the West Bank and Gaza in response to favorable economic conditions, as expected by economic theory, Kleiman concluded that "institutional capital flows ... seem to have gone in the opposite direction" (Kleiman 1993: 316). Palestinian workers employed in Israel "are excluded from many of the benefits provided by National Insurance for Israeli workers" (Institute for Social and Economic Policy 1993: 69). Though Palestinian workers hired through the Israeli employment service are required, like their Israeli counterparts, to pay the full amount of social insurance taxes, they "do not receive commensurate benefits." They are eligible for severance pay in case of the employer's bankruptcy and for compensations for work-related accidents, but not for unemployment insurance, child allowances, and age-old pensions, and are entitled to maternity benefits only if the child is born in Israel (Histadrut 1993: 11; Institute for Social and Economic Policy 1993: 69–70). According to the Harvard report, the gap between the insurance taxes paid and the benefits received by Palestinian workers employed in Israel in the first twenty-five years of the occupation amounted to $250 million. The Histadrut estimated the gap to be $400 million between 1967 and 1993 (Institute for Social and Economic Policy 1993: 31; Histadrut 1993: 12). The Israeli government has argued that a portion of these national insurance payments was used to finance the civil administration, without specifying, however, for which expenses were these sums credited. It would probably be more accurate to argue that the Palestinian workers have been paying an occupation premium to the Israeli authorities.

This pattern of overpayment by Palestinians is repeated in many other areas as well. According to Kleiman's liberal estimates, Israel collected value added tax (VAT) from the residents of the OT to the tune of $150 million in 1986, and $180 million in 1987 (Kleiman 1993: 316). The custom dues paid for goods and services imported to the OT through Israel was even higher. A significant portion of Israel's exports to the OT consisted of reexports to the OT by Israeli importers who, by virtue of holding the monopoly to represent their foreign companies in Israel, also had exclusive rights to export to the OT. The importance of this source of income is revealed in the concern expressed in the report of the Israeli economic organizations from February 1993 that "the implementation of [Palestinian] autonomy is likely to hurt the exclusive representatives of foreign companies that operate in Israel," and the absurd recommendation that Israel demand that in this context "the autonomy is recognized as an integral part of Israel" (Coordinating Bureau 1992: 3).

It was in view of the lack of infrastructural development, absence of protection for and planning of agricultural production, restriction in access to water resources (Dillman 1989; Gwirtzman 1993; Bellisari 1994; Hess 1998), and refusal to grant permits to operate industrial enterprises and financial corporations that Israel was so willing, as the Ben-Shahar report proudly stated, to accommodate the expansion of the Palestinian labor force within its own economy. The concentration of half of the Palestinian workers in the construction industry, however, an industry known for its sharp oscillations, its laying off of workers during periods of economic slowdown, and its publicized desire to replace Palestinian workers with Jewish immigrants, points to the dangers inherent in this kind and level of dependence. These characteristics of the Palestinian labor force make it "highly vulnerable," in Kleiman's conclusion, "to the threat of the host [country] to expel or restrict it, in an attempt to bring pressure upon, or punish, the territories, often at a low cost" to the host economy (Kleiman 1993: 312). In the Paris Agreement of 1994, the PLO and Israel agreed to the continued employment of up to 100,000 Palestinian workers in Israel. In fact, however, already during the Gulf war of 1990–1, and later on, in the wake of the suicide bombings that followed the Oslo Accords, Israel repeatedly imposed closures on the OT and prevented the entry and employment of Palestinian workers within its borders. Over time Israel replaced a growing share of the Palestinian workers from the OT with overseas labor migrants (Elmusa and al-Jaafari 1995; *Haaretz*, July 31, 1998; chap. 12, below).

Political rights and colonization

As early as June 7, 1967, Israel appointed its first military governor of the West Bank and vested in him "all powers of government, legislation, appointment, and administration" that had belonged to the Jordanian district commissioner. In effect, this made the military governors of both the West Bank and Gaza into heads of state without any countervailing powers to check them (save, as it would later turn out, the Israeli Supreme Court, which half-heartedly took it upon itself to oversee the legality of the military administration's actions) (Association for Civil Rights in Israel 1985; Peretz 1986: 80; Shamir 1990; Shelef 1993).

The Labor governments' policies with regard to the Palestinians after 1967 were assessed, on the twentieth anniversary of the 1967 war, by General (Res.) Shlomo Gazit, coordinator of Israeli government operations in the administered territories between 1967 and 1974. In Gazit's assessment, Israeli policies in the West Bank were based on two principles. The first was minimal interference in the lives of the local population which, he argues, created "almost complete normalization between Israel and the inhabitants of the territories." And again: "There is no doubt that twenty years of relative quiet in the territories is Israel's most important achievement." It would be cruel to belabor the absurdity of this conclusion, slapped in the face as soon as the book went into print, by the outbreak of the first intifada. But Gazit's self-congratulatory article also indicates, indirectly at least, one of the major reasons for the failure of Israeli policy in the West Bank. "A political solution," according to the second postulate that underlay Israeli policy since 1967, "will be achieved through negotiations between Israel and the leaders of the Arab states beyond Israel's border (Egypt, Jordan, Syria), whereas the inhabitants of the territories will be unable to play a part or carry much weight in the formulation of a future settlement." Accordingly, Israel imposed a "total prohibition" on political organization on the West Bank, and potential local partners to negotiations were not encouraged, until it was too late. When such attempts were made by Palestinians, whether in the form of political organizations or of consultative assemblies or associations of local leaders, they were "consistently banned." In general, organizations that sought to create a single political framework for the OT were not allowed to emerge (Gazit 1988).

The one area in which existing government bodies were left in place were the municipal authorities. The military government initially adopted a policy of non-intervention in their affairs. Consequently, it was in the municipal councils that the politicization already evinced during the Jordanian period gradually grew in scope, an arena of struggle against the occupation evolved, and internal Palestinian debates, leading to the emergence of a powerful Palestinian nationalist movement, were played out. These took place in the context of the two electoral campaigns for municipal councils and mayors that were held under Israel's rule. Shortly after the occupation, the military administration decided to extend the tenure of the elected municipal councils. In view of the political calm, the repression of the PLO in 1970–1 in Jordan (especially during what came to be known as "Black September"), and tacit Jordanian assent, new elections were held in early 1972 which, for the most part, led to the reelection of the incumbent mayors and councils. These bodies, composed of members of the wealthy and moderate pro-Jordanian traditional elites, remained the recipients of Jordanian government subsidies into the 1980s (Younis 2000: 114).

In the early 1970s the PLO attained growing international and inter-Arab support which allowed it to enhance its influence within the OT. In August 1973 the PLO succeeded in establishing the Palestinian National Front (PNF) as a coalition of the major Palestinian resistance organizations in the West Bank and Gaza and launched a struggle against both the traditional, pro-Hashemite elites and the occupation authorities. Israel, weakened by the 1973 war, and unable to ignore the growing influence of the nationalist camp, sought to use the inter-Palestinian struggle to its benefit by capturing the allegiance of part of the Palestinian public for itself. Defense Minister Peres decided to hold elections again in 1976, with an electorate expanded to three times its former size by granting the suffrage to women and lowering the tax limit for qualifying to vote. In addition, Peres promised to transfer the management of civil affairs to the municipalities, with the intention of establishing Palestinian autonomy under the aegis of an Israeli civil administration (Peretz 1986: 96). But the days of Palestinian submission in the municipal sphere were over; the nationalist bloc won strong majorities in all cities, with the exception of Bethlehem, and replaced the leadership of the traditional notables. As Israel learned to its dismay, "democratization from above," which elsewhere enhanced the loyalty of newly enfranchised citizens, is not an option for colonial regimes (Younis 2000: 146–7).

The new, radical mayors viewed their positions as launching pads for a struggle against the occupation. With the coming to power of the first Likud government in 1977, followed by extensive land expropriation and settlement drive, the confrontation between Israelis and Palestinians in the OT intensified. Some of the mayors were deported; assassination attempts were made against two others by settler underground organizations. Confrontation came to a head in March 1981, when, in the wake of the Camp David accord, Menachem Begin decided to implement the Likud's earlier autonomy plan. His objective was to ostensibly carry out Camp David's provisions for the withdrawal of Israeli military and civilian administration from the OT, while circumventing it in practice. According to Likud's autonomy plan, the Israeli military was supposed to have retained control over security and remain in the OT permanently; water and state lands would have remained in Israeli hands; and Israeli citizens would have had a free hand to buy land and settle in the OT. The military government was to be replaced by a civil administration which would have conferred authority on an elected Palestinian administrative council, to be put in charge of municipal, educational, welfare, and economic issues. The autonomy bestowed on the Palestinian residents was to be personal, rather than territorial – that is, it was not to be bounded within distinct geographical limits or apply to the Israeli settlers.

In implementing this plan, Defense Minister Ariel Sharon and the head of the new civil administration, Professor Menachem Milson, never intended to carry out the transfer of powers to freely elected Palestinian representatives, or even remove the military government. In Milson's tortured interpretation, "civil administration is not an administration operated by civilians but an administration dealing with the affairs of civilians" (Oren 1983). Milson himself was appointed to his office by the "Commander of the Israeli Forces in Judea and Samaria" who now replaced the military governor of the area, though retaining his powers under the original proclamation of June 7, 1967 (Peretz 1986: 83–4). Milson abandoned Dayan's non-interventionist approach to local affairs which, in his view, had allowed the PLO to consolidate its position in the towns, and sought to turn the clock back on the PLO through a new creation: the Village Leagues (Milson 1981). The rural population, in Milson's view, was more amenable to Israeli influence and willing to co-operate with it, and he sought to gain their allegiance through financial patronage (Younis 2000: 147–56).

Not surprisingly, the elected Palestinian mayors and municipal councils boycotted the new civil administration which, on its part, deposed nine mayors and saw the remaining ones cease their operations. Palestinian resistance to the Israeli measures led from non-cooperation to rioting and to bloody clashes that were more intense than in previous years. The repressive measures taken against the protesters included curfews, expulsions, imprisonment without trial, house demolitions, and the closure of universities for months on end. Jewish settlers were armed by the IDF and organized into regional defense units, which acted in vigilante fashion against Palestinians. The Israeli authorities used this opportunity to replace the ousted mayors with officers of the Israeli military, and by so doing abolished all vestiges of Palestinian municipal autonomy. The Village Leagues also did not fulfill the hopes vested in them. Their members were viewed as collaborators by the Palestinian population and their leaders as corrupt. When Rabin became defense minister in the national unity government of 1984, the Village Leagues were quickly abandoned. The new structure of ruling the OT, however, was left intact.

A major reason for Palestinian resistance to Israeli rule was the third aspect of Israeli policy – settlement in the newly occupied territories – which Gazit mentioned but did not raise to the level of an equally important principle. Jewish settlement appeared to him merely as a "possibility" which somehow got out of hand and intensified the "rage and frustration of the Arab population of Judea and Samaria" (which, he stated, it was Israel's "most important achievement" to have normalized and routinized) (Gazit 1988).

Given the role played by colonization in the history of Israeli state formation, the new settlement drive could not have remained of marginal significance. As we saw in chapter 6, post-1967 settlement was aimed at establishing a permanent Israeli presence, and was set under way in the framework of the LSM's well-established demographic reasoning. Likud's autonomy plan coincided with the newly inaugurated Drobless settlement plan, which was based on a new legal conception of state lands as well. According to the new doctrine, Israel was the repository of state lands as these were defined by the Ottoman Land Law of 1858. Using the most sweeping interpretation of the Ottoman law, Israel laid claim to about 35 percent of the West Bank's land area, to be used for Jewish settlements (Benvenisti and Khayat 1988: 61).

A corollary of the new colonization policy was the 1982 invasion of Lebanon. After the failure to suppress the PLO in the West Bank, the invasion was undertaken with the aim of destroying its infrastructure in Lebanon and reducing its influence in the OT. In Sharon's words to Ambassador Samuel Lewis of the United States, the invasion was to "solve the problems of the West Bank and Gaza" (*New York Times*, May 28, 1985; cf. Shifer 1984: 93).

In the early 1980s the Palestinians were devoid of political rights. The various autonomy plans, aimed at finding a *modus vivendi* in which political power would remain in Israeli hands in return for partial self-government for the Palestinians, were rejected not only by the Palestinian resistance organizations but by a massive cross-section of the population in the OT. The Palestinians thus became superfluous within the Israeli citizenship incorporation framework, with the exception of the economic sphere, where, as we saw, they were exploited as workers, consumers, and tax-payers.

The limits of civility

The autonomy of the Israeli judicial system in addressing legal issues stemming from the occupation was very limited. There is little reason to believe that such autonomy is, or would be, stronger in most other countries. Still, one cannot but be struck by the unabashedly open fashion in which Israeli legal reasoning has come to reflect and justify the reality of military force (Benvenisti 1990; Shamir 1990; Shelef 1993).

By international law, in situations such as Israel's conquest of the West Bank and Gaza Strip, military authorities are required to enforce the legal system that existed prior to the conquest, and observe the international law of belligerent occupation in order to maintain "public order and security." Settling the occupier's own citizens on the occupied territory is illegal from the viewpoint of this body of law. Since Israel claimed to be observing the law of belligerent occupation as a good-will gesture (never having admitted that these territories were "occupied"; see below), it was required to resort to legal acrobatics in order to justify Jewish settlement in the OT. According to Eyal Benvenisti (1990), there were four areas in which Israeli law and courts had been used and misused in ways relevant to the OT:

(1) *The prescription of Israeli law to the Jewish settlements*: As if in a mirror image of the personal autonomy proposed for the Palestinians, various Israeli legal frameworks were extended to the persons of the Jewish settlers, as well as to the territory of their settlements, in order

to enable them to live in a "state within a state." This process was carried out by the military governors, acting as legislators, through "almost evasive techniques," in order to maintain the fiction of compliance with international law.

Israeli settlements were incorporated according to Israeli municipal law, excluding Arab-owned land even when surrounded by Jewish-owned land, and going beyond Israeli municipal law when that suited the settlers' interests. Thus, military governors have habitually appointed judges from Israeli courts to the civil courts that operate in the settlements. (Palestinians in the OT were tried in military courts.) These judges carry out their "extracurricular" activities outside the proper area of Israeli jurisdiction, but apply Israeli laws that have been incorporated in their entirety in the settlements in an extraterritorial manner. The Ministry of Education (controlled from 1977 to 1992, and then again from 1996 to 1999, by the NRP) went even further and placed the educational institutions of the settlements under its direct authority. For purposes of investment, the settlements have been considered "development regions" within Israel and receive the same preferential treatment.

(2) *Extraterritorial prescription of Israeli law*: Israeli law is also applied on a personal basis to non-settler Israelis when they are in the West Bank and is used to confer additional rights on the settlers. Individuals listed in the Israel Population Registry may exercise their right to vote in polling stations located in the OT. At the same time, they are within the jurisdiction of Israeli police and tax collectors.

With regard to legal issues concerning both Israelis and Palestinians, the choice of the law to be applied is highly selective. In most cases the Israeli law would apply. But labor contracts between Israeli employers and Palestinian workers, whether in the territories or within Israel, are governed by the law of Jordan or Gaza. In consequence, social benefits payable to Palestinian workers are handed over to the Israeli Treasury.

(3) *Prescription of Israeli laws to the Palestinian population*: The application of selective Israeli laws to the Palestinian population had the effect of making the economy of the OT subordinate to the Israeli economy. The legal tender in Gaza was the Israeli shekel; in the West Bank both the shekel and the Jordanian dinar. Imports from Israel to the OT were exempted from duties; direct Jordanian imports were subjected to the same duties as goods imported into Israel. Probably most far-reaching in revealing the depth of the ties between the two economies was the decision of the Supreme Court to uphold the order of the military authorities to extend the new Israeli VAT to

the OT. The reasoning of President of the Supreme Court Shamgar was that an exemption of the OT from the VAT would sever the ties between the two economies and adversely affect the welfare of the Palestinian population. Eyal Benvenisti cogently observed that the court took for granted the unification of the two markets, which had been implemented by the Israeli occupier.

(4) *The jurisdiction of the Supreme Court in the occupied territories*: The most vexing question concerning the "legal dualism" created by Israel in the OT has to do with the decision of the Israeli Supreme Court to extend its jurisdiction to the OT. The position of all Israeli governments has been that no legitimate sovereignty had been ousted by Israel from the West Bank and the Gaza Strip. While this position implies that the Fourth Geneva Convention of 1949 regarding belligerent occupation (incorporating the Hague Regulations of 1907) is not applicable in these regions, Israeli governments voluntarily consented to have this body of law applied by Israeli courts to its actions there. This policy of "having your cake and eating it too" spurred the Supreme Court's legally courageous decision to extend its jurisdiction to the new territories. And yet, the Supreme Court, not wanting its hands tied, adopted an equally ambivalent stand. As part of this approach the court held that the Geneva Convention was not customary law but conventional law, and therefore had to be incorporated by the Knesset into Israeli law in order to become binding in Israeli courts. Even though such incorporation never took place, the court decided to use the Convention, in addition to relevant Israeli law, in examining the actions of the authorities. The reasoning of the court was that it sought to give priority to humanitarian concerns even above and beyond international norms that call for the preservation of the status quo.

At the same time, "one of the court's clearest policies has been deference to the discretion of the military authorities whenever it invoked military considerations" (Benvenisti 1990: 53). It overturned only two decisions, in which security considerations were found to be an excuse for other motives – the Elon Moreh and the Jerusalem Electrical Co. cases – and only because it learned of the subterfuge from the authorities which, in these controversial cases, were divided among themselves. In consequence, the ability of the Palestinians to use the legal system to check abuses of power and arbitrary actions has been severely limited. The courts, observed Benvenisti, could not create legal equality under conditions of occupation. They could not even maintain its semblance: for example, when notices of land confiscation were not served to their Palestinian owners according to the law, the military authorities changed the law retroactively and rendered the courts ineffective (see also Shamir 1990; Shelef 1993).

While in general legality has served Israeli interests, in certain areas the extension of Israeli legislation had beneficial effects for individual Palestinians. The military government guaranteed paid sick leave and increased workmen's compensation; public health services were introduced; suffrage in municipal elections was extended to women and the poor; and capital punishment, legal under Jordanian law, was abolished. The Israeli court system was also seen by some Palestinian residents as of a higher quality than the local courts that use Jordanian law, but Israeli courts discouraged attempts to file in them claims against other Palestinians.

In spite of the few legal benefits the Palestinians did derive from the Israeli occupation, the overall effect of Israeli legal practice in the OT was clearly negative. In essence, the OT were annexed to Israel in the sphere of law, while the fiction of formal adherence to the law of belligerent occupation was maintained. What existed until the establishment of the Palestinian National Authority (and still exists in large areas of the West Bank still under Israeli rule), was not two legal systems, one in Israel and the other in the OT, but a dual system, under which Israeli law applied in full in Israel and selectively in the OT, in a manner designed to advance the interests of Israeli settlement. The supposed existence of two legal systems served to maintain the fiction of separateness and its derivative illusion of enlightened occupation. This fictitious legal narrative explains, in Benvenisti's words, why "political pressure within the Israeli body politic never reached unmanageable levels" (Benvenisti 1990: 58).

The two intifadas: Palestinian civil society and its impact on Israel

For twenty years, from 1967 to 1987, Israel was able to maintain a low-cost, low-casualty occupation. As Dayan had anticipated, "in return for employment possibilities in Israel and opportunities for trade and travel across the Jordan River, the Arabs of the territories assumed a generally passive role" (Lustick 1993b: 564). As with other authoritarian regimes, economic growth and attendant social rights, coupled with political repression, led to a temporary *modus vivendi* between oppressor and oppressed. An important factor in producing this unstable balance was the seeming absence of a clear Israeli annexation plan and the attendant uncertainty and openness with regard to the OT's future disposition. The individual legal limbo in which the Arab inhabitants of the West Bank and

Gaza found themselves thus reflected the ambiguous legal status of these areas as a whole. This strategy, of gradually constructing a new demographic and political reality while maintaining ambiguity about the final aim of the process, had served Zionist colonization well in the pre-1948 era. In the OT, however, the strategy began to be undermined by the massive land expropriations and indiscriminate repression that marked the Sharon–Milson era, during the second Begin government.

Prior to the first intifada, Palestinian resistance to Israeli occupation and colonization had assumed two forms. Armed resistance was carried out by Palestinian guerrilla organizations, affiliated with the PLO, that operated almost exclusively from outside the OT. Civil resistance was aimed at a host of targets but, with the exception of the periods right after the occupation and 1981–2, remained sporadic. Nonetheless, the Israeli authorities saw civil resistance as a threat to be suppressed, and continued to try and suppress it, with increased violence, over the years. While recognizing their failure to eradicate it, the authorities felt that they had at least effectively contained it.

Thus, when the first intifada broke out, demonstrating an ability to carry out sustained acts of resistance in spite of severe losses in casualties and income, the Israeli government's response was surprise and repeated assurances that the "disturbances" were being brought under control. Israelis failed to anticipate the ability of Palestinian society to sustain the intifada, because they could not accept either one of the two premises out of which it emerged and on which it was built.

The first premise was the definition of Palestinian aspirations in nationalist terms, inevitably leading to a Palestinian state in which Palestinians will enjoy the comprehensive rights of citizenship denied them under Israeli occupation. The four major constitutive political bodies associated with the PLO, the Fatah, the Democratic Front for the Liberation of Palestine, the Popular Front for the Liberation of Palestine, and the Palestinian Communist Party, had done the important preparatory work of articulating the national-political aspirations of a population devoid of legitimate political identity and expression. But the PLO had been severely mauled and set back by the 1982 Israeli invasion of Lebanon and the consequent relocation of its headquarters to Tunis. In fact, the intifada was a reaction not only against the intensification of Israeli attempts "to swallow" the OT, but against the PLO's inability to effectively halt that process as well.

The second premise was the self-organization of Palestinians, in spite of the repressive conditions of the occupation, in a congeries of organizations that McDowall has termed "the popular movement" (McDowall 1989: 110–17). The first intifada moved rapidly from a series of spontaneous and sporadic acts of confrontation to an organized uprising with its distinct dynamics and leadership structure. This expansion and continuity were based on a dense network of preexisting voluntary organizations that had sought to provide alternatives to, or lead to the attainment of, the very citizenship rights Israel was denying the Palestinians or granting as privileges to its collaborators. These bodies added up to an underground society of voluntary self-help institutions. Thus the first intifada was a civic uprising, and was carried on the back of civic institutions. In McDowall's cogent summary:

While the health, agricultural and voluntary work committees remained social rather than political in their programs, they blazed a trail that others widened into a national highway. As a result, almost as soon as Israel tried to suppress the Uprising with curfews, blockades and violent policing, the community organized itself along the lines the popular movement already prescribed. (McDowall 1989: 118)

The organizational principles on which these civic institutions were based varied: some were geographically based in refugee camps, villages, or neighborhoods; others were functional or occupational; many were affiliated with political parties or religious bodies (Peretz 1990: 87). Among them were trade unions, women's organizations, youth groups in the refugee camps, physicians', lawyers', and students' bodies, and manifold other grassroots organizations. This was at once "the backbone of the uprising" (Kuttab 1988) and the framework of Palestinian society as it sought to dissociate itself from the institutions of the Israeli occupation.

Just as in Israel the construction of citizenship was initially affiliated with the institutions of nationalist pioneering, so within occupied Palestine institution building was a major element in the project of nation building. The creation of a self-organized Palestinian society, a civil society (in the sense of being autonomous from the Israeli state), was done in the framework of the nationalist struggle and carried its imprint, for better or worse.

The outbreak of a Palestinian civil rebellion undergirded by nationalist aspirations was a historic landmark for Palestinian society. But the first intifada, as Lustick pointed out, was chronologically also "the first of many mass-based, illegal, non-violent or semiviolent challenges to non-democratic governing structures to burst upon the world scene at the end of the 1980s." It was at one with the Algerian, Jordanian, Burmese, Baltic, and East European movements which were widely described as "struggles by oppressed peoples rising up against the coercive power of states to demand political and economic rights" (Lustick 1993b: 561).

As in these other cases, the first intifada was civil resistance by people deprived of rights, and in this sense similar to democratic protests, though nationally motivated. A few weeks into it, a small, self-selected group of Palestinian intellectuals, operating with the consent of the unified leadership of the uprising, published a list of the movement's fourteen demands. The group asserted that Israeli recognition of the PLO, and of the Palestinians' national right of self-determination leading to the establishment of a Palestinian state, were the paramount goals of the uprising. The demands, however, also included the full range of citizenship rights in their manifold manifestations, of which Palestinians had been deprived. In the economic sphere, it was demanded that Israel remove restrictions on industrial and agricultural development, and release the funds deducted from the wages of Palestinian workers employed in Israel as national insurance fees; in the political domain, an end to political restrictions and new municipal elections were demanded; and in the domain of civil rights, an end was sought to the oppressive measures used in the attempts to suppress the intifada. In more general fashion, the document demanded that the international conventions that are supposed to regulate the treatment of civilians under military occupation be respected (Peretz 1990: 107–8).

The first intifada strained the resources of the Israeli state, both materially and morally, at the same time as the state's mobilizational capacity was being undermined by economic and social liberalization (see chap. 9, below). Economically, the intifada affected Israeli society within the pre-1967 borders in five different ways: it caused an increase in military expenditures and a decline in Israeli exports to the OT, in the inflow of labor and tax revenues from them, and in the volume of tourism. The overall economic effect of these changes is hard to determine, because the Israeli economy had gone into recession in the middle of 1987. Still, it is estimated that Israel lost about 2–2.5 percent of its gross domestic product (or about one billion US dollars) in 1988–9 due to the intifada, most of it in 1988. After 1989 the Israeli economy adjusted itself successfully to the new situation and entered a period of economic growth due, primarily, to massive immigration from the former Soviet Union (Razin and Sadka 1993; Rosen 1991; Tessler 1991; Lustick 1993a: 394; chap. 12, below).

The political effects of the first intifada have been longer lasting. The uprising resurrected the Green Line in the consciousness of most Israelis and brought to almost complete halt travel by Israeli Jews, other than settlers, in the OT. This highlighted the failure of the efforts, led since 1977 by Likud governments, to establish the inseparability of the West Bank and Gaza from Israel as a hegemonic notion in Israeli political culture. As personal security for Jews deteriorated on both sides of the Green Line, the argument that holding on to the OT was essential for Israel's security also lost much of its force (Tessler 1991; Lustick 1993a).

Morally, the brutal methods used by Israel's security forces to try and suppress the intifada forced the Israeli public to face, in a way it had never had to do before, the discrepancy between the two systems of rule prevailing on the two sides of the Green Line. This resulted, among other things, in a small but expanding movement of primarily reserve soldiers refusing to serve in the OT. Other reservists were complaining loudly about the increased burden of active service caused by the uprising. In addition, the amount of time devoted to training, by both regular and reserve army units, suffered serious cutbacks, leading military experts to predict a decline in military preparedness.

Thus, "the intifada appears to have further highlighted the inherent 'curse' of the occupation of the territories, whereas the 'blessing' aspects were more evident early on" (Shamir and Shamir 2000: 182). As a result, public support for continuation of the status quo in the OT declined from about 40 percent in 1987 to about 25 percent at the end of 1989. Similarly, the percentage of Israeli Jews refusing to relinquish control over the West Bank and Gaza declined from over 50 percent in 1987 to about 40 percent at the end of 1990, while the number of those willing to do so grew from about 30 percent to over 50 percent during the same time period. Agreement to the establishment of a Palestinian state and to negotiations with the PLO also widened from the beginning of the intifada, from 20 to 30 percent and from 40 to 60 percent, respectively (Shamir and Shamir 2000: 170–4; Tessler 1991: 75; Arian 1995; cf., however, Yuchtman-Yaar 1993).

In sum, the first intifada, by undermining political stability within the Israeli control system, began to enhance the realization that the benefits of colonial control were outweighed by its costs. The curtailment of the employment of non-citizen Palestinians had a passing economic effect on Israel (and a very significant and lasting one on the Palestinians), but it revived a political lesson from the pre-1948 period – that the goal of "pure" or "homogenous settlement" aiming at the separation of the two peoples was the only way of ensuring security for the Jews. In this way, the protracted Palestinian uprising set limits to the colonial project and contributed decisively to Israel's willingness to move in the direction of recognizing the PLO and Palestinian national rights. The Oslo Declaration of Principles (DOP) of September 1993 was still only an interim plan, motivated in large measure by Israel's desire to bring the intifada to a halt. In that spirit, Israel agreed to withdraw in short order from the Gaza Strip and Jericho, and followed that by withdrawal from all other Arab cities in 1995 and 1996 and from most of Hebron in 1997. The DOP, however, did not lay down the conditions for the partitioning of Palestine.

The DOP provided a framework for a transitional period of five years, at the end of which negotiations on the permanent status of the OT would lead to the implementation of Security Council resolutions 242 and 338. Section 3 of article V of the DOP stated that "these negotiations shall cover remaining issues, including: Jerusalem, refugees, settlements, security arrangements, borders ..." During the interim period control was to be divided between Israel and the PLO. For example, article VIII set up a dual system of policing: A "strong Palestinian police force" was to be established to guarantee the public order and internal security of the Palestinians, while Israel was to continue "to carry ... the responsibility for overall security of Israelis" in the West Bank and Gaza. As it turned out, however, instead of building trust between Israelis and Palestinians, the interim period was punctured by a series of postponements, crises, and acts of violence which destroyed the trust that had been established by the DOP.

It is not our intention to provide an overview of Israeli–Palestinian relations from 1993 to 2000, only to examine those causes for the failure of the Oslo process that impinge on our analysis of Israeli citizenships and their transformations. With Ehud Barak's election as prime minister in 1999, it seemed that a push would be made for completing the Oslo process and turning to the resolution of the outstanding issues between the two sides. Such an attempt was made at the second Camp David conference in July 2000, but it failed to produce an agreement. On September 28, 2000 the intifada which the Oslo DOP was supposed to have ended began anew.

The al-Aksa intifada, as the second uprising is called, was not only more surprising to most Israelis, but also more disappointing than the first. It demonstrated the extent to which the Palestinians had lost faith in the peace process and, therefore, that the Oslo process was a wasted opportunity. The new intifada has been conducted not by Palestinian civil society alone, but by the Palestinian Authority, with its many police forces, as well. (The precise division of labor between the two entities is not yet clear at the time of writing.) It is therefore more threatening and violent than the first. Israeli retaliation, most likely impelled by the disappointment of Camp David as well, has also been more lethal than during the first intifada. Within the first fourteen weeks of the uprising, 301 non-citizen Palestinians, 43 Israeli Jews, and 13 citizen Palestinians were killed and numerous more wounded. By May 24, 2001, 481 non-citizen Palestinians and 78 Israelis had been killed (*Haaretz*, May 25, 2001).

What was most shocking to Israelis was that Barak's seemingly maximalist concessions, which included compromising over Jerusalem and uprooting a sizable portion of the settlements, led to violence, rather than peace. The magnitude of Barak's concessions, especially on Jerusalem, had shattered his parliamentary majority even before the Camp David summit. But their rejection by the Palestinians, and the outbreak of a new intifada, undermined his public support completely and forced him to resign and call new elections, at a moment when his chances of reelection had become minuscule. Paradoxically, while the al-Aksa intifada has sown confusion in the minds of many Israelis, no other event in recent history has thrown more sharply into relief the distinction between Israel's Jewish and liberal-democratic facets and their respective citizenship discourses, while at the same time demonstrating that the fundamentals of Israel's underlying colonial character continue to constrain the possibilities of choosing between these two contradictory options (Ophir 2001).

The al-Aksa intifada began in response to Ariel Sharon's visit to the Temple Mount on September 28, 2000, a provocative visit because this was the site over which the Camp David talks had reportedly collapsed. Although incited by Sharon's visit, the al-Aksa intifada was an expression of frustration with the solutions offered to all three unsolved issues – refugees, settlements, and Jerusalem – that had clouded the Camp David summit. We will examine each one of these issues in turn, relying, necessarily, on media reports of President Clinton's verbal "bridging proposals" of December 2000. Since the exact terms of Clinton's proposals have not been made public, our examination will be of a general nature only. (The best accounts to appear so far are in Malley and Agha 2001; Sontag 2001.)

Jerusalem

The basic principle underlying the proposed territorial arrangement in Jerusalem is the traditional Zionist principle of pure settlement colonialism – national separation: Arab-populated areas are Palestinian, while Jewish-populated areas are Israeli (*Haaretz* editorial, December 26, 2000; BADIL Resource Center 2001). Such territorial partition would translate into political terms the current geographical layout of the city's demographic reality. This approach is not new; most of Israel's boundaries were determined during the 1948 war by the layout of Jewish settlements and towns. Now the same principle would be applied to Jerusalem, and as we shall see in the next section, would mean that Jerusalem was no different than the rest of the West Bank territories conquered during the 1967 war. From Israel's perspective the Jerusalem that would be under its control would be the largest in Jewish history, and the vast settlements around it, which house nearly 200,000 Israeli settlers, would not only be left in place, but would be used to demarcate the Israeli border. Within the Old City the proposal seems to call for the application of the same principle: The Jewish Quarter would be under Israeli sovereignty (with a corridor to the Western Wall, leading through the Armenian Quarter) and the Muslim and Christian Quarters would come under Palestinian sovereignty. Although such a territorial partition would recognize Israeli expansion since 1967, the withdrawal from Arab neighborhoods would crown it "concessions."

At the same time, Jewish construction in the Jerusalem area, namely, the ringing of Arab East Jerusalem by Jewish townships, makes it difficult to apply to the Palestinian population the principle of maximum territorial contiguity laid down by the Clinton proposals. Whereas some of the Palestinian neighborhoods would remain isolated islands, Israeli sovereign territory would be contiguous. At the same time, the same principle of partition would compromise the security of some of the new Jewish townships, which would be adjacent to sovereign Palestinian territory both in Jerusalem and in the West Bank.

The distinct aspect of Jerusalem's territorial partition concerns its religious sites, above all the Temple Mount/Haram al-Sharif plateau. The proposed division of sovereignty on the Temple Mount is not clear from the published reports, but it seems that the Palestinians, or some representative body of the Arab world, would have a measure of sovereignty over the Haram, while Israel would have sovereignty over the Western Wall, one of the walls supporting the compound. Though the details will affect the likelihood of reaching an agreement, for our purposes the significant development is Israel's willingness to consider giving up its symbolic sovereignty over the Temple Mount (the area has remained under effective Muslim control since 1967). This willingness expresses a preference for the principle of modern statehood over religious identity. The clash between the two principles was captured in two commentaries published in *Haaretz* on the same day. Uzi Benziman wrote that "the dispute over the Temple Mount is reminiscent of a tribal fight more than a struggle over the borders and identities of two modern nations; it is more appropriate to the age of the Crusades than to the computer age" (*Haaretz*, December 31, 2000). In contrast, Yair Sheleg stated that a voluntary concession of parts of the Old City and Temple Mount to a vastly inferior adversary defies the logic of Jewish history, to stubbornly refuse "to surrender conspicuous emblems of identity, even if the cost of such obstinacy is life itself" (*Haaretz*, December 31, 2000). As these contending positions illustrate, by subjugating sovereignty over the Temple Mount to the goal of diffusing the Israeli–Palestinian conflict, the state of Israel would win out over *Eretz Yisrael*, and liberal citizenship would win out over religiously accented ethno-nationalist citizenship. It is far from clear, however, that there is a majority in Israel that would support such a decision, or that the decision would not generate a strong backlash and movement to reverse it.

Settlements

The plan discussed at the second Camp David summit and the subsequent bridging proposal would allow Israel to annex settlements housing about 80 percent of the Israeli settlers, which lie in three blocs along the Green Line and comprise about 4–6 percent of the area of the West Bank (10 percent if the territory annexed as part of Jerusalem is included). Israel would be expected to compensate the Palestinians for the annexation through an equivalent of 1–3 percent of the West Bank area along the Gaza Strip. The settlements in the Jordan rift and the rift itself would remain under Israeli control for three to six years and then revert to Palestinian sovereignty. All settlements in the Gaza Strip, and the West Bank settlements not included in the three annexed blocs, comprising about 50,000 settlers, most of them in Gush Emunim settlements, would be evacuated. Such an approach would, as in Jerusalem, codify the accomplishments of Israeli colonization, leading to the extension of the pure, or homogenous, settlement model. It would also, however, "punish" Israel for its limited application of the model. The decline of the republican colonization drive, undertaken in the past by a virtuous citizenry, and the limited appeal of the mixed religio-colonial and liberal–colonial drives, set the parameters of Israel's proposed borders. A *Haaretz* editorial cogently assessed the logic behind these boundaries: "Demographics, diplomatic conditions and psychological reasons resulted in the failure of Israel's ambition to annex – if not legally, then practically – the West Bank and the Gaza Strip. The occupied territories remained Palestinian for the most part, and this fundamental fact dictates the need for an agreement, and also its nature" (*Haaretz*, editorial, December 26, 2000).

But what appears to the Israeli side as a weak and ultimately failed settlement drive is far too much for the Palestinians. They demand the return of all territories occupied in 1967 as a principle guiding the agreement, and reject the use of the settlement blocs, set up through an illegal colonial undertaking, as a basis for border rectification between the two sides. One of the greatest frustrations of the Palestinians with the peace process since Oslo has been the ever-continuing expansion of the Israeli settlement map. No matter whether Rabin, Peres, Netanyahu, or Barak served as Israel's prime minister, the result was always the same: by the end of their terms Palestinians controlled less land than before, and the number of Jewish settlers grew. As we have seen in chapter 6, the number of Jewish settlers doubled since the Oslo process began; it was as if the Oslo framework had been used by Israel as a cover for digging in more deeply in the OT, rather than as the beginning of Israeli withdrawal; as if a drunk had promised to quit but could not keep away from the bottle. Nothing better illustrates the grotesque and irrational character of continued settlement than the village of Netzarim, a site of repeated and lethal confrontations during the al-Aksa intifada. Though Netzarim is situated on an important junction in the Gaza Strip, it is an isolated outpost: surrounded on all sides by territory under the control of the Palestinian Authority. Nevertheless, this small settlement has grown by more than 100 percent, to about four hundred people, since the Oslo process began. In early summer 2000 a new neighborhood of private homes was dedicated in the settlement, in the presence of Barak's housing minister, Yitzhak Levy of the NRP.

The extent to which Israeli colonization has disrupted Palestinian personal and communal life, and generated Palestinian hostility, has been dramatically demonstrated by the clear focus of the al-Aksa intifada on settlements, settlers, and the roads connecting the settlements with Israel and with one another.

For many days the [settlers] were virtual prisoners in their communities, if not in their very homes. Mail and public transport were disrupted, and travel in armed convoys was "advised" by the IDF . . . [Unlike the first] intifada, which progressed in incremental stages both in intensity and breadth, this latest revolt descended upon the settlements in a bolt of full fury. West Bank settlers, who adjusted to the power of the intifada over time, by, for example, installing shatterproof glass in vehicles in response to the evolution of Palestinian tactics, were initially stunned into paralysis by both the scale and tactics of recent violence. (Aronson 2000)

Israeli troops defend these settlements, and without their around-the-clock protection the future of the settlements would be sealed.

The partitioning of Palestine between Israel and a new Palestinian state is a process of partial decolonization that would mark the end of the Zionist colonization process that began over a century ago. This would signal, simultaneously, the final demise of the republican project of state building through settlement and of any claims to the virtuous citizenship that sustained it and derived its prestige and hegemony from it.

Refugees

Whereas during the second Camp David summit the main bone of contention seems to have been the disposition of sovereignty over the Temple Mount, since then the "right of return" of the Palestinian refugees forced out of their homes in 1948 has come to center stage. This was a result of demonstrations and petition-drives by Palestinian refugees themselves, who were fearful that their leadership and the international community would ignore them. So far in this study we have discussed two Palestinian populations: those who are Israeli citizens and those Palestinians who live in the OT. Each of these groups appeared in a different peripheral concentric circle around the Jewish core of Israeli society and possessed different rights: The Israeli citizens belong in the liberal framework and, consequently, have most civil rights, limited political, and even more limited social rights; the OT residents, bereft of citizenship, possess only the most minimal rights, occasional protection by the Supreme Court, and, if they work in Israel, also some social rights. But there is also a third group: Palestinians in refugee camps outside the OT, who are not within the Israeli "control system," but whose fate, nevertheless, has been influenced, not to say fundamentally determined, by Israeli policies, and whose own actions had an impact on Israel. Most of the *fedayeen* in the 1950s, the fighters of the PLO and its affiliates, and the man- and womanpower of the first and second intifadas were supplied by Palestinians in refugee camps (both within and outside the OT), who are at the bottom of their respective societies and have the least to lose from the disruption of the status quo. Their commitment to remember their homes, in the absence of new ones, and willingness to fight, have been the major motor force of Palestinian resistance to Israel.

The only "right" these stateless and citizenshipless refugees possess is the "right of return" anchored in paragraph 3 of UN General Assembly resolution 194 of December 1948. The maximalist version of that resolution seems to grant a right to the refugees, some 200,000 to 300,000 of whom are estimated to still be alive today, and to their descendants, to return to their homes and properties, or receive compensation for them. But there are also other, less stringent, interpretations, which render this right more conditional. The total number of people involved is also given to dispute, with conservative estimates putting it at 3.5 million. Those who fare worst among them are the 300,000 refugees living in Lebanon, since as non-citizens they are barred from receiving social services and are allowed only menial jobs. In Jordan the refugees have been admitted to citizenship and are partly assimilated into a Hashemite Jordanian identity. Among Palestinians who succeeded in leaving the camps, some have provided funds, others intellectual leadership to the struggle for return.

Even if a mutually acceptable territorial formula is found, the issue of refugees has a life and logic of its own. The refugee question has been "invisible" to most Israelis, but not to others. Israel, even under Barak, has not accepted any share of the responsibility for the birth of the refugee problem during the 1948 war, although it did express some empathy with their predicament. On Israel's understanding, the "subtext" of the Oslo agreement was that in return for recognition of a Palestinian state in part of the OT, the PLO would drop the demand for recognizing the refugees' "right of return." This view dovetailed with the Israeli peace camp's slogan of "two states for two people," which would leave intact Israel's Jewish ethno-nationalist character. A recent manifesto by Peace Now, signed by some of the most prominent intellectuals in the Israeli peace camp and addressed to the Palestinian leadership, clarified that "we shall never be able to agree to the return of the refugees into the borders of Israel, for the meaning of such a return would be the elimination of the State of Israel" (advertisement in *Haaretz*, January 2, 2001). The signatories agreed to individual humanitarian gestures for family reunification, but not to massive return.

Evidently, then, the limit to Israel's willingness to decolonize the OT is the protection of its ethno-nationalist character. Palestinians can be citizens of Israel within the liberal citizenship framework, but that framework is to remain secondary to the ethno-national one. Israel cannot let refugees in, because it cannot "digest" them for another reason: Palestinians are peripheral citizens in Israel, and increasing the number of such citizens, who are less likely to be intimidated politically than those fewer Palestinians who had lived under Israeli military government until 1966, would pose a grave political threat. Recognition of the right of return could happen only within a strictly liberal citizenship framework, but this has not yet been extended even to Israel's own Palestinian citizens. Israeli liberalism, as we have been arguing, is based on colonial exclusion.

President Clinton's bridging proposal endorsed the right of the refugees to return, but instead of returning to their "homes" (which, in most cases, exist no more) they could go "back" to their "homeland," in effect to part of it – to the Palestinian state. It is expected that the majority of the refugees, on whose behalf the Palestinian resistance has been waged, would choose either compensation or resettlement in other countries. Compensation would be provided by the international community. Resettlement could take place in present host countries, such as Jordan and Syria, or in other countries willing to absorb the refugees. Lebanon has adamantly refused to integrate its Palestinian refugee population, and it is far from clear that other Arab countries would be willing to do so. It is expected that over ten years about 500,000 refugees, mostly from the Lebanese camps, would be resettled in the state of Palestine. Israel, on its part, would admit around 100,000 refugees through a combination of family reunification and a lottery system, and settle them near the Gaza

Strip. The majority of Palestinians, however, would be unlikely to seek new homes in Israel.

Without addressing the needs and aspirations of the Palestinians who have fewest rights – the inhabitants of the refugee camps – no closure is possible for the conflict. In a world of nation-states, a population without citizenship and a national home is a vulnerable population and a source of grave instability to the states where it resides. Although it seems that the focus on the plight and rights of the refugees of the 1948 war has led to an impasse, the refugee population is not made of one cloth. Danny Rabinowitz has suggested an innovative approach to the problem, based on a number of distinctions:

between Palestinian refugees who lack citizenship and those who have received citizenship from any country since 1948, . . . according to their living conditions and their chances of rehabilitation in their current homes, . . . between those who were exiled in 1948 and family members who were born in exile, between the right to citizenship and the right of residence, and to link all of these distinctions to the matter of monetary compensation. (*Haaretz*, January 4, 2001)

His overall argument is that Israelis are implicated in the refugee problem and should begin to address it seriously.

It also seems that the central attention given to the refugees' right of return derives in part from the seemingly unresolvable issues of Jerusalem and settlements. When the peace process is at an impasse and violence flares up, those least reconciled to compromise on the Palestinian side revisit the "original" grievance, the *Nakba*, or dispossession, of 1948, just as the extremists on the Israeli side go back to the religious dimension of the Holy Land. Linked compromises on the three issues – Jerusalem, settlements and boundaries, and the refugees' "right of return" – could go a long way towards removing seemingly immovable obstacles in all three areas.

Conclusion

The two intifadas raise the question, already touched on in chapter 4, above, of why only the Palestinians in the OT have taken active part in the uprisings, while Israel's Palestinian citizens have not. This question strikes at the heart of the concept of "incorporation regime" and, thus, at the heart of the conceptual framework developed in this book. Palestinian refugees outside the OT, who have no access to any rights in Israel, remain implacably hostile to it. For them, any accommodation between Israel and those Palestinians who stand to gain citizenship rights in their own state, at the expense of the refugees' only right – "the right of return" – will not be acceptable. The Palestinians of the OT were allowed to partake of only marginal aspects of Israeli citizenship. Even co-operation with Israel's occupation regime could not lead them to admission into the Israeli body politic and, therefore, collaborators were left as obvious and easy targets for nationalist retribution. Their demand for territorial and political separation indicates that where the gap in citizenship rights is widest – that is, where two legal systems, granting different rights, are applied to two collectivities within the same incorporation regime – resistance among the excluded will be strongest. Citizen Palestinians, who do enjoy a modicum of Israeli citizenship rights, chose to utilize these rights in order to support the intifada materially and politically, without, however, joining the uprising itself. Their choice was endorsed by the leadership of the intifada and the PLO (Rouhana 1991).

Thus, while the colonial dimension of Zionism indeed makes it unwilling "in principle as well as in practice, to consider non-Jews, and particularly Arabs, as capable of becoming full-fledged members of the Israeli-Jewish national community" (Lustick 1993b: 577), this holds true with respect only to the republican and ethno-nationalist discourses of citizenship. Israel's liberal citizenship discourse does afford non-Jews certain citizenship rights, including the right of political expression. And indeed, Israel's Palestinian citizens who stayed away from active participation in the first intifada played a crucial role in shoring up Rabin's minority government during the time of the signing and initial implementation of the Oslo Accords.

Part 3

The emergence of civil society

8 Agents of political change

Ian Lustick has listed three conditions as necessary in order "to overthrow an established ideologically hegemonic conception or explain its breakdown":

- A severe contradiction between the conception advanced as hegemonic and the stubborn realities it purports to describe;
- An appropriately fashioned alternative interpretation of political reality capable of reorganizing competition to the advantage of particular groups;
- Dedicated political-ideological entrepreneurs who can operate successfully where fundamental assumptions of political life have been thrown open to question, and who see better opportunities in competition over basic "rules of the game" than in competition for marginal advantage 123–4)

So far in this book we have shown how the republican citizenship discourse had been confronted with greater and greater difficulties in trying to balance the "stubborn realities" of Israel's hierarchical and "sticky" incorporation regime with the democratic aspects of its government. We have also described the two competing conceptions vying to take the place of the republican discourse as the hegemonic conception – the ethno-national and liberal discourses – and the groups that stood to gain from a redefinition of the rules of the game in one or the other direction. In this chapter we provide a glimpse into the sense of malaise that came to afflict important sections of the veteran Ashkenazi elite, the main bearer and beneficiary of the republican discourse, and then focus on the political entrepreneurs who have been, or sought to be, the agents of change in a liberal direction. In the rest of part 3 we analyze the interrelated changes that have taken place in three key areas of social life: the economy, constitutional law, and the provision of social rights.

The specter of decline

The 1973 war and the oil-price revolution that was attendant upon it plunged Israel into a comprehensive crisis which would cause the downfall of the Labor Party and, ultimately, compel a far-reaching reexamination and transformation of significant elements of the country's incorporation regime. The central arch of Israel's citizenship structure, the republican pioneering discourse, came to be viewed more and more as a dead-weight remnant of the past, and the institutions that sustained it gradually began to lose tasks, budgets, and prestige. As a result, their ability to operate as a coherent regime, that is, their interlocking and mutually supportive character, which was one of the keys to their longevity and endurance (even after the loss of political power by Labor) was seriously impaired. Institutions formed after 1948 and not fully integrated into the republican institutional regime, or working at cross-purposes to it, consequently acquired greater freedom of operation. A period of institutional struggle, entrepreneurship, and innovation ensued, replacing the LSM's institutional regime with a plural and conflictual institutional patchwork and a looser citizenship structure.

A brief survey of leading Israeli opinion in the 1980s, a decade whose first half was marked by the Lebanon war and by very high monetary inflation, will reveal gloomy assessments as to the state of Israeli society. Interestingly, however, this pessimism already revealed signs of the direction of Israel's future transformation, because it was based on a comparative perspective that placed Israel in a global framework.

Arie Shachar and Maya Choshen used the World Bank's national indicators for measuring the change in Israel's relative position in the global context between 1965 and 1989. Their study found that in terms of the provision of certain social services, such as health care and higher education, Israel ranked among the very top throughout the whole period: it was 23rd in 1965 and 22nd in 1986. And yet their detailed analysis demonstrated that Israel had been, and remained, lodged between the upper layer of the developing and the bottom layer of the developed countries. Not only had it failed to make it into the ranks of the developed countries by 1989, but "the disparities between Israel and the countries of the developed world are growing, while the disparities with the upper section of the developing countries are decreasing." The prolonged continuation of this trend was likely, therefore, to move Israel from its "intermediate position ... into the large group of developing countries" (Shachar and Choshen 1993: 324).

In a more narrowly but aptly conceived comparison, Yoram Ben-Porath, a leading Israeli economist and rector of the Hebrew University, wrote in 1986 that "Israel, which until recently seemed to belong to the ... group [of East Asian states], displays symptoms of premature aging, combining the structural problems of some of the richer and older European countries with inflation, balance-of-payment crises, and foreign indebtedness observed in some Latin American countries" (Ben-Porath 1986: 13; see also, Barnett 1996: 56). Dov Lautman, president of the Manufacturers' Association of Israel (MAI), surveying a single year's economic performance, spoke of 1988 as a year of missed opportunities, as manifested in a series of disheartening statistics. Though pleading the special case of industry, and especially of its export sector, whose profitability, he argued, was impaired by government indifference, Lautman placed these in a broader context. Even though the previous year had been a boom year globally, he argued, Israeli exporters were unable to take advantage of this boom, and consequently, in his words: "international trade continues to grow, while we are at zero percent growth. Another year like this one and it will be exceedingly difficult to get out of this imbroglio" (Manufacturers' Association of Israel 1989). In his assessment, as in that of many others, continued stagnation was doubly perilous, since the world economy, and especially international trade, were expanding and thus increasing the gap between Israel's economy and the economies of other countries that were better able to ride the wave of expansion.

This mood was typical of the fifteen years between 1974 and 1989, when important sectors of the Israeli economy were battered by severe downturns. The GDP remained relatively stagnant (Economic Models 1993: 6)[1] and the first half of the 1980s, according to Economic Models Inc., an economic forecasting firm, "was the worst period in the history of Israeli economy [as] both inflation and the foreign debt seemed to spiral out of control" (Economic Models 1993: 31). According to economists Assaf Razin and Efraim Sadka, "the period which started with the [1973] Yom Kippur War and lasted until the ... wave of immigration [from the former Soviet Union] which began in 1990 is known as the 'lost years'" (Razin and Sadka 1993: 16).

The sense of anxiety and helplessness in the face of decline were palpable among the participants at a conference devoted to "Trends in the Transformation of Israeli Society" held on December 21–22, 1989 at the Hebrew University in Jerusalem.[2] Using different theoretical perspectives and conceptual frameworks to assess the directions in which Israeli

---

[1] Even "the growth of industrial production ... fell from an average of 12% in the 1960s and early 1970s to 3.8% in 1973–1987, accompanied by falling productivity" (Bar 1990: 34).

[2] This conference was attended by Gershon Shafir.

society was likely to move in the 1990s, the speakers, some of Israel's leading academics and intellectuals among them, mounted the rostrum and one after another displayed a rare consensus that Israeli society was in dire straits, losing its place and way in the world.

Nathan Rotenstreich, a renowned philosopher, argued that "Israel is an increasingly backward society fighting an outdated war [i.e. the first intifada] which, like a self-fulfilling prophecy, may indeed become a war of survival with the chance of winning decreasing with time." A political scientist, Yechezkel Dror, concluded that Israel suffered from "stalemate and blockage" because of the Palestinian issue, the demographic threat of high Arab birthrates, and a possible chain of wars with Arab states. Israel's creation involved massive intervention in history, he added, which always leaves a legacy of long-term problems. In Israel's case these are far from being solved; on the contrary, Israel has not yet created a critical mass of accomplishments which could guarantee its survival.

Other participants asserted that in a world in upheaval, which was, nevertheless, full of promise, Israel was singled out by its rigidity. One reason given was a restatement of the functionalist "overburden" thesis: the transfer of governmental power from Labor to Likud in 1977, it was argued, did not entail a corresponding transfer of real power. Instead, a political stalemate prevailed between the two leading parties with regard to the future of the OT, which finds its expression "in the waning of political authority in Israeli society." Loss of authority was seen as undermining not only attempts to solve, or at least regulate, the Israeli–Palestinian conflict, over which Israelis disagreed, but also issues over which there was overwhelming consensus. Many of the participants painfully pointed to what they perceived as Israel's demonstrated inability to prepare for the expected influx of hundreds of thousands of Jewish immigrants from the Soviet Union. This was seen as particularly tragic, since not only was Israel created in order to absorb persecuted Jews, but such massive influx was likely to stimulate the economy and shore up Israel's ability to cope with its external enemies. In Israel of the late 1980s, however, immigration was seen as a burden, not a boon.

Lack of development and forward movement in a dynamic world, it was repeatedly emphasized, meant decline and backtracking. Several professors provided a sad litany of deterioration in their respective fields: Israeli higher education was in a precarious state, environmental issues were receiving scant attention, the ethos of science was eroding, the bonds between military and civilian society were full of cracks, Israel's strategic doctrine had collapsed, the Supreme Court was allowing the reality of de facto annexation to pull the law in its train, and the ongoing post-1973 recession was dragging the GDP into permanent stagnation.

In the summary plenum, S. N. Eisenstadt pointed out that he had not seen such uniform gloom in past conferences. Why now? he demanded to know. Although in the participants' view the major causes of the impasse lay in the past, either in the 1967 war or in the rise of Likud to power in 1977, in his view, it was the intifada that tipped the scale and subdued the spirit of his colleagues. Taking the argument further, Zeev Sternhell argued that the brutality of the Israeli response to the intifada was the outcome of Israel's post-1967 colonial path. In other societies in such profound crisis, even if they were previously thoroughly liberal, intolerant nationalism had invariably prevailed and in many places democracy itself was overthrown. If the situation did not change, he concluded, it was hard to believe that the results in Israel would be any different.

This crisis of confidence, which characterized the decade-and-a-half from 1973 to 1989, reflected, however, not so much an "overburdened" Israeli polity as the crisis of the LSM's colonial state-building institutions, which were based (and not only since 1967) on the notions of pioneering virtue and republican citizenship. During the previous three-and-a-half decades most institutions of the LSM had shed their state-building role and become ever more explicitly sites of patronage and control. None of these institutions functioned as effectively as they had in the past, and many of them racked up large financial deficits. Appeals to their historical glory rang ever more hollow, and the LSM's privileges which they protected were ever more resented. But their "stickiness" and inertia were all evident. The day of reckoning, through which some of them could have perhaps been salvaged, kept being postponed. Moreover, in a manner similar to the USSR, efforts to stem their decline frequently had the opposite effect: they exposed long-evolving debilities or indirectly weakened the institutions. Some purported reforms amounted to conscious assaults on the institutions they allegedly sought to rescue. Each component of the LSM's institutional regime experienced this crisis and willy-nilly entered, or was compelled onto, the path of transformation.

Beneath the crisis, however, new possibilities were evolving. Institutions that were not part of the LSM, but were created after the establishment of the state, and thus less saddled with the burden of the past and only partially integrated into its institutional regime – the Supreme Court, the Bank of Israel, newly established liberal political parties and groups, and the business community's various bodies, as well as religious institutions that had come into prominence since 1967 – became entrepreneurs and innovators in seeking to position themselves at the center of a new institutional framework. Even from within the Labor Party the feeling that saving the party meant abandoning its republican institutions and heritage was brewing. In retrospect it can be seen that these institutional initiatives and transformations precipitated the demise of the LSM's institutional regime and so marked the end of the vestigial era of republican pioneering citizenship.

The liberal discourse reinvigorated

In Israel the liberal citizenship discourse was historically the weakest of the three in terms of its social grounding and organized political expression. Even though most of the Jewish capital invested in Palestine in the period of the Yishuv was private, most owners of that capital stayed away from the country and funneled their investments through the Zionist institutions. The ascendancy of the LSM to a position of hegemony in the Yishuv and in the world Zionist movement by the mid-1930s made it the vehicle through which most Jewish capital reaching Palestine had to flow. As a result, the development of a middle class in the Yishuv was stifled, and General Zionism, the liberal tendency that represented middle-class interests, was weak and internally divided in Palestine, as later in Israel, in spite of its prominence among Zionists abroad (Neuberger 1991: 85–91; Shalev 1992: 91–4; Shapiro 1996a: 14–18; 1996b; chap. 2, above).

The General Zionists, who in 1961 united and renamed themselves the Liberal Party, and in 1965 united with Herut to form Gahal (which became the Likud in 1973), represented, essentially, the old private sector of the Yishuv. That private sector was seriously weakened in the post–1948 period by the rapid expansion of the Histadrut and state sectors. In the mid-1960s, however, after Ben-Gurion was replaced by Levi Eshkol as leader of Mapai and the state, and in the face of a brewing economic crisis, Mapai made a strategic decision to relax the state's control of the economy and encourage the development of the private sector.

The initial result of this new economic policy was the state-induced recession (*mitun*) that began in 1965. That recession ended with the 1967 war which greatly expanded the Israeli economy, both territorially and demographically. Only the post-1967 prosperity began raising the confidence of the new, state-generated private sector, and reinforced the demands of the managers of the Histadrut and state sectors for economic, rather than political, rationality in the conduct of their enterprises. When the old Labor leadership faltered in 1973, the political space was opened for the appearance of the new, liberal political entrepreneurs that are the subject of this chapter (Shalev 1992: 208–34; Levy 1997: 117–31).

We will discuss in this chapter three political parties, Shinuy (change), the Democratic Movement for Change (DMC), and Meretz, and two ideological–political circles within the Labor Party, Chug Mashov and Chug Hakfar Hayarok, that have played a key role in promoting the liberal discourse as a contender for hegemony over Israel's political culture.[3] The three political parties we will discuss have not really been three distinct entities. One of them, Shinuy, was instrumental in founding the DMC in 1976, remained a constitutive element of it for two years, and was the only faction of the DMC that survived the elections of 1981. In 1992 the majority in Shinuy joined two other political parties, Ratz and Mapam, to form Meretz, while a rump faction, retaining the party name, reconstituted itself as the radical anti-clerical party mentioned in chapter 5.

Shinuy and the DMC

Shinuy came on the scene as one of the many "protest movements" that sprouted up after the disastrous 1973 war, and was the only one of these movements to have survived for any length of time. It was founded by two professors at Tel Aviv University, the sociologist Yonathan Shapiro and Amnon Rubinstein, dean of the law school, and by Mordechai Virshuvski, who then served as legal counsel to the city of Tel Aviv. (Shapiro left Shinuy soon afterwards to join Ratz.) The first sizable meeting of the new movement took place in March 1974, and was attended by about a hundred people, "all of them belonging to the successful, bourgeois class of Ashkenazi Israel" (Urieli and Barzilay 1982: 88; Shapiro 1980). In Shapiro's overview:

Shinuy's initial political goals were distinctly liberal, yet unfocused: It concentrated on issues of social integrity and on honesty and rationality in government. It was satisfied with the demand for a rational approach in both domestic and foreign policy and for greater democracy in the state. It did not deal with the questions of Israel's integration into the region ... nor did it demand radical change in the pseudo-socialist structure of the economy ... Most of its practical proposals dealt with changing this or that law or with an amorphous demand for

---

[3] In some sense these groupings had a precursor in Rafi (Israel's Workers' List), a splinter group headed by David Ben-Gurion, Moshe Dayan, and Shimon Peres that had left Mapai in 1965 over Ben-Gurion's refusal to recognize the leadership of his successor as prime minister and head of that party, Levi Eshkol. Rafi was opposed to the Histadrut and advocated a "pragmatic, non-ideological" economic policy, rationality and efficiency in government, electoral reform, and a harder line on the Arab–Israeli conflict. It was supported mainly by members of the public-sector technocratic elite, and won ten Knesset seats in the elections of 1965. By 1967 Rafi, in effect, ceased to exist when Dayan joined the government of national unity on the eve of the war. The majority in Rafi, not including Ben-Gurion, rejoined Mapai officially in 1968, to form the Israeli Labor Party (Neuberger 1991: 51–4; Shapiro 1996a: 107–8; Arian 1998: 133–7).

change in the general atmosphere. (Shapiro 1980: 102; see also A. Rubinstein 1982: 45–6)

In 1976 Shinuy joined a number of other groups and prominent individuals, many of them members of the upper managerial strata of the Histadrut and state sectors, to form the DMC. The new party was headed by Yigael Yadin, a Hebrew University archaeologist and highly esteemed former chief of the IDF general staff (Torgovnik 1980; Urieli and Barzilay 1982; A. Rubinstein 1982). The DMC was truly a center party, in that its platform combined a liberal critique of the prevailing economic institutions of the LSM, in the spirit of Likud, with a "moderate" stance on the Arab–Israeli conflict akin to that of Labor. (Moderation in those days meant willingness to forgo Israel's "historical right" to the OT and accept the need for territorial compromise, and an agreement to establish new settlements in the OT for security reasons only, that is, in accordance with the Allon Plan.) But the party's main focus was clearly on the domestic front. Out of seven key points in its platform, only one dealt with foreign policy, while the other six were equally divided between issues of economic policy and demands for governmental and electoral reform (Urieli and Barzilay 1982: 204; Torgovnik 1980: 87; Arian 1998: 133–7).

This formula appealed to many members of the second-generation Ashkenazi elite who supported Labor's way of managing the Arab–Israeli conflict but were increasingly disillusioned with the constraints put on the market by the institutions of the pioneering era. They concluded that radical economic reform required as a precondition the loosening of the control of Labor over the economy, and perhaps even its removal from political office, because the party had too many vested interests in the existing institutional and socio-economic system. In the general elections of 1977 the DMC won 11.6 percent of the vote and fifteen Knesset seats, an unprecedented showing for a first-time contender (Arian 1980; Torgovnik 1980; Shalev 1992: 289; Arian and Shamir 1995).

After arduous negotiations that lasted five months the DMC joined the coalition government headed by Menachem Begin, without having secured any of the political principles it had defined as its minimum requirements for joining the coalition. This caused the party to disintegrate, with Shinuy the only one of its factions to survive and return to the Knesset in 1981. Although Shinuy was able to retain only two Knesset seats in 1981 its political programme merits some discussion, for two reasons: the fact that it served as a link between the DMC and Meretz, which would receive twelve Knesset seats in 1992; and its political principles that, for the first time, accorded the liberal discourse a significant place in Israeli politics (Shira 1980; A. Rubinstein 1982; Urieli and Barzilay 1982).

From its founding in 1974, until its merger with Ratz and Mapam to form Meretz in 1992, Shinuy's political program was based on three principles: "democratic state," "free economy," and "striving for peace" (Neuberger 1991: 146). The clarity and concreteness with which these principles had been articulated became more pronounced as time went on. As noted by Shapiro, Shinuy's initial program, which served as the basis for the DMC platform as well, was characterized by vague generalities. Its eight-point summary called for:

(1) peace negotiations with the Arabs based on territorial compromise;
(2) electoral reform;
(3) a written constitution that would guarantee basic civil rights;
(4) limiting the government's intervention in the economy;
(5) personal accountability in the public service;
(6) improvements in education;
(7) reducing the social gaps;
(8) fundamental change in "ways of life and the provision of public services." (Shira 1980: 13)

In 1988, the time of the last election campaign in which it participated as an independent party, Shinuy called for recognition of the Palestinians' right to self-determination, negotiations with the PLO, and cessation of Jewish settlement in the occupied territories. In the economic sphere it demanded privatization of state-owned enterprises, reduction of subsidies on consumer products, tax cuts, and "assistance to the unemployed but not to work-dodgers." In the civil rights area it formulated concrete demands relating to religious legislation and the rights of Palestinians, both citizens and non-citizens. Shinuy also continued to be active in the efforts to institute electoral reform (Neuberger 1991: 145–6).

Meretz

Meretz was formed on the eve of the 1992 general election by the coming together of three established political parties: Ratz, Mapam (United Workers' Party), and Shinuy. Ratz was founded in 1973, largely as a result of a falling out between Shulamit Aloni, an outspoken liberal member of Knesset for Labor, and Golda Meir, the prime minister and party leader. Aloni's defense of civil rights, including freedom from religion, had infuriated Meir who, in 1969, excluded her from Labor's list of candidates for the Knesset. In response, Aloni formed her own list in

1973 and, in the crisis atmosphere that prevailed after the war of that year, was able to win three seats in the Knesset (Neuberger 1991: 64; Avneri 1993).

Ratz's electoral fortunes had known ups and downs through the years, but it gradually established itself as the most liberal element in the Labor Zionist camp. Starting with the defense of civil rights proper, it gradually began to champion other elements of the liberal credo. While keeping up its commitment to civil rights and fierce opposition to religious legislation, Ratz gradually added to its platform clear "dovish" positions on the Arab–Israeli conflict, and liberal social and economic demands. Thus Ratz had called for reducing the government's role in the economy, partial privatization of the state sector, separation of Chevrat Haovdim from the Histadrut, mandatory arbitration in labor disputes and national health insurance (Neuberger 1991: 64–7).

Mapam, in 1992, was in effect the political arm of the Kibbutz Artzi settlement movement, which had been founded by the Hashomer Hatzair youth movement in 1927. Throughout its existence, whether as an independent political party or as a constituent element in larger political bodies, Mapam was always the most ideologically socialist of all Labor Zionist movements. Between 1969 and 1984 Mapam was aligned with the Labor Party in the Labor Alignment, and between 1984 and 1992 it had its own independent representation in the Knesset. Mapam shared with Ratz and Shinuy a moderate position on the Arab–Israeli conflict, but unlike them it called for a welfarist social–economic policy (Neuberger 1991: 40–6). Still, as Kibbutz Artzi was, and is, deeply involved as a capital owner in the market economy, Mapam's commitment to a welfarist economic policy was taken by many with a grain of salt. In joining Ratz and Shinuy to form Meretz, Mapam clearly preferred its commitment to peace between Israel and the Arabs to its declared social and economic concerns.

Meretz's 1992 election platform admitted that its three constituent parties had some disagreements in the socio-economic field. Due to these disagreements, the social and economic planks of the platform were formulated as rather vague generalities. They called for an "open, free and pluralistic economy," the reduction of both inflation and unemployment, and the institution of both national health and national pension insurance. Significantly, there was no mention of the Histadrut or of labor unions in general in the platform.

The economic chapter of the platform was very clear in tying together the issues of peace and economic development:

We see [our] social goals intertwined with the progress of the economy and with the policy of striving for peace. Without a peace policy there is no [economic] growth and without growth there is no economic wellbeing . . .

Making peace in the region and termination of the Arab boycott will make possible free and open trade with additional countries in the world and integration into the Middle Eastern economy, and will open up for Israel new and large markets that are closed to us today . . .

Peace agreement with our neighbors and an Israeli policy consistent with the values and interests of the democratic world will enable Israel to integrate into the world economy and into a stronger and expanding European Community, to become the recipient of investments and credit and to possess a progressive and export-oriented economy. (Meretz 1992)

Reaching peace is described, in sum, as imperative not only for gaining security but also for realizing Meretz's socio-economic vision: globalization of the Israeli economy and the attainment of the European Community's standard of living by the year 2000. This formulation constituted an effort to redefine the Arab–Israeli conflict in economic, rather than political–strategic, terms. It was precisely this redefinition, as we will argue in greater detail in chapter 9, that was one of the keys to the breakthrough in Israeli–Palestinian relations in 1993.

In order to reach peace with the Arabs, the platform formulated a plan that foretold the policy of the future Rabin government. It called for recognizing the principles of territories for peace, including on the Golan Heights, and of Palestinian self-determination, including the possibility of an independent Palestinian state; the cessation of Jewish settlement in the OT; autonomy for the Palestinians as an interim step towards a peace agreement; and possible negotiations with the PLO. The platform also included the typical liberal demands for a written constitution, including a bill of rights, electoral reform, equality for women and for Palestinian citizens, and for "separation of religion from politics and politics from religion, and . . . of the institutions of religion from the institutions of the state." The platform reaffirmed, however, Israel's character as a Jewish and democratic state (in that order) and the Law of Return (Meretz 1992).

Mashov and Hakfar Hayarok circles

The evolution of a distinctly liberal political program within the Labor Zionist movement did not occur only outside the Labor Party. Two important ideological coteries inside that party, Chug Mashov (Feedback Circle) and Chug Hakfar Hayarok (the Green Village Circle, named after the agricultural school that was the site of its founding meeting), had been working assiduously since the early 1980s to bring the party to explicitly support both peacemaking and economic and social liberalization. Of the two circles, Mashov, headed by Yossi Beilin, was more ideological in character, while Hakfar Hayarok, led by Chayim Ramon and Nissim Zevili, functioned as a political base for a particular age group within the party (those born in the late 1940s and 1950s). There was some overlap in the membership of these two circles (Beilin, for example, was member in both) and both drew their ideas from the ideological work done by Mashov (Barzilay 1996: 81, 114–15).

No studies of these two circles have been published yet, but the programmatic documents produced by Mashov portray a fascinating process of the gradual erosion of the hegemony of the republican discourse among the third generation of the Labor Party elite, who constituted the two circles' membership. Mashov's "founding charter," a one-page, typewritten document, calls for a reexamination of the Labor ideology "formulated at the time of the Yishuv," and a clarification of "the meaning of the socialist message" in contemporary Israel. It declares the group's intention to present the party with new ideas in the social sphere, concentrating on issues relating to the party itself and to the Histadrut (Mashov 1981).

Mashov's first conference did not take place until April 1983. The conference adopted resolutions calling for transforming the character of Chevrat Haovdim, taking a bold initiative for resolving the conflict with the Palestinians, and holding primary elections within the party. The conference heard reports from various committees that spoke in much clearer language about issues such as the need to reevaluate the Histadrut's role as both employer and labor union and consider the possibility of severing it from Chevrat Haovdim; a peace initiative based on fulfilling the legitimate rights of the Palestinians; encouraging "Arab" economic activity in the OT in order to, among other things, "develop free economic ties between Israel and the Arab world"; and instituting a national health insurance scheme (Mashov 1983).

Through the ten years of its existence prior to Labor's return to power in 1992, the rhetoric used by Mashov continued to employ the key social-democratic terms of the republican discourse, while gradually subverting their meaning. Thus "socialism" became "socialism of choice"; "equality" was redefined as "equality of opportunity"; workers, it was argued, needed to be regarded as "consumers and citizens" as well; "public companies" were redefined as companies traded publicly on the stock exchange; using unemployment to fight inflation was opposed, "except in rare cases"; and it was in the interests of the public health-care system, it was claimed, that "the rich turn to real private medicine" so as not to burden the system (Mashov 1985; 1986; 1987; 1989; 1991a; 1991b).[4]

By the time of Mashov's May 1991 conference, the liberal character of its program had become crystal clear. In his keynote address on "society and the economy," Mashov's founder and leader, Yossi Beilin, surveyed the failings of the planned socialist economy, and after decorously praising the Histadrut for its illustrious past, proceeded to offer a list of concrete reforms that would essentially gut that historic institution. Among the draft resolutions considered by that conference were the transfer of control over Chevrat Haovdim enterprises to a variety of owners, including in some cases the enterprises' own workers (only in cases of "small companies and/or those with a simple hierarchical structure"), and the separation of Kupat Cholim from the Histadrut through the institution of national health insurance (Mashov 1989; 1991a; 1991b).

Without its sick fund and economic enterprises the Histadrut would, obviously, become (as it actually did become in 1994), at best, a mere labor union federation. Heretofore, the demand to separate the Histadrut's economic and social service enterprises from its labor-union activities had been associated with the right wing of the Israeli political spectrum. Carrying out this radical transformation, however, required control over the Histadrut itself, not just the government, which was the reason why Likud was not able to accomplish this task. Still, the economic policies pursued by Likud since its assumption of power in 1977, and the ensuing economic crisis, had weakened the Histadrut enterprises to the point where Labor had to invest more and more of its dwindling political power just to secure their economic viability (see chap. 9, below; Barzilay 1996: 92–105, 109–12). This, in addition to their general liberal outlook, convinced the young Labor reformers that the party's own good, and its ability to struggle for peace, as well as for the real interests of the Histadrut's "clients," required that the burdens of Chevrat Haovdim and Kupat Cholim be lifted from its shoulders.

Mashov's 1991 conference also adopted positions on the peace process which, while never adopted by Labor into its own platform in 1992, turned out to be very influential in laying out the groundwork for the Oslo Accords. Thus the conference called upon the government to:

> – recognize the Palestinians' right of self-determination and nego-
> tiate with whoever they designated as their authorized repre-
> sentatives, provided those representatives would meet certain

---

[4] For an analysis of the transformation of the discourse of Western labor parties, including the Israeli Labor Party, from social-democratic to liberal democratic, see Khenin 2000.

preconditions (these preconditions had already been met by
the PLO and, in effect, this was a call for negotiating with the
PLO);
– institute a "Gaza first" interim withdrawal plan with full autonomy for the Palestinians in Gaza;
– consider the possibility of setting up a common political framework for Gaza and the West Bank (in effect, a Palestinian state).
(Mashov 1991b)

The most innovative aspect of Mashov's 1991 program, however,
was the express linkage it made between the economic and political
dimensions of peacemaking. In similar vein to Meretz's platform of
1992, Mashov's resolutions stated: "The chance to successfully address
the challenges of the Israeli economy, and especially mass immigration
and the necessity of growth, depends on our ability to take the path of
peace." Peacemaking, it was argued, would enhance Israel's "ability to
transfer resources towards these tasks and mobilize external economic
assistance which is contingent on our international standing." A closely
related demand was that: "to advance the peace process an economic
program will be undertaken to ensure the development of sources of livelihood and economic infrastructure for the Palestinian community and
to simultaneously foster Israeli–Arab economic cooperation" (Mashov
1991b).

Posing so clearly and dramatically the relationship between peace and
economic prosperity was yet another manifestation of the desire, shared
by liberal reformers within and without the Labor Party, to redefine the
Israeli–Palestinian conflict in such a way that its economic dimensions
would appear paramount. This was precisely the kind of redefinition of
the rules of the game that, according to Lustick, is one of the required
conditions for the replacement of one hegemonic project by another (see
above, p. 213). By redefining the conflict in essentially economic rather
than geo-strategic terms, and advocating its resolution as one element
in a package of economic and social reforms, these young liberals succeeded in articulating the concerns of a large and important segment of
Israeli society and turning them into a coherent program of social transformation. Their ability to formulate this program in a language that
challenged the hegemonic discourse of citizenship was greatly enhanced
by the economic reforms instituted in 1985 (the EESP; see chap. 9,
below) which began freeing the private sector from the financial tute-
lage of the state. Once Labor and Meretz formed a government, after
the 1992 elections, the reformers turned immediately to execute their
program.

In the Labor–Meretz government constituted in 1992 Yossi Beilin became deputy foreign minister, Chayim Ramon, leader of Chug Hakfar Hayarok, became minister of health, and Dedi Zucker of Meretz became chair of the all-important Constitution, Law, and Justice Committee of the Knesset. A division of labor thus developed between the three bodies, with Beilin and Mashov working on the issue of peace, Ramon with some of his political allies working on a national health insurance plan that would remove Kupat Cholim from the control of the Histadrut, and Meretz dealing with constitutional issues.

Meretz's involvement with the "constitutional revolution" (see chap. 10, below) actually predated the election victory of 1992. Amnon Rubinstein, leader of Shinuy, was one of the four sponsors of the law for the direct popular election of the prime minister, a law that was passed in the twelfth Knesset (elected in 1988) with the support of nine of the ten members who then constituted the Meretz faction (Allon 1995: 23). Rubinstein was also the one who successfully navigated two constitutional laws dealing with civil rights – Basic Law: Freedom of Occupation and Basic Law: Human Dignity and Freedom – through the twelfth Knesset, towards the very end of its term (Bechor 1996: 198). This legislative record was not matched by Meretz, or by any other party for that matter, in the thirteenth Knesset, elected in 1992.

As minister of health Ramon's primary objective was to pass a national health insurance plan that would separate membership in Kupat Cholim from membership in the Histadrut, thus drastically cutting the latter's membership rolls and ensuring its downfall as a major economic, social, and political institution. Ramon and his allies had done a great deal of preparatory work even before taking power. In order to weaken the power of the Histadrut apparatus within the Labor Party, they convinced the party to eliminate the requirement that party members be members of the Histadrut and change the locus where candidates for important elected positions were selected, from the party's central institutions to the entire membership. This dual move failed to secure passage of the national health insurance plan within Labor. But, as it turned out, it was responsible for the victory of Yitzhak Rabin, who was more popular among party voters and more sympathetic to the reformers, over Shimon Peres, who was supported by the party and Histadrut apparati, in the first primary elections, in 1992 (Barzilay 1996: 218–21; 245–7).

Ramon's national health insurance bill, whose linchpin was the severance of membership in Kupat Cholim from membership in the Histadrut, was approved by the cabinet in March 1993. However, the party leadership was later forced by the central party institutions, dominated by the Histadrut apparatus, to revoke its support for the bill. This made Ramon and his allies realize that in order to break the Histadrut they would have to take it over first.

Their first attempt to do so was by having one of their own, Amir Peretz, challenge the incumbent Histadrut secretary general, Chayim Haberfeld, in the Labor Party primaries. Peretz, however, failed to depose Haberfeld, and as a result Ramon himself, in a dramatic move, decided to resign his post as minister of health and run against Haberfeld in the Histadrut general elections. For this purpose Ramon formed a coalition with Meretz, Shas, and some of his own Labor Party allies, which ran in the Histadrut elections, while in the Knesset he continued to be an important member of the Labor faction. This unprecedented arrangement, and the persistent rumors that Ramon's move was actually supported by Rabin (Barzilay 1996: 388–9), was yet another illustration of the decline of political parties and the personalization of politics that resulted from the introduction of primary elections (see chap. 10, below). Even more significantly, Ramon's move against the Histadrut, supported as it was by both liberal Meretz and ethno-nationalist Shas, was a rare moment of unity between these two discourses against the flagship institution of the republican discourse. Their extraordinary co-operation demonstrated how hated the Histadrut and how bankrupt republicanism had become in Israeli society, thus marking the end of an era.

In the Histadrut general elections, held in May 1994, Ramon's list, "New life in the Histadrut,"[5] won 46 percent of the vote to Labor's 32 percent (Barzilay 1996: 288–395). Ramon became the Histadrut's new secretary general, a post he immediately retitled "chair" while also renaming the organization itself the "New Histadrut," in order to dissociate himself from the old, socialist-sounding terminology. He also did away with the red flag and the Internationale anthem as symbols of the new institution.

Now that it was no longer in control of the Histadrut, an institution it had founded in 1920 and dominated for seventy-four years, the Labor Party had no reason to oppose Ramon's national health insurance bill. The bill was passed into law by the Knesset in June 1994, with only Likud, the historical champion of national health insurance, voting against it. The law in effect nationalized the responsibility for health-care insurance and the collection of premium payments from the insured, while maintaining the existing HMOs (the Histadrut's Kupat Cholim Klalit and three smaller sick funds) as health-care providers, to be paid

---

[5] The list's name in Hebrew, Chayim Chadashim, was a play on the fact that both Ramon's and Haberfeld's first names were Chayim.

by the state at a fixed rate per member (with variations for age, area of residence, etc.).

Under the new law, the requirement that membership in an HMO be conditional on membership in any other organization was made illegal. The opportunity this created, of receiving health-care insurance without belonging to the Histadrut, resulted in a drop of two-thirds in Histadrut membership, from 1.6 million eligible voters in the Histadrut elections of 1994 to 600,000 in 1998. It also resulted in the universalization of access to health-care insurance (previously between 250,000 and 300,000 people did not have any health insurance) and in the onset of free competition between the different HMOs for the enrollment of new members (Barzilay 1996: 398–404; for the actual effects of the new law on the provision of health-care services, see chap. 11, below).

Most famous of the young guard's achievements in the Labor–Meretz government of 1992–6, however, was the Oslo Accord, brainchild of Yossi Beilin and his Mashov colleagues. The story of Oslo has been told many times already and we do not wish to repeat it here (see, e.g., Corbin 1994; Peres 1993; Beilin 1999; Savir 1998). We would like to draw attention, however, to the prominent place devoted in the DOP (the Declaration of Principles signed in Oslo) to economic co-operation between Israel and the Palestinian National Authority, and between both parties and regional economic bodies. The prominence of these economic issues is not at all surprising in view of the fact that the DOP was negotiated between a member of Mashov, Yair Hirschfeld (author of a study commissioned by the EU on Israeli–Palestinian economic relations, titled *From Dependency to Interdependence*) and his colleague Ron Pundik, and Abu Ala (Ahmed Qurei), the director of Sumud, an important economic arm of the PLO (Corbin 1994). While the Palestinians were more interested in the political dimension of the agreement, and in spite of some heated arguments about the need to end Israeli economic exploitation, they were willing to accommodate Israel's demands for regional economic co-operation and an integrated Israeli–Palestinian economy, in return for political recognition of their rights and Israel's withdrawal from parts of the OT (see chap. 9, below).

Conclusion

It is one of the ironies of Israel's national development that the project of making liberalism the hegemonic discourse of citizenship has not been promoted by the right, which is too committed to the ethno-national discourse to truly care about liberal citizenship rights, but rather by the left, which has adopted liberalism as a revival ideology for the

Labor Zionist movement. This attests, as well, to the endurance of the republican discourse and the institutional regime that supported it. The republican bastion could not be taken from the outside, even after it had long deteriorated by hypocrisy, atrophy, and corruption; it could only be captured from within. And the forces that would capture it from within, in order to demolish it, were generated by the very economic development that was the pride and glory of Israeli republicanism.

The political agents discussed in this chapter began their activity on the margins of the Labor Zionist movement, but succeeded in remaking that movement in their own image. Their program of peace and socio-economic liberalization was adopted and implemented, to an extent, by the Labor Party. The Likud government of Benjamin Netanyahu, which was in power between 1996 and 1999, did not stray too much from that program either, despite its ethno-nationalist rhetoric. This is the best indication that the program has indeed become hegemonic, at least among the leading strata of Israeli society. The fact that its hegemony has not extended beyond these strata, and that its opponents have rallied around the ethno-national discourse and seek to make it into the hegemonic discourse, explains the political turbulence that Israel is facing as it enters the twenty-first century.

9 Economic liberalization and peacemaking

In this chapter we examine in detail the nature of the crisis that beset Israeli society and its economy between the mid-1970s and the early 1990s, and of the institutional transformation that was consequent upon it, as well as their interaction with, and impact upon, Israeli citizenship. The institutions we chose to examine are the military, the Histadrut, and what we would broadly call the institutions of the capital market and the business community. We will inquire how the decline of the republican institutions, foremost among them the Histadrut, reshaped the relationship between the state and the market. Of the various aspects of the deregulation and liberalization of the economy we will focus on one: the gradual but by now decisive liberalization of the capital market. In our view it is this aspect of liberalization that created, by the early 1990s, the conditions for the emergence, for the first time, of an Israeli business community – a more-or-less cohesive social sector made up of professional business executives interested primarily in profit making (and their counterparts in the state administration) and not beholden to the state, the Histadrut, or the values of pioneering republican virtue. Indeed, the very term "business community" is new in Israel, and we date its origins to the past decade. We will trace the emergence of this community by focusing on the shifting fortunes of the largest Israeli corporation: Koor Industries, once the flagship of the Histadrut's Chevrat Haovdim, now Israel's largest multinational holding company.

In contrast to the inward-looking Histadrut, strategic sectors of the business community were intent on taking advantage of the opportunities offered by the rapidly growing global economy of the 1990s. In order to do that the business community added its voice to those who were calling for accommodation with the Palestinians, and helped catalyze the Labor Party's turn towards direct negotiations with the PLO. The close association of state and business, which replaced the state–Histadrut alliance (see, e.g., Lane 1998), does have its share of ironies, however. Israeli business has not only become more concentrated in the wake of economic liberalization (Shalev 2000: 141), but, in spite of becoming

231

vocal supporters of peace economics, many of its members continue to be involved in weapons production and trade.

The DOP signed in Oslo between Israel and the PLO was an important signpost. By expressing Israel's willingness to withdraw from large sections of the West Bank and Gaza Strip, that is, to at least partially decolonize these regions, the government in effect declared that the process of state building had come to an end and, with it, the rationale for maintaining the republican pioneering type of citizenship. This has had important implications for many of the social citizenship rights that were inherent to the discourse of republican virtue and were safeguarded by its institutions. The co-operation of the Labor Party and the business community in opening the door for Israeli–Palestinian peace thus also challenged and transformed the old citizenship framework, in terms of both rights and institutions. While social rights have been questioned and diminished in the 1990s, civil citizenship has been gaining ground. Two institutions, the Supreme Court and the Bank of Israel, emerged as among the most autonomous, influential, and controversial institutions of the "new Israel." Institutional change will be the focus of this chapter; the corresponding transformation of the citizenship discourse will be the subject of chapters 10 and 11.

Preconditions for change

The late 1980s and early 1990s are commonly seen as a period of profound transformation and new beginning. In the economic arena it has become customary to point to the successful July 1985 Emergency Economic Stabilization Plan (EESP), undertaken by Shimon Peres's national unity government to reduce double-digit inflation, as the turning point in adopting a new socio-economic regime, reducing state intervention, liberalizing the capital markets, and preparing the groundwork for additional steps required to open the economy to the world. The EESP is often associated with the same government's narrowly adopted decision, taken in the same year, to partially withdraw its troops from Lebanon, to mark a political–economic watershed.

Both the direct impact of and the guiding vision behind the EESP are usually overstated, however. Attempts to integrate Israel into the world economy had already begun in the 1970s, with the signing of partial free-trade agreements with the European Community (now European Union) in 1975 and with the US in 1985, making Israel the only country to have such agreements with both. The EESP, as its name implies, was a short-term emergency plan that dramatically reduced spiraling inflation. The symbolic date of July 1985 highlighted, then, rather than commenced, the new era in the Israeli economy, by publicly acknowledging that "things could not go on as before" and by manifesting a determination to reverse the specter of decline. Even after 1985, however, it was not clear that the economy would actually improve and, in fact, by mid-1987 it had plunged into a recession from which it picked up only with the onset of Soviet Jewish immigration in the 1990s (Economic Models 1993: 32).

The widespread sense of malaise at the end of the 1980s indicated that the new institutions, with their burgeoning liberal citizenship discourse, were not yet seen as heralding a new socio-economic future. The pre-conditions for transformation were in place, but additional reforms were required for them to begin to bear fruit. In short, the significant transformations that ushered in a new era for the Israeli economy, society, and politics began before and continued after 1985. Nor should the withdrawal from Lebanon undertaken by Peres's national unity government be seen as reflecting an integrated socio-economic vision. In the political arena, the Camp David Accord with Egypt had already been signed in 1979, the domestic controversy over the 1982 invasion of Lebanon had generated deep polarization, and the outbreak of the intifada in late 1987 demonstrated that the withdrawal of Israeli troops into the buffer zone in southern Lebanon was an episode, rather than an epoch-making event. (Full withdrawal from Lebanon took place only in 2000.) Only in the 1990s were economic policy and political moderation linked.

Beverly Silver (1990) has accented the political–economic connection by placing Israel within Immanuel Wallerstein's three-tiered world-system theory, in order to explain its transition from economic miracle to economic decline. Her conclusions were similar to those of the Israelis who lamented the "lost decade," but in contrast to their hopelessness, Silver accompanied her observations with a proposed remedy. Israeli success in attracting immigrants and foreign capital subsidies led her into "the perimeter of the [world system's] core" (Arrighi and Drangel 1986) but were also the direct cause of inflaming the conflict with the Palestinians and with Arab nationalism generally. The increased channeling of the mobilized human and material resources into military expenditures – paying for policing the OT, defraying the costs of the 1973 and 1982 wars, and building and nourishing a large-scale military industry that depended on American goodwill for supplies and for marketing its products – undermined Israel's success in the semi-periphery, making it harder for her to attract immigrants or foreign capital (Silver 1990: 176–8). Silver concluded that "the current crisis can only be resolved if Israel can disengage itself from the military conflict." Finally, she challenged Israelis to find out whether peace had the same magnetic qualities for attracting resources as war did (Silver 1990: 178).

Though Silver's essay is as profound as it is prophetic, its chronology is anachronistic in important respects. The turn away from exclusive reliance on military power had begun with the 1979 Israeli–Egyptian peace treaty and the subsequent Israeli withdrawal from the Sinai Peninsula. Israel's military expenses were further reduced in 1984 and 1985. And Israel's military industry, which expanded rapidly in the 1970s and early 1980s and served as an engine of economic growth at least until the mid-1980s, found itself in deep recession. The decline in three areas: (1) the share of the military budget in the GNP; (2) the soundness of the military industries; and (3) the social prestige of the IDF indicated that the pride of place occupied by the military sphere in Israel's society, economy, and culture had been eroding (Levy 1997).

The military budget

Historically, the share of military expenses in Israel's GNP had been fluctuating widely, in response to the level of conflict with the Arab states and, to a lesser extent, with the Palestinians. Until 1967 the military burden amounted to about 10 percent of GNP; between 1967 and 1973 it was in the 20 percent range; and in the wake of the 1973 war it jumped to over 30 percent. That level could not be sustained for long, however, and the military budget's share of the GNP returned to its previous range of around 20 percent after 1976.

In 1984 and 1985 the government undertook a drastic reduction in the share of the GNP it allocated to military expenditures, reducing it to 10 percent in the 1986–8 period and to close to 8 percent in 1991 and 1992. The obvious reason for the cut was the stagnation of the Israeli economy, but the conditions that made this reduction possible were the peace treaty with Egypt, the end of the redeployment of Israeli troops from the Sinai, the Iran–Iraq war, and the transformation of American military aid from loans to grants (Brodet 1994: 225; Ben-Zvi 1994: 227–8.)

The importance of the 1979 peace accord with Egypt (completely missed, as we have indicated in the introduction, by functionalist students of Israeli society) for Israel's economic development cannot be overstated. The accord provided Israel with a genuine "peace dividend," by allowing it to lower its military expenses back to their 1960s level. Free of the fear of external military conflict, the economic reformers could reduce budgetary outlays and begin to tackle the inflationary and structural crises. By sustaining this relatively low-level military budget the reformers were also able to transform the momentum of economic reform from a short-term anti-inflationary struggle to a long-term process of economic liberalization.

Significantly, the absolute size of Israel's military expenditures had not declined in the 1990s, because of renewed economic growth (Brodet 1994: 224). Israel could, therefore, purchase a fixed amount of security for declining shares of its GNP and, in essence, had "solved" the problem of its military expenditures. A fixed rate of military expenditure, even if three times as high as the European and twice as high as the American rate, is not a pressing problem for Israeli decision makers. Thus there was no pressure on the military budgets for seeking accommodation with the PLO. Israel had already benefited from the "peace dividend" by making peace with Egypt, and additional gains were forthcoming not from reduced military budgets but from continued growth.

The military–industrial complex

The rapid expansion of a military–industrial complex (MIC) after the 1967 war led to economies of scale which allowed Israel to become a major arms exporter (Levy 1997: 147). The central place occupied by the MIC in Israel's economy in the 1970s and 1980s was but another aspect of the militarization of Israeli society: the linking of the livelihood of a significant portion of the civilian labor force – 25 percent of the industrial labor force in the peak year of 1982/3 – to the needs of the military (Levy 1997: 121). Some scholars, however, have exaggerated the impact of the MIC by expecting it to dominate the political arena as well. Michael Barnett, for example, argued that the customary expectation that war would strengthen the state had not worked in the Israeli case. Instead, the MIC had cast its shadow over the state. The Israeli state experienced a "sorcerer's apprentice effect": it created the MIC which had outgrown its creator by evolving independent sources of financing and, consequently, not only eroded the state's control but made the state beholden to military production for continued economic development and capital accumulation (Barnett 1992: 233–7). In actual reality, the picture of these industries in the mid-1990s was clearly not one of a monster ready to swallow or harm its master. Barnett's 1992 book used data from the 1948–77 period only, and therefore missed the reversal of the trends he described.

The creation of Israel's modern military industries was triggered by the imposition of the French embargo in June 1967,[1] but their explosive expansion was a response to a growing global market for arms, with expanding profit margins (Y. Levy 1995: 121; Barkai 1988). In the

---

[1] The embargo imposed on Israel after the 1948 war had not led it to develop a military industry, nor did Israel seek to build up its MIC after the 1956 war (with the exception of its nuclear capability).

mid-1980s, however, that is, even before the end of the Cold War, Israeli domestic military purchases declined considerably and, although different enterprises were affected to different degrees, the decline plunged the MIC into a veritable crisis (Lifshitz 1995: 9). As minister of defense in 1989 Rabin canceled the production of the Lavie fighter plane, thus both conceding that Israel could not play in the big league of major weapons systems producers and admitting the necessity of shrinking its MIC (Inbar 1996: 62–3). The canceling of the Lavie project led to the loss of much of the Israeli MIC's luster and, as many companies were already battling for survival with the help of government subsidies, the driving force of military industrialization seemed spent. Whereas in the mid-1980s the labor force of the military industries numbered over 65,000, in 1991 it stood at 40,000, and by early 1995 declined to 24,000 and was expected to be further reduced to around 18,000–19,000 employees by mid-1996 (Levy 1997: 192). In 1997, of the two main companies in the Israeli MIC, the Israel Aircraft Industries had only 13,690 employees, while Taas had 4,900 (Lifshitz 2000: 369, table *yod*-3). As part of this process the government was involved in bailing out the ailing military industries to the tune of almost $2.5 billion ($525 million to the Israel Aircraft Industries, $1.1 billion to Taas, and $650 million to Rafael) in addition to government guarantees. The end of the Cold War has further shrunk the market for the products of Israel's military industries. In 1995 the director general of the Ministry of Finance expected that in the longer run the reforms would lead to the development of a more business-oriented approach in the Israeli MIC (*Haaretz*, January 4, 1995). Not until 1997 did the Israel Aircraft Industries, the MIC's largest concern, show any profit.

Among the reasons cited for the crisis of the Israeli MIC, the three most common are the decline in the global arms market, the bureaucratic rigidity of such large-scale enterprises, and the power of the skilled high-tech unions in a small market. Yaacov Lifshitz added yet another factor, whose significance will become even clearer as we discuss the evolution of the economy in the 1990s. Though many MIC companies became global players, they had not, Lifshitz indicated, freed themselves from dependence on the public purse. The military industries were formed with relatively limited equity, and most of their capital generation remained internal. They lacked access to the private capital market and could not reach the capital reserves that were required for their rapid growth. When, in the mid-1980s, they needed to undertake expensive readjustment programs, their equity was eroded and could not be replenished without the addition of private partners or other forms of privatization (Lifshitz 1995: 16). Lack of direct access to the capital market played a central role in their crisis and, in some cases, in their demise.

Military prestige

The IDF's once exorbitant prestige began shrinking as a consequence of two of its own actions: the invasion of Lebanon in 1982, where it was faulted for engaging not in a defensive but in an offensive action, and its role in attempting to suppress the first intifada. After 1967, when the IDF first became an occupying army, and especially since the beginning of the intifada, when it became the tool of its suppression, the previously high rate of volunteering for elite units started to fall (Inbar 1996: 54–7). The military began to express, sometimes publicly, its conviction that the intifada could only be brought to an end through a political solution. Such an argument, of course, sidelined the role of the military itself. The Oslo peace talks, conducted entirely by civilians, and without prior knowledge of the military, were an example of the IDF's more limited role in the new era. It was reintroduced into subsequent technical negotiations over the implementation accords, in which it again played a crucial role. After Likud's 1996 election victory its bitter attacks on the IDF, which was described as "prisoner" (*shafut*) of the Oslo concept, further eroded its status.

The depreciation of IDF's prestige, however, was the result not only of the changing character of its tasks, but also of the changing nature of Israeli society. The children of the pioneering groups, aided by their secure access to citizenship rights, were quick to take advantage of new occupational opportunities, as alternative sources of prestige emerged. Among those still seeking to serve in elite units, the allure of republican virtue has declined (as it has in many other social spheres), to be replaced, in part, by individualistic or ethno-nationalist and religious motivations. On the one hand, aspiring volunteers prepare themselves, while still in high school, in expensive private boot camps, for military service that, they expect, would enhance their manliness and prove their ability to overcome obstacles. On the other hand, national-religious youth, many of them in *yeshivot hesder*, seek positions in front-line military units out of religiously defined nationalist motivations. The traditional path of mobility through a military career was thus left for these new groups, especially Mizrachim and the national-religious, at a time when the military began to lose some of its luster. After the Lebanon war and during the intifada the composition of volunteer units and of the officer corps, especially, began to change: the percentage of Mizrachi and national-religious youth increased, while the traditional source of volunteers from the LSM's co-operative settlements began to dry up. Cognizant of these changes, and of the general decline in the willingness of young Israelis to serve, the IDF command has resorted to various "motivation increasing" measures, but has also floated suggestions for transforming the IDF into a professional force (Cohen 1997b; *Haaretz*, January 13, 1998; March 24, 1998; April 7, 1998; Shochat 1998; Golan 1998). As these processes jointly illustrate, the institutional and cultural predominance enjoyed for decades by the IDF, rooted in the conviction that military solutions were the only "answer" to the dilemmas of the Israeli–Arab conflict, is being eroded by the changing nature of the conflict and by the liberalization of the society (Levy 1997).

Capital market liberalization

Our discussion of Israel's capital market deregulation and liberalization will be fairly detailed, as it has many technical aspects that need to be clarified, or else we will remain mired in generalizations rather than in concrete analysis. Both the Yishuv and Israel had always been dependent on foreign capital. Capital was required to subsidize "pure settlement colonization," that is, to aid in the absorption of propertyless immigrants, maintain a European standard of living, and foot military bills. Thus, the Yishuv was, as Israel still is, a major recipient of one-way transfers from abroad. For about a decade-and-a-half after 1950 Israel received German reparations, and it continues to receive tax-free contributions and proceeds from the sale of its bonds in the US, and, since 1967, US military and civilian assistance as well. This financial dependence on outside sources of capital has prevented Israel from being inward looking (as it was regarded in functionalist analysis), and served as one basis for its being viewed, mostly by its Arab critics, as a "foreign transplant."

Israel did not, however, become the recipient of direct foreign investment. With the exception of a small amount of mostly "Jewish" funds, capital flows to Israel were by and large not market driven but unilateral. These one-way capital transfers made Israel a relatively high-wage economy, thus blocking its use for offshore production. Foreign capital, in Barnett's summary, has generally bypassed Israel as a place to relocate its high-wage sectors because of lack of natural resources, comparatively low domestic demand, and the Arab–Israeli conflict (Barnett 1996: 119). Consequently, Israel ranked second from the bottom, compared to all Third World countries, in its share of firms fully owned by foreigners (Mardon 1990: 129). No more than 5 percent of all investment in Israel until the mid-1970s was provided by multinational corporations (Michaely 1975). In short, as long as the Arab boycott was in effect,

Israel was able to take only partial advantage of its willingness to open to the outside world. In the 1990s, therefore, as we shall see, the emergent business community joined those already calling for Israel to embark on a peace process with the Palestinians, which would undermine the Arab boycott, and enable Israel to join in the process of economic globalization.

Domestic capital formation in Israel, as we have seen in chapter 2, was a circular affair which made available to the government the Histadrut's pension and provident funds for loans to public and private investors for investments approved by the government itself. A major result for domestic capital formation was that "the economy's chief source of investment credit" remained under effective government control, regardless of whether the investment was effected in the public, Histadrut, or private sector (Grinberg 1991: 91). As long as the private sector was dependent on government-allocated credit it could not attain autonomy. What seemed like a private sector was, in fact, tied to the state's apron strings.

When Likud came to power in 1977, Simcha Ehrlich, leader of its liberal wing, became finance minister and embarked on self-conscious economic liberalization. Ehrlich's aim, however, was limited, since he represented mostly commercial interests, and his plan was poorly designed and executed. By easing foreign-currency restrictions Ehrlich arrogantly promised to make Israel the "Switzerland of the Middle East." Since his reforms were not comprehensive, as he did not, for example, put a limit on the budgetary deficit or retain a fixed exchange rate for the shekel, his plan led to big arbitrage deals and significantly enhanced inflation. In fact, the professional consensus is that the first Likud government failed to carry out any privatization or restructuring of the economy to fit its liberal pronouncements. According to Stanley Fischer, professor of economics at MIT and former chief economist at the World Bank, the Likud years represented a "wasted opportunity by a government that should have known better" (Fischer interview; see also Passell 1992a; 1992b), a view shared by Israeli economists.

Nevertheless, one policy change of the first Likud government, the implications of which were not fully understood at the time, undermined the Histadrut's privileged position in the capital market, though still leaving it under virtual government control. In October 1980 Yigal Horowitz, Likud's second finance minister, canceled the 50 percent share Chevrat Haovdim had enjoyed in the approved investment plan (see chap. 2, above), and thus deprived the Histadrut of its source of cheap and secure credit (Grinberg 1991: 91; Aharoni 1991: 118–19). The Histadrut responded to the loss of its cheap and risk-free credit by turning to its own Bank Hapoalim for other forms of favorable funding. Under cover of the massive inflation of the first half of the 1980s, the extent of the damage done to Chevrat Haovdim enterprises, to the Histadrut's social services, and to the kibbutzim and moshavim that borrowed from Bank Hapoalim, remained veiled. It was revealed, however, by the EESP of 1985. The adoption of the EESP placed the Histadrut in a precarious position, which contributed significantly to its loss of power.

The occasion for the second liberalization plan, the EESP, was not a change of ruling parties but runaway inflation. The main goal of the EESP was the restoration of price stability, and it successfully reduced inflation from an annual rate of 466 percent to 25 percent, as measured in the period August 1985–March 1986. (For a detailed description of the plan by one of its architects, see Bruno 1986.) The Stabilization Plan itself was complex: it involved the freezing of the interest and exchange rates, wages, and prices, and was successful due to the US government's special aid of $1.5 billion, in the form of the conversion of US loans into grants. The plan was further aided by the fortuitous decline in the world price of oil and the strengthening of the major European currencies and the yen, in relation to the dollar, which effectively devalued the shekel (which was pegged to the dollar) (Grinberg 1991: 151).

The EESP resulted from, and was an admission of, a crisis situation in the old institutional ways of running the country. As such, it opened the door for new approaches and new institutions, and by the early 1990s gave rise to a new economic policy regime. But the EESP was only a short-range policy, whereas the new regime was the result of a complex transformation. How, then, has the former led into the latter?

It has been argued, among others by Michael Keren, that the Stabilization Plan was the brainchild of Israeli economists who warned about the disastrous consequences of inflation spiraling out of control and rallied in an unprecedented manner around the leadership of Shimon Peres, prime minister of the national unity government, in 1985. Consequently, the success of the plan reflected and reinforced their high status as a professional group (Keren 1995). But while the economists as a group indeed played a crucial role in mobilizing public support in 1985, their uncharacteristic unanimity was short lived. Beyond the immediate goal of price stability to be attained within a year, the economists' views frequently diverged. They could only rarely agree on specific measures, such as the elimination of non-tradable government bonds, and were unable to provide a single road map for further reform. This originated in another institution – Israel's central bank, the Bank of Israel (BOI) – that initiated most of the subsequent steps, first deregulation (namely, eliminating special administrative controls that shielded various sectors and fragmented the market) and, later on, liberalization (namely, opening up to the world) of the capital market (Klein 1996).

Though, in retrospect, it seems that after 1985 the BOI purposefully transformed its own *raison d'être*, from maintaining price stability to the general direction of the economy, in fact its approach was piecemeal. The BOI had to take advantage of possibilities made available by regulation to prepare tools for liberalization. In an economy in which about 80 percent of credit was "directed," or earmarked by government policy, no monetary policy was possible. Only once a capital market was established could interest rates be used as an effective policy instrument. At first, the main mooring of monetary policy remained foreign-exchange controls, but with the opening up of the closed currency market the value of this anchor declined. But by then it became possible to rely on the short-term interest rate charged by the BOI to commercial banks as the new bulwark of monetary policy. The growing independence of the BOI began to matter only in the early 1990s, because the deregulation of the financial market lent real weight to its decisions.

The central role played by the BOI in determining interest rates was accepted in Israel no more enthusiastically than elsewhere, since the emphasis on price stability subordinated other worthy goals, such as employment. But in the post-1985 era the BOI was willing to tie its reputation to an effective anti-inflationary policy. The transition commenced in the late 1980s, at the end of Michael Bruno's term as governor of the BOI, and was accelerated at the beginning of Yaacov Frankel's term. The BOI began to argue that to accomplish its goal of price stability it needed policy tools such as control over the interest rates, that is, in effect, the bank needed to be independent of the government. This independence, it insisted, would serve a common good: in the long term price stability would make the economy more efficient (Klein interview).

The BOI has relied on two sources of authority: legal and wrested, or usurped. First, the Bank of Israel Law was revised, forbidding the bank "to print money," that is, to finance the government deficit. This laid the basis for an independent monetary policy for the first time. A second, further, tightening took place with the adoption in 1991 of a law stipulating that the budget deficit could not exceed a certain percentage of the state budget (thus anticipating a crucial part of the Maastricht plan). Finally, a purportedly technical change, altering the mechanism for setting the exchange rate, which was enacted in December 1991, handed the bank a new tool for policy making. A horizontal exchange-rate band (with upper and lower limits of 3 percent around a central parity, ensuring a 3 percent yearly devaluation) was replaced with a diagonal, or upward-crawling, band, the slope of which was determined by the difference between the local and international inflation rates. But since accepting the prevailing local rate would have been counterproductive, a yearly "inflationary target" (*yaad inflatziyoni*) was used instead. This technical target now assumed a life of its own: it became a political necessity to offer a lower or at least equivalent yearly goal. When Rabin's finance minister, Avraham Shochat, sought to undermine the use of such official "targets" he found that not to be possible any more. Like the Supreme Court's policy of judicial activism (see chap. 10, below), the BOI's newly minted coin of inflationary target has served to enhance its goal of anti-inflationary policy and wrested for the BOI, its foremost guardian, real autonomy and a central role in discussions of economic policy.

The initiatives of the BOI required government support, especially the support of the ministers of finance. This was frequently attained over the opposition of the ministry's upper echelon of civil servants. Even economists from the BOI's own research department sometimes opposed the initiatives of the BOI's leadership. The new policy contradicted the developmentalist perspective of the previous economic regime, that foreign currency was rare and needed to be husbanded vigilantly, and, more broadly, that policy making was best left to the government and its ministries. The BOI's preference for market discipline limited the influence of other civil servants, among them economists in other institutions, and could not command the unified support of all Israeli economists, divided as they were by institutional affiliations.

Nowhere were the results of financial liberalization more obvious than in the growing importance of the Israeli stock market. The removal of the requirement that provident and pension funds and insurance companies invest in non-tradable government bonds, and the gradual reduction in the amount of government-issued non-negotiable bonds, slowly produced more competitive terms for the government and the private sector in the bond market. At the end of 1986 the Ministry of Finance suspended the sale of non-tradable bonds to provident funds, but continued to sell them to certain kinds of pension and life-insurance funds (Aharoni 1991: 119). The share of non-negotiable bonds had declined in the pension funds' portfolios, but was significantly reduced only in 1990 (Rolnik 1995). Consequently, between 1985 and 1990 the share of government securities held by the public fell from 83 percent to 65 percent of the stock of financial assets. Similarly, the share of direct and indirect government loans to the private sector fell from 57.6 percent to 29.7 percent in just three years, from 1987 to 1990 (Razin and Sadka 1993: 193).

"The private sector's sources of finance changed radically after the July 1985 stabilization program" (Razin and Sadka 1993: 191). With the elimination of the guaranteed rate on government-issued bonds, the large Israeli corporations were compelled to look for new sources of financing. Of the three largest, Klal, Discount Investments, and the Histadrut's own

Koor, the former two chose to turn to what was then a fledgling Israeli stock market, as did many other Israeli corporations. The Tel Aviv Stock Exchange (TASE) almost doubled its value between early 1989 and early 1991 and had doubled it again by 1994. The rise in terms of both yield and value of the public's portfolio was dramatic, for example by the end of 1993 the total value of shares held by the public was 3.5 times its value in early 1991 (Gaon 1994a).

An even more important role in freeing the capital markets was played by the relaxation of controls over the borrowing of foreign capital. Israeli corporations began floating their securities on the New York Stock Exchange, and these added up to 36 percent of the total market value of publicly held Israeli nonfinancial corporations as of January 1992. Firms received permission to invest up to 40 percent of their equity abroad (Razin and Sadka 1993: 195). In 1993–6, Israeli industrial firms purchased $1 billion equity in foreign companies (MAI Strategic Planning Committee 1996). Since early 1991 "there has been an unprecedented number of Wall Street IPO's of Israeli companies." By March 31, 1992 there were thirty-eight such companies trading on Wall Street with a market value of $6 billion (Gaon 1992: 6–7). By 1995 over six hundred Israeli companies traded for around $55 billion on the TASE, and another sixty to sixty-eight companies traded for $10–15 billion on Wall Street (short-term capital transactions and investment abroad are still regulated) (Razin and Sadka 1993: 191–2). In both 1996 and 1997 Israeli companies raised more than $1 billion on Wall Street (*Globes*, December 31, 1997).

Foreign investment in Israel began in special country funds (established in 1992), as well as a few sectoral funds, and later led to the entry of strategic investors. In 1993 foreign, mostly financial, investment rose to $4.3 billion, an increase of 42 percent over the previous year. Direct investment in Israeli concerns rose from $17 million in 1993 to $584 million in 1996 (MAI Strategic Planning Committee 1996). In the first ten months of 2000 total foreign direct investment in Israeli companies, portfolios, and property reached a record amount of $8.6 billion, but commencing in the second quarter of 2000, FDI in the TASE began declining. The shortfall in 2000 was $404 million; since the outbreak of the second Palestinian intifada in October 2000 it amounted to $252 million, and in November alone $92 million were withdrawn (*Jerusalem Post*, December 24, 2000).

In contrast with the private corporations, the Histadrut refused, or was unable, to go down that road. In part, as a self-declared socialist body its leaders felt that this would be inappropriate. In part, entry into the stock market would have required the transformation of the management and control patterns of Chevrat Haovdim which, for the first time, would have been required to open its books to public scrutiny. The Histadrut did not experience the acute pressure felt by private corporations, because it had an alternative source of financing. Chevrat Haovdim boasted its own bank, Bank Hapoalim. Exploiting the inflationary conditions prevailing in the first half of the 1980s, Histadrut-owned companies borrowed money from this bank at fixed interest rates, not indexed to the rate of inflation, thus, in effect, continuing to receive what seemed like free money. Only after 1985, when runaway inflation was halted, bank credits were drastically cut, and interest rates rose, causing a credit crunch in which interest and principal had to be repaid at realistic rates, did the folly of the Histadrut companies' "free loans" become obvious (Reiner interview; Barkey 1994: 49–50).

The BOI was able to emerge as a major innovator because of the reduced role of the Histadrut and the state in the capital market. The reduction of government intervention in the disposition of savings allowed private-sector borrowers to obtain financing through private intermediaries. Furthermore, private enterprises were able to be capitalized by issuing securities through the stock exchange, thus freeing themselves of government control. Whereas in the past the financial market was fragmented by huge interest-rate differentials, these have shrunk considerably in recent years (Razin and Sadka 1993: 186–7, 194–5). The ability to borrow directly from the public, or through private intermediaries, or abroad has freed up Israeli businesses from their customary dependence on the state.

While the Histadrut's reduced influence became obvious in the early 1990s, its decline resulted from deep-seated structural causes. The modernization and industrialization of the Israeli economy and especially the growing demand for skilled employees led over time to a dramatic fall in the numbers and influence of unskilled Jewish workers. In the Yishuv these workers competed with low-paid Arab workers and found protection behind the walls of Histadrut's subsidized institutions. The virtual collapse of the Histadrut's subsidized enterprises diminished the advantages previously conferred by the LSM on its members. With the decline of old opportunities the younger generation turned to new venues. Whereas in the past the privileges of membership of the LSM's institutional network were used as stepping stones for bureaucratic power, they increasingly came to be converted into educational, financial, and professional accomplishment. Side by side, a private economic elite "continued to expand after other elites had reached their saturation point" and became "a highly esteemed status group" (Horowitz and Lissak 1989: 97).

The battered and debt-ridden Histadrut and the LSM's institutional domain in general were now seen as obstacles to political popularity at home and to auspicious global transformations. The main influence of economic globalization was to shift the balance between economic and political institutions and processes. The impact of global economic forces on the Israeli economy made less viable the unique extra-market features that were the result of Israel's establishment and reproduction as a colonial society. These were the massive, but inefficient and costly, extra-market mechanisms and institutions that provided Jewish settler-immigrants and their offspring with conditions favorable for settlement and prosperity. These institutions gave Israel probably the largest public-sector employment outside the communist countries. Created to bypass market mechanisms, they played a crucial role as providers of subsidized employment and services for Jewish immigrants to Palestine, and have come to represent the idiosyncrasies of their socio-economic organization. The attack on these extra-market mechanisms and institutions strengthened Israel's business community.

The privatization of Koor

The history of Koor is the history of Israeli industry in microcosm. From the Histadrut's, indeed Israel's, largest industrial conglomerate, it became Israel's first multinational holding company. Reviewing this history will thus open a window on the growing role of foreign capital in the economy, as well as on the business community's newly found and vigorously pursued emphasis on Israeli–Palestinian peace as a necessary step along the road to integration into the global economy.

Koor was established in 1944 with the intention of building labor-intensive factories to provide employment to Jewish immigrants, in the time-honored fashion of the Histadrut. With privileged access to labor, land, and capital, it had emerged by the mid-1950s as a major conglomerate. Its role as provider of jobs, rather than growth or profits, was illustrated, for example, in its purchase in 1983 of Alliance, a tire manufacturer that had been threatened with liquidation by its creditors. Koor's unusual structure further reflected its republican origins. Owned by a trade union which was also an employer – the Histadrut – Koor's employees were its nominal owners. The salaried and hourly paid workers at each plant elected representatives to workers' committees. These formed a central committee to represent all Koor workers, which, although it had no management responsibility, played an important role in negotiating the workers' benefits. The central workers' committee nominated six rank-and-file workers to serve four-year terms on Koor's twenty-one-person board of directors, and one worker to its six-person executive (*International Management* 1974: 19). Finally, Koor's subsidiaries mutually guaranteed each other's debts, their internal clearing-house subsidized the loss-making ones and ensured that wages remained roughly equal among workers in different industries and enterprises (Gross 1994: 1).

Without any strategic plan or vision Koor entered into many unrelated fields, but assigned an especially important role to its military industries. Even in its early years, by setting up Soltam for producing artillery and ammunition and Telrad for the production of telecommunication equipment (adding Tadiran in the early 1960s), Koor became a mainstay of the Israeli arms industry (Asa-El 1997).

In the 1970s, under the management of Meir Amit, a retired general, Koor began to emphasize profits, seeking, in his words, to balance profit and the company's social mission by, for example, experimenting with profit sharing. This goal was combined with enhanced power for management. On one occasion, for example, the Histadrut consented to the closing of an unprofitable plant and the firing of its 100 workers. But these remained piecemeal changes and the "most important matters [continued to be] cleared with the union," which was the company's legal owner (*International Management* 1974: 18).

Koor relied on bank loans to raise capital throughout its existence, with the exception of two periods. In the early 1960s it issued securities through TASE, but these gave no voting rights. TASE repeatedly demanded the transformation of these into regular stocks, but Chevrat Haovdim was determined to keep complete control over Koor and refused all such initiatives. Koor turned for the first time to the US markets in 1986 and raised $105 million, at a high interest rate, in the junk-bond market through Drexel Burnham Lambert's Michael Milken. Shortly afterwards the BOI forbade Israeli companies to raise capital at such high prices (Gross 1994: 2–3). These two ventures indicated that, even when turning to security markets, Koor was not yet willing, or able, to be a full and regular participant.

For most of its period of existence Koor reported profits. Its 1987 sales of $2.7 billion represented more than 10 percent of Israel's GNP, while its employees accounted for nearly 11 percent of the country's labor force. In 1986 Koor incurred a loss of $100 million, which climbed, in 1987, to $188 million and in 1988 to $369 million. In 1988 126 out of Koor's 130 subsidiaries were losing money and were bailed out by the four profit-making ones, most of them in military production. In October 1988 Koor defaulted on its loans and its ratio of debt to equity was 72:1. Koor's future became doubtful when the financial reports of 1987 revealed a debt of $1.4 billion and one of its American debtors asked for its liquidation (*Multinational Business* 1989; Asa-El 1997).

Benny Gaon, who in 1976 had set up Koor's foreign trade division, the largest Israeli company in Europe, with fifteen branch offices and $100 million in yearly sales, and later helped restructure the Histadrut's Co-op – Israel's largest supermarket chain – was appointed Koor's CEO in June 1988. Between May 1988 and September 27 1991, nerve-racking negotiations were conducted with thirty-two Israeli and foreign banks. At what seemed like the last possible moment these negotiations led to a comprehensive agreement with Koor's debtors. The agreement wrote off a large share of Koor's bad debt ($330 million), with the Israeli government and the Histadrut, reluctantly and after much foot dragging, providing small bridge loans (NIS 175 million) for the duration of the reorganization period (Asa-El 1997). The protracted crisis and the refusal of both the government and the Histadrut to help Koor made it obvious that, in spite of the expectation of Koor's management that the company's large size would leave the Israeli government no choice but to come to its aid, "Big Brother [was] not going to support us anymore" (Waldman 1991). The Histadrut itself was not able to help in any serious fashion, since many of its companies were simultaneously in crisis, and in 1986 it chose to invest its capital reserves in Solel Bone. Whatever government and Histadrut support was forthcoming was relatively small and was offered in the context of changing Koor's ownership structure.

Under Gaon's management Koor was radically and brutally transformed. The mutual guarantee and the internal clearing arrangement among Koor's subsidiaries, which ensured the employment and relative wage equality of its workers, was abolished. The Histadrut conceded that profitability must be viewed as the top priority. Consequently, it consented to the sale of many of Koor's assets, the shutting down of loss makers, and the largest ever layoff in Israeli history – the firing of 40 percent of Koor's workers, who made up 4 percent of Israel's civilian labor force. Even the *Wall Street Journal* compared the effect of the newfound "capitalist creed" on Koor, which saved the company by shedding so much of its labor force, to that of a "neutron bomb" (Waldman 1991). And the *New York Times* quipped that Koor turned into a "lean-and-mean conglomerate that sheds money-losing businesses faster than you can say 'Charles Darwin'" (Passell 1992a). Although the layoffs were accompanied by worker demonstrations and protests, the repudiation of worker control, the firing of the very workers who under Chevrat Haovdim's constitution were Koor's putative owners, and the company's transfer, in the words of the *Jerusalem Post*, to "the unabashedly greedy ownership of Wall Street financiers – [they] hardly [caused] anyone to raise an eyebrow" (Asa-El 1997).

Chevrat Haovdim's 97 percent stake in Koor, already reduced to 71 percent in the reorganization's wake, was dramatically truncated by selling close to 60 percent to the public and to the Shamrock Group of the Shamrock Holdings investment company, wholly owned by the Disney family. In March 1995 Shamrock purchased Chevrat Haovdim's remaining shares, thus ending Koor's close to fifty-year association with the Histadrut. The new Koor was structured as a loose holding company in which individual firms were separately managed and managers were told they would be measured by their ability to maintain profitability. The sale of many of Koor's subsidiaries, and the very reorganization of Koor itself, though called in Hebrew *havraa* (recovery), was for all practical intents a process of privatization, a fact sometimes obscured by the reservation of the term "privatization" for the sale of government assets only.

In 1991 Koor reported a net profit for the first time in five years, and began a process of financial restructuring (Waldman 1991; Carnegy 1991; Passell 1992a; Enchin 1992). The restructuring was initially a financial success story: the new holding company, consisting of thirty individual firms, remained Israel's largest and for half a decade was its most profitable industrial conglomerate, led by its electronic and high-tech subsidiary, Tadiran.

"The turning point of its reorganization" and the key to its success and, concomitantly, to its independence from the government and the Histadrut was Koor's ability to tap the international financial market directly (Gross 1994: 13). By late 1992 Koor had raised about $220 million through stock issues in the US and Israel, and another $120 million in late 1995 in the US (Ozanne 1995). Benny Gaon pointed to the "discovery of the capital market by the Israeli business sector," starting in 1988–90, as the beginning of the economic transformation that had led to the transition to a market-based economy and signaled the shift of the center of gravity from banks to corporations, both holding and investment companies. "Israel's business community," Gaon summed up, "has discovered the capital market ... gradually disengaging ... from a traditional dependency on the banks in favor of the stock market" (Gaon 1993; Gaon interview). Shlomo Ben-Ami, director of Koor's Middle Eastern ventures in 1994–5, concurred with this conclusion (Ben-Ami interview).

Both Gaon and Ben-Ami argue that Israeli companies were able to raise great sums of money through the Israeli and US stock exchanges, and by the mid-1990s were awash with funds (Gaon and Ben-Ami interviews). This capital abundance, without the mediation and control of the government, has played a crucial role in the growing weight of the business community and the mounting influence of business interests on public decision making in Israel (see Lane 1998). It is also the basis on which a new collective identity – the Israeli business community – was formed. This identity was partially borrowed: in Ben-Ami's view Israeli business people have simply undergone a process of Americanization (Ben-Ami interview).

The discourse that accompanied and was used to justify Koor Industries' restructuring sheds critical light on its broader significance. "Within the 1985 conceptual and operational framework," Gaon argued, "no hope was left for Koor or for Israeli industry in general." Under Koor's new management reform was not effected in a patchwork form but was "a true, comprehensive, turnaround program" (Koor 1992). Koor, stated the *Wall Street Journal* during the restructuring, "adopted a new approach to doing business: the profit motive." Koor, it wrote, "got into trouble in the same way socialist enterprises have foundered elsewhere: it tried to create jobs instead of profits" (Waldman 1991). As we have shown throughout this book, Israeli socialism was above all a form of nationalism which sought to provide employment for nationalist reasons and, hence, enjoyed government support. Gaon is correct, then, in arguing that political considerations had historically overridden economic calculations (Gaon interview). Consequently, "a revolution in corporate culture had to be achieved" (Carnegy 1991).

In a speech in Washington, to celebrate the end of one stage of Koor's restructuring in April 1994, Gaon claimed that "the restructuring of Koor signaled the end of the concept of social welfare overriding profits, and the establishment of a market driven economy." These sober reflections gave way to a different tone, one more typical of the newfound self-confidence and bravado of the Israeli business community's leaders. In another speech, at the Waldorf-Astoria, to Koor's American shareholders and bankers involved in Koor's rescue, Gaon stated that "we have been in the forefront of Israel's turning away from a socialistic approach to our economy to one which rewards enterprise and hard work" (Gaon 1994a). The boastful and crude character of this statement is indicative of a desire to impress the US businesspeople in the audience, but also of the triumphant mood of the new Israeli economic elites. Given the centrality of Koor to the Histadrut, Gaon's observations on its pivotal role in Israel's socio-economic transformation are not too far fetched.

As a "key part" of its recovery plan Koor Industries under Gaon emphasized an export-oriented approach by seeking out "new markets for our goods and joint ventures with new partners." The "capitalistic profit-oriented" approach was the basis for Koor's aim "to ensure itself a competitive place in the world's markets as they open up in the West and East alike," that is, to partake in the process most commonly referred to as "globalization" (Koor 1992). In reporting the results for 1993 Gaon singled out for praise the telecommunications and electronics high-tech, construction materials, and agro-chemical companies, whose successful performance in the export market demonstrated the competitive character of Koor products at a time the company "accelerate[s its] efforts to enter new growth businesses serving emerging markets in Israel and around the world" (Koor 1994). The "future of the company," argued Gaon, "lies in globalization."

By 1995 Koor was in the process of "turning itself into a multinational concern and forging strategic partnerships with international companies" (Ozanne 1995). In 1993, for example, Koor's exports rose by 13 percent, with most of the growth coming from markets recently opened in India, China, Vietnam, and the Commonwealth of Independent States. Finally, Koor made an international stock offering, "thus becoming the first Israeli multinational company to be traded worldwide." These initiatives formed part of an overall plan: "The integration of Koor Industries into the global business community will form the essence of our strategy over the forthcoming years" (Gaon, Tel Aviv Hilton, June 22, 1995).

In 1997 Shamrock sold its shares in Koor to Claridge Israel and in July 1998 Jonathan Kolber took over from Benny Gaon as head of the company. During 1998 and 1999 Koor transformed itself from a diversified "Israel Fund" to a focused high-tech high-growth holding company. In July 1998 45 percent of Koor's products were exported; by August 2000 the percentage rose to 85. The new Koor's best year on record was 1997, with sales amounting to NIS 12.6 billion. In 1998 sales fell to NIS 11.5 billion ($2.82 billion), and further slowdown led to sales of only NIS 2.95 billion in the third quarter of 1999 and NIS 2 billion in the equivalent period in 2000 (out of 6.33 billion for the first nine months of 2000). In 2000 Koor's workforce was only 20,000. Whereas in 1998 almost all of Koor's employees were unionized, in August 2000 less then half of them were.

Koor's downward trend continued in 2001. In the first quarter of the year it registered the biggest loss in its history, and, in fact, in the history of any Israeli company – one billion shekels (close to $250,000,000). The loss stemmed from Kolber's policy of shedding "old industry" companies and concentrating on high-tech ones. As part of this policy Koor invested heavily in ECI, a telecommunications company that was hit very badly by the global crisis in the high-tech industries in 2000. Koor's losses also affected the profitability of Israel's largest bank – Bank Hapoalim – the former Histadrut bank, which had also been privatized. Bank Hapoalim became a major shareholder in Koor as part of the settlement of Koor's crisis of the 1980s and is also the main creditor of Koor, ECI, and Kolber. Evidently, privatization and institution of economic rather than political rationality were not sufficient in and of themselves to guarantee economic performance.

Summing up the situation of the Israeli economy and capital market in 1994, Gaon repeated that "there is no doubt that the continued expansion of the economy depends on the significant widening of the Israeli market to foreign investment and in furnishing opportunities and assistance for the strategic investment of Israeli corporations abroad" (Gaon, lecture at IMC, May 24, 1994). Global ties and investment fulfilled two roles: they provided strong financial backing, as well as new management experience and links to international marketing and data bases, whereas Israeli investment in foreign subsidiaries or in purchasing equity in foreign companies provided a stepping stone for increasing technological know-how and penetration into new markets (Gaon, Jerusalem Business Conference 1994).

The obstacle to the achievement of either of these goals – opening new markets for Israeli industry and attracting foreign capital – had been the Israeli–Palestinian conflict. Many Israeli business leaders realized that the Arab boycott was a major obstacle on the road to integrating the Israeli economy into the world market; as long as it remained in effect all efforts in this direction yielded only limited results. Even after Israeli companies had been launched in the American stock market, international capital still remained aloof from Israel, due to the political instability in the Middle East. Only the stability ensured by peace could bring foreign investment and foreign corporations into Israel on a significant scale (Hurvitz, Lautman, Gaon interviews).

Economic liberalization thus provided an impetus for peace by mobilizing strategic sectors of the emerging Israeli business community, Gaon most prominently among them, in support of achieving a breakthrough in Israeli–Palestinian relations. The politicization of the business community around this issue was simultaneously an indication of its newfound autonomy and a major contribution to breaking the stalemate between Israel and the Palestinians.

The Israeli–Palestinian conflict had remained at an impasse as long as it was viewed solely as a security matter. It became "solvable" when it was reconceptualized as an obstacle to the integration of Israeli business into the global economy, at a moment of acute consciousness of the difference between "winning" and "losing" countries in the world economic arena. Within this new framework the old issues of the colonial era became secondary to questions of economic growth and development. This created the potential for replacing the traditional, zero–sum game, in which one side's gain was the other side's loss, with a more open-ended game, in which both sides could be winners. This process of redefinition was greatly aided by the outward-looking sectors of the business community, in league with the professional and technocratic elites of the civil service (especially its legal and economic sectors) and the political leadership, after Labor's election victory in 1992. It involved an attempt to extend the boundaries of the "economic" at the expense of the "political," and of the "civic" and "individualistic" at the expense of the "pioneering" and "collective," in short, of the liberal discourse of citizenship at the expense of the ethno-national and republican ones. This view dovetailed with the experience of financial, trade, legal, and cultural globalization that has pointed up, for most countries of the world, the limits of nation-state autonomy.

Peace and profits

The expression of independent business opinions on the Israeli–Arab and Israeli–Palestinian conflicts, and the crossing of the line between economic and politics, was at first timid but the move from lobbying to public campaign was unprecedented – this was the first time Israeli business leaders came out to campaign for an issue until then defined strictly as political. At first this independence was tested with regard to the safer question of the absorption of the masses of Jewish immigrants who began arriving in 1989 from the ex-USSR, an issue well within the national consensus, but linked by businessmen to the peace process. In his survey article of December 4, 1989, John Rossant of the *Business Week* found that: "To make Israel more attractive to the immigrants, many Israeli businessmen insist that peace is needed. The pragmatic Israeli business community is putting behind-the-scene pressure on the Shamir government to negotiate with the Palestinians" (Rossant 1989: 58). "Israeli businessmen know that without peace with the Arabs," Rossant found, "there is little chance of the country building a stable civilian economy." It is against this conviction, at a time when the economy had already been restructured into "Israel Inc.," much to the delight of business, and was slated for take-off, that "many Israeli businessmen are joining the Bush Administration in leaning on Prime Minister Yitzhak Shamir to become more flexible in his approach to negotiations." Eli Hurvitz, CEO of Teva Pharmaceuticals, Israel's largest drug company, and past president of the Manufacturers' Association of Israel (MAI), expressed this consensus by stating that from this economic perspective "the future is problematic without peace" (Rossant 1989: 54).

Most outspoken on this issue was Dov Lautman, CEO of Delta Textiles. Between 1987 and 1993 Lautman was president of the MAI and chair of the Coordinating Bureau of the Economic Organizations – the broad-based association of Israeli business organizations that includes, in addition to the MAI, the Federation of Chambers of Commerce, as well as the umbrella organizations of building contractors, banks, private farmers, life-insurance companies, the self-employed, diamond manufacturers, hotels, etc. In the early 1990s, the last years of Shamir's government, Lautman was a major critic of government economic policies which, in his view, did not procure the increased productivity and exports that he viewed as preconditions for the absorption of the masses of Soviet Jewish immigrants. The pressing need to absorb the immigrants served as a shield behind which it was possible to criticize the government's lack of proper economic policies, and, indirectly, its lack of enthusiasm for the peace process.

At the annual Jerusalem Business Conference, held in 1992 one week before the crucial elections in which Shamir squared off against Rabin, Lautman issued his first open linkage of peace with economic growth, and issued an indirect call to advance the negotiations that had been going on in Madrid since late 1991. In his words, the major obstacle to foreign investment in the Israeli economy was regional instability, and only the combination of a proper economic policy with progress in the peace talks could make Israel attractive to foreign investors (*Haaretz*, June 17, 1992).

In November 1992 Lautman added the Arab boycott to his list of conditions that hurt Israel economically, and argued that the business community had made a mistake in the past decade by not highlighting the linkage between peace and economic growth (*Haaretz*, November 17, 1992). He was seconded in this opinion by Danny Gilerman, president of the Israeli Chambers of Commerce, who, relying on a study conducted by his organization, alleged that Israel had lost $44 billion as a result of the Arab boycott. Gilerman called on Rabin, the new prime minister, to consider the abolition of the boycott a top priority *(Haaretz*, August 7, 1992). Finally, in January 1993, Lautman threw in the trump card by promising that a breakthrough in the peace "talks in 1993 will serve as a tremendous turning point (*mifne adir*) in the fortunes of the Israeli economy in general and of industry in particular, by 1994" (*Haaretz*, January 1, 1993).

The innovation in the interconnectedness between the Israeli economy and the peace process was captured by Yoram Peri, then editor of the Histadrut daily, *Davar*. In May 1993, at a reception organized by Koor for the Israeli economic elite, Stanley Fischer, deputy director of the IMF and co-chair of the steering committee of the Project on the Economics of Transition at the Institute for Social and Economic Policy in the Middle East at Harvard's Kennedy School of Government, gave an early overview of the study's perspective on Israel's peace economy (see Fischer et al. 1993; Institute for Social and Economic Policy in the Middle East 1993). Peri marveled at the gap between those attending the reception – who since the 1992 elections which brought Rabin and Labor to power "live in tomorrow's world" where "peace was already viewed as a fait accompli," with only its details needing to be worked out – and the "man in the street" and the vast majority of Israeli politicians, for whom the Israeli–Arab conflict was still the overwhelming reality. The two groups, in his words, resided on "separate planets." Since the politicians refused to talk the language of the future, the new "truth is articulated by economists and businessmen, diplomats and even . . . generals" (Peri 1993).

As soon as the news of the pending, but yet unfinished and still potentially collapsible, accord between Israel and the PLO leaked to the public, the elite of Israel's business leaders called on Rabin and Peres, in a paid advertisement, "to bring peace for the sake of good years" (*Haaretz*, September 2, 1993). As a sequel, some of the signatories established a committee to support the government's peace policy, for example by plastering billboards with the slogan "Israel awaits peace" (*Haaretz*, September 5, 1993). When Rabin and Peres returned from Washington, after signing of the DOP, some of the same individuals were invited to the welcoming ceremony, in order to underline the centrality of the economic dimension of the agreement (*Haaretz*, September 19, 1993). Lautman was mentioned as a possible chair of the Israeli delegation to the economic talks with the Palestinians that followed the DOP, and Eli Hurvitz, CEO of the large pharmaceutical concern Teva, was actually offered that job, but declined due to the extensive time commitment it required (*Haaretz*, October 11, 1993; November 16, 1993; Hurvitz interview).

Support for the peace process, and implicitly for recognition of Palestinian national rights, was by no means unanimous among Israeli businesspeople, however. The self-selected business leaders, who expressed their vigorous support and sought to rally others, on the grounds that peace would open up the world economy to Israel, were drawn from industries that could benefit from export-oriented growth. They were stubbornly opposed by executives from labor-intensive industries, whose purview was more domestic. This division was clearly revealed in the differing attitudes of the two groups toward the new economic possibilities an autonomous Palestinian authority would present.

In mid-1992 Lautman set up a committee of the Coordinating Bureau of the Economic Organizations, chaired by Dan Gilerman of the FCC, to study the "Economic Implications of the Establishment of Autonomy in the Territories and Ways for its Integration with the Israeli Economy." Although the leadership of the Coordinating Bureau and the MAI was clearly supportive of such autonomy, many in the rank and file were fearful of its impact on their particular sectors and expressed their reservations. Both a survey conducted by the MAI (MAI 1994) and a special issue of its quarterly, devoted to the "autonomy," revealed that textiles, food, wood, leather, and plastic products were seen as vulnerable to competition from Palestinian workers, whose wages were only a fraction of the wages of Israeli workers in these industries. Ironically, building contractors, the biggest employers of Palestinian workers, were concerned about losing their workers to what they expected would become a booming Palestinian economy, while private and collective farmers thought they might both lose workers and be exposed to cheaper agricultural imports (Coordinating Bureau of the Economic Organizations 1992; 1993). Summing up the demands and concerns of the Gilerman Report (which were largely incorporated into the Israeli position at the Paris economic talks in 1994), industrialist Mozi Wertheimer concluded that their acceptance would replace autonomy with Israeli economic domination over the Palestinians (Wertheimer 1993; Ben-Shahar 1995; "Protocol on Economic Relations" 1995; Savir 1998: 122–3). Although the vocal supporters of the peace process were drawn from the very apex of the business community, a considerable part of their efforts was spent in seeking to reduce the anxiety of other industrialists, farmers, and merchants, fearful of the potentially adverse economic effects of a peace accord on their branches of the economy (Menashe interview). The complaints and fears of the opponents from within the MAI were played down, however, by Lautman, who led the MAI towards a policy "of free trade and open markets" with the Palestinians (Lautman interview).

In parallel with the public opinion campaign the MAI, under Lautman and others, and the Israel Management Center (IMC) sought to commence talks with Palestinian businesspeople in order to facilitate economic co-operation and, through it, advance the political talks as well (Lautman and Kamenitz interviews). Some thought that voluntary assistance for a Palestinian organization for export, for a clearing house for Israeli–Palestinian trade, or for setting up a Palestinian stock exchange would serve as proof that progress could be attained. "Palestinian industrialists," argued Yoram Blizovsky, director general of the MAI, "view us, industrialists, as a more credible partner than the government, since we are perceived as a more neutral factor" (Blizovsky interview). This sentiment was shared by other Israeli business leaders, who believed that business ties and co-operation between individuals and enterprises would make it possible to bypass political problems. In the words of Uri Menashe, who was in charge of these talks, it was expected that the changing economic reality could marginalize political problems and have politicians follow the lead of economic co-operation (Menashe interview).

Soon after Labor won the 1992 elections Lautman called for negotiations over Palestinian autonomy with the goal of facilitating the co-
ordination of the two economies (Reiner 1992). For the first time the
grand vision of economic growth in the context of Middle East peace
and the immediate reality of Israeli–Palestinian conflict were linked in a
single strategic framework. The eventual talks between the two economic
elites remained sporadic and inconclusive, however, due to the inability
of the Palestinian side, still under Israeli military occupation, to separate
its economic from its political concerns, and due to restrictions imposed
by their political leadership (Menashe interview; *Haaretz*, December 18,
1992). In addition, Palestinian businesspeople were well aware of the past
opposition of Israeli industrialists to the establishment of industrial enterprises in the West Bank and were less than keen on an open border
policy. Under these conditions, two separate decisions to establish a permanent forum for consultation between the two elites did not take effect
(*Haaretz*, February 17, 1993).

It was in the immediate aftermath of the DOP that the voice of business
support for peace economics grew loudest. In the fall of 1993 *Globes*, the
main Israeli business daily, was full of glorious and euphoric predictions
of the economic benefits of the peace process, propagated by businesspeople and government officials (*Globes*, September 15 and November 2,
1993). There was a veritable stampede of lesser business leaders and
economists rushing in the footsteps of the trailblazers. "The sky is the
limit" of the peace economy, was their approach, and the economic benefits of peace served as its main selling point. One of the most telling
examples of the euphoria was a brochure prepared by the IMC for its
annual meeting in December 1993, in which the keynote speaker was
Rabin, and the other speakers were the president of Israel, the minister
of finance, the president of the MAI, and the chairman of the IMC. The
brochure was decorated with the picture of the famous Rabin–Arafat
handshake on the White House lawn, with President Clinton looking
on, under the logo "The Economic Turn Begins": not the political turn,
mind you, but the economic turn! The extensive participation of government representatives demonstrated the extent to which this approach
and this sentiment were shared by the government. The government
mobilized the industrialists to sell the peace, after the industrialists had
identified themselves with the process of peacemaking. Rabin relied on
their power, influence, and the public climate they created, in order to
continue with the peace process. Thus, he and Peres gathered the top
echelon of Israeli businesspeople in August 1994 and asked them to back
the peace process, for the hope of economic prosperity it would bring
(Tal-Shir 1994).

Of the various Israeli corporations, Koor was best equipped to turn to Arab and Middle Eastern markets because it had some limited experience in this area. As head of Koor's foreign trade operations, Gaon had set up a Koor office in Egypt after the Camp David Accord, the first Israeli company to do so. Due to Egyptian reluctance, however, hopes for expanding trade relations were quickly shattered. However, though there were no open trade relations between Israel and the Arab world until 1994, it is estimated that in the previous decade about $500 million of Israeli exports annually were destined for Arab countries. (This sum constitutes half of the close to $1 billion in the unclassified category of Israeli exports in Israel's *Foreign Trade Statistical Quarterly*.) For example, in the 1980s Iraq imported hydraulic lifts and agricultural products, as well as pharmaceutical products (Fishelson interview), while Morocco purchased fertilizers, agricultural implements and seeds, and air-conditioners, to the tune of $80 million per year (Barak interview). Many of these products were supplied by Koor subsidiaries.

Koor's Peace Project was launched shortly after the signing of the DOP in Oslo in September 1993. Simultaneously Koor tried, ultimately without success, to set up a project for regional co-operation, Salam-2000, in cooperation with Omnium Nord Africa (ONA), Morocco's largest private concern, and a group of Palestinian businessmen (Ben-Ami interview). Another effort was to form Jordanian–Palestinian–Israeli partnerships to invest mostly in West Bank and Gaza infrastructure and in the Arab world, in both trade and industry. In anticipation of a breakthrough in the peace process, Koor entered the tourism industry. It was also the main company to have established ongoing economic relations with the Palestinian National Authority, exporting cement, construction iron, and telecommunications equipment, worth $80 million in 1994 (Gaon and Ben-Ami interviews).

Gaon posited Koor as a leader in promoting the peace-and-profit nexus. In a country with a small number of industrial concerns, such as Israel, he stated, "it is the responsibility of companies such as Koor ... to forge new joint projects, to divert funds from war to peace, to deepen the economic bonds between regional economies and the western world and to develop a regional economy of peace." He called on "the leading industrial concerns," i.e. IDB, Israel Corp., Israel Chemicals, Klal, and Koor itself, "to take the lead, to take the risk, and invite foreign capital for joint investment projects in Israel as well as in the region" (Gaon, Jerusalem Business Conference, 1994).

For Israeli companies the Arab economies held promise as potential markets, suppliers of cheap labor, sub-contractors, business partners, and objects or targets of investment. In 1993 this multiple set of interests animated many of the meetings of the regional and topical forums of the dense business network operating under the aegis of Israel Management Center (IMC). Haim Kamenitz, the IMC director, recalls that the gatherings of its tourism, marketing, senior managers, and many other groups, were dissatisfied with the pace of the peace process. The hope repeatedly expressed in these meetings was that managers might be able to advance what politicians could not, and that economic ties would provide a good foundation for political arrangements (Kamenitz interview). Producers of luxury goods recognized the Arab market as stratified and aimed their products at the affluent stratum, as well as the more affluent Arab states in the Gulf region (Nurith Nachum interview). Low-tech producers, among them food manufacturers such as Elite and Osem, that occupied semi-monopolistic status in the Israeli economy anticipated being hurt by the reduction of tariff barriers as part of trade liberalization, and were eager to enter into markets of non-industrial societies.

But the ambitions of the Israeli business leaders reached even higher. Gaon summed up the attractions of the Middle East for Israeli investors: "Israel's technological and financial know-how, coupled to the financial resources of the Gulf states and to the inexpensive labor available in the area, offers investors a combination of commercial attributes that is probably unique in the world" (Gaon 1993). In the vision of the overconfident business leaders Israel appeared as the hub and coordinator of a new regional economic grouping, without any consideration of the potential conflicts between countries with widely disparate resources. It is hard to escape the conclusion that in peacemaking, as in conflict, the Israeli approach of qualitative superiority continued to prevail. In fact, no such regional economic order has developed yet, although a small number of Israeli companies, mostly in textiles, transferred their plants from development and citizen Palestinian towns and even from the Gaza Strip to Jordan and Egypt (*Mitzad Sheni*, January/February 1997: 16–19).

The main economic benefits, however, were expected to come not from the Arab markets, but from other foreign markets that had been closed to Israel due to the secondary Arab boycott (in which third parties doing business with Israel were penalized). In a speech delivered at the annual conference of the IMC in May 1994, and repeated at the Jerusalem Business Conference of 1994, Gaon pointed out that the peace process "has opened additional avenues of growth for the Israeli economy." In addition to the immediate circle of Palestinians, Jordan, and Syria he listed the outer circle of the North African and Gulf countries and Turkey, as well the Asian countries of Indonesia, Malaysia, India, Vietnam, Japan, and Korea, as potential commercial targets. Economic relations with Arab countries "represent only a fraction of the benefits that Israel stands to gain from peace in the Middle East" and the other, more lucrative, possibilities "would not have been likely before the peace process began" (Gaon, lecture at the IMC, 1994).

Conclusion

The role played by the business community, so clearly united behind the breakthrough with the Palestinians, raises some interesting questions concerning its impact on the possible continuation of the peace process. Israeli business has not been completely transformed since the Israeli–Palestinian DOP. Koor is still a champion of peace, but also continues to be an important arms manufacturer. And while the disappearance of the secondary Arab boycott satisfied many of the interests of the business community in finding new strategic partnerships and markets in East Asia and Europe, it also made them less vulnerable to the continuing vagaries of the peace process. The political stability of the Middle East, however, remains a key precondition for its more complete integration into the world economy and for raising the standard of living of its inhabitants. The most significant contribution of business and its allies to the peace process was probably the redefinition of political issues as economic issues, that is, the adoption of the business community's perspective for more general purposes. This is a potent illustration of this group's influence in an era in which it acquired a considerable measure of autonomy, as well as of a potential way of ignoring the full weight of the political issues with which economic considerations intersect.

Ultimately, the peace-and-profit nexus is part of a broader set of issues, addressed in this study as Israel's incorporation regime and multiple citizenship discourses. The role played by the business community and the other advocates of disengagement and withdrawal from the West Bank cannot be separated from the conflict now looming between alternative incorporation regimes, based on two different citizenship discourses, the liberal and ethno-national. The intensification of the Israeli–Palestinian conflict and the suspension of the peace process since the outbreak of the al-Aksa intifada, as well as the renewed crisis of Koor, demonstrate that the victory of the liberal discourse over the ethno-national one is by no means guaranteed. Another major arena where the conflict between them is played out – the arena of social citizenship rights – will be the subject matter of chapter 11.

10   The "constitutional revolution"

The United Nations partition resolution for Palestine, which was adopted on November 29, 1947, called upon the two states whose establishment it advocated – a Jewish state and an Arab state – to adopt written constitutions that would guarantee, among other things, "equal non-discriminatory rights in religious, economic, and political areas to all persons, including human rights, freedom of religion, language, speech, education, publication, assembly, and association" (Medding 1990: 11–12; Mahler 1990: 81). In accordance with this resolution, Israel's declaration of independence, adopted on May 14, 1948, stipulated that "a Constitution [would] be drawn up by a Constituent Assembly not later than the first day of October 1948" (Medding 1990: 238). In July 1948 a constitutional committee was established to prepare a draft constitution, and the constituent assembly was elected in January 1949. Instead of adopting a constitution, however, the constituent assembly declared itself to be the first Knesset on March 8, 1949.[1] On June 13, 1950 "the Knesset voted by a 50–30 margin to postpone indefinitely the adoption of a formal written constitution and decided instead to allow for its gradual creation, with the individual pieces to be designated Fundamental [or Basic] Laws" (Mahler 1990: 83).

The debate leading up to the decision not to formulate a complete written constitution in the main pitted against each other politicians advocating a liberal conception of citizenship and making formal, principled arguments and those seeking to promote an ethno-nationalist or republican conception and arguing in the name of pragmatic considerations. Institutionally, the former position implied, at least, a preference for a legislature and an executive constrained by constitutional limitations

---

[1] An interesting constitutional question raised by the constituent assembly turning itself into the first Knesset is: Did the assembly transfer its constituent powers to the Knesset, or did it void them? This question would figure prominently in the future debate about the "constitutional revolution" of the 1990s (Gavison 1997; Klein 1997; Kretzmer 1997; Barak 1998).

and hence, necessarily, by the judiciary; the latter position meant greater freedom of action for the Knesset and the executive branch and a weaker judicial branch. And indeed, the judiciary began as the weakest of Israel's governmental institutions (Lahav 1993).

Not surprisingly, the most formidable opponent of the constitution was David Ben-Gurion himself. Arguing in terms of the majoritarian principle of democracy and the need of the state to have maximum freedom of action, Ben-Gurion objected to any self-limitation on the power of the Knesset, whether through laws entrenched with privileged majority requirements, judicial review of legislation, or a bill of rights. His claim was that such limitations would impede the ability of the state to act decisively, an ability that was crucial for a state whose demographic and territorial composition was still in flux. To illustrate his point Ben-Gurion reminded his adversaries of the conservative role played by the Supreme Court of the United States in trying to block the progressive social legislation of the New Deal as unconstitutional. In the Knesset debate Ben-Gurion and Mapai were joined by the religious parties, whose representatives argued that Israel did not need a man-made constitution, since it already had a God-made one – the Torah (Knesset 1950; Medding 1990: 37–42; Mahler 1990: 81–4; Shapiro 1996a: 30–3; Gavison 1997: 75–9; Gross 1998a).

Ben-Gurion's arguments against the necessity of a bill of rights clearly revealed his continued commitment to the republican discourse of citizenship and to its civic virtue – *chalutziyut*. In a free society, he argued, where the people rule, there is no need for a bill of rights, because the citizens' rights would not be threatened by their own democratically elected government. What there was a need for, on the other hand, was a bill of *duties*. This was particularly true of Israel, a free and democratic country that

will not be built, will not be defended and will not fulfill its mission in Israeli [i.e., Jewish] history – without intensified *chalutziyut*, and *chalutziyut* means accepting the burden of duties ... The great and difficult tasks history has imposed on the generation of the founders, builders and defenders of the state [i.e., "security, *aliya* and settlement"] will be impossible without a bill of duties we will impose on ourselves, out of our own free will. (Knesset 1950: 819)

It is noteworthy that Ben-Gurion stressed only the duties entailed by the virtue of *chalutziyut*, not the aspect of voluntary self-fulfillment, *hagshama atzmit* (see chap. 2, above). This is understandable in view of the conception the LSM had of the newly arriving immigrants in the 1950s, particularly the Mizrachim among them, as "immigrants" rather than "*olim*" (see chap. 3, above).

In the absence of a full-fledged constitution a number of laws designated "basic laws" have been passed since 1950, but with few notable exceptions none of them were entrenched by either formal or substantive requirements, and none were given the power to override other, non-basic pieces of primary legislation. Without an overarching standard to refer to, judicial review of legislation was, of course, impossible. (The court itself initially rejected the idea that the declaration of independence could provide such a standard.) This highlighted the weakness of the Supreme Court, the only branch of government without roots in the pioneering era of the Yishuv, and an institution staffed primarily by non-pioneering Jews of German or English-speaking origin. Symbolically, as Pnina Lahav has noted, it was not until 1992 (by chance, the year of the "constitutional revolution"), long after the other two branches of government, that the Supreme Court was provided with a building of its own (Lahav 1993: 127).

In 1953 the court took its first bold step against the executive branch, in invalidating a suspension order issued by the minister of the interior against two dailies, in Hebrew and Arabic, published by the Israeli Communist Party. In order to do that, the court for the first time invoked Israel's declaration of independence as a normative basis for the protection of freedom of speech. This bold act was preceded by the enactment of the Judges' Law, which guaranteed judges life-time tenure and immunity from interference by the executive in their salaries and working conditions, and by the inauguration of a new system of selecting judges, through an appointment committee in which judges and lawyers have a guaranteed majority (Lahav 1993: 129–39).

One law that was entrenched in the 1950s was the clause in Basic Law: The Knesset (1958) that established the electoral system as national, equal, direct, secret, and proportional. That clause could be changed only by an absolute majority of members of the Knesset (i.e., sixty-one votes). On the basis of this requirement, in 1969 the Supreme Court took another step on its road to becoming a powerful institution, and forced the Knesset to amend a new law providing for the public funding of political parties. That law, it was argued, violated the equality clause of the Basic Law since it discriminated in favor of political parties already represented in the Knesset in the allocation of public funds. Because it had been passed by fewer than sixty-one votes the new law could not override the equality provision of Basic Law: The Knesset and had to be amended. This case, known as the *Bergman* case, set a precedent and established the right of the court to exercise judicial review over primary legislation. That right, however, had lain in abeyance for over twenty years, until the "constitutional revolution" of 1992 (Mahler 1990: 85–91; Lahav 1993; Gavison 1997: 82; Kretzmer 1997).

The political, economic, and intellectual crisis generated by the 1973 Arab–Israeli war, the Lebanon war of 1982, and the rapid monetary inflation of the early 1980s was a watershed event in the constitutional history of Israel. In 1986 a group of law professors from Tel Aviv University wrote a draft constitution and launched a public campaign for its adoption. The draft formally codified many of the existing constitutional arrangements, but departed from them in several important respects. It called for the direct election of the prime minister by the electorate, turning Israel's system of government from a parliamentary to a semi-presidential one. It also sought to change the system of electing the Knesset itself, turning it from a fully proportional system based on a single national constituency to one based on a combination of proportional and district representation. The draft constitution also included a bill of rights, with a number of social rights among them (the full text of the draft constitution is in Bechor 1996: 207–56).

Building on the disaffection of many Israelis with a political system they considered corrupt and too easily manipulated by small, primarily religious parties, the formulators of the draft constitution were able to mobilize hundreds of thousands of people in support of their Constitution for Israel campaign (Bechor 1996; Hazan 1996: 24). The campaign failed to bring about the adoption of a constitution or a bill of rights, but succeeded in transforming Israel's political and constitutional systems in two important respects: between 1996 and 2001 the prime minister was no longer elected by the Knesset, but directly by the electorate (this was changed back in 2001), and two basic laws pertaining to human rights, Basic Law: Freedom of Occupation and Basic Law: Human Dignity and Freedom, were enacted. These three constitutional acts, all legislated in 1992 and subsequently amended, were described by Aharon Barak, then an associate justice of the Supreme Court and since 1995 its president, as a "constitutional revolution" (Barak 1992; the texts of all three basic laws are in Bechor 1996: 257–82; see also Barzilai 2000). As we shall see, this revolution had the effect of enhancing liberal citizenship rights in the civil, political, social, and economic spheres, to the detriment of republican and ethno-national rights. At the same time, certain ethno-nationalist and republican legacies were protected, with the result that the coherence that characterized the institutional regime in the period of LSM hegemony was undermined, and the institutional fragmentation of a system in which alternative citizenship discourses coexist was made more explicit.

The electoral system

The initial thrust of electoral reform in Israel was a multilevel transfer of influence from collective bodies to individuals. The reform actually began in the mid-1970s, when the DMC instituted primary elections as a means of selecting its candidates for the Knesset (Urieli and Barzilay 1982; A. Rubinstein 1982; chap. 8, above; many of the promoters of the "constitutional revolution" had been members of the DMC). The DMC had disintegrated after only one term in the Knesset, but its legacy as a model of internal party democracy survived. In 1992 the Labor Party adopted the system of primary elections, to replace the old method of candidate selection by the party's central institutions. In 1996 both major parties held primary elections to select their candidates for prime minister and for the Knesset, as did a number of smaller parties (Doron 1996; Hazan 1997a; Arian 1998: 163–5, 189–205; Korn 1998).

The second prong of electoral reform was the amendment of Basic Law: The Cabinet (as well as Basic Law: The Knesset and a number of other laws) in 1992, so between 1996 and 2001 the prime minister (PM) was elected directly by the electorate, rather than by the Knesset as before (Allon 1995; Bechor 1996). (This reform followed the model of direct popular election of mayors, introduced in 1978 and considered a great success: Hazan 1996: 25–6.) Other elements of the governmental system, including the way the Knesset is elected, were not changed, however, so that a hybrid parliamentary–presidential system unique to Israel emerged. This new system failed to achieve the stated purpose of its initiators: to weaken the smaller, primarily religious parties' bargaining power vis-à-vis the PM, and ensure greater efficiency and stability in government (Hazan 1997a; 1997b; Nachmias and Sened 1999). In 2001, therefore, the old electoral system was restored, an outcome that can be understood if we look at the actual electoral results of the new and, as it turned out, short-lived liberal reform.

The actual result of the reform was that the electoral strength of the small, sectoral parties, especially the religious ones, increased significantly, at the expense of the major parties. In the 1996 Knesset elections the Labor Party lost ten seats, compared to 1992 (forty-four to thirty-four), while Likud, together with its affiliated party, Tzomet, lost eight seats (forty to thirty-two). All the Jewish religious parties combined gained seven seats (sixteen to twenty-three), while two new political parties, one representing immigrants from the former Soviet Union (Yisrael Baaliya) and the other a hawkish spinoff from Labor (the Third Way), won seven and four seats, respectively. Lastly, parties representing primarily Palestinian voters gained four seats (five to nine) (Arian 1998: 208–9;

Hazan 1997b: 347). This trend continued in the 1999 elections, after which there were no more major political parties in the Knesset. Rather, three medium-sized parties had the largest factions – Labor with twenty-six seats (later reduced to twenty-three), Likud with nineteen, and Shas with seventeen.

These results were clearly the direct, if unintended, outcome of the new electoral system. Under the old system the leader of the largest faction in the Knesset would normally become PM. Voters had an incentive, therefore, to vote for the large parties, in order to influence the selection of the head of government. Under the new system voters could split their vote between their preferred candidate for PM and their favorite political party, so they could support small, ideological, or sectoral parties for the Knesset and still affect the choice of PM (Nachmias and Sened 1999).

Moreover, the small parties' bargaining power increased even beyond their electoral success, because a candidate for PM now needed to build two coalitions, instead of only one: one coalition prior to the elections, in order to win the popular vote, and a second coalition, of at least sixty-one members of Knesset, after s/he was elected, in order to gain a confidence vote for the cabinet. (If no candidate had received more than 50 percent of the vote in the first round of election for PM, a second round would have had to be held. In this case the winning candidate would have had to form a coalition three times, not only two.) Naturally, the PM's position in this bargaining process was weakened along with the electoral strength of the major political parties (Diskin 1998; Arian 1998: 178–205; Nachmias and Sened 1999).

The electoral reforms also weakened the internal party institutions of the two major parties, especially that of Labor, whose legendary party machine had been among the most powerful institutions in the society. Since under the new system neither the party leader, who was its prime ministerial candidate, nor the party's candidates to the Knesset were selected by party institutions these institutions, made up of long-time party activists, lost much of their reason for being. Intra-party politics became personalized and politicians' fortunes came to depend on their fundraising abilities and on their media exposure, rather than on their loyalty to the party's ideological principles or central institutions. This also weakened the parties' ability to function as cohesive bodies in the Knesset (Begin 1996; Hazan 1997b; Hofnung 1998; Rahat and Sher-Hadar 1999).

These electoral reforms were thus characterized by a number of internal contradictions, which made them unstable and likely to be modified. The liberal principle of personal election was applied in the prime ministerial and internal party elections only. In Knesset elections the republican proportional system was maintained. Thus, whereas the party leader needed to face between two and four rounds of personal elections, Knesset candidates had to face only one round, in the primaries, and once elected to the party's list of candidates did not have to go out and try to gain the confidence of a wider constituency. Their chances of actually being elected to the Knesset depended, from that point on, on the work of the party organization, to which they were no longer beholden, because of the primaries. By the same token, the weakening of party institutions meant that the party leader lost much of the ability to control its Knesset members and because more vulnerable than before to political pressure on their part.

The upshot of these electoral reforms, then, was that a new, seemingly powerful institution – a popularly elected prime minister – was created, to join two previously existing institutions that have been greatly strengthened in the period of liberalization – the Bank of Israel (discussed in chap. 9) and the Supreme Court (to be discussed below). However, the new power given the PM was subverted by the continued dependence of the cabinet on the confidence of the Knesset and by the weakening of both the major parties and party discipline. Thus, two of the three PMs elected under this internally contradictory system – Netanyahu and Barak – failed to complete their terms of office.

In response to these anomalies, after its victory in 1996 Likud decided to do away with primary elections of Knesset candidates and revert to their election by the party center. Following that decision by Likud, voices demanding similar changes have increasingly been heard in the Labor Party as well. Most importantly, after Ariel Sharon was elected prime minister, in February 2001, the direct election of the prime minister was abolished and the old, parliamentary electoral system was restored.

Human rights legislation

Judicial activism and the rise of the Supreme Court

In the absence of a formal bill of rights, human rights had been protected in Israel by a "judicial bill of rights," a body of judicial decisions that had gradually established the basic liberal freedoms as norms governing the conduct of the state. The protection provided by this judicial bill of rights was very uneven, however, with considerations of "national security" and the ethno-national interests of Jews overriding individual rights in many cases (Lahav 1993; Gavison 1997; Gross 1998a). Still, the revolutionary nature of the two basic laws of 1992 pertaining to human rights did not lie in the introduction of rights discourse into Israel's political and legal culture. It lay, rather, in the enhanced stature the Supreme Court was able to claim as a result of them. According to Aharon Barak, in 1992 the Knesset for the first time limited its own power to interfere with certain fundamental human rights:

The fundamental rights now obligate the legislator himself. Israel can no longer be said not to have a "written constitution" (formal and rigid) in the sphere of human rights. The new legislation took Israel out of its isolation, and placed us in the large camp of countries in which human rights are grounded in a "written" and "rigid" constitution, that is, in a document possessing normative priority or superiority. (Barak 1992: 13)

The extent to which the Knesset indeed intended to limit its own power to change or contravene these two laws is not that clear, however. Of the two, only Basic Law: Freedom of Occupation was entrenched, rather weakly, with a stipulation that it could be amended only by another basic law enacted by a majority of Knesset members. Basic Law: Human Dignity and Freedom, which protects the rights to life, liberty, honor, the integrity of the body, private property, privacy, and movement in and out of the country, was not entrenched in this way, because of its possible implications for the validity of Israel's religious legislation. Furthermore, the rights guaranteed by the two laws can be infringed by subsequent primary legislation, provided that such legislation is consistent with the values of Israel as a Jewish and democratic state, is enacted for a worthy purpose, and the infringement does not exceed what is necessary for that purpose. In addition, all legislation that had been on the book prior to the enactment of the two basic laws is immune forever against scrutiny for its accordance with Basic Law: Human Dignity and Freedom, and for four years under Basic Law: Freedom of Occupation (that four-year period has been extended already to 2002) (Kretzmer 1992: 240–2; Gavison 1997: 93–100; Gross 1998a; Barak 1998).

While the two basic laws do not provide explicitly for judicial review either, the limitations they placed on future legislation have laid the ground for the Supreme Court to claim for itself the right to intervene in cases where conflicts are alleged to exist between such legislation and the basic laws. The court has already acted to establish this right in practice, in the *Mizrachi Bank* (or Gal Law) case, where the majority (of eight to one) argued, in a 367-page decision, that the court had the right to nullify a statute it found to contradict Basic Law: Human Dignity and Freedom (although the court did not make such a finding in that particular case). Later on the court did act to nullify a clause in a statute it deemed to be in contradiction to Basic Law: Freedom of Occupation – a technical clause in a statute designed to regulate the profession of financial advisors. The court's action drew angry responses from the speaker of the Knesset and from the chair of its Constitution, Law and Justice committee (Allon 1997; Dotan 1997; Hofnung 1997; Kretzmer 1997; Gross 1998a).

The reaffirmation of the court's prerogative to review primary legislation (claimed for the first time, as we saw, in the *Bergman* case in 1969) was the culmination of a process of increased activism by the court, especially in its role as the High Court of Justice, that had taken place during the 1980s. This activism consisted in the court applying legal norms to more and more areas of social life and in its willingness to intervene in issue areas that had not been considered appropriate for judicial intervention in the past (Mautner 1993: 108–17; Lahav 1993; Gavison et al. 2000).

As formulated by Barak, the program of judicial activism, which he considers essential for maintaining the rule of law, has four elements to it:

(1) ensuring maximum access to the court;
(2) relaxing the standing requirements that plaintiffs had to meet in order to appeal to the court (such as showing direct material interest in the case);
(3) decreasing the number of issues that are deemed to be "unjusticiable";
(4) subjecting every governmental agency, including the Knesset, to judicial review. (Barak 1993; see also Gavison et al. 2000)

In an important study comparing the court's demeanor in the 1950s and in the 1980s, Menachem Mautner examined the increasing activism of the court, focusing primarily on the argumentation it used to justify its decisions. He found that in the 1950s the court had relied primarily on formal legal arguments, while in the 1980s it resorted much more openly to the language of values. Mautner's explanation is that in the 1950s the court's liberal values diverged quite widely from the dominant values of the society at large, which he characterized as "collectivist." Because of this divergence the court had to rely on formal arguments in order to justify its decisions. By the 1980s the court's liberal values had come to be shared by a significant segment of the society, the so-called "enlightened public," so that the court no longer had a reason to hide its liberal values behind a facade of formalities. The values of this "enlightened public" are increasingly referred to by the court as a source of legitimation for its decisions (Mautner 1993; 1994; Shamir 1994; Avnon 1996).

Commenting on Mautner's thesis, Ruth Gavison has argued that what changed was not only the court's rhetoric, but its conception of its own role in society: from adjudicating disputes to providing moral leadership (Gavison et al. 2000: 75). In a comparative study of "constitutional revolutions" in Israel and several other colonial-settler states, Ran Hirschl has identified the social interests that lie behind this reconceptualization of the role of the judiciary. The "enlightened public," whose values are used by the court now as its moral frame of reference, Hirschl argues, is "a relatively coherent social class of secular neoliberals of European origin, composed of politicians, business people, and professionals striving to maintain their political hegemony" (Hirschl 2000a: 95). The judicalization of politics, and the correspondent power shift from the legislative and executive branches to the judiciary, entailed by the "constitutional revolution," serve the interest of these elites by insulating their rights and privileges from majoritarian institutions, where these rights and privileges can be assailed due to the growing electoral weight of peripheral groups. Hirschl has calculated that the number of MKs representing elite interests has shrunk from 95 in 1981 to 80 in 1992 and then, following the institution of direct popular election of the PM, to 58 in 1999, while the number representing peripheral groups has risen in the same time period from 25 to 40 to 62 (Hirschl 2000a: 148, table 1).[2] Not surprisingly, the elite is making every effort to transfer more and more decision-making powers to non-elected government institutions, such as the BOI and the Supreme Court, and has restored the old electoral system which had provided it with better representation in the Knesset.

Mautner and Hirschl have each highlighted the changes in one aspect of the Israeli incorporation regime – citizenship discourse and institutional relations, respectively. Combining their insights, we can argue that as long as the institutions of the LSM and the republican discourse of citizenship were hegemonic, the Ashkenazi elite was interested in allowing majoritarian institutions, all firmly under the control of Mapai, as much freedom of action as possible, and was opposed to limiting their power through a constitution and a powerful judiciary. This interest was clearly expressed by Ben-Gurion during the original debate over the constitution (p. 261, above). With the shift from republicanism to liberalism as the discourse favored by the Ashkenazi elite, and the consequent flaring up of the conflict between the liberal and ethno-nationalist discourses, the elite can no longer trust the majoritarian institutions and is therefore shifting the political weight to non-elected ones.[3]

---

[2] As mentioned above, the later, more pronounced, jumps were an unintended consequence of the change of the electoral system.

[3] Accusing the Knesset of financial irresponsibility, in legislating "populist" laws that

The "constitutional revolution" and social rights

The dimension of citizenship where the social interests behind the "constitutional revolution" are most apparent is the sphere of social rights. Since the mid-1980s the orientation of Israeli labor law, and labor relations in general, has been changing from the collectivist, corporatist orientation that characterized the republican discourse of citizenship to an individualist, liberal orientation. Thus the dominant labor-relations discourse has shifted from an emphasis on national goals, social improvement, and a decent standard of living to stressing contractual relations, individual rights, and market forces. The decline of the Histadrut and of collective bargaining and collective labor agreements has been reflected in a new conception of employment relations as governed by individual contracts, hence as largely immune from state intervention (Yadlin 2000).

Prior to this change, in cases where rights such as workers' right to strike were curtailed, this was done in the name of collective interests, such as national security or the provision of essential services. Nowadays these rights are increasingly viewed as "balanceable" by other rights, such as the public's right to receive services (where "the public" is conceived of as made up of consumers, not workers) and the employers' right of private property, interpreted as their right to be protected from any economic loss. Clearly, rights are in a weaker moral position when balanced against other rights than when balanced against mere interests. And as Hirschl has pointed out, "when an 'equation' between different rights is drawn, the decision about which right should prevail depends, at least to some extent, on the 'holders' of that right ... [This] gives a preliminary advantage to the public (supposedly 'universal') interest over workers' ('particularistic') concerns" (Hirschl 1997: 141; Ben-Israel 1997; Gross 1998a).

The two basic laws of 1992, as interpreted by the court, have tilted the balance of rights even further towards the rights of employers and property owners. As mentioned already, one of the rights guaranteed by Basic Law: Human Dignity and Freedom is the right to private property. The link between human dignity and private property, according to Barak, is personal autonomy: the possession of property is a condition for the exercise of autonomy (Barak 1998: 368–9; cf. Ezrahi 1997: 32–46). This conception could possibly have led to redistributive conclusions as well, since personal autonomy is the right of every person in a liberal society. However, the court chose to interpret the right to property

---

cost taxpayers a great deal of money, is a favorite pastime of economists, elite-oriented politicians, and the liberal media in Israel.

in a possessive way, that is, to give preference to the maintenance of the current property regime over the right of every person to own some property. The irony of this interpretation is particularly telling with respect to property in land, for the current property regime in land is in itself the result of widespread expropriations of Palestinian-owned land since 1948. Thus the right to property is in effect used to legitimize the widespread violation of Palestinian property rights in the past (Gross 1998a; 1998b; chap. 4, above).

Freedom of occupation could also be interpreted in ways that would balance the rights of employers and employees. For example, it could be seen as protecting employees from ethnic, national, or gender discrimination and from arbitrary dismissal from their jobs. However, the basic law guaranteeing this freedom has been interpreted by Barak in the following way:

> Freedom of occupation is not the right to be employed, nor the right to work. Freedom of occupation is also not the right not to be dismissed from a job; tenure in a job does not derive from freedom of occupation but from freedom of contract. Freedom of occupation is the freedom to employ or not to employ. (Barak 1998: 369–70; cited in Hirschl 1997:142)

This formulation diverges quite significantly from the way freedom of occupation had been conceived in Israeli jurisprudence. From 1949 this freedom was understood to mean "the freedom of individuals to freely choose a profession, work in that profession, and earn a living therefrom" (Gross 1998a: 94). Only gradually did the understanding of this freedom expand to include free competition and the freedom from regulation in the conduct of one's business. Now, under Barak's interpretation, "free competition is at the basis of freedom of occupation. If the state intervenes in free competition it infringes on freedom of occupation, and it must justify this intervention within the limitations clause" of the law. Examples of state intervention that need to be justified, according to Barak, include the regulation of wages, prices, working hours and conditions, production quantities and marketing methods, and the imposition of taxes, subsidies, or limitations on entry into a particular field of business (cited in Gross 1998a: 94–7; see also Gross 2000b).

Moreover, not only have the two basic laws neglected to safeguard the interests of workers, they may actually endanger many of the basic rights Israeli workers have enjoyed in the past. Thus, for Barak, the connection between a worker's right to strike (and, for good measure, an employer's right to institute a lockout) and human dignity is still an open question. So it is not certain yet whether Basic Law: Human Dignity and Freedom could be used to safeguard workers' right to strike (Barak 1998: 368–9).

Even if it turns out that the law can be used in this way, however, since a strike inevitably involves economic loss for the owners, and sometimes for consumers as well, the private-property clause of this very law could be used to "balance" and limit the workers' right to strike.

As importantly, if less dramatically, many of the prevailing labor arrangements, such as collective agreements, minimum wage, union representation, pension schemes, etc., may be in jeopardy as a result of the two basic laws. For in the past these arrangements were legally based on "extension orders," a form of secondary legislation that extended to the entire workforce in a particular industry or industrial sector a collective agreement that was reached between some members of that sector. Extension orders replicated in the labor market the symbiotic relations that prevailed between the state and the Histadrut in the old capital "market." They were used to grant collective agreements negotiated by the Histadrut the force of law, and thus extend their applicability from the contracting parties to workplaces that had not participated in the negotiations. This enabled the Histadrut to negotiate with a limited number of large employers (that is, in many cases, with itself), and then have the resulting agreement applied, with the force of law, to an entire industrial sector. Thus the uniformity of wages and working conditions was ensured throughout that sector (Ben-Israel 1997; Hirschl 2000b: 195).

Like all labor legislation, extension orders placed limitations on the contractual freedom of employers and employees and on the former's rights of private property and freedom of occupation. Since the two basic laws establish that such limitations can only be enacted, or authorized, by primary legislation, under the conditions specified above (p. 267), the constitutionality of these extension orders may be challenged in court. Thus, the entire edifice of labor relations as developed within the republican discourse of citizenship may be found unconstitutional. Already, the National Labor Court, in a case involving the Zim shipping company, declared union security arrangements of the closed shop and union shop type to be unconstitutional. But even if most prevailing features of labor relations do pass the test of constitutionality, on the strength of the limitation clauses that appear in the two basic laws, their legal standing would have been seriously weakened as compared to their standing prior to the "constitutional revolution" (Ben-Israel 1997; Marmor 1997; Gross 1998a; 1998b; Hirschl 2000b).

Civil rights and Jewish ethno-nationalism

The two basic laws that constitute the heart of the "constitutional revolution" have clauses that define their respective purposes as, ultimately, "grounding in a basic law the values of the State of Israel as a Jewish and democratic state" (Bechor 1996: 279, 281). The two laws do not specify what is meant by Israel's values "as a Jewish and democratic state," nor how these two sets of values are to be reconciled; this task was left to the discretion of the courts.

President of the Supreme Court Barak, who is also a distinguished professor of law, has been the most influential interpreter and promoter of the idea of a constitutional revolution. His views on how the state's democratic and Jewish values are to be reconciled merit, therefore, citation at some length:

Can there be a contradiction between the Jewishness of the state and its democratic character for the purpose of deriving fundamental values? ... In my opinion, the utterance "Jewish and democratic" does not encompass two opposites, but rather complementarity and harmony. The content of the utterance "Jewish State" will be determined by the level of abstraction assigned to it. In my opinion, this utterance must be assigned its meaning at a high level of abstraction, which will unite all members of the society and find what is common to them. The level of abstraction must be sufficiently high as to be compatible with the democratic character of the state. Indeed, *the state is Jewish not in the halachic-religious sense, but in the sense that Jews have the right to immigrate [laalot] to it, and their national being is the being of the state (this is manifested, inter alia, in the language and in the days of rest)*. The fundamental values of Judaism are the fundamental values of the state. I mean the values of the love of mankind, the sanctity of life, social justice ... human dignity, the rule of law over the legislator ... values that Judaism has given the entire world ... *the values of the State of Israel as a Jewish state must not be identified with Jewish law. We must not forget that there is a substantial non-Jewish minority in Israel.* Indeed, the values of the state of Israel as a Jewish state are those universal values that are common to all members of democratic society and that grew out of Jewish tradition and Jewish history. (Barak 1992: 30–1; emphasis added)

Barak's way of reconciling Jewish and democratic values, then, is by viewing Judaism at such a high level of abstraction that it collapses into liberalism. This, certainly, is not the only way to view Judaism, for if it were there would have been no need to specify "Jewish and democratic" values as two separate categories. Most interpreters assume that there is at least some tension between Jewish and democratic values as guidelines for state action, in a society where about one quarter of the population is not Jewish; these interpreters have looked to reconcile the two imperatives in ways that do not collapse one into the other (*Tel Aviv University Law Review* 1995).[4]

What is most notable in Barak's argument is the fact that he appears to have abandoned the traditional way of reconciling "Jewish"

---

[4] For criticisms of Barak's view, including the claim that he has not consistently maintained this view, see Avnon 1996; Marmor 1997; Gross 1998a; Gavison et al. 2000.

and "democratic," through a combined ethno-republican discourse, and adopted a thoroughgoing liberal, some would even say libertarian, discourse instead (Marmor 1997).[5] Initially, however, the practical import of this change, as of the "constitutional revolution" in general, was not manifested evenly in all areas of the law. Two areas where change was minimal or non-existent were the civil rights of non-Jews and the place of religion in public life. In the former case, "security" arguments grounded in the republican discourse continued to override the court's liberal values (Shelef 1993), while in the latter, the religious status quo was largely protected, by the ethno-national discourse, from the requirements of the basic laws. The new liberal discourse was manifested primarily in the socio-economic sphere and in enhancing what Andrei Marmor has called, somewhat unkindly, "Yuppie rights" – personal freedoms derived from the conception of autonomy as "self-ownership" (Marmor 1997).

Even after the enactment of the two basic laws, in cases that involved the right of Palestinian citizens to have equal access to state land or to be protected from the expropriation of their own land for Jewish use, as well as in cases involving the rights of non-citizen Arabs, the court had consistently rejected the claims of Arab petitioners based on their rights to property and to human dignity and freedom (Gross 1998a). However, as we have been arguing all along in this volume, once a particular discourse of citizenship is adopted it becomes very difficult to contain it within clearly delineated limits. Thus, in recent years the liberal values espoused by the "constitutional revolution" have been making important inroads into the home territory of the ethno-national discourse – Jewish–Arab relations and the status of Jewish religion in the public sphere.[6]

The most important legal development bearing on the rights of Palestinian citizens has clearly been the decision of the High Court of Justice in the *Qaadan* case, related in chapter 4 above. To reiterate, in that decision the court determined that the ethno-national interest of Zionism in "Judaizing" the country cannot override the principle of equality, even when it comes to the allocation of state land, and even if the discriminatory allocation of land is effected through Jewish "national institutions." In another landmark decision in 2000, the court reversed itself on the legality of state action in abducting and holding Lebanese citizens not suspected of any wrongdoing as bargaining chips for use in future negotiations for the release of Israeli prisoners allegedly held by

---

[5] We say that Barak only "appears to have abandoned" the ethno-republican discourse because in another pronouncement of the same period he defined the Jewish state as a state for which "the settlement of Jews in its fields, towns and villages is at the center of its interests" (cited in Gross 1998a: 103).

[6] For an early and quite solitary prediction that this would indeed be the case, see Saban 1996.

Lebanese militias. In 1997 the court, in a two-to-one majority led by Barak, allowed the state to continue to incarcerate such people, some of whom had been held for over ten years. Barak argued then that the infringement of the detainees' human dignity and freedom was justified in this case by the principle that a democracy "should not commit suicide in order to prove its [democratic] viability" (AMM 10/94, par. 13; for the history of the case up to that point, see E. Barak 1999). The attorneys representing the hostages asked for reconsideration of the decision, and this resulted in its reversal. President Barak himself had changed his mind in the meantime (DNP 7048/97, par. 22), and a majority of the nine justices now on the bench agreed with him that there was no basis in law for the state holding innocent people as hostages. In September 1999, departing from a long record of refusing to pass judgment in this matter, the court also decided that Shabak (General Security Service) officers did not have the authority to use torture in interrogating Palestinian suspects (Bagatz 5100/94). Regardless of this decision, human rights organizations in Israel and abroad allege that the Shabak continues to torture Palestinian prisoners.

In the religious sphere too the court has been displaying increasing activism in recent years. In 1993 it declared the prohibition on the importation of non-kosher meat, a long-standing feature of the religious status quo, unconstitutional, because it contradicted Basic Law: Freedom of Occupation. As a result, that law has been amended twice already by the Knesset, in 1994 and 1998, in order to maintain the prohibition. The court also invalidated the arrangement through which yeshiva students have been receiving deferments of their military service (see chap. 5, above), forced local government bodies to include women and non-Orthodox Jews in local religious councils, intervened in decisions of rabbinic courts in areas where these courts enjoy statutory jurisdiction, and in general has sought to inject liberal norms into the conduct of public religiosity (Hirschl 2000a: 118–20; Gavison et al. 2000: 49–51; Lahav 2000).

Conclusion

The collapse of the hegemony of the LSM, and the impact of this collapse on Israeli citizenship, have been most clearly visible in the area of law. The two prongs of the "constitutional revolution" – electoral reform and human rights legislation – have been important milestones on Israel's way to becoming a civil society in the narrow, Lockean sense: a society that provides ample space for the operation of private interests, unhindered by the state. The electoral reforms have personalized the electoral process, and thus greatly widened the opportunities for private capital, including transnational, even illicit transnational capital, to influence the political outcome. This corresponded, quite naturally, with the expansion of market opportunities that can be exploited more easily by big political donors. As an unintended consequence the reforms also weakened the major political parties, with claims to represent the general interest of society, in favor of sectoral parties openly representing particularistic interests. Because of this the electoral reforms have been largely done away with.

In the human rights sphere, the most significant development has been the entry of the right to property, the right to freedom of contract, and the right to freedom of occupation, interpreted by the court as rights protecting the current regime of possessions, rather than rights mandating a redistribution of resources, into Israel's constitutional discourse (Gross 1998a: 92). Needless to say, this development is perfectly consonant with the process of political and economic liberalization analyzed in this book.

On both the electoral and the judicial fronts liberalization has not gone unopposed. As we have seen, the electroral reforms have been rolled back, while the Supreme Court has come under fierce political attack, primarily by Orthodox religious groups that have identified the court, correctly, as spearheading the liberalization of Israeli society. Not surprisingly, the political party that has emerged as the court's chief opponent is Shas, an Orthodox political party whose political power base lies in the most peripheral Jewish group – Mizrachim of low socio-economic status – and that represents for the adherents of liberalism everything they fear in Israeli society. In February 1999 Shas led a massive demonstration against the Supreme Court, in which the justices were attacked as heretics and *ignorami* and the court itself as unrepresentative of the Israeli public. Shas has also been active in trying to promote legislation that would make the court more representative (Hirschl 2000a: 121–3; Gavison et al. 2000: 51–2).[7]

Criticism of the court has been mainly confined, however, to issues of interest to the ethno-nationalist discourse of citizenship. The systematic dismantling of the socio-economic rights and institutions of the pioneering era has received little attention from the court's political (as opposed to academic) critics, because there are no longer any significant social forces that are committed to the republican discourse. This asymmetry

---

[7] Shas has a particular gripe against the court because of the role played by the judicial system in the investigation and trial of its former political leader, Arie Deri (Bilsky, forthcoming). At the time of writing Deri's appeal for a retrial is pending before the Supreme Court.

has led to the ironic consequence that Basic Law: Social Rights, which has been on the legislative agenda since 1994, has not been enacted because of the opposition of Shas. This opposition stems from the fear that the enactment of *any* basic law would further empower the court and enhance the momentum of liberalization. (Deri has reportedly vowed to oppose any basic law that comes up in the Knesset, even a law that enshrines the Ten Commandments in Israel's constitution) (Mautner 1993; Marmor 1997; Hofnung 1997; Ben-Israel 1997: 36–7; Yishuvi 1997).

Although the court's liberal activism has resulted in some loss of its legitimacy among the public, and Barak has already recanted on his use of the controversial terms "everything is justiciable" and "the enlightened public," the ability of its critics to change the course of Israel's constitutional development is quite doubtful. The judicial system is in the process of adopting the liberal preferences that already dominate so much of Israeli social and economic reality, and in the sphere of citizenship rights, the most important changes, those that facilitate the operation of the market, have already taken place and are not the ones being attacked by opponents of the court.

11 Shrinking social rights

The radical transformations outlined in chapters 9 and 10, from institutions of solidarity to institutions of competition, reflecting a process of transition from a republican to a liberal citizenship discourse, had the effect of extending civil rights and shrinking social rights. The tensions between institutions representing republican, ethno-national, and liberal citizenship conceptions, and sometimes within these institutions as well, we have argued, were clearly demonstrated in the allocation of rights to Israeli citizens according to their group affiliations. Whereas in the Yishuv and Israel's early decades the tensions between republican and ethno-national rights were the most pronounced, beginning with the 1967 war, and more clearly in the 1990s, the ethno-nationalist and liberal conceptions have been the ones more frequently pitted against each other. And whereas in the past the intensity of the struggle was muted, due to the prominence of republican citizenship, which served as the hegemonic mediating center around which other rights were grouped in a single incorporation regime, now the struggle is more open and institutions offering alternative approaches are locked in open conflict with one another.

Inequality and the new wage structure

In Marshall's memorable words, social rights "mean the whole range from the right to a modicum of economic welfare and security to the right to share to the full in the social heritage and to live the life of a civilized being according to the standards prevailing in the society." He suggested that "the institutions most closely connected with [such rights] are the educational system and the social services" (Marshall 1973: 72). These are the institutions that seek to lessen the impact of, or at least compensate for, social inequality generated in the marketplace. Since institutions of social citizenship are an outgrowth of the battle against inequality, their effectiveness must be directly related to the general level of such inequality. The greater the inequality, the more interventionist these institutions must become in order to counter its polarizing effects. Before

278

an analysis of the social rights of education, healthcare, and housing in the third section of this chapter we will, therefore, examine the formation and trends of social inequality itself in this section, and the incidence of poverty in the next section.

Inequality in modern societies is determined in large measure by employment structures and opportunities, i.e., by the market, but is moderated through the progressive character of income tax and transfer payments which affect disposable income. Comparisons of total, economic, and disposable incomes, and wage inequality in general, as well as the percentage of families under the poverty line, provide important indicators of access to social rights.

The most common measure of income distribution inequality is the Gini index, which shows the degree of divergence from absolute equality in the distribution of income, ranging from 0, when income is equally distributed, to 1, when all income is concentrated in the hands of a single individual or family. Based on this index, the history of inequality in Israel may be divided into four periods: the Mandatory period for which we have limited information; 1954 to 1967 – rising inequality; 1967 to 1976 – declining inequality (with a slight increase in 1971–4); and, finally, rising inequality again beginning in 1976 (with a slight fall in 1984–5 and in 1995–6).

In the second period inequality in gross income distribution rose by 26 percent, in the third period it fell by 21 percent, and in the fourth period it rose again by 13 percent. In 1994 income distribution inequality was roughly where it had been in 1967. After a brief introduction to the Mandatory period, we will focus our attention on the first and third periods, each of which corresponds to a wave of industrialization – the first based on import substitution, the second on high-tech industries and export.

It is important to keep in mind, while reading the indicators in table 11.1, that the measurements used and the population covered in the early and later periods have changed considerably and, consequently, comparisons of the intervals across these two periods remain problematic. There were many changes within the most recent period as well. The Gini coefficients are calculated on the basis on the Central Bureau of Statistics's (CBS) annual income surveys, which until 1994 covered households headed by wage-earners or the unemployed, but not the rural and self-employed populations. In addition, until 1994 Israel's Palestinian citizens were also underrepresented, because only households in Palestinian towns of over 10,000, of which there are very few, were included. Altogether, the annual income surveys excluded about one-quarter of the households. From 1995 Palestinian towns of 2,000–10,000

Table 11.1 *Gross and disposable income distribution of the population in Israel in quintiles, 1954–1997*[*]

	1954	1964	1969	1989	1994	1997	1997 new series	1989	1994	1997	1997 new series
Lowest	7	5.1	5.8	1.3	1	0.9	1.0	7.2	6.7	7.2	6.7
Second	13.9	11.5	10.9	8.9	8.1	7.9	7.5	12.2	11.7	11.8	11.2
Third	18.2	16.9	16.1	15.8	15	14.8	14.1	17.2	16.9	17	16.3
Fourth	22.9	23.6	23.2	25.3	24.5	24.7	23.9	24	23.9	23.8	23.7
Fifth	38	42.9	44	48.7	51.4	51.7	53.4	39.4	40.8	40.2	42.1
Total	100	100	100	100	100	100	99.9	100	100	100	100
Gini index	0.293	0.369	0.372	0.474	0.502	0.505	0.520	0.325	0.344	0.332	0.357

[*] per "standardized individual"

Sources: 1954–69 data from Lerner and Ben-Shahar 1975, table 20–1, p. 147; 1989, 1994, and 1997, 1997 (new series) data were calculated respectively from NII 1990, table 20, p. 71; 1995, table 24, p. 81, 1998; table 26, p. 83; 2000, table 15, p. 71.

people have been added to the surveys as well. Thus, in the 1995 survey, 10.7 percent of the households covered were "non-Jewish," the conventional euphemism used in Israeli statistical publications for Palestinian citizens (NII 1996: 147, 180). The inclusion of a larger share of them in the survey, as we shall explain below, coincided with their growing, though still partial and contradictory, incorporation into governing coalitions and the welfare state. Needless to say, neither non-citizen Palestinians nor labor migrants, whose numbers have been rising steadily since the Oslo agreement (chap. 12, below), are included in the surveys. Their inclusion would have increased the observable income gap even further. In addition, beginning in 1998 a new method of data collection was adopted, combining the annual income surveys with the CBS's quarterly survey, which also contains the relevant questions. The new survey also includes most of the rural population, the self-employed and the population of East Jerusalem, covering altogether 95 percent of the households in Israel. Only kibbutz members and nomadic Bedouin are now not surveyed. Because the new sample is 1.8 higher larger than the old one, comparisons between this and previous years are unreliable (NII 2000: 38). However, since for 1997 we have both the old and new series, we can draw some conclusions, if not about trends at least about the depth of inequality.

1929–1976

It was, and still is, commonly argued that in Israel's early years "the degree of inequality . . . had been one of the lowest in the world" and an international comparison of "the share of total income going to the richest tenth of the population show that Israel's income distribution is as close to equality as that of any other nation for which data are available" (Lerner and Ben-Shahar 1975: 146; see also Halevi and Klinov-Malul 1968: 117). The conventional explanation for this phenomenon was that the universalism of the LSM, its ideological commitment to equality, led to a relatively egalitarian wage structure within the Histadrut's own economic sector and beyond. The Histadrut indeed attempted to institute within its own domain a wage system based on family size, and sought to equalize wages in the construction industry. Nevertheless, the only serious study on the wage structure of the Yishuv, by Zvi Sussman, found that "the Histadrut's wage policy . . . was significantly influenced by the economic forces operating in the labor market" (Sussman 1974: 131). One of the main influences, customarily ignored by researchers, as Sussman complained, was the pressure of low-paid, unskilled Arab labor, which lowered the wages of unskilled Jewish workers as well. The Histadrut's main effort in the labor market – to ensure a European minimum wage for unskilled Jewish workers – had only a limited impact. As Sussman concluded: "A detailed examination of wage statistics, collected between 1920 and 1939, demonstrates that the notion that the measure of equality among Histadrut members in particular and Jewish wage earners in general was very high, is without foundation when compared either with later periods or with other countries" (Sussman 1974: 130; cf. Sternhel 1998, chap. 6). Sussman's observation may serve as a general warning: when Palestinians are included in the analysis of Israeli society, the results not only vary, but are often inverted.

Sussman's study has shown that we need to take the purported equality in the Yishuv with a grain of salt. For example, in 1950–1, years of austerity and strict rationing, economic welfare, as measured by food consumption (of the urban Jewish population only), was more egalitarian than in either 1943 or 1946 (Halevi and Klinov-Malul 1968: 117–19). Looking at table 11.1 now, the Gini index indicates a rise from 0.293 in 1954 to 0.369 in 1964, that is, an increase in inequality of 26 percent over a decade. Inequality continued to rise until 1967, afterwards declining for a while (Lerner and Ben-Shahar 1975: 146). Between 1954 and 1969 the income share of the lowest fifth declined from 7 percent to 5.8 percent and that of the highest fifth rose from 38 percent to 44 percent, increasing the index of differentials (which measures the total income that would need to be transferred in order to achieve full equality) from 20.4 percent in 1954 to 27.2 percent in 1969 (Lerner and Ben-Shahar 1975: 147). In 1965–7, when Israel suffered from a depression (*mitun*), accompanied by the highest rate of unemployment experienced until then, inequality grew rapidly. Unemployment was responsible for most of the increase in inequality, since, as the National Insurance Institute (NII) surveys have shown, it is among the unemployed that the rate of poverty is the highest in each time period. In short, the years 1965–7, when unemployment rose rapidly, and 1967–71, when it returned to its previous level, were exceptional years. A comparison of the Gini indexes for 1965 and 1971 demonstrates that in the early years of rapid industrialization and population growth Israeli inequality did rise, but not as steeply as it has since 1976, that is, in the recent period of growing inequality.

So far we have discussed gross family income. We will now turn to disposable income, and examine the effects of income tax and social services on inequality. Lerner and Ben-Shahar's examination of data from 1960 led them to conclude that the progressive effect of income tax was largely erased by the regressive impact of indirect taxes, leaving a cumulative reduction of inequality by only 4.5 percent. The provision of social services by the government, however, did reduce inequality from 0.300 to 0.234, that is by 22 percent (Lerner and Ben-Shahar 1975: 147).

Nevertheless, although international comparisons of income distribution indicate that in the 1950s and 1960s inequality fell in the developed countries (Kuznets 1963), in Israel it had grown during that period. Social services and transfer payments lagged behind the market forces that generated inequality. Even so, Israel maintained a relatively low level of social inequality in its first two decades, and its republican institutions, therefore, did not come under any serious challenge.

1976–1998

In the 1985–97 period the Gini coefficient fluctuated, but its overall tendency was upwards. It shot up in a secular rise (with the exception of 1993) from 0.312 in 1985 all the way to 0.344 in 1994, began declining to 0.336 in 1995 and 0.3285 in 1996, but reverted back to 0.332 by 1997 (NII 1997: 93, table 32).

Data on and studies of inequality in the past twenty-five years are more abundant and detailed than for earlier periods and reveal a number of contradictory trends. The Gini inequality coefficient of gross incomes grow from 0.432 in 1979 to 0.505 in 1997, namely by 17 percent, but disposable income inequality grew from 0.318 in 1979 to 0.333 in 1997, that is by 4.5 percent only. The ratio between the gross income of the top and bottom quintiles grew from 38 in 1989 to 56.8 in 1979, but between disposable income grew from 5.4 in 1989 to only 5.6 in 1997. At the same time, the tendency was partially and temporarily reversed in 1995 and 1996. The most recent data indicate the continuation of growing inequality as measured both before and after direct taxes and transfer payments, though the two grew, for the first time, at the same rate. The Gini coefficient for gross income rose from 0.509 in 1997 to 0.512 in 1998 and then to 0.517 in 1999; that is altogether by 1.6 percent. The Gini coefficient measuring the distribution of disposable income rose from 0.352 in 1998 to 0.359 in 1999, namely by 1.7 percent (see HYPERLINK http://www.btl.gov.il/whats_new/Poverty_00.htm). The past twenty-five years, then, witnessed a secular rise in inequality (and, as we shall see, of increased poverty as well). Increased inequality is a fact of life in liberalizing Israel, but its dimensions are being fought over.

Other data and studies support and fine-tune this conclusion. The new income survey series, on which the calculation of the Gini coefficient is based since 1997, includes the self-employed (as well as residents of Arab East Jerusalem) and for 1997 – the one year for which we possess data from both the old and new series – the gap between the data is wide. The Gini coefficient for gross income from the old series was 0.505 and from the new 0.520; whereas for disposable income the coefficients were 0.332 and

0.357, respectively. The old series, then, underreported the inequality of income distribution by 3 percent and 7 percent for gross and disposable income, respectively (NII 1998: 83, table 26; 2000: 71, table 15).

A study by Zvi Sussman and Dan Zakai found indications pointing to an erosion of income among public-sector wage earners. The wage differential within this category was 2.2 times higher in 1994 than it was in 1974. Further, the basic salary component amounted to 77 percent of their total wages in 1974, and only 46 percent in 1994. In short, the income portion that was equal for all employees fell, whereas those additions to the basic wage that allow differentiation between the workers, such as fringe benefits and overtime, effort, car expense reimbursement, etc., grew. This was reflected in the strike activity of workers in the public sector: though they make up only 30 percent of the labor force, between 1991 and 1994 they accounted for 70–100 percent of all days lost due to strike action (Meltz 1996). In 1994 one such strike yielded results, and public-sector employees received a significant increase, thus restoring some of their previous losses.

The conclusion of a report by Bank Hapoalim, which surveyed the overall trends revealed in the Gini index of disposable income for the Israeli population, was that "the extent of inequality in the distribution of income in Israel . . . grew in the past 5–10 years. Especially noteworthy is the steep increase in the index from the beginning of the decade [i.e., since 1990]" (Bank Hapoalim 1996: 12–13). The bank's evaluation recognized that part of the increase was temporary, due to the lower wages of the 700,000 new immigrants from the former USSR, who constituted 12 percent of the population, and to some biases in the technical measures of inequality. It concluded, however, that in addition to these factors, structural changes and legislation, such as the freeing of the capital market and privatization, had favored the upper income earners and, consequently, "inequality has grown" (Bank Hapoalim 1996: 16).

The State Revenue Administration reported in December 1994 that despite the progressive character of the income tax "the distribution of income in Israel (before and after tax) is characterized by greater inequality than in Western countries other than the US" (State Revenue Administration 1994: iii). This happened in spite of the fact that in Israel the income tax is judged to be highly progressive and reduces the inequality in the distribution of income by approximately 13 percent. In 1993, for example, the Gini coefficient, which measures the extent of direct taxes' progressivity, indicated that they reduced inequality from 0.577 to 0.447, that is, by 22.5 percent (State Revenue Administration 1995: 96).

Nevertheless, changes in the income tax have not kept up with the growth of inequality and, in fact, it has become less effective as an equalizing mechanism. The income-tax reform of 1987 eliminated the top marginal tax categories of 50 percent and 60 percent and set the top one at 48 percent. Subsequent changes in 1990 partially reversed the reform, by reinstating the 50 percent marginal tax category as the top rate, and reduced the marginal tax category for the lowest tax-paying income categories from 20 percent to 15 percent (NII 1996: 192–3). Overall, however, the goal of income-tax reform has been the reduction of the tax burden on high income earners (NII 1995: 50).

As we have shown in chapter 3, inequality in Israel has a clear ethnic dimension. We can use Istvan Kalor's study of the relationship between income inequality and family size for indirect observation on the impact of transfer payments on the status of Mizrachi families. Kalor decomposed the Gini index in order to examine the usefulness of using family size as an indirect indicator for "tagging" poor families. This method could be used to "tag" Mizrachi families as well, because they tend to be larger than Ashkenazi families (other groups with large families, namely citizen Palestinians and *charedim*, make up much smaller portions of the population). Kalor found that inequality declined in the 1980s when measured in terms of standardized individuals, but increased for households. He concluded that this discrepancy indicated that poverty and family size were less strongly correlated in the 1980s than they had been in the 1970s (without seeking to explain the reasons for this decoupling) (Kalor 1997: 2, 17–19). The growing inequality measured for households indicates that Mizrachim (as well as Palestinian citizens and *charedim*) continue to be more adversely affected by increased inequality of income distribution.

What are the reasons for increased inequality in the post-1976 period? Sussman points to two factors. Changes in the structure of the economy, due to the growing weight of high-tech industries and the upgrading of production processes in traditional industries, are increasing the demand and pay for highly skilled and educated workers. In contrast, the organizational power of unskilled and semi-skilled workers is declining, as illustrated in the falling number of collective wage agreements which had traditionally protected the more vulnerable workers. The replacement of such agreements with unorganized employment through manpower companies and employment agencies, without long-term security and reduced social benefits, lowers the income of the lower-paid groups at the same time as the income of the upper income groups, whose members sign individual contracts or are self-employed, is rising (Sussman 1996).

A comparison of income-distribution trends in Israel with Western industrial countries, by Yasser Awad and Nirit Israeli, using standardized data collected by the Luxembourg Income Study, yields a somewhat more favorable picture. The international comparison of Gini coefficients in the 1980s and 1990s divided countries into three categories. In the 1980s the coefficient of disposable income distinguished between countries with (1) high inequality – the US, Israel, Italy, and Australia; (2) medium inequality – Great Britain, France, Canada, the Netherlands, and Germany; and (3) low inequality – Belgium, Norway, and Sweden. In the 1980s Israel, with a Gini coefficient of 0.3241, was second only to the US's 0.3467. A similar comparison of early 1990s data showed the movement of Great Britain and France into the group of high inequality, whereas Italy moved in the opposite direction, into the medium inequality group (Awad and Israeli 1996).

This international comparison placed Israel among the countries with highest inequality by the 1980s, where it stayed in the 1990s as well. However, Israel fell from the second to the fourth place in that group, following France, the US, and Great Britain, in all of which the Gini coefficient rose, whereas in Israel it declined to 0.3180 (Awad and Israeli 1996: 229, table 7). Standardized income data still leave Israel in the group of the least equal industrial countries but, in comparative terms, indicate that inequality in Israel rose more slowly then in other members of that group, hence Israel's relative position improved somewhat. A summary of these historical trends is provided in Bank Hapoalim's report: "In the 1960s income distribution in Israel was among the most egalitarian in the Western world. In the middle of the 1990s, there exist few Western countries in which inequality is greater" (Bank Hapoalim 1996: 16). As we mentioned, these trends would have been even more pronounced had labor migrants and non-citizen Palestinians been included in the calculations.

Poverty amelioration and taxation

Another indicator of rising income inequality in Israel is the growing number of families under the poverty line. The NII sets the poverty line at half of the median disposable income (i.e., the income level dividing the population into two equal groups). A family is considered to be living in poverty if, after totaling income from work and/or transfer payments from the NII and deducting income and health taxes, it has less than half the median disposable income in the economy. This form of measurement, in contrast to a fixed line based on the price of a basket of goods used, for example, in the US, is relative, adjusting the poverty line upwards as the population's standard of living rises. The American method, by controlling for inflation, makes sure that the absolute condition of the poor does not worsen; the Israeli method tracks the economy and allows the poor to share in its prosperity. At the same time, the Israeli poverty line is adjusted for family size, since it is calculated according to the number of "adult equivalents" (or "standardized individuals"), thus taking into account relative savings for family size.

From 1989 to 1994 the number of families below the poverty line rose from 118,00 to 205,200; in 1999 the number was 308,000. While the total population grew as well, due to both natural increase and immigration, the share of poor families still increased. During the 1985–95 decade their percentage in the population rose from 11.4 percent to 16.8 percent, despite an increase in the budget share devoted to fighting poverty, from 9.4 percent to 11.2 percent (Sussman 1996; numbers slightly amended, on the basis of the data in table 11.2). Subdividing the population under the poverty line into groups, we find that in 1995 it included 59 percent of the unemployed, 40 percent of families with four children or more, 31 percent of citizen Palestinians, 23.5 percent of the elderly, and only 7.8 percent of wage earners (NII 1996: 161). By 1999 the share of the poor rose to about 20 percent of the Israeli population, and a quarter of the children live in poor families (*Haaretz*, December 20, 2000).

Table 11.2 *Percentage of families under the poverty line in Israel, 1979–1997*

(1)	(2)	(3)	(4)	(5)	(6)
Year	Before Transfer Payments	After Transfer Payments	After Transfer Payments & Direct Taxes	Percent Reduction due to Direct Taxes	Percent Reduction due to TF & DT
1979	27.9	16.4	17.2	41.1	38.4
1980	28.1	13.9	15.7	50.6	44.1
1981	28.8	14.2	15.7	50.8	45.4
1982	29.8	9.1	10.8	69.5	64.0
1983	29.5	11.1	12.5	62.4	57.7
1984	30.7	12.9	14.6	58.0	52.5
1985	31.3	10.3	11.4	67.1	63.5
1988	32.6	13.3	14.3	59.2	56.0
1989	33.0	11.7	12.8	64.5	61.2
1990	34.3	13.4	14.3	60.9	58.2
1991	35.1	14.2	14.9	59.5	57.5
1992	34.7	16.4	17.2	52.7	50.4
1993	34.6	16.0	16.7	53.8	51.7
1994	34.2	17.6	18.0	48.5	47.2
1995	33.7	14.7	16.8	56.4	50.1
1996	34.3	13.6	16.0	60.3	53.4
1997	34.3	13.6	16.2	60.5	52.7

Source: NII 1997, table 23, p. 79; 2000 table 11, p. 61.
(TF = transfer payments; DT = direct taxes)

The longitudinal series presented in table 11.2 shows the changing rate of the incidence of poverty in Israeli society, as measured by the annual income survey (with the exception of 1986, in which it was not conducted). The data in column 6 show a secular rise in poverty between 1979 and 1991 and its slow reversal beginning in 1991, only to rise again since 1995, reaching a plateau in 1996. There is greater variation in the rate of poverty measured after transfer payments and direct taxes, with the exception of two periods: poverty was reduced in the four years between 1979 and 1982 and increased in five of the six years from 1989 to 1994, whereas there is no discernible pattern in the period in between.

In 1995 the share of households under the poverty line declined, for the first time since the upward turn of the economy that began in 1989, from 18 percent in the previous year to 16.8 percent. This was the direct result of the August 1994 Law for the Reduction of Poverty and Income Gaps and the June 1995 Law for Reducing the Magnitude of Poverty (NII 1996: 149–50). This change, however, was very limited. The rate of individuals in poverty declined only fractionally and the rate of children in poverty remained roughly the same. Furthermore, among wage earners the inequality in the distribution of economic income (i.e. pre-tax and pre-transfer payments income) rose, whereas in disposable income it dropped minimally (NII 1996: 153–4). In 1996 the reduction of poverty continued, thus offsetting some of the losses of the previous years. Thus it would seem that the safety net under Israel's poor has been lowered, but is periodically being yanked up.

Poverty reduction relies on two methods: (a) progressive taxation on income; and (b) income-maintaining transfer payment programs administered by the NII and social services. The main forms of transfer payments in Israel include child and old-age allowances, as well as maternity and disability allowances. Services, mostly in kind, that are funded directly by the government include education and health – the largest outlays – and housing, employment, immigrant absorption, and personal welfare services, which are aimed at vulnerable populations, such as the retarded, the blind, and families in distress. Transfer payments are paid directly to the recipient and are not deducted from their taxes. Outlays for services consist mostly of wages to teachers, medical personnel, social workers, etc. In the context of this study we will focus on child and old-age allowances and on education and health services. These are the most relevant and revealing for the comprehension of rights as conceptualized and allotted by the multiple Israeli citizenship discourses.

Different transfer payments benefit different population groups. Among recipients of old-age allowance Ashkenazim are more heavily represented, whereas a larger share of children's allowances go to Mizrachim (Kop 1986: 66), though this difference narrows over time. Children's allowances, argues Shlomo Swirski, are a powerful illustration of the layered character of Israel's welfare state: they are the "lower and ethnically specific tier of the Israeli safety net." Children's allowances, adopted by the Knesset in 1959, in the wake of the Wadi Salib uprising – the first large-scale violent Mizrachi protest in Israel – saw the beginning of the incorporation of the ethnic dimension into the welfare state (Swirski 1998). Furthermore, eligibility for children's allowances was made conditional on military service, thus until recently effectively excluding Israel's Palestinian citizens from this social citizenship right. In short, children's allowances are one of clearest illustrations of the operation of multiple citizenship in the allocation of social rights. In Israel the politically more manipulable children's allowances also serve as a substitute for the income-tax deductions parents receive in other countries. Their modifications, therefore, serve as indications of changes in access to national institutions and citizenship practices (Rosenhek and Shalev 2000).

Children's allowances, especially when compared with old-age and survivor allowances, were the stepchild of Israeli social citizenship. For a decade and a half, children's allowances were calculated according to a variety of shifting criteria and combined with tax deductions. In 1975, following the recommendation of the Ben-Shahar Committee, a policy of universal children's allowances was adopted for the first time. They have been thereafter administered through the NII, which paid an allowance for all children and increased it according to the number of children in the family, and continued paying it for recently demobilized soldiers (Gabay and Lavon 1996: 4–5; Rosenhek and Shalev 2000). At the same time, in spite of rapid inflation, children's allowances were updated only once, in 1984, and thus lost, in real terms, half of their value between 1979 and 1985 (families with over four children were less affected) (NII 1996: 191). In contrast, old-age and survivor allowances, which benefit Ashkenazim more than Mizrachim, were regularly updated and raised in the 1979–84 period. As part of the EESP of 1985 the universalism of children's allowances, adopted only a decade earlier, fell victim to cost-cutting measures. Children's allowances for the first child in families with up to three children, except for low-income families, were abolished, and in 1991 the allowance for the second child was also eliminated (NII 1996: 192). Only when it was realized that about one-third of the eligible families, ashamed to reveal their poverty, did not apply for the allowance, were universal allowances restored, in 1993. Again, the universality of old-age and survivor allowances has never been tampered with.

In 1993 the Rabin government also equalized the children's allowances paid to Israel's Jewish and Palestinian citizens, severing this social right from the duty of military service (NII 1996: 150, 181; Rosenhek and Shalev 2000: 314). This policy was carried out in four steps between January 1994 and January 1997. As a consequence, poverty among Israel's Arab population declined somewhat. In 1995 the rate of poverty (for disposable income) among the "non-Jewish" population fell even more drastically than in the general population, from 38.5 percent in 1994 to 31.2 percent in 1995. Transfer payments extricated from poverty 1.5 times more "non-Jewish" families in 1995 than they did in 1994 (NII 1996: 183). The increase of child and old-age allowances was particularly important for the "non-Jewish" population because transfer payments constitute 20.5 percent of its income, in contrast to 14.9 percent in the general population (NII 1996: 180–1). When the gap between the Jewish and Palestinian citizens declined, it became possible (or less embarrassing) to count the latter in the income surveys. The extension of social citizenship rights to the Palestinian Arab citizens, and their greater visibility in political life, as well as in official statistics, attest to the increased weight of the liberal citizenship discourse in Israel's incorporation regime.

An international comparison of poverty rates, based on the data of the Luxembourg Income Study, standardized to the Israeli definition of poverty, indicates that Israel had among the highest poverty rates among Western industrial countries in the 1980s and 1990s, although the rate declined somewhat in the latter period. The comparative incidence of poverty in Israel dovetailed with its relative place in the inequality of income distribution. In the 1980s, with a poverty rate of 16.2 percent, Israel was placed in the group with the highest rate of poverty, just behind the US, with 19.8 percent. The lowest incidence of poverty, 3.7/3.8 percent, was in Sweden and Norway, respectively. In the 1990s the gaps between the countries surveyed closed somewhat, with a rise in the Scandinavian countries, France, and Great Britain, and a decline in Israel and Canada and practically no change in the US. As a consequence Israel dropped to fourth place, with a 14 percent poverty rate (Awad and Israeli 1996: 218, table 2).

Probably more telling than the relative placing of each of these countries is the relative effectiveness of their poverty-reduction policies. This may be measured by the percentage of the population that was elevated out of poverty by the combined impact of transfer payments and direct taxes. In the 1980s the US had the least potent policy, which pulled 21.4 percent of the poor above the poverty line, and was followed as a distant second by Israel, where the rate was 40.7 percent, closely followed by Canada and Australia. All other countries in the survey, from Italy to Sweden, had significantly higher rates of poverty alleviation and in Belgium and the Scandinavian countries it was in the 80–85 percent range. In the 1990s the percentage of individuals removed from the ranks of the poor rose to 26.2 percent in the US, still lowest in the industrialized world, followed by Germany at 46.5 percent, Israel with 48.0 percent, and Australia with 49.2 percent. The rate dropped in all other countries, but was still in the 80–84 percent range. The Israeli welfare state, in short, was among the least interventionist in the industrialized world in the 1980s, and despite some improvement, remained near the bottom in the 1990s as well.

As we have seen in these two sections, gross economic inequality and the percentage of families under the poverty line is rising relentlessly in Israel, even in comparison with other industrialized countries. At the same time, direct taxation and especially transfer payments have been used, if not always systematically, then at least in spurts, to keep the disposable-income gap and the gap between the haves and the poor from widening excessively. In the past fifteen years transfer payments have regularly reduced inequality by about 20 percent and reduced poverty, though by fits and starts, by about 60 percent. The amount of resources devoted to abating the gap, however, has to expand to keep the gap from widening. The share of "social expenses" (i.e. social security, education, health, etc.) from the GNP rose from 15 percent of GNP in 1985 to 20 percent in 1999 (Strassler, *Haaretz*, July 11, 1999), most of it for unemployment benefits and income supplementation (Shalev, *Haaretz*, July 15, 1999), and whereas the GNP grew by 2.1 during these twenty years, the amount of transfer payments grew by a factor of 3.6. (Barkai, *Haaretz*, September 19, 2000). The question needs to be asked, therefore, how likely is it that an ever-growing relative and absolute share of resources will continue to be devoted to keeping growing inequality down, without any discernible hope of making a dent in it?

The prevalent assessment is that instead of devoting more resources to poverty abatement, fewer additional resources will be available in the future for keeping these growing gaps at the current levels. Ben-Shahar and Helpman observe that the source of the funds used to cover the ever-growing transfer payments is reductions in the military budget. In short, the "peace dividend" that allowed the reduction of the share of the military in the budget since the peace with Egypt in 1979 has been used for social causes. As mentioned in chapter 9 above, in 1985 the military budget consumed 22 percent of the GNP, today around 10 percent. The room for further reductions in the military budget, however, is not endless, and in Ben-Shahar and Helpman's view was already exhausted (Ben-Shahar and Helpman, *Haaretz*, June 8, 2000; see also Strassler, *Haaretz*, November 11, 1999). Barkai adds that transfer payments already amount to 11 percent of the GNP, and he also believes that this rate cannot be pushed much higher (Barkai, *Haaretz*, September 19, 2000). Where else could the additional resources come from? While the three economists' evaluations of the availability of further resources for transfer payments can be debated, as can the optimal size of the Israeli military budget and transfer payments, the most relevant predictors might not be narrowly economic, but the transformation in the citizenship discourses. The replacement of republican citizenship and its communitarian dimension by a business-oriented liberal citizenship discourse, as expressed in the tangled income/taxation/transfer payment complex, does not augur well for the hope of keeping inequality and poverty within the present bounds.

Although Israel underwent a veritable revolution, similar to the East Asian tigers, in terms of its GDP per capita – from $5,585 in 1980 to $16,754 in 1998 (Shalev 2000: 129; World Bank 2000, tables 2.1, 4.2) – the disparity in the income of wage earners and the upper stratum has been staggering. In April 1999 companies owned by only five families owned 40 percent of the capitalization value of the TASE (Koren, *Haaretz*, August 2, 1999). Salary costs of the top executives of publicly traded Israeli companies are higher than those of their counterparts in England and Germany: whereas in 1994 it was thirteen times the average income, by 1999 it rose to twenty-two times that income (*Globes*, April 19, 1999; April 19, 2000). Though the majority of the poor come from the elderly and the unemployed, one-third of Israeli wage earners also fall below the poverty line (Swirski, *Haaretz*, June 6, 1999). Furthermore, whereas Israeli executives receive European salaries, the wages of Israeli production workers remain below those of their European counterparts.

Most significantly, the taxes imposed on Israeli companies have fallen dramatically since the EESP of 1985, relieving them of the burden of social costs paid by employers elsewhere. The rationale for this relief was the improvement of their international competitiveness. Corporate income tax (*mas chavarot*) was reduced from 61 percent in 1986 to 36 percent in the 1996–2000 period, bringing it into parity with other industrial countries. Employers' tax (*mas maasikim*), which stood at 7 percent in 1986, was abolished in 1992. Most tellingly, the contribution of employers to social security fell from 15.6 percent in 1986 to 4.93 percent in 1995, while the employers' "parallel tax" for health insurance was shouldered by the government, leaving Israel as a unique place where employers do not contribute to their employees' health expenses (Kim, *Haaretz*, June 8, 1999; Shalev, *Haaretz*, July 15, 1999). All these reductions, at a time when poverty and inequality are rising, constitute a significant transfer of wealth to the economic elites. To find new resources for transfer payments, this pattern would need to be reversed.

It is also entirely within the realm of possibility (as it had been done in 1985–93) that the universality of children's allowances will be rescinded, with first and second child's allowances abolished and the saved resources reallocated to parents with larger, and usually needier, families. Such an approach, by getting rid of the universal criteria of allocation, would end a universal citizenship right and replace it with the more traditional method of charity. This change would make it even harder to guarantee the continuation of the allowances in the long run.

In sum, the secular growth of gross income inequality is partially reduced by a sometimes energetic, if not always consistent, policy of transfer payments and direct taxes. The incorporation of Israel's Palestinian citizens, as we shall see in the rest of this chapter, into the social security system seems to enhance its universalism. It would seem, then, that there are limits to the levels of inequality that would be acceptable in Israeli society. At the same time, worrying signs abound. The importance of state institutions for providing an effective social protection net should be obvious from our discussion (see also Shalev 2000: 149); and yet its activist role in a liberalized economy is more problematic. Overall, the disappearance of republican citizenship and its institutions, together with their communitarian orientation towards, admittedly, a segment, but on occasion also towards the whole, of the Jewish population, and the concomitant rise of a liberal citizenship discourse, provide for a much weakened resolve to try and ensure the stability of the inequality and poverty rates. This weakened resolve might not suffice to generate the resources for the growth of transfer payments needed to keep up with growing inequality and poverty. In fact, the effects of this transition in the predominant citizenship discourse are already evident in shrinking social rights.

Contraction of social citizenship rights

The Israeli welfare, health, and education systems, that is, the realm of social citizenship rights, has been downsized in recent decades. From expanding the broad-based, though never universal, administration of these rights until the late 1970s, there has been a transition to selectively targeting social services at the weaker social groups, while encouraging those who can afford it to opt out of state-provided services. These changes have led to the increased privatization of many social services, with the result of providing them to the lower socio-economic strata at lower standards or replacing them with traditional charity, while allowing the wealthy to use the privatized services to their advantage. In this way the health, welfare, and education systems have been bifurcated between the rich and poor, leaving the middle class trapped in between.

Education

Until recently, the most far-reaching direct and indirect privatization attempts have taken place in the educational sphere. As a result, the role of education as a tool of social mobility and social integration has diminished. One mechanism for educational privatization in Israel, prevalent especially in the 1980s, was the reduction of instructional time in the schools, leading to the appearance of so-called "gray education": payment by parents for educational activities eliminated because of these reductions. These enrichment courses, provided by private educational bodies, amount to the direct financing of part of the school budget by parents who could afford it, and, in effect, to the formation of a parallel private education system within the official one. Other mechanisms of privatization have been the granting of financial autonomy to individual schools and the encouragement of greater parental involvement. The overall result has been that the payment assumed by households for education rose by 1992 to 24 percent of the national education budget, while the percentage of schools with "gray education" rose from 38 percent in 1988 to 63 percent in 1994 (Swirski 1999: 230).

Two commissions appointed by the Ministry of Education in 1993 recommended the furthering of these processes. The Gafny Commission, charged with examining the possibility of raising funds for educational purposes from non-public sources, recorded its concern over the danger of the erosion of equality among schools under such an arrangement. It nevertheless recommended that schools be encouraged to mobilize financial resources and resources in kind from contributions, in-house activities, and other sources. The Wollonsky Commission, which studied schools under self-management, suggested means and ways of reducing public responsibility for education (Adva 1993).

In 1990, in an attempt to reduce the educational resource gap between children in "weak" schools located in underprivileged areas and children whose parents could afford to pay for "gray education," the Knesset passed a law mandating longer school days in the poorer schools. However, only half of the funds required for implementing this law were allocated between 1990 and 1995, and in 1996 no funding was provided (Adva 1996b: 28). As a consequence, in 1994 only a third of the privately funded teaching hours were offered in the geographically peripheral schools (Swirski 1999: 230).

In the 1990s the trend was reversed and the education budget began to rise again. In the first three years of the Rabin government it rose quite substantially, by about 14 percent a year, so that in 1996 the education budget constituted 9.5 percent of the state budget. Most of the increase, however, was dedicated to the absorption of immigrant children from the former USSR and, in 1993/4, to salary increases for teachers. Consequently, the budget share allocated to programs aimed at equalizing the educational level of different sectors of the population actually shrank (Adva 1996b: 10). Ruth Klinov's prediction from 1989, that "there is no way or chance that state funding of education will ever replace private funding" has been borne out in the intervening years (Klinov 1989: 133).

The most significant changes have occurred at the top and bottom of the education system. Starting in the early 1990s, just as the Ministry of Education's budgetary outlays for programs akin to Head Start in the US, and for special "fostering" (tipuach), or compensatory, education programs began to be cut back by between a fifth and a quarter, it launched a five-year plan to decrease the chasm in the allocation of funds to Jewish and Israeli Palestinian-Arab schools, which had previously been funded according to different criteria. Thus, in 1994 citizen Palestinian children became eligible for the first time to be included in the "fostering" programs, previously reserved for Mizrachi children only. Although this change increased the size of the eligible population, the actual budget for this program continued to fall as late as 1996 (Adva Center 1996b: 36).

The long school day in mostly Mizrachi low-income schools and the inclusion of Arab students in fostering programs and enhanced budgets have somewhat diminished the discrimination built into the education system, which favored the principle of ethno-nationalism over liberal criteria. Still, the gaps between schools that cater for Ashkenazim, Mizrachim, and Palestinian citizens, as indicated, for example, by rates of graduation from high schools, have barely been narrowed. Graduation from Israeli high schools and eligibility for university admission depends on passing the matriculation examinations (bagrut). In 1998 only 38.5 percent of high-school seniors received matriculation certificates. Of this already low percentage, the highest rates were in the older cities and towns in the center of the country. Among the twelve development towns, of mostly Mizrachi populations, only eight had rates above the national average, due to high rates of success among immigrants from the former Soviet Union. In only one citizen Palestinian locality was the rate of success above the national average. One reason for this disparity is the differential drop-out rate: in largely Ashkenazi middle-class neighborhoods it stands at 6 percent, in mostly Mizrachi development towns it is 21 percent, and in citizen Palestinian localities 42 percent. Another reason is the channeling of a higher percentage of Mizrachi, and increasingly also of Palestinian, high-school students to vocational schools, in which only a fraction of the students are prepared for matriculation, and on average only 29 percent pass these examinations. Not surprisingly, the matriculation rate among Palestinian high-school students remains 20 percent, about half of the rate for the general population (Adva Center 1999; Swirski 1999: 234).

While the equalization of schools has given limited benefits to students in development towns and Arab locales, in the name of the free choice promised by the liberal discourse the commitment to integrate Jewish junior high and high schools has diminished and additional benefits have accrued to the top tier of the school system. Thus, the state religious schools (*mamlachti dati*) have been bifurcated between religiously more observant schools (*mamlachti dati torani*), catering mostly for the children of religious middle-class Ashkenazi parents, and the regular religious schools, where most of the Mizrachi children remain. Within the state secular schools an elite layer of elementary and junior-high magnet-type schools with distinctive curricula was chartered, most of them in Tel Aviv, growing from two in the late 1980s to about forty in 1991, educating about 2 percent of the total enrollment of the respective age groups. The Kashti Commission concluded that "the spread of [such magnet] schools represents a trend towards social separation and segregation" (Swirski 1999: 232).

Health-care insurance

In contrast to the public education system, which has been characterized by piecemeal privatization, the transformation of the public health-care system had been debated since the establishment of Israel (Aridor 1993), but was accomplished practically overnight in a particularly dramatic and telling fashion. The transformation of Israel's health-care system was probably the most complex of all the institutional changes effected since 1985; one with truly far-reaching consequences for Israel's incorporation regime and for its multiple citizenship discourses. This transformation was also, on the face of it, the most muddled one in terms of its direction and immediate effects on citizenship rights. It is, therefore, in clear need of interpretation. In our view, notwithstanding the fact that health care in Israel was nationalized and thus seemingly universalized as a right, health-care reform should be seen as part and parcel of the general wave of liberalizing measures and as a major component in the assault on social rights.

Israel's health-care crisis was an aspect of the Histadrut's crisis of the late 1980s, and was rooted in a deeper dispute over the very purpose of that institution. The proud legacy and institutional expression of republican virtue in the sphere of public health was the Histadrut's Kupat Cholim Klalit (General Sick Fund), established in 1911 (that is, before the Histadrut itself) by the "Association of the Agricultural Workers of

Judea," and affiliated with the Histadrut in 1920. Kupat Cholim was based on the LSM's communal principle of "mutual aid" among its citizens. The level of services provided was uniform and did not depend on the rate of dues paid by individual members. In the spirit of communal solidarity, Kupat Cholim sought to provide services to all (initially only Jews) in all geographical regions, and could not refuse admission to people with prior medical conditions. This was in sharp contrast to other, later, public health-care providers, which targeted younger, healthier, and more affluent populations in the central areas of the country (Ben-Meir 1978: 242).

Since 1937 union dues and membership fees in the sick fund were collected jointly, under the name "unified tax" (*mas achid*) (Ben-Meir 1978: 294). A parallel tax (*mas makbil*) was paid by the members' employers. By joining the Histadrut one became immediately eligible to receive health-care from its Kupat Cholim; by becoming a member of Kupat Cholim *eo ipso* one became a member of Histadrut. In fact, the membership card (*pinkas chaver*) in the Histadrut and Kupat Cholim was a single document. In this way Kupat Cholim became the Histadrut's primary vehicle of recruitment. Not surprisingly, therefore, in its heyday membership in the Histadrut was over 100 percent of the labor force, and included homemakers and a share of the self-employed. In 1977 the Histadrut membership was 2,652,000 (including 283,000 citizen Palestinians), namely 74 percent of Israel's population (78 percent of the Jewish and 50 percent of the citizen Palestinian population) (Ben-Meir 1978: 243).

The "unified tax" was a progressive tax, and the Histadrut's main source of revenue (Ben-Meir 1978: 295). About 60–70 percent of the tax paid to the Histadrut was transferred by it to Kupat Cholim, and the rest was kept for its own expenses. This arrangement provided the Histadrut with a captive membership and with a clear rationale to oppose changes to the prevailing health-care financing system. As long as Israelis needed health care, the Histadrut's future seemed ensured.

In contrast to the Yishuv period, when health care was scant and provided as part of a voluntary network of "mutual help," after 1948 the republican health-care institutions had to coordinate themselves within a newly formed dense and tangled institutional field. In 1948 health policy came under a weak Ministry of Health, and various health-care institutions, which did not form part of Kupat Cholim, or were only partially incorporated into it, were established. For example, a network of free maternity and early childhood health facilities (*tipat chalav*) was established and funded by the state. Similarly, mental-health facilities were created, run, and funded jointly by the Health Ministry, the NII, the sick funds, and private and non-profit organizations. About half of the hospital-related expenses were covered by the government, which also owned close to half of all general hospital beds.

Chernichovsky and Chinitz provide a long list of problems this Byzantine institutional system begot: Entitlement to health care had not been clearly defined and remained confusing for the average citizen; "no national policies concerning the aged, manpower, or medical education" could be adopted; the financial liability and accountability of health-care providers was left open; institutional barriers created duplications and discontinuities; centralized management ignored local needs and initiatives; and health-care provision was politicized (Chernichovsky and Chinitz 1995: 130–1). Consequently, "sick funds, the major one [i.e. the Histadrut's] in particular, centrally financed and managed, have been accountable to neither their members nor to the state" (Chernichovsky and Chinitz 1995: 131). But as long as the Histadrut itself was not in financial difficulties, and for a long while afterwards, it successfully prevented attempts to link or integrate health services and institutions in a way that would weaken its control over Kupat Cholim.

The Kupat Cholim crisis was precipitated by the reduction in government spending on health care as part of its 1985 general economic stabilization policy. Whereas in 1978/9 the government footed 45 percent of the health-care system's expenses from its general revenues, by 1987/8 its share fell to 21 percent. Conversely, the share of the compulsory payroll tax by employers rose from 17 percent to 30 percent, and the members' share through direct (out-of-pocket) expenses rose from 20 percent to 31 percent. Membership dues were the only component whose share of the total remained fixed: 18 percent (Chernichovsky and Chinitz 1995: 129, table 2).

At the same time demographic changes, such as the aging of the population, as well as growing demand for better care and improved service, coupled with the decline of the government's share in health-related expenditures, led to the expansion of private medicine and the development of "gray" markets within public hospitals and clinics. This caused "increasing inequality in access to care" and undermined "the philosophical and ethical foundations of the [existing] system" (Chernichovsky and Chinitz 1995: 134). The crisis, then, consisted in a "decline in the rate of growth of resources allocated to health, and the shift from public to private finance, [which] exposed the basic deficiencies of the system" (Chernichovsky and Chinitz 1995: 132).

While all branches of the health-care system suffered from tighter budgets, the Histadrut's Kupat Cholim, providing services, by then, to only 70 percent of the population, including its older, sicker, poorer, and peripheral sectors, and whose membership fees, based on a progressive taxation system, were lower, was under the greatest fiscal pressure. Since it preferred to borrow money, rather than raise its membership fees, in order to stay competitive, an accumulated debt of $700 million in 1988, which grew to $1 billion dollars by 1994, threatened its solvency.

In June 1988 a commission headed by Shoshana Netanyahu, a Supreme Court justice, was appointed to investigate the public health-care system. In August 1990 the commission proposed to reform the health-care system along the lines that, as we shall see, were adopted with some minor changes in 1994. The commission proposed to guarantee by legislation "access to a basic package of care financed through taxes as a citizen's right," similar to the European social democratic approach (Chernichovsky and Chinitz 1995: 137). In contrast to the British system, however, in which the government is the provider of health care, the commission preferred the HMO model of regulated but competing sick funds. In contrast to the US model, these sick funds, the existing *kupot cholim*, were to continue to be non-profit organizations. As a public right, health-care financing was to retain its public character through the combination of government contribution and sick-fund membership dues that would be turned into a health tax, collected by the NII along the same progressive lines as the income tax (Chernichovsky and Chinitz 1995: 134–7). All Israeli citizens were to be responsible for joining one of the sick funds which, on their part, could not deny membership to anyone and were to compete for members by offering various levels of co-payment and quality of service.

The reforms proposed by the Netanyahu Commission (and later adopted in the National Health Insurance Law) corresponded to the recommendations made to the commission by the Union of Government Physicians, but were opposed by the Histadrut and the unions of other health-care workers. The latter were concerned "with lay-offs, development of wage differentials between workers in different sectors, and the weakening of their national unions as a result of the formation of stronger local unions in the individual hospitals" (Chernichovsky and Chinitz 1995: 137). But the Histadrut, fearing loss of control over its sick fund – the final act in its transformation into a regular trade union – was the main opponent of national health insurance.

The NHI bill was submitted to the Knesset by the Likud government in early 1992, but the change of government required that the process be restarted by the Rabin government. In that government Chayim Ramon was appointed minister of health and he expected to pass the NHI bill, sever Kupat Cholim from the Histadrut, and complete the Labor Party's internal reform. The public debate on national health insurance was reopened and focused on the reform's implication for

Kupat Cholim–Histadrut ties and the separation of tax collection for health care and the Histadrut, rather than on the hoped-for resolution of the health-care system's chronic deficits.

The leadership and apparatus of the Histadrut used their full weight to defeat the bill, even after finance minister Shochat proposed to separate the collection of Histadrut dues and health-care fees but still retain the Histadrut–Kupat Cholim ties, namely, to ensure that membership in the Histadrut would continue to be required for insurance by its Kupat Cholim Klalit, and vice versa. The support mobilized by the Histadrut in the Labor Party led to Rabin's withdrawal of his support for the bill and to Ramon's resignation of his post, in January 1994.

The political process through which Ramon then became chair of the New Histadrut and the NHI was passed in June 1994, was outlined in chapter 8 above. While from the perspective of other societies, primarily the US, it would seem that a national health insurance is the very opposite of health-care privatization, in Israel, we would argue, the NHI law constituted a major blow to public health-care provision, and an important signpost on the road to privatization. Admittedly, the new health-care system codified access to "a socially acceptable basket of medical services [as] a citizen's right" financed through a national tax, run by multiple and competing non-profit HMOs (Chernichovsky and Chinitz 1995: 134). Certainly, the setting of national standards and the universalization of access to health care indeed do not signal a movement toward a liberal market model. On the contrary, it could be, and has been argued, that in this case the social democratic element was divorced from the republican one and extended, in a liberal fashion, to truly universal dimensions.

And yet there are strong indications that the NHI law, as implemented, is headed in the direction of a market-driven health-care system (Filk 2000). The basket of health benefits adopted by the law was based on the Histadrut's Kupat Cholim's existing basket. This meant that dental and mental health services, for example, as well as geriatric institutionalization, that had not been provided by any Kupat Cholim prior to the law remained outside its purview. Those seeking additional, or better, services than those provided under the government's standards, namely, most members of the middle class, are paying additional membership fees to their sick funds and take out supplementary private health insurance, thus bifurcating the system. Updating the basket was left up to the government, which does so reluctantly, if at all, for budgetary reasons (Gross and Barmali 1996).

An even more significant factor leading to the bifurcation of the system is the reluctance of the state (operating, in this case, through the senior members of the Finance Ministry bureaucracy) to pay its share of the cost of health-care provision. When the NHI law was enacted, it was stipulated that its financing would come from several sources: the newly established health tax that replaced the membership fees in Kupat Cholim, the employers' parallel tax, various NII payments, patients' out-of-pocket fees, and "complementary sums out of the state budget to be determined each year in the annual budget law that will complete (*yashlimu*) the financing of the cost of the basket of health services" (*Rashumot* 1469, June 26, 1994: 160, 13(5)). In January 1997 the Knesset abolished the employers' "parallel tax" and placed upon the government the responsibility to cover the lost revenues, thus increasing the government's share in financing the NHI law. However, since the law did not obligate the government to cover the entire difference between the cost of health-care provision and the revenues generated by all other sources, the Finance Ministry has been trying to reduce the government's share, and increase the share of the insured, in paying the costs of health care. As a result, since the law went into effect the fiscal crisis of the health-care system not only has not been alleviated, but has been exacerbated instead. This has led the sick funds to refuse to provide new, expensive treatments and medications, and even to cut back on services they had previously provided (Filk 2000).

In 1998 the sick funds (whose "inefficiency" was cited for the government's reluctance to cover their deficits) were authorized to collect additional payments from their insured, in the form of both periodical fees and payments for specific services and medications. Since, unlike the health tax, these payments are uniform and not related to income, they "introduced a regressive element into the system of health services financing" (State Comptroller 1998: 166). (The NHI law forbids health-care providers to refuse services for lack of payment, so it is not clear how the new payments can be enforced. The Histadrut indeed called on the public to refuse to pay them.) So far, the Finance Ministry's 1998 proposals, to require each sick fund to offer its own basic basket of benefits and give official recognition to for-profit HMOs, have been blocked by the Knesset.

If the gradual withdrawal of the government from financing the real cost of health-care provision continues, as does the trend for patients' out-of-pocket payments to assume an ever-larger share of the cost, the health-care system will follow the education system in its rate of privatization. By paying for added benefits, whether directly or through higher insurance fees, some will be able to enjoy privatized services from publicly funded health-care providers. The corporatization of government hospitals, already commenced by the previous Likud government, further subjects the provision of health services to allocation by price. The result of nationalizing health insurance, in sum, is not likely to be increased access to its services but rather the reduction of its publicly paid costs. In this case, social citizenship rights would suffer another blow, under the cover of a particularly cruel deception. This should not be too much of a surprise if the context in which nationalization took place is kept in mind: it was an essential measure, indeed a necessary precondition, for the assault on the Histadrut. With the accomplishment of that goal, the safeguarding of the new health-care system is likely to assume secondary importance for many of the Histadrut's opponents.

Housing rights

Israel has one of the highest rates of private home ownership in the world, much of it achieved through public assistance. Data from the 1983 census show that 73 percent of the population owned their homes, 13 percent rented on the private market, and the remaining 14 percent were tenants in public housing. In the US the comparable percentages (for 1988) were 66, 32, and 2 percent, in Great Britain (in 1989) 67, 7, and 26 percent, while in France (in 1988) they were 51, 25, and 24 percent, respectively (Werczberger 1991). The 1986/7 household expenditure survey conducted by the CBS indicated that home ownership in Israel rose in the intervening years to 76 percent (Lewin-Epstein, Elmelech and Semyonov 1997: 1456).

The privatization of dwellings, through the construction of public housing and the sale of units at under-market prices to their inhabitants, had been a long-standing policy of the LSM and Israel's governments that, in other spheres, favored republican institutions. In regard to housing, however, not only the needs of the republican community but of the broader circle of the ethno-national citizenry, all Jews, were addressed. The goal was to attach not only the members of the LSM but also immigrants who could not be integrated into the republican institutions in Israel, by providing them a stake in the nation-state through home ownership. This goal, as the numbers indicate, was attained to a large degree. But this success was accompanied by a differentiation between public and private housing and by geographical divisions that correspond to ethnic and national differences. Private construction took place primarily in central parts of the country, mostly in the coastal plain, whereas public housing was concentrated in peripheral or frontier areas (Law Yone and Kalush 1995: 3).

About 95 percent of publicly constructed and owned housing is managed by two companies: the government-owned Amidar and the Jewish Agency-owned Amigur. The number of units managed by these two bodies peaked in 1979 at 206,000. Rents in public housing are expected to cover management and maintenance costs, but not the original capital outlays, and were initially set not to exceed about half of the construction costs. Until 1987 rents in public housing were not being adjusted for inflation (Werczberger 1995: 97).

From the very beginning of public housing construction apartments had been available for purchase by their tenants, and between 2 and 5 percent were sold annually. Over the years reasons for their privatization multiplied, and the efforts to sell them intensified. The progression of the rationales for selling the apartments show the transition from nationalist goals to liberal justifications. To the goal of enhancing home ownership were added, in the 1960s, the more economic goals of reducing management and maintenance costs, which the rents could not cover. By the end of the 1980s privatization was presented as an end in itself, and a major drive to sell to occupying tenants was launched. Only a 10 percent downpayment was required (which was waived for new immigrants), the prices were discounted 25 percent below the market price, and subsidized loans were made available for the remainder. The rate of sales climbed to 6 percent, but remained limited by the less than enthusiastic co-operation of the housing management corporations, which privatization was meant to put out of business, and by the fact that many of the tenants were financially unable to purchase their homes. In 1992 the discounts were eliminated, but the subsidized loans for purchase were maintained (Werczberger 1995: 98–9).

In 1998 the Knesset passed a Public Housing Law, which enabled tenants in public housing projects to purchase their apartments for heavily subsidized prices (up to 85 percent below the value of the unit, depending on the length of tenancy). This law was passed despite the opposition of the government and under pressure from extraparliamentary groups, most prominently the Democratic Mizrachi Rainbow, a group of mostly Mizrachi intellectuals that seeks to promote social rights and the cultural rights of Mizrachim. The success of these efforts stemmed, at least in part, from the fact that they were undertaken in the context of a move by the government, since the early 1990s, to massively privatize ILA land. This privatization would be effected by allowing the holders of agricultural leases (mostly kibbutzim, moshavim, and private agro-business concerns) to construct housing and commercial spaces on large portions of the land they hold and pocket large portions of the windfall profits that would ensue from this conversion. This move, which amounts to nothing less than the unilateral transfer of huge amounts of "national" capital to the private ownership of the most privileged groups in society, is yet another blatant manifestation of the retreat of the national-republican discourse in the face of the liberal one. It is instructive, however, that in the public debate now raging around this transfer, spokespeople for the kibbutzim hark back to their pioneering record in trying to justify their massive appropriation of public assets (Yiftachel and Kedar 2000; Yonah and Saporta 2000).

Not surprisingly, the triumph of the liberal over the republican discourse spells the precisely opposite results for the mostly Mizrachi poor tenants of public housing. Since the enactment of the Public Housing Law, the government, under both Likud and Labor, has done everything in its power to sabotage its implementation, claiming it would have adverse budgetary consequences. As a result of these efforts, take-up rates of the opportunities provided by the law have been exceedingly low (Eliash 2000).

In the late 1960s public housing construction and tenanting were transferred to private building companies, whereas the government retained the selection of building sites in national priority areas, and focused on the determination of eligibility, housing subsidies, and regulation of the industry. Under the new system contractors were being allocated nationally owned land through the ILA, without competitive bidding, and were reimbursed for development costs, while housing prices were allowed to be determined at real costs. Housing subsidies were thus transferred from the tenants to the builders of public housing (Law Yone and Kalush 1995: 5).

The next significant step in disconnecting housing from public construction, and limiting the nationalist justification for providing housing services, was taken during the massive immigration of Jews from the former USSR in the early 1990s. These immigrants, as Smooha has pointed out, were not burdened with national tasks. They were not expected to settle on the frontiers, help in the development of industry, or enlarge the pool of soldiers. If Likud hoped to settle them in large numbers in the occupied territories, this goal could not be realized either (Smooha 1994b: 6). The absorption of immigrants was undertaken, in disregard of the Histadrut's proposal to centralize the process (*Haaretz*, August 2, 1990), through a method of "direct absorption." The absorption process encompassed several stages in which subsidies and tax exemptions were initially granted, such as subsidies to employers who employed immigrants, and then eliminated in stages. While some categories of immigrants were sent to absorption centers, most received a rent subsidy or, after July 1990, an "absorption basket" which they could use at their discretion (Moskovitch 1990: 17–18). Eligibility for housing, in short, was applicable in both the public and private housing markets. Public housing for immigrants became a residual sector and privatization has exacerbated social differentiation (Werczberger 1995: 105; chap. 12, below).

Under the sway of the republican and ethno-nationalist discourses, housing policies had contributed to the social distinctions that made up Israel's incorporation regime. A study by Lewin-Epstein et al. found that disparities in housing wealth, defined as the combination of home ownership and the value of the home, independently of demographic factors (i.e., age and marital status) and labor market outcomes (i.e., earnings) have stratified Israel's Jewish population according to their ethnic origins (Lewin-Epstein, Elmelech, and Semyonov 1997: 1458). Whereas in 1986/7 80.8 percent of Jews of European descent, closely followed by 78.6 percent of Jews from Asia (mostly Iraq), owned their homes, only 59.4 percent of Jews from North Africa (mostly Morocco) did so. Furthermore, the value of housing also differed, this time placing Asian Jews closer to the North Africans: Whereas the average value of European Jews' homes was NIS 99,713, Asian Jewish homes were valued at NIS 80,746, and North African Jewish homes at NIS 69,968 (Lewin-Epstein, Elmelech, and Semyonov 1997: 1448, table 2).

Differential access to housing ownership and to higher value housing resulted, in large part, from the timing of immigration. European and Asian Jews arrived in big waves before 1948 or in the few years afterwards, whereas the arrival of immigrants from North Africa was spread out more evenly between 1947 and 1970, with 40 percent of them arriving between 1961 and 1970. More significantly than the simple factor of timing, in 1953 the government adopted a conscious policy of population dispersion, that is, settling immigrants in frontier regions, where development towns were being built. The arrival of the first large group of North African Jews, vulnerable as immigrants to social engineering of the republican type, coincided with this plan. This policy was not enforced with equal rigor on Jewish immigrants from Europe who arrived in the same time period, so they "were able to overcome the disadvantage of later immigration by other means" (Lewin-Epstein, Elmelech, and Semyonov 1997: 1452). Consequently, as many as 38.1 percent of North African Jews, but only 13.8 percent of Asian Jews and as few as 8 percent of European Jews lived in development towns before the massive Soviet immigration of the 1990s (Lewin-Epstein, Elmelech, and Semyonov 1997: 1448). Thus, in addition to time of immigration, place of residence is a major predictor of both home ownership and value of housing: in peripheral towns, the rate of home ownership is lower than in other regions, as is the value of the homes owned (Lewin-Epstein, Elmelech, and Semyonov 1997: 1453).

The "dire implications" of the cumulative effect of home ownership and the value of housing, namely, the fact that the group with the lowest rate of home ownership also owns the less valuable homes, are spelled out by Lewin-Epstein and his co-authors: "Housing wealth constitutes the primary form of household wealth for the overwhelming majority of the population and is a major determinant of intergenerational assistance and inheritance. Disparities in home ownership, then, may generate the reproduction of ethnic inequality in wealth and standard of living across generations" (Lewin-Epstein, Elmelech, and Semyonov 1997: 1458; cf. Spilerman 1996). Access to public housing services is so clearly polarized between Jewish and Palestinian citizens that it is, in effect, a distinct "Jewish social citizenship right." In 1970/1, for example, only 1 percent of the Ministry of Housing's budget, which finances public housing projects, was spent in Palestinian communities. In 1993 still only 2.2. percent of the housing units being constructed under the initiative of the Housing Ministry were in these communities (Sikkuy 1996: 11; cf. Sikkuy 2000: 18–19). Eligibility for subsidized mortgages to newly married couples, a major form of housing assistance, is based on a point system in which military service is a weighty factor. This ranks most Palestinian applicants below Jewish ones. Thus, in 1995 Palestinian couples constituted only 2.3 percent of couples who actually received such mortgages, and in 1999 they still constituted only 8 percent (Adva Center 1996c; Adalah 1998: 61; Sikkuy 2000: 18; Rosenhek and Shalev 2000). Finally, housing subsidies in development areas *eo ipso* exclude Palestinian citizens, whose towns and villages in the very same regions are excluded from the definitions of such areas, making them eligible only for more modest mortgage assistance (Kretzmer 1990: 122).

Palestinian citizens enjoy lower standards of social citizenship not only in comparison with Jews in general, but with Mizrachi Jews in particular. Project Renewal for the renovation of dilapidated neighborhoods, commenced by the first Likud government jointly with the Jewish Agency, directly targeted eighty such locations with high concentrations of Mizrachim, but no Palestinian neighborhoods were chosen. The justification for choosing solely Jewish neighborhoods was that funding for this project came from the Jewish Agency, a "private" organization concerned with the welfare of Jews, and not from the state.[1] In fact, the government's outlay on Project Renewal exceeded that of the Jewish Agency, except in the area of public buildings. As a result of a public outcry, Arab neighborhoods in the mixed cities and towns of Tel Aviv–Jaffa, Haifa, Lod, Ramle, and Maalot–Tarshicha, but not

---

[1] Funneling funds through purportedly non-state Zionist institutions, such as the Jewish Agency, the JNF, or the WZO, is a widely used method of circumventing the legal requirement of equal treatment of Jewish and Palestinian citizens (Kretzmer 1990: 96–8; Adalah 1998: 51–4). This is another reason why the *Qaadan* ruling of the High Court of Justice, discussed in chapter 4 above, is so significant.

exclusively Arab localities, were eventually included in Project Renewal (Kretzmer 1990: 119–20).

Conclusion

The decline of the LSM's republican institutions of "mutual aid" has been accompanied by a rise in the saliency of the discourse of liberal citizenship in state institutions that are expected to provide equal access to their services across social divides. At the same time the liberal discourse of civil society, when the latter is conceived as encompassing the market and economic relations, is used to assault the rights to social services people enjoy by virtue of their membership in a particular community. The main conclusion of our examination of social citizenship rights in the context of this transition seems to be that the decline of the LSM and its pioneering-cum-colonizing ethos and institutions undermined the broad commitment to social democratic rights in many spheres. Only in a few spheres, and even there more rhetorically than in practice, have these republican communal rights been replaced with effective, universal, liberal rights.

At the same time, once rights have been historically guaranteed, it becomes difficult, in Israel as elsewhere, to eliminate them. They are eroded and their scope may fluctuate, but most survive, even if in a diminished form. It is the political right to vote that makes possible the protection of some of the social rights, and those groups – in the Israeli case Mizrachim in support of Likud and Shas, and Palestinian citizens in support of Labor – that can use it effectively may even benefit. But as the liberal discourse of the market seems to predominate, citizenship itself becomes more privatized and the overall commitment to social solidarity and to social rights is gradually diminished.

12 Emergent citizenship groups? Immigrants from the FSU and Ethiopia and overseas labor migrants

During the 1990s, liberalization processes, both global and local, have resulted in the incorporation into Israeli society of new population groups that have further challenged the frontier incorporation regime and the republican citizenship discourse: Jewish and non-Jewish immigrants from the former Soviet Union (FSU), immigrants from Ethiopia whose Jewishness has been questioned by the rabbinic authorities, and overseas (i.e. non-Jewish, non-Palestinian) labor migrants.

The incorporation of immigrants from the FSU into Israeli society has been effected largely through liberal market mechanisms from which most of them have been well equipped to benefit. Their incorporation has been justified, however, in classic ethno-national terms, that most of them seem to endorse, even though a significant minority among them are not Jewish. Thus, the "Russian" immigrants occupy a unique place with respect to the liberal–ethno-nationalist dilemma. Furthermore, since immigrants from the FSU have been motivated much more by "push" than by "pull" factors, and have arrived in such massive numbers, they may yet form an ethnic enclave within the society. Inward-looking and isolationist, even "separatist," tendencies can already be identified among them, so it is still impossible to predict whether they will adopt one of the existent competing citizenship discourses, or develop one of their own (Nudelman 1997).

In marked contrast to the Jewish immigrants from the FSU stand the Jewish immigrants from Ethiopia. Their numbers are much smaller and they have brought few marketable skills with them. More importantly, like the non-Jewish immigrants from the FSU, who gain entry by virtue of being related to religiously defined Jews, Ethiopian immigrants pose a problem in terms of their incorporation into Israeli society and its institutions. Since the Ethiopians' version of Judaism is not the rabbinic one they are the only Jewish community for which the ethno-national criterion of incorporation has not been sufficient. Thus, with respect to both of these groups, the religious definition of Judaism has been challenged by an ethno-national one, signaling a possible future rift between Jewishness and Israeliness.

Since 1967 Israeli companies, especially in the secondary labor markets, have employed large numbers of non-citizen Palestinian workers who, as we related in chapter 7, have lived under military occupation and enjoyed few rights. Since the outbreak of the first intifada in 1987, and especially since the Oslo Accords of 1993, many of these Palestinian workers, although by no means all of them, have been replaced by workers from Eastern Europe, the Far East, Latin America, and Africa. The incorporation conditions of these overseas workers bear many similarities to those of the Palestinians they replaced, with one significant difference: Palestinian workers were daily commuters, while overseas workers are residents of Israel.

None of Israel's existing citizenship discourses accords these overseas workers any rights, so they have sought rights by virtue of the new discourse of deterritorialized "universal personhood." This universal-rights discourse is an important facet of the massive labor migration that has taken place in the world since the 1960s and of globalization in general. For reasons that have to do with the Israeli–Palestinian conflict neither the older Israeli legal framework nor the current, more liberal, one recognizes the status of "refugee" or accepts appeals to universal human rights as valid under Israeli law. Therefore, if large numbers of labor migrants, over half of whom are undocumented, seek to settle in Israel, as their counterparts have done in Western Europe, their legal status will become a troublesome issue. For they are the only migrants who do not fit into this classic immigration country: As non-Jews they cannot gain admission through the ethno-national door, but the liberal door is also shut in their face. They are thus in a legal limbo. And whereas Jewish immigrants from the FSU seem to enjoy multiple citizenship options, overseas labor migrants seem to have none.

The ways in which these new groups have been incorporated into Israeli society potentially point in the direction of greater pluralism, even multiculturalism, in the emergent discourse of citizenship. But they also highlight the dangers to groups that find themselves on the margins of the existing discourses. The reasons for the arrival of these groups, the modes of their incorporation, and the ways in which they have affected Israel's incorporation regime will be explored in this chapter.

Immigrants from the FSU

An atypical immigration wave

The immediate reason for the migration of about 950,000 people from the FSU to Israel during the 1990s was the collapse of the Soviet system, the greatest liberal triumph in the global arena at least since the Second World War. This immigration "wave" has had four distinct and unusual characteristics that, in combination, have shaped its mode of incorporation into the society and its effects on it: its sheer numbers, relative to the size of the veteran population; its non-ideological motivation; the amount of human capital it brought into the country; and the high percentage of non-Jews among the immigrants.

The two peak years of immigration from the FSU were 1990 and 1991, with 185,000 and 148,000 immigrants, respectively. The numbers declined by more than a half by 1992, but still, by the end of 1996 more than 656,000 immigrants had arrived, increasing the total population of Israel by about 12 percent (Habib et al. 1998: 1; Friedberg 1998: 1). These vast numbers of people were "pushed" out of the FSU by the drastically worsening economic, social, and political conditions and by the increase in the open expressions of anti-Semitism that were attendant upon the collapse of the USSR; but they were not really "pulled" to Israel. Unlike the much smaller wave of Soviet immigration to Israel in the 1970s, which numbered about 150,000 people (Paltiel et al. 1997: 287), the 1990s immigrants were motivated neither by Zionist ideology nor by any particular desire to live in Israel for religious or other reasons. Their wish was to emigrate to the West, preferably to the United States. In the terminology of the functionalist school, then, they were clearly "immigrants" rather than "*olim*" (Lissak 1995: 4; Gitelman 1995: 15, 27; Horowitz and Leshem 1998: 300; al-Haj and Leshem 2000; see also chap. 3, above).

For its part, the Israeli state was not about to let the opportunity of significantly increasing Israel's Jewish population slip through its hands. Equally important, it seems, was the expectation that the immigrants, 80 percent of whom hailed from the European republics of the USSR, would also restore the declining share of Ashkenazim in the Jewish population. According to Yehuda Dominitz, who from 1979 to 1986 was director general of the Jewish Agency's department of immigration and absorption, "the start of the Soviet Jewish exodus to Israel [in the 1970s] was considered an historic opportunity to increase the Jewish population of Israel, build the nation and strengthen Israel's social fabric and cultural foundations. To forfeit such an opportunity by letting tens of thousands of Jews opt for other countries of migration would be unforgivable." Therefore, "on a number of occasions [in the 1980s] the government of Israel ... expressed its concern at the generosity of the American government in allowing so many Soviet Jews with Israeli visas to immigrate as refugees to the United States" (Dominitz 1997: 121–2; see also Margalit 1991; Jones 1996: 48).[1]

---

[1] Entry visas to Israel were required for emigration out of the Soviet Union until October

In 1989 the entreaties of the Israeli government, the passing of the Soviet Union as a political and ideological rival of the United States, and the prospects of a greatly liberalized Soviet emigration policy caused the number of formerly Soviet immigrants allowed into the United States to be limited to 50,000 a year. This had the effect of directing most of the emigrants from the FSU to Israel (Gitelman 1995: 13–17; Liebman 1995: 5; Jones 1996: 48–56).

Demographically, the immigrant population has been older, more highly educated, and held higher-status occupations in its countries of origin than the average Jewish population of Israel (not to say the population of Israel as a whole). At the end of 1992 the ratio of persons aged sixty-five and over per thousand persons aged fifteen to sixty-four was 139 in the Jewish population as a whole (including the immigrants) and 218 among the immigrants. In 1995 55 percent of the immigrants aged fifteen and over had more than thirteen years of schooling, as compared with 28 percent of the entire Jewish population of Israel in 1989. By the end of 1993 the number of engineers and architects among the immigrants was double their number in the Israeli labor force, while the number of medical doctors and dentists was 70 percent of their number in Israel. With all the inaccuracies that are bound to occur in these statistics (because of self-reporting etc.), the inflow of human capital into the Israeli economy as a result of this immigration was nothing short of staggering (Paltiel et al. 1997: 292–9; Sikron 1998).

Finally, a high proportion of the FSU immigrants, ranging from about 5.5 percent in 1990 to over 50 percent since 1998, have been non-Jews according to *halacha* (including many who were not Jewish either according to the criteria that prevailed in the Soviet Union). As a result, by 1999 Israel had a new minority group of about 250,000 non-Jewish non-Arab citizens, causing Ian Lustick to describe Israel as a "non-Arab," rather than a Jewish, state (Lustick 1999; *Haaretz*, March 5, 2000; Khanin 2000; Gitelman and Goldstein 2001: 209–10).

This unexpected consequence resulted from the amendment, in 1970, of the definition of "who is a Jew" in the Law of Return, making it compatible with *halacha* (with one minor exception – still recognizing non-Orthodox conversions to Judaism performed outside Israel). While this redefinition signaled the apparent victory of the ethno-national citizenship discourse over the liberal one, a (republican) compromise was struck in order to prevent the impeding of the demographic needs of Israel as a settler society. Since the Orthodox religious definition of "Jew" was

---

1989. Therefore, describing the emigration as "exodus to Israel," while relating the efforts made by the Israeli government to actually channel its flow to Israel, is not technically an inconsistency.

bound to significantly reduce the pool of potential immigrants in the Soviet Union, the criteria of eligibility for the benefits provided by the Law of Return were broadened, to include the children and grandchildren of Jews, with their own spouses and minor children (see chap. 5, above). Obviously, the assumption behind this amendment was that non-Jews who would immigrate to Israel under the Law of Return would embrace a Jewish, rather than a Palestinian, political identity. Thus, for the first time, the identity between the ethno-national and religious definitions of "Jew" was relaxed somewhat. With conditions in the FSU and in Israel being what they were in the 1990s, it is not surprising that many non-Jews decided to take advantage of the opportunity presented by this relaxation.

Citizenship rights

As immigrants to Israel by virtue of the Law of Return, immigrants from the FSU have been granted Israeli citizenship upon arrival. Like any other group, however, the actual practice of their citizenship rights has been characterized by its own peculiarities and idiosyncrasies, reflecting their placement in the incorporation regime. Our analysis of the FSU immigrants' citizenship rights will begin with their social rights, the rights most immediately important to an immigrant population (with special emphasis on their employment situation); continue with their civil rights; and conclude with the area in which the immigrants have left their most distinct mark – political rights and political activity.

The 1990s immigrant wave came into a relatively affluent and rapidly liberalizing Israeli society, which has become even more affluent and arguably more liberal as a result of their arrival. The largely positive effects the immigrants have had on the Israeli economy as a whole (Sussman 1998) did not result solely from their numbers or their educational endowments, however. Their economic integration was eased by a $10 billion loan guarantee provided by the US government, specifically for the purpose of "absorbing" these immigrants. The circumstances surrounding the granting of this loan guarantee are worth relating in some detail, as they demonstrate the close interconnection between the domestic and international arenas, and between the peace process and Israel's economic fortunes.

In September 1991 the Likud government, headed by Yitzhak Shamir, formally requested $10 billion in loan guarantees from the US, in order to help settle the FSU immigrants. The rationale behind that request was that the US's strong support for Jewish emigration out of the Soviet Union, dating back to the 1970s, coupled with the restrictions recently placed on the entry of these emigrants into the US, created a moral obligation for the US government to provide humanitarian aid for their resettlement in Israel. The (first) Bush administration, however, freshly victorious in the Gulf war and working to convene the Middle East peace conference in Madrid, made the provision of these loan guarantees conditional upon the complete cessation of Israeli settlement activity in the OT (Jones 1996: 87–93).

The refusal of the Likud government then in power to accede to this American demand, and its consequent failure to receive the loan guarantees, were among the reasons that led to its demise in the 1992 elections. Nearly 60 percent of the FSU immigrants voted for Labor or Meretz in those elections (Gitelman and Goldstein 2001: 205), affording the new coalition government of Yitzhak Rabin a secure base in the Knesset. The new government immediately declared a freeze on construction activity in the OT settlements, and in October 1992 the US Congress approved the $10 billion loan guarantees, to be used for immigrant resettlement and absorption "in areas which 'were subject to the administration of the Government of Israel before June 5, 1967'" (Jones 1996: 204, 207). Less than a year later the Rabin government signed the DOP with the PLO in Oslo.

Social citizenship rights have been conferred on the 1990s FSU immigrants through a new, liberal, free-market concept known as "direct absorption," adopted in 1989. Rather than being provided with housing or employment directly by the state, each immigrant family received an "absorption basket" consisting of income support and rental subsidies, amounting to about $10,000 per family of four, for their first year in Israel. In addition, each family could receive a subsidized mortgage equal to about 50 percent of the purchase price of an apartment. With these funds the immigrants were free to find housing and employment wherever they could. They also received free health-care insurance for the first year, as well as free Hebrew-language instruction for the first five months of their stay in Israel (Adler 1997: 141–3; Paltiel et al. 1997: 300; Leshem 1998; Gal and Leshem 1999).

The policy of "direct absorption" notwithstanding, the Likud government (and its housing minister, Ariel Sharon) still spent $5 billion on the construction of 140,000 apartments and the purchase of 25,000 mobile homes in order to provide the immigrants, whose numbers were initially expected to be much higher than they actually were, with the most basic Zionist social right – housing. Much of this investment turned out to have been wasted, however, since housing was made available mostly in peripheral areas of the country, where there were no employment opportunities for the immigrants. Still, within two years of their arrival in Israel, over 30 percent of the immigrants (and over 50 percent of immigrant families with two income earners) came to own their apartments (Gitelman 1995: 18, 43; Borukhov 1998).

Employment has been and remains the most pressing issue in the immigrants' life in Israel (Gitelman 1995: 18). While the human capital they brought with them was very valuable in the Soviet context, not all of it was convertible to the Israeli labor market. Many of the skills the immigrants possessed were irrelevant to the Israeli economy because of differences in language, technology, specialization, institutional setting, etc., in addition to the simple calculus of supply and demand. Clearly, the Israeli economy could not absorb twice as many engineers as it already had, or an equal number of medical doctors. This problem was reflected in lower levels of labor-force participation among the immigrants in Israel than those they had experienced in the FSU; in high initial levels of unemployment; and in downward occupational mobility, in terms of both occupational branches and the status gained within each occupation (Sikron 1998; Sussman 1998).

In the FSU the rate of labor-force participation among the would-be emigrants aged fifteen and over was 70 percent. In Israel their rate of participation stabilized at around 55 percent within two to three years of immigration, compared to an Israeli rate of 53 percent (not including the military). Women encounter greater obstacles than men, and older people have had greater difficulties than younger ones in joining the labor force. Immigrants who joined the labor force experienced high levels of unemployment and underemployment for the first three years, but their levels of unemployment were equalized with the general unemployment rate after their third year in the country. Here, again, women and older people fared worse than younger men (Sikron 1998: 139–46).

Most of the immigrants experienced some downward occupational mobility, either between or within occupations, but were not declassed on a massive scale. In 1994 10 percent of the immigrants who had arrived since 1990 were employed in academic and scientific occupations, and an additional 13 percent were employed in professional and technical ones. This compared with 34 percent that had been employed in *each* of these two occupational categories in the FSU. By the same token, 30 percent of the immigrants were employed as skilled workers and 22 percent were employed in services, compared to 15 percent and 4 percent in the FSU, respectively. These changes in the occupational patterns of the immigrants reflected not only the devaluation of their human capital as a result of migration, but also the effectiveness of the labor unions representing veteran primary-sector workers in protecting their members' employment and pay levels (Sussman 1998: 204).

Overall, in 1990–2, the average immigrant, having 14.1 years of schooling, was employed in occupations requiring 12.2 years of schooling and was earning 10 percent less than s/he would have earned if employed at the level appropriate to her/his education. This educational–occupational mismatch increased with age and with years of schooling (Sikron 1998: 148–51).

Like previous immigration waves, this wave too had generally favorable effects on the Israeli economy. Economic growth was resumed in 1989, and the unemployment rate among veteran Israelis declined from 8.9 percent in 1989, on the eve of the immigration, to 5.8 percent in 1995. This resulted primarily from the creation of new jobs in housing and in the production of consumer goods for the immigrants. Despite the great influx of academically and technically trained immigrants, labor-force participation rose, and unemployment declined, among similarly trained veterans. These highly educated veterans' real wages rose as well, both absolutely and relative to those of other workers. Because of the downward occupational mobility experienced by academically and technically trained immigrants they competed not with their educational peers, but with less-educated veterans, and were thus partially responsible for the decline in the latter's real wages. (The other reason for this decline was the massive introduction of overseas workers into the Israeli economy; see below.) Thus, the immigration added to the growing inequality in income distribution that characterized the Israeli economy in the 1990s.

The single most important issue relating to the civil rights of FSU immigrants has had to do with the non-Jews among them. While the Nationality Law confers immediate Israeli citizenship on every immigrant who arrives in Israel by virtue of the Law of Return, it is up to the Ministry of the Interior to register the newcomers as Israeli citizens and as Jews (or members of other religions). Through the entire decade of the 1990s the Ministry of the Interior was under the control of Shas, and its registrars made every effort not to register non-Jews or doubtful Jews as citizens. Needless to say, the denial, or even delay, of the granting of citizenship can have very serious consequences for a person's ability to enjoy certain rights. It was for this reason that in 1999 the main political party representing the immigrants, Yisrael Baaliya, made control over the Interior Ministry the key point of its election campaign (Gitelman and Goldstein 2001: 212). The Yisrael Baaliya leader, Nathan Sharansky, was indeed appointed minister of the interior following the 1999 elections, but until his resignation, on the eve of the Camp David summit meeting between Ehud Barak and Yassir Arafat in July 2000, no noticeable change had occurred in the practices of the population registrars (Gaon 1999).

Non-Jews who are registered as Israeli citizens still encounter great difficulties in practicing some of their civil rights, primarily those relating to personal status, such as marriage, divorce, burial, and family unification. As related in chapter 5 above, religious courts have a virtual monopoly on most matters of family law, and the *halacha* does not sanction interreligious marriages. Non-Jews who wish to marry Jews must therefore go outside the officially recognized institutions, although the state does recognize those unofficial forms of marriage as binding. Ironically, some FSU immigrants go back to the FSU in order to get married, thus circumventing the religious courts (Ilan 2000b).

Non-religious burial grounds have only recently and hesitantly been introduced, largely as a result of the problems raised by the need to bury non-Jewish immigrants from the FSU, including several soldiers who fell while serving in the IDF. Non-Jewish citizens also have serious difficulties when they request that non-Jewish spouses, parents, or children be admitted to citizenship. This is a source of great misery to many of them, given the high rates of intermarriage and of divorce that prevailed in the USSR (Jones 1996: 132–40; Gitelman and Goldstein 2001: 212).

The most distinctive mark made on Israeli political life by the FSU immigrants had to do with their providing the swing vote in several national elections and with their unprecedented success in organizing their own political parties. In the four national elections held since their arrival – 1992, 1996, 1999, and 2001 – most FSU immigrants voted against the party in power and against the incumbent prime minister. (In each case, the candidate who won among the immigrants won the premiership.) This voting pattern seems to suggest that their political behavior has been motivated by dissatisfaction with their treatment by all Israeli governments that have held power since their arrival. Closer analysis, however, reveals that dissatisfaction with government performance on issues related to the immigrants was indeed the crucial factor in determining their vote in 1992 and 1996. But in 1999, in the race for prime minister, the immigrants' voting pattern was remarkably similar to that of the general electorate and was motivated by the same sorts of concerns. Therefore, unlike 1992 and 1996, in 1999 the immigrant vote did not determine the outcome of the elections (Gitelman and Goldstein 2001).

In 1996 a new phenomenon appeared on the Israeli political scene, the (successful) ethnic "Russian" party. The first such party that succeeded in entering the Knesset was Yisrael Baaliya, headed by Nathan (Anatoli) Sharansky, a well-known civil-rights and Zionist activist in the USSR. In the 1996 elections that party received over 40 percent of the immigrant vote, which gained it seven parliamentary seats. In 1999 Yisrael Baaliya was joined by a competitor, Yisrael Beitenu, placed to the right of it on the political–ideological scale. These two parties received over 50 percent of the immigrant vote between them, which translated to ten Knesset seats, six for Yisrael Baaliya and four for Yisrael Beitenu. Following the elections, two members of the Yisrael Baaliya Knesset faction with close affinity to Labor seceded from the party and formed their own faction, Democratic Choice (Gitelman and Goldstein 2001; Khanin 2000).

The success of political parties catering specifically to FSU immigrants is partially accounted for by the changes in the electoral system that took effect in 1996. The institution of direct popular election of the prime minister enabled voters, for the first time, to split their vote between the prime minister and the Knesset (see chap. 10, above). Still, the rapidity with which the FSU immigrants were able to organize themselves effectively in political parties is revealing, especially when compared to the length of time it took Mizrachim and citizen Palestinians to do the same. The first somewhat successful Mizrachi political party, Tami, appeared in 1981 and disappeared completely before the 1988 elections. Shas, the first long-lasting Mizrachi party, appeared only in 1984, over thirty years after the onset of massive Mizrachi immigration. Citizen Palestinians succeeded in running their first avowedly national political party, the Progressive List for Peace, also in 1984, thirty-five years after their incorporation in the state of Israel. These differences clearly relate to the changing character and declining role of the state in Israeli society, but also, importantly, to the favorable way in which FSU immigrants are viewed by the veteran Ashkenazi elite.

In 1999, in both the Knesset and the prime ministerial races, the "Russian" vote was motivated by a combination of concerns that were quite similar to those that motivated veteran Israelis. The issues uppermost in the minds of immigrant voters were job creation (25 percent), military security (23 percent), and the changing role of religion in public life (20 percent). The first two of these concerns were shared by the general electorate (Arian and Shamir 2001b). Only the saliency of the state–religion issue was peculiar to the immigrants, for reasons that have been clarified above. Improving the immigrant-absorption process was the most important issue for only 6 percent of the immigrants (Gitelman and Goldstein 2001: 217).

Challenges to the incorporation regime

The integration of the FSU immigrants into the society is still very much an ongoing process, if for no other reason than because their immigration continues, at the rate of several tens of thousands a year. It is difficult to predict, therefore, whether Israel's Russian-speaking population will crystallize into a distinct ethnic group, or will disperse and join existing groups along the axes of class, ethnicity, gender, religiosity, and ideology. However, a few preliminary observations can already be made about the effects this immigration has had, and is likely to have, on Israel's incorporation regime and on the status of its competing citizenship discourses.

The most visible effect of the immigration in this regard has been the further problematization of Israel's self-definition as a Jewish state. (As we relate below, this problematization is reinforced by the Ethiopian immigration and by the presence of large numbers of overseas workers.) As Lustick has shown, the fastest-growing religious community in Israel is the Christian, despite the low birth rate and high emigration rate that characterize Israel's Christian Arab population (Lustick 1999: 428–9).

Given the high rate of non-Jews among the FSU immigrants (25 percent), and considering that many of these non-Jews have Jewish family members in Israel, so that the problems of the non-Jewish immigrants impact on many more than one quarter of the immigrant families (Khanin forthcoming), it might come as a surprise that Jewishness is a very significant component of the immigrants' identity. In a survey conducted in May 1999 by Sabina Lisiza and Yochanan Peres, 47 percent of the FSU immigrants identified themselves as "Russian," while 45 percent defined themselves as Jews, and only 8 percent as Israelis. By comparison, among veteran Israelis 61 percent of Ashkenazim and 45 percent of Mizrachim identified themselves as Israelis, 24 percent and 43 percent, respectively, identified themselves as Jews, and 23 percent and 11 percent, respectively, identified themselves in terms of their inter-Jewish ethnic background. When asked to identify themselves by two cultural markers, 57 percent of the FSU immigrants chose a combination of Russian and Jewish. Twenty-two percent chose a combination of Russian and Israeli, corresponding, roughly, to the share of non-Jews according to *halacha* among the immigrants. Length of stay in Israel tended to increase the immigrants' identification as Jews, at the expense of the Russian component of their identity, with only a slight increase in their self-identification as Israelis (Lisiza and Peres 2000; cf. Leshem 1994: 40; al-Haj and Leshem 2000: 29–30).

These puzzling data become clearer when a closer look is taken at the meaning that the immigrants assign to their Jewish identity. Much more than among veteran Israelis, FSU immigrants do not conceive of their ethno-national Jewish identity in religious terms. In 1993 64 percent of the immigrants who were Jewish according to *halacha* defined themselves as secular, compared to 21 percent among the Jewish population of Israel as a whole. This self-definition was borne out when break respondents were asked about their observance of specific religious commandments (Leshem 1994: 42–3; cf. al-Haj and Leshem 2000: 41–2). In the Gitelman–Goldstein survey of 1999, "over two-thirds described themselves as either not religious (52 percent) or atheists (17 percent). This is consistent with earlier surveys that show the proportion of those believing in God ranging from one in five to one in three, though only a small minority of these people practice any form of religion" (Gitelman and Goldstein 2001: 210).

This secular ethno-national identity shapes the immigrants' attitudes towards the two citizenship discourses that currently contend for hegemony in Israeli society, the liberal and the ethno-national. The immigrants hold strongly liberal positions on the issue of relations between state and religion, with 78 percent (in 1993) of all respondents, and 67 percent of those who are Jewish according to *halacha*, supporting the demand to reduce or abolish religious legislation by the state. Significantly, opposition to religious legislation increases with length of stay in Israel, as, presumably, the actual consequences of this legislation become clearer to the immigrants. Thus, almost 100 percent of the immigrants surveyed by Leshem in 1993 supported the institution of civil marriage and divorce in Israel (Leshem 1994: 44–9; cf. Gitelman 1995: 27–37; al-Haj and Leshem 2000: 44–7).

In the other key issue-area in contention between the liberal and the ethno-national discourses, the peace process, the FSU immigrants tend to hold strongly ethno-nationalist positions. In the Gitelman–Goldstein survey in 1999, in which keeping all of the OT under Israeli control was not even presented as an option, only small minorities were willing to give up all (3 percent) or part (16 percent) of the territories for peace, while 60 percent were willing to give up only a small part (Gitelman and Goldstein 2001: 211). These findings are consistent with the findings of many other surveys taken on this issue, with the strongly nationalist tenor of the Russian press in Israel and with the political activities of many immigrant organizations, including both "Russian" political parties, against the peace process (Ben-Simon 1999; Khanin forthcoming; *Yediot Achronot*, April 14, 2000; al-Haj and Leshem 2000: 58).

Several reasons can account for the FSU immigrants' "hawkish" positions on the Arab–Israeli conflict: Soviet political culture, in which territorial acquisition and the establishment of spheres of influence were considered essential for national security; inadequate knowledge of the history of the conflict; and immigrants' natural inclination to identify with the more nationalist elements of their new society in order to gain acceptance in it. It is important to note, as well, that the FSU immigrants do not hold liberal positions on any other questions, except for state–religion relations and the economy (al-Haj and Leshem 2000: 66–8).

The separate political organization of a large cross-section of the immigrants is based, in part, on separatist cultural tendencies. Russian speakers have already established an impressive array of cultural institutions, ranging from a prolific press to a network of high-quality schools. In a survey conducted by Majid al-Haj and Elazar Leshem in 1999, 80 percent of the respondents indicated that the continued existence of these institutions was very important to them. Almost 90 percent assigned very high value to the preservation of Russian culture among their children (al-Haj and Leshem 2000: 35). The Russian-language press, especially the most widely circulated *Vesti*, holds a particularly important position, and is read regularly by 60 percent of the immigrants, even after they learn Hebrew. The FSU immigrants also maintain close ties to their countries of origin through cable and satellite television (regularly viewed by 77 percent of the immigrants) and through extensive mutual visits of both ordinary tourists and cultural figures. This cultural activity is motivated not only by the difficulties experienced by the immigrants in integrating into the society and by their need for a congenial cultural context, but also by the conviction of most FSU immigrants that European, and especially Russian, culture is vastly superior to Israeli culture. The achievements of many immigrants and immigrant institutions in fields such as music, theater, science, and athletics give additional credence to this conviction (Zilberg and Leshem 1996; Nudelman 1997: 32; Kimmerling 1998: 283–91; al-Haj and Leshem 2000: 19–23).

If this communal cohesion, which is greatly enhanced by the existence of immigrant political parties, is maintained over time, it may sooner or later lead to a demand for formal recognition by the state. The demand for recognizing Russian as a third official language, alongside Hebrew and Arabic, has already been voiced (Zilberg and Leshem 1999: 27). Such a development would add weight to a cluster of political demands and evolving social institutions that are leading towards the emergence of the multicultural discourse of citizenship as a serious claimant of attention in Israeli political culture. We will discuss the potential development of multiculturalism in Israel in the conclusion.

Ethiopian immigrants

We expected Jerusalem. All Gold. No Tel Aviv, no Haifa, no Sefad. All Jews. To live with Jews in Jerusalem. Also, without work. There are orange trees and, without working, you go and pick and eat. Life like, I don't know, the Garden of Eden. We came with that thought. And where is the reality? (An Ethiopian immigrant in 1993 (cited in Reiff 1997: 134))

Demographically, the immigrants from Ethiopia who arrived in the 1980s and 1990s present a mirror image of the immigrants from the FSU: in 1997 they numbered only 65,000, out of whom 16,000 were Israel-born; they are a very young community, with 50 percent aged eighteen or under;

their birth rate, thirty per thousand, is 50 percent higher than the average Israeli rate; and they brought with them practically no human capital with any relevance to the Israeli economy. In 1997 over 50 percent of Ethiopian families in Israel had no breadwinner, and only among men aged twenty-five to forty-five were employment rates comparable to those of the general population. As a result, in July 1997 their average family income was higher by only NIS 700 than the minimum wage of NIS 2,097 per month. In 1996, out of every fifteen children born in Israel with the HI virus, fourteen were Ethiopian (Kaplan and Salamon 1998; Kimmerling 1998: 291–306; *Haaretz*, December 30, 1998).

Ethiopian Jews were known in Ethiopia as *falasha* – landless – and constituted a low-status minority group of artisans. Their religious practices diverged from those of the surrounding Christian population and were reminiscent of pre-*halachic* Jewish practices. It is important to note, however, that Orthodox Christianity in Ethiopia had, or claims to have had, Jewish roots, and that many of its religious practices resemble Jewish practices. Intermarriage, conversions, and shared rituals and texts were common among the various religious communities in Ethiopia, so that the *falasha*, or Beta Israel as they prefer to be called, constituted one group among several on a continuum between Orthodox Christianity and pre-*halachic* Judaism (Pankhurst 1997: 14; Kimmerling 1998: 294–7).

Contact between Beta Israel and modern Jewry was established only in 1904, and from then they began to adopt some practices of rabbinic Judaism and abandon some Ethiopian Christian practices. In the mid-1970s the Israeli chief rabbinate recognized the Beta Israel community (although not each individual member) as Jewish, opening the way for their recognition by the government as Jews for the purpose of the Law of Return. Famines and wars that were rampant in Ethiopia in the 1980s caused many Ethiopians, including Ethiopian Jews, to seek refuge in Sudan, where they lived in miserable conditions in refugee camps and city slums. This tragedy greatly reinforced the pressures exerted on the Israeli government to arrange for the immigration of Ethiopian Jews to Israel. These pressures were exerted by American Jewish organizations seeking a display of Jewish–Black solidarity, and by religious Zionist groups in Israel, seeking to augment the Jewish population of Israel and, especially, of the OT. As a result, between 1980 and 1992 45,000 Ethiopian Jews were brought to Israel, about half of them in two airlifts, from Sudan in 1984–5 and from Addis Ababa in 1990 (Kimmerling 1998: 293–9; Kaplan and Salamon 1998: 5–6, 23).

As Kimmerling has noted, the incorporation of Ethiopian Jews in Israeli society has been affected by three features, each one of which would have been sufficient by itself to exclude them from the center of society: their dark skin color, their doubtful Jewishness, and their poor human capital (Kimmerling 1998: 299). Because of these multiple handicaps, "direct absorption," the mechanism through which FSU immigrants were incorporated in the society, was clearly irrelevant in the case of the Ethiopian immigrants. Rather, their "absorption" was effected by the same institutional methods utilized to incorporate the Mizrachi immigrants in the 1950s.

Because of this similarity, it is tempting to explain the incorporation patterns of Ethiopian immigrants as stemming from the same causes that shaped the incorporation of Mizrachi immigrants in the 1950s (see Reiff 1997: 103–7). There are vast differences between these two groups, however. The Mizrachim arrived in very large numbers – 331,000 between 1948 and 1951 alone, and 751,000 between 1948 and 1975 – and came to constitute a majority among Jews in Israel (Smooha 1978: 281). The Ethiopians arrived in very small numbers, and constitute only 1.1 percent of the current population of Israel. Both the demographic presence of the Mizrachim, as Jews, and their labor power could be utilized on a massive scale for the fulfillment of various state ends (see chap. 3, above). The Ethiopians are too few in number, and too poorly endowed with relevant skills, to be exploited in the same manner. Thus, "when closures of the occupied territories have created labor shortages, the authorities have responded not by hiring replacements from the large numbers of unemployed Ethiopians but by allowing the entry of labor migrants" (Kaplan and Salamon 1998: 22; see below).

Another difference between the Mizrachi and Ethiopian immigrants is that the former were always unquestionably Jewish in the eyes of the rabbinic authorities, while the latter were not. Since Ethiopian Judaism was based on the Torah (first five books of the Old Testament) alone, while all other religious Jews live by the *halacha* – a body of law produced by about two thousand years of textual interpretation of the Torah – the rabbinic authorities suspected that improper procedures of conversion and divorce may have produced illegitimate Jews and illegitimate children (*mamzerim*) among the Ethiopians. They therefore demanded that all Ethiopian immigrants undergo symbolic conversion to Judaism, a demand later limited only to those wishing to be married in rabbinic courts. Similarly, the Rabbinate did not recognize the Ethiopian religious leaders – *kessotch* – as rabbis, so they were forbidden to perform religious functions such as marriage, divorce, funerals, and, of course, conversions. Since, initially at least, all Ethiopian immigrants were observant Jews in their own eyes, their treatment as doubtfully Jewish added insult to injury in the already difficult process of their incorporation in the society (Reiff 1997: 139–42).

Where the interplay between an ethno-nationalist discourse of membership, a Eurocentric conception of religious boundaries, and the realities of Ethiopian society produced particularly tragic results is in the matter of the non-Jewish descendants of Ethiopian Jews, known as *feres-mura*. The basic social unit in Ethiopia is the extended, rather than the nuclear family. Because the boundaries between the various Ethiopian religious communities are so porous, and because of the great social dislocation that occurred before and during immigration, it could and did happen that members of the same extended family were classified by Israeli officials as belonging to two religious categories, Jews and *feres-mura*. Determining who of the *feres-mura* is entitled to the privileges of the Law of Return by virtue of having Jewish family members is a near-impossible task, for several reasons. Birth registration and naming practices are different in Ethiopia and Israel, while marriage practices include polygamy and child marriage, which are not recognized by Israeli law. Moreover, bureaucratic documentation of all of these practices is sketchy at best, particularly in view of the long period of upheaval experienced by Ethiopian society. Thus in many cases close relatives, even spouses or parents and children, have been assigned different statuses of eligibility for immigration. Not infrequently this happened after they had already left their villages and spent several years in Addis Ababa waiting to go to Israel (Reiff 1997: 114–33; Dayan 2000b).

In 1998 the Israeli government decided, as a one-time gesture, to allow 4000 *feres-mura* who had been living in a compound near the Israeli embassy in Addis Ababa to come to Israel. However, those who had married non-Jews during their years of waiting in the compound were required to divorce their non-Jewish spouses as a condition of gaining an entry visa. This blatantly illegal requirement was motivated by the fear of Israeli officials that strict adherence to the letter of the Law of Return would result in a deluge of Ethiopians flooding the country (Dayan 2000b). Thus, the demand of Ethiopian Jews that the rights granted by the Law of Return be respected in their case as they are in the case of the FSU immigrants is probably the most painful manifestation of the Ethiopians' problematic location in the Israeli incorporation regime.

Labor migrants

The problem of overseas labor migrants would not have existed in contemporary Israel but for the opening of the borders to 120,000 workers from the administered [i.e. occupied] territories since the Six Day War. (Kondor 1997: 45)

Palestinian and overseas labor migrants

In 1988 legally employed overseas, that is non-Palestinian, non-Israeli workers made up less than one half of one percent of the Israeli labor force (Bartram 1998: 309). In August 2000 the daily *Yediot Achronot* concluded that "relative to the population, the number of labor migrants [in Israel] is the highest in the western world" (*Yediot Achronot*, August 24, 2000). The Ministry of Labor and Welfare estimated the number of documented labor migrants in the last quarter of 1999 at 67,000, and the undocumented ones at 80,000 (Manpower Planning Authority 2000: 5). The state comptroller, however, based on a report of the Interior Ministry, put the number at 100,000 undocumented workers five years prior to that (State Comptroller 1995: 490). Unofficial estimates almost double the number of workers without permits, putting it at 141,000 in 2000. In addition, 40,000 documented and about 80,000 undocumented Palestinians were employed in Israel prior to the outbreak of the al-Aksa intifada in October 2000 (Kav Laoved, *Information Sheet*, May 2000). Finally, the daily *Haaretz* reported in March 2001 that as many as 200,000 documented and undocumented non-Jewish overseas migrant workers live and work in Israel (*Haaretz*, March 14, 2001), while a study by the National Insurance Institute put the number of undocumented workers at 320,000 by 1996 (Kondor 1997: 68). By these greatly varying estimates, in 1999 overseas workers, both documented and undocumented, comprised anywhere between 7 percent and 14 percent of the Israeli labor force of 2,344,000 (Bank Hapoalim 2000).

Labor migrants inhabit recognizable neighborhoods of Tel Aviv and other cities and have come to constitute a distinct segment of the society (Schnell forthcoming). Their presence means that a new category of foreign residents, attractive for employers because of their low wages and limited ability to defend themselves due to lack of citizenship, has been incorporated into Israeli society.

The key to understanding the rapid expansion of the overseas labor force, as well as the way it has been incorporated into the society, is the realization that it was meant to replace the commuter Palestinian workers from the OT. The reasons for the exclusion of the Palestinian workers were numerous, as we shall see. But once this exclusion had been effected, the urgency of replacing them stemmed from the pressure to supply the FSU immigrants with housing (Borukhov 1998). In order to construct this housing, Israeli leaders put aside their concerns about the introduction of a large non-Jewish population of migrant workers into a society typified by exclusivist ethno-national legal boundaries, and ignored the warning that, like in Western Europe, these "guest workers" were there to stay.

The most common explanations for the need to replace Palestinian workers with overseas ones were that (1) with the outbreak of the first intifada, in 1987, Palestinian workers ceased coming to their places of employment in a regular and reliable fashion; and (2) Palestinian workers posed a security risk. Indeed, the security argument carried a lot of weight in this case, as it always does in Israel, but excessive reliance on it raises many puzzles and it can, ultimately, provide only a partial explanation. The size of the Palestinian labor force employed in Israel remained about 100,000 for the first three years of the first intifada (Kondor 1997: 47, table 1; Bartram 1998: 307, table 1). As late as 1990 Israel employed 107,700 documented Palestinian workers from the OT in the lower, un-skilled segment of the labor market, mostly in construction, agriculture, and services (Bartram 1998: 307, table 1). In the same year only 4,200 permits were issued for overseas workers (Bartram 1998: 313, table 3).

Even the near-total closure imposed by the Israeli government on the OT during the Gulf war in 1991 did not result in a massive replacement of Palestinian workers. When the war ended Palestinian workers returned, although border controls were tightened and the share of undocumented workers among them fell. In Bartram's summary: "until this point, access to Palestinian labor was hindered but not severely disrupted" (Bartram 1998: 312).

With the start of the massive wave of Jewish immigration from the FSU, the government wished to find employment rapidly for the new arrivals. It encouraged Israeli employers, in the time-honored fashion of direct subsidies, to hire immigrants instead of Palestinians, many of whom were veteran employees. The Farmers' Association's citrus forum indeed pledged to do so, and similar efforts were undertaken in the con-struction industry. "Replacing Palestinians with Russian Jews," Bartram concluded, "became something of a national mission" (Bartram 1998: 310). But only a few thousand immigrants began working in construction, and even they did so on a temporary basis, until they could find work that matched their professional skills. The FSU immigrants were, after all, Jews, and "had no more reason than other Jews to want 'Arab jobs'" (Bartram 1998: 310). Thus, in spite of the arrival of over 350,000 Jewish immigrants in 1990–1, by 1992 the number of documented Palestinian workers in Israel reached its all-time high of 115,600 (Bartram 1998: 307, table 1).

Not surprisingly, the first round of replacement efforts ended in failure. As Piore (1979) and other theorists of the dual labor market demon-strated, potential workers who are citizens prefer to stay unemployed rather than take on employment in the lower tier of the market, where work is low paid, unstable, and sometimes dangerous and dirty. Where ethnic divisions correspond to labor-market segments, such employment is further construed as degrading. Citizens have an alternative: they possess social rights which ensure them social protection even under conditions of unemployment. By the same token, the same ethnic division that leads employers to seek out vulnerable non-citizen workers in the first place predisposes them to look for replacement workers of the same kind.

The turning point came in 1993. In response to a series of murders committed by Palestinians within Israel, the Israeli government imposed a general closure on the OT. However, the replacement of Palestinian labor migrants with overseas labor migrants was still not a foregone conclusion. Eleven percent of Israel's labor force, and an even higher percentage of the immigrants from the FSU (not to mention those from Ethiopia), were unemployed. Given such high rates of unemployment, it was proposed that the unemployed be directed to the construction industry, and those refusing their assignment would lose their unemployment benefits. The labor minister was opposed to granting any permits for the importation of foreign labor. But in April 1993 the Rabin government began issuing an ever-growing number of such permits, first for construction workers and later on for other, mostly agricultural, workers as well. But the real opening of the sluice gate to overseas workers was a result of the Oslo DOP, signed later that year, and of Israel's interpretation of the meaning of Israeli–Palestinian peace.

The DOP confirmed the abandonment of both the Greater Israel project of territorial expansion into the OT and the idea that their population be integrated into Israel by making it dependent on Israeli employment. This involved a return not only to territorial partition but, concomitantly, also to the LSM's traditional approach of "separatism" (Bartram 1998: 314). Breaking the twenty-five-year-long Israeli dependence on Palestinian workers now led to massive unemployment in Gaza and the West Bank and to an equally massive importation of overseas labor migrants to Israel (Kondor 1997: 48).

In the three years following the signing of the DOP about 30,000 permits per annum were issued for overseas workers, bringing their number from 9,600 in 1993 to 103,000 in 1996 (Bartram 1998: 313, table 3). From the viewpoint of the Israeli institutions that enforce the relevant aspect of the incorporation regime, the new overseas workers were a direct substitution for Palestinians from the OT. The Rabin government basically "accepted employers' arguments that it was responsible for finding a substitute workforce for the Palestinians." Thus, after it initially issued permits to construction workers only, the government found it easy to back down when the farmers' organization sued it in the High Court of Justice in 1993. The farmers argued that "the government had a responsibility to ensure a labor supply after interrupting access to their traditional labor supply by closing the borders," so the government issued similar permits to agricultural workers as well. In fact, the permits issued to employers for overseas workers were allocated in direct ratio to "to previous legal employment of Palestinians" (Bartram 1998: 321, 313–14, 317).

Once the domestic labor market had become segmented between citizen and non-citizen labor forces, the replacement of the latter with the former became economically too costly for employers. Citizens did not want to perform the menial jobs that came to be associated with Palestinian labor, and paying citizens "Israeli" wages would have raised their cost substantially. Replacing cheap unskilled Palestinian labor migrants with overseas foreigners left the status quo intact.

A comparison of the wages paid in industry and construction before and after the 1967 war amply illustrates this point. In 1964–7 the average wage paid in construction was 4–6 percent higher than in industry. Between 1967 and 1991 the share of Palestinian workers from the OT in construction rose to 46 percent, while the average wage fell from 104 percent to 77 percent of the industrial wage. In agriculture it fell from 62 percent to 50 percent (Kondor 1997: 51). Since the construction industry in Israel is closely tied to the immigration rate it is highly cyclical and contractors prefer to pay low wages rather than modernize the industry and tie up their capital. Not surprisingly, overall productivity in the construction industry fell by one quarter in the six years from 1994, and capital and other inputs per worker are among the lowest in the industrial countries (Ben-David and Ben-Shachar 2000).

To prevent "unfair competition" between Israeli and Palestinian workers, employers were required to pay workers from the OT the minimum wage of the (Israeli) collective wage agreement reached in their respective industries. Even so, the official gross average pay to Palestinians from the OT at the beginning of the 1990s stood at two-fifths of the average Israeli salary. The majority of the wage differential was explained with reference to the concentration of the Palestinians in low-paying industries, notwithstanding the circular nature of the argument – namely, the direct relation between the rising percentage of Palestinians in an industry and its falling wages. The difference in disposable income between Israeli and Palestinian workers was even higher, due to discriminatory taxation. Like Israeli workers, the latter were required to pay social security taxes, although, in contrast to Israelis, who enjoyed the social services they were entitled to as citizens, payments by Palestinians were kept by the Finance Ministry (Kondor 1997: 49). Furthermore, it would be consistent with the general picture to assume that Israeli citizens rose within construction and agriculture to higher positions even as the average wages in those industries fell (Kondor 1997: 41). In short, everyone but unskilled Israeli workers seem to have benefited at the expense of the Palestinian workers: employers, the state, and most Israeli workers.

Similarly, as two respected economists, Ben-David and Ben-Shachar, report, "since the labor laws applied to Israelis are not exercised in regard to foreigners [i.e. labor migrants], the costs of their employment are much lower than the minimum wage" (Ben-David and Ben-Shachar 2000). A 1995 estimate, which adds unreported living expenses paid by employers to workers' wages, still puts the wages of overseas workers at just above half of the average Israeli wage. Though this seems to be higher than wages paid to the Palestinian workers, in Kondor's estimation overseas laborers work more hours than did Palestinian workers and, consequently, their effective wages are actually lower (Kondor 1997: 59).

Ben-David and Ben-Shachar also concluded that overseas workers displaced not only Palestinian but also unskilled or low-skilled Israeli citizens, thus increasing the rate of unemployment and reducing wages at the lower end of the pay scale. Consequently, gross income distribution grew more unequal and led to increased unemployment benefits and income supplements to those below the poverty line. The employment of labor migrants means, therefore, that "the government, in fact, subsidizes [their] employers and is also forced to carry the burden of transfer payments to the social strata harmed by their presence" (Ben-David and Ben-Shachar 2000).

Conditions of employment

Labor migrants in Israel are drawn from many sources and are concentrated in three main industries. Workers from Romania are employed primarily in construction; from Thailand in agriculture; and from the Philippines in nursing and domestic services. But there are others, from Latin America, sub-Saharan Africa, Eastern Europe and the FSU, as well as from Jordan, Egypt, and Morocco. The documented workers are brought through "manpower companies" (many of which branched out of travel agencies) which are expected to carry out the same role vis-à-vis overseas workers that the Ministry of Labor's Labor Bureau does for Israeli citizens and Palestinians from the OT. In fact, many of the manpower companies act not only as go-betweens but frequently also double as employers. Since the labor permits are issued to the employer and not to the employee, these bodies have tremendous leverage over their "employees." In numerous cases such companies were reported to have taken possession of their workers' passports. Most of the undocumented workers arrive as tourists and overstay their three-month visas. Documented workers receive a ten-month permit, with an option of renewal for another ten months, but many of these also stay longer.

Israel is a signatory to the ILO's international treaties on social security which require it to ensure the non-discriminatory employment of labor migrants. The Employment Service requires that employers of documented labor migrants provide them with adequate housing and private health insurance equal to the basic basket of the national health insurance enjoyed by Israeli citizens (Peleg 1999: 5, 30). There is, however, only scant inspection of the implementation of these provisions and almost no enforcement or punishment of its violators. The state comptroller reported that in 1995 the accommodations of fewer than 2,000 workers were inspected by the Ministry of Labor and Welfare. Although 75 percent of these accommodations were found to be deficient, no employer's right to hire labor migrants was revoked (State Comptroller 1995: 494). The quality of overseas workers' health insurance is also low. Employers, finally, are required to pay the National Insurance Institute to insure labor migrants against work injuries and to cover maternity costs (Peleg 1999: 5). Since work permits are given only to individuals, the need for the latter is scant, however. The most important social citizenship rights that are based on contributory programs – child allowances, old age and survivor pensions, and unemployment benefits – are not extended to labor migrants as they were also not available for Palestinian workers.

Among undocumented workers there are families with children, and these children are officially covered by the Mandatory Education Law and, since February 2001, are entitled to free medical care as well. The state is reluctant, however, to provide adult workers with social services, for fear that they might *de facto* legalize their presence and contribute to their desire to settle in the country. The implementation of the social rights enjoyed by labor migrants' children is also uneven and varies from one locality to the next. The city of Tel Aviv, with the highest concentration of labor migrants, has been relatively diligent in providing the services required by law. However, such policies, like the occasional calls for the legalization of undocumented overseas workers' communities, for example by the mayor of Tel Aviv, are not justified in terms of citizenship rights based on personhood, but rather on the potential adverse effects their neglect might have on the citizen residents of Tel Aviv (Rosenhek 2000).

Universal personhood rights

So far we have emphasized the similarities between the modes of incorporation of Palestinian and overseas labor migrants in the Israeli economy.

The major difference between the two groups, however, is that Palestinian workers were commuters who were required to return home every night. Overseas workers are foreign residents, and this means, according to Kemp et al. (2000), that "the host society [does] not just benefit from their participation in the production process; it must also take responsibility for their reproduction cost." Israelis and overseas workers meet not only in the labor market but also in other institutional settings. This more permanent association created "a new category of foreign residents with all its implications" (Kemp et al. 2000). Although migrant workers are not considered prospective citizens, they are expected to be protected by international legal and labor agreements to which Israel is a signatory. In Western Europe labor migrants are not considered simply "aliens" any more, but are sometimes called "denizens," implying a certain level of more permanent bond; in Israel they still occupy an uncertain and undetermined institutional domain (Hammar 1990).

The parameters of this domain will be defined by two factors. On the one hand, by the depth of the overseas workers' desire to make their new home in Israel, and on the other, by the spread of the new citizenship discourse of "universal personhood" and by the overseas workers' ability and willingness to use it effectively. Being undocumented makes overseas workers "invisible" in the eyes of state apparatuses in regard to social, political, and civil rights (Kemp et al. 2000). Only the recognition of their rights of "universal personhood" can make them visible again. Right now it is far from clear how strong their desire to stay in Israel is, nor is it obvious whether the liberalization process that is redefining the Israeli legal system, which so far has had only marginal effects on Palestinian rights, will be extended to non-Palestinian workers (Rosenhek 2000).

Still, there are some early indications of institutional developments that are already taking place in these areas, which impact on the overseas workers' citizenship rights and on the Israeli incorporation regime. These developments have taken place in direct response to the Israeli discourse on the place of labor migrants and to occasional drives to reduce their numbers by expelling undocumented ones. The public discourse in Israel is polarized between employers, who seek to maintain access to a steady supply of overseas workers, and their opponents, who warn of the consequences associated with the permanent settlement of these workers. Thus employers' organizations engaged in a public pressure campaign on Prime Minister Netanyahu and his minister of labor and social welfare, through newspaper ads, accusing them of bringing construction to a halt and, even more dramatically, of liquidating agriculture altogether (*Maariv*, December 12, 30, and 31, 1996). Contractors went as far as threatening not to submit bids to government tenders in general, and to security-related tenders in particular, unless they were allowed to import additional workers (*Yediot Achronot*, August 27, September 2, 1997). A government appointed interministerial committee proposed at the end of 1996 that a special tax be imposed on employers of overseas workers and on the workers themselves. This proposal led nowhere, in consequence of the employer associations' vigorous, not to say hysterical, ad campaign. The demand for a special overseas workers' tax on employers was repeated recently by economists such as Ben-David and Ben-Shachar, arguing that this tax was needed "as a compensation . . . for the social burden that results from the employment of labor migrants," and as an incentive for employers to replace these workers with Israeli citizens (Ben-David and Ben-Shachar 2000).

In 1996 the interministerial committee recommended the arrest and expulsion of between 500 and 2,000 overseas workers per month. Concern over adverse foreign responses reduced the target numbers, but in 1997 about fifteen undocumented workers began to be expelled daily (Kondor 1997: 56). Around the same time, a few hundred undocumented workers were arrested in the Tel Aviv neighborhoods where they resided and were subsequently expelled, but this drive was brought to a halt after a few days as a result of public demonstrations and the opposition of some liberal Knesset members (*Yediot Achronot*, March 26, April 4, and July 7, 1997).

In reaction to the adoption of the deportation policy, African workers in Israel launched an organizing drive and, with the help of a sympathetic Israeli journalist, began articulating demands on behalf of their members. As the Kemp study demonstrates, African migrant workers had already created an organizational network that consisted of national and regional associations, churches, sports and music clubs, and mutual-aid societies. These were able to serve as institutional bases for political mobilization and the formation of the African Workers' Union (AWU) in September 1997. The new body emerged out of meetings with Israeli human rights activists, NGOs, and official representatives, which led to a meeting with Knesset members from a number of political parties. The AWU demanded what amounted to an official policy of institutional incorporation, namely, legitimization of the presence of the undocumented workers and expanded rights for the documented ones. The AWU envisioned a policy which would give three- to five-year work permits, and provide access to the social services of the National Insurance Institution, including national health insurance. In addition, they asked for freedom of exit and entry and the protection of police and other institutions (Kemp et al. 2000). Subsequently, Latin American and other workers formed their own supranational organization, many of them church based and concerned with providing after-school education to their children. At a joint meeting of Latin American and African workers' representatives with the Knesset Committee on Migrant Workers in May 1998, the workers' representatives proposed that undocumented workers be legalized by granting them one-year permits in return for a deposit of $5,000 to be refunded when the permit expired and the worker left the country. The government did not accept this proposal (Kemp et al. 2000).

The citizenship discourse invoked by leaders of the AWU and by community members writing in *Hair*, a local Tel Aviv weekly, incorporated various versions of the universal human rights theme. Rights derived not only from membership in a national community, they pointed out, but also from the law of nature, or "legal citizenship on Mother Earth." In addition, they sought to compel the state of Israel to recognize the status of refugee by raising claims for asylum from political persecution and hunger. These were particularly poignant issues at the time of the civil wars in Nigeria and Sierra Leone. Finally, parallels were drawn between slavery and the slave trade, on the one hand, and the Jewish Holocaust on the other (Kemp et al. 2000).

In general, labor migrants in Israel have not created ethnic or national communities but preferred to seek rights on the basis of their "universal personhood." So far, there are no real indications that such demands have been successful: the Israeli government still does not admit documented labor migrants into membership in the National Insurance Institute and their social citizenship rights remain minimal and are frequently ignored and not enforced. There are clear risks associated with the organization of undocumented workers and limits to its possible reach. The leaders of both African and Latin American workers expressed concern that speaking on behalf of a "generalized category of migrant workers" might be counterproductive and see greater benefit to speaking for workers from their respective continents (Kemp et al. 2000). Finally, as we have seen, those institutions willing to extend health care and education to undocumented workers do not share in the discourse of universal human rights, but are motivated by an instrumental institutional logic. Overseas labor migrants, like the Palestinian before them, are *in* Israel but, in spite of their residence, not *of* it. The process of economic liberalization and globalization that brought them to Israel, and which they invoke in their claim for social citizenship rights and universal personhood, have not transformed the legal system under which they are incorporated into Israel. The undocumented among them are still "invisible" as far as any of the citizenship discourses are concerned.

Conclusion

The ambivalent and contradictory locations accorded the three groups discussed in this chapter in the Israeli incorporation regime highlight the problematic nature of that regime and point to the possibility of its transformation. The ways the three groups are being treated by the key defining document of the incorporation regime – the Law of Return – illustrate this point.

The Law of Return was amended in 1970 specifically in order to facilitate the immigration to Israel of non-Jews from the USSR, who, it was assumed, would become politically and ethnically Jewish upon their arrival. Thus a potential rift was created between the religious and the national concepts of "Jewish" by means of the very law that had been designed to cement the identity between them. The provisions granting the children and grandchildren of Jews the right of "return" were formulated with a typical European, urban, secular family in mind. When these rights are demanded by Ethiopian immigrants, whose families are neither European, nor urban, nor secular, this demand conjures up the specter of a black deluge flooding the country, and is largely ignored. Thus, Ethiopian Jews, who are collectively, though not necessarily individually, recognized as Jewish, are being openly told that their non-European origin makes their citizenship inferior to that of European Jews. Finally, the Law of Return does not relate at all to non-Jewish migrants. Therefore, the establishment of a sizable community of such migrants attests to the declining significance of that law in defining Israel's migration regime.

The growing irrelevance of the Law of Return to actual migratory flows, coupled with the Palestinian demand for recognizing the right of the 1948 Palestinian refugees to return to Israel, point to the need to replace this ethno-nationalist law with a legal instrument that could accommodate present social, political, and ecological realities. All three groups discussed in this chapter would like to see a more liberal immigration law replacing, or at least supplementing, the Law of Return, while Israeli ethno-nationalists would like to see its scope limited by enhancing its ethno-nationalist character. However, because the Law of Return symbolizes Israel's self-definition as a Jewish state, any tampering with it would be interpreted as challenging this self-definition and would therefore be fiercely opposed by many Israelis.

In actual fact, however, Israel's character as a Jewish state is being challenged already by the very presence of these three groups, regardless of the changes that will or will not be made in the Law of Return. Recently, non-Jewish recruits to the IDF, who are immigrants from the FSU, caused a furor when they asked to be given the New Testament, rather than the Old, in their swearing-in ceremony. It should be noted that these non-Jewish youngsters did not object to being drafted to the military force of the Jewish state; they only wanted to be given a book that was religiously meaningful to them. This symbolizes the distance that is being opened now between the religious and the national (or civil) definitions of "Jewish." This distance is bound to grow as more and more non-Jews arrive from the FSU, as the labor migrant population continues to grow, and as more and more non-Jewish relatives of Ethiopian immigrants are allowed in the country.

Paradoxically, it is the tenacity with which Israel still clings to vestiges of its occupation of the OT that undermines its character as a Jewish state. If Israel were to be more generous in its negotiations with the Palestinians, enabling the peace process to be successfully concluded, Palestinians could resume their employment in Israel, and the need for overseas workers would decline. By the same token, peace with the Palestinians may result, over time, in a relaxation of Israel's demographic concerns, and may allow it to replace the Law of Return with a more rational immigration law. It may also allow the incorporation regime to be restructured as a democratic, multicultural regime, a reconstruction the general contours of which will be presented in the conclusion.

13 Conclusion

Our purpose in this book was to offer a comprehensive long-term historical–sociological analysis of Israeli society that could explain its trajectory of development, from its origins in the Yishuv up to its currently ongoing liberalization and setting out on the way of peace-making with the Arabs. To achieve this goal we developed a conceptual framework that departed in several important respects from previous comprehensive studies of Israeli society. Following a critical evaluation of these studies, we rejected the functionalist mode of explanation; the view of Israeli society as exclusively Jewish; the view of the Arab–Israeli conflict as exogenous to the society; the view of the Labor Zionist elite as a "service elite" devoid of its own particular interests and unconcerned with the pursuit of power; and the conceptualization of Israeli political culture as comprised of only two ideological elements – Jewish nationalism and liberal democracy.

Our own theoretical framework has centered on the concepts of "citizenship discourse" and "incorporation regime." An incorporation regime, as defined by Yasemin Soysal, is a regime of social, political, economic, and cultural institutions that may stratify a society's putatively universalist citizenship by differentially dispensing rights, privileges, and obligations to distinct groups within it. This differential allocation is legitimated, we argued, through the use of particular ways of conceiving of the membership of individuals and groups in the society and the state. These conceptions of membership, which define the rights and duties each side has towards the other, we have termed "discourses of citizenship." Israeli political culture, we argued, is made up not of two but of three such discourses – Jewish ethno-nationalism, democratic liberalism, and a colonial version of civic republicanism. The latter discourse was, until recently, the dominant of the three, and the one that mediated between them and structured their particular modes of operation in Israeli society. Its practical manifestation was a colonial drive that characterized Zionist settlement from its outset and continues to operate even now, after a process of partial decolonization has been launched by the Oslo Accords of 1993. A clear indication that the colonial drive has not spent itself yet is the doubling of the Israeli settler population in the OT since 1993. This was one of the main reasons for the resumption, in September 2000, of the intifada that the Oslo Accords were meant to end.

T. H. Marshall's distinction between three generations of citizenship rights – civil, political, and social – allowed us to demonstrate which group receives what kinds of rights within the Israeli incorporation regime. With the aid of this theoretical framework we analyzed two distinct but inter-twined processes: the evolution of Israeli society as a colonial frontier society, and its gradual transformation, since 1967, towards a civil society in the liberal sense of the term.

As the nation-building elite of a colonial frontier society, the primary task facing the Labor Zionist movement (which we termed Labor Settlement Movement, or LSM), first in the Yishuv and later on in the state of Israel, was the mobilization of societal resources for the purpose of state building in the context of the Jewish–Palestinian (and later on Arab–Israeli) colonial conflict. The LSM elite felt particularly fit to lead this struggle, because their own co-operative "pioneering" settlement project seemed most effective in the gradual transfer of land and labor resources into the hands of the Jewish Yishuv. The "pioneering" method of realizing the commonly shared nationalist goal conferred on the LSM, by the mid-1930s, a hegemonic aura. However, the elitist cast of the LSM's approach, its dependence on the WZO for funds and its reliance on non-pioneering Jewish groups for human power prevented the assimilation of other groups into its institutions. Thus the LSM's Zionist revolution remained, in Gramsci's terms, a "passive revolution."

Rather than assimilating non-elite groups into its own institutions, the LSM sought to incorporate them into the society by utilizing their resources to the maximum extent possible and giving them in return the minimal rewards required to ensure their compliance. This was the logic behind the development of the main institutional characteristics of Israeli society: the non-separation of state and religion; the existence of a large public (Histadrut and state) economic sector; a welfare state of a particular, non-universal kind; a military system based on conscrip-tion and lifelong service in the reserves; the predominance of political parties in almost all areas of social life; and the imposition of martial law first on the citizen, then on the non-citizen, Palestinians. Culturally, this institutional complex was legitimated through a composite citizenship discourse, combining liberal, republican, and ethno-national elements.

This incorporation regime, which combined force, benefits, and an effective legitimational discourse, made it practically impossible for non-elite groups to challenge the hegemony of the LSM, and thus attained remarkable stability. Its great mobilizational capacity was demonstrated in 1948/9, when Israel was established through a violent conflagration, and again in 1967, when Israel's boundaries were extended and the territories of the ancient Jewish homeland were joined to the modern state of Israel. That, however, was the high point of the frontier-incorporation regime, and the beginning of its dissolution.

The results of the 1967 war challenged the Israeli incorporation regime in two novel ways:

(1) For the first time in its history, the Zionist leadership came to rule over a sizable group – the Palestinians residing in the OT – that it could not incorporate into the society. Incorporating over one million additional Palestinians into the society as citizens would have violated the most essential precept of the ethno-national discourse, namely, that Israel should be a Jewish state; incorporating them with no citizenship rights would have violated the most fundamental canon of liberalism. At the same time, successive colonial drives gave rise to Jewish territorial aspirations within the OT, and their Palestinian population was kept as almost completely rightless subjects of Israel's military regime. These non-citizen Palestinians were integrated, however, into the Israeli economy as workers, consumers, and tax payers. This meant that for the first time in the history of Zionist settlement in Palestine, a group with no stake in the system became part of Israeli society. Thus, a reinvigorated colonial dynamic introduced an inherent element of potential instability into the system, as was proven with the outbreak of the intifada in 1987 and again in 2000.

(2) The expansion of the domestic market that resulted from the integration of the OT into the Israeli economy, coupled with the accelerating process of economic globalization, began to turn the corporatist economic institutions of the frontier incorporation regime from a blessing to a burden for the economic elite, of both the public and private sectors. This elite began to push for economic liberalization, that is, for doing away with the old incorporation regime.

After a number of abortive attempts, liberalization was successfully launched with the Emergency Economic Stabilization Plan of 1985. When the intifada broke out two years later, the measures required to quell it could no longer be utilized. For they were in contradiction to the logic of liberalization, which could not be confined to the economic sphere alone. Moreover, key segments of the elite – military, political, and, of course, economic – realized that the "control system" established in 1967 was inherently unstable because of the non-incorporation of the non-citizen Palestinians into the framework of political legitimacy. In addition, they came to see the occupation itself, and the broader Israeli–Arab conflict, as obstacles on their way to a greater role in the regional and world economies.

The Gulf war of 1991, which for the first time exposed Israel's civilian population to massive attacks with no effective response, coupled with Israel's inability to quell the intifada, were the immediate reasons for Israel's agreement to participate in the Madrid peace conference that was convened in 1991. Although that agreement was probably tactical and meant as a play for time only, it recommitted Israel formally to solving the Palestinian issue diplomatically. (The first such commitment was made in the Camp David Accords of 1979, but was never put into effect.) With Labor's election victory of 1992, its group of young, liberal political entrepreneurs, who now became managers of Israel's foreign affairs, realized that only direct secret negotiations with the PLO could move the peace process along (Savir 1998). Once they convinced Prime Minister Rabin of that, the way to the Oslo agreement was open.

Ideologically, the decline of the LSM's hegemonic incorporation regime meant the decline of the republican discourse, the only citizenship discourse in Israel's political culture that related rights to contribution to the common good. (In the liberal discourse rights inhere in the citizen as such; in the ethno-national discourse they inhere in Jews as such.) As a result, two opposite approaches came to contend for support among Israelis: an individualistic, market-oriented and contract-based liberal discourse, which has little to say about the question of social solidarity, and the solidaristic ethno-national discourse, which is concerned exclusively with the rights of Jews. Not surprisingly, those benefiting from liberalization, economically, politically, or culturally, rallied around the liberal discourse and the peace process. The victims of liberalization, on the other hand, rallied around the ethno-national discourse and opposition to the peace process. Since, as demonstrated in all Knesset election results since 1973, these two camps are more or less equal in size, Israeli politics have become suffused with a crisis atmosphere. Difficult decisions, such as peace with Egypt in 1979, the invasion of Lebanon in 1982, the economic plan of 1985, the Oslo agreement of 1993, and the withdrawal from southern Lebanon in 2000, took place only when situations reached crisis dimensions and *ad hoc* coalitions could be built to solve them. The institution of direct popular election of the prime minister, in 1996, was meant to reduce this instability, but has had exactly the opposite effect. By the year 2000 neither of the two popularly elected prime ministers, Netanyahu and Barak, was able to complete his term of office. As a result of this and other factors, the direct election of the prime minister was revoked, and the old parliamentary system restored, in early 2001, to take effect in the next general elections.

Since the signing of the Oslo Accords in September 1993, the tactical conflict between "doves" and "hawks" over the means of attaining security has given way to a strategic conflict between neo-Zionists, who have replenished old Zionism with a fundamentalist religious and anti-Western twist, and post-Zionists, who view the stage of conquest, colonization, and state building as over (Ram 1996; Kelman 1998). These contradictory perspectives are articulated most clearly in the two competing citizenship discourses that structure, stratify, and provide ideological expression to the hopes and fears of all social groups: Ashkenazim, Mizrachim, Orthodox Jews, citizen and non-citizen Palestinians, and women.

The Ashkenazi LSM elite has outgrown the confines of its colonial phase of development and now seeks to venture out into the world. It was for this reason that it lost its interest in maintaining the privileged republican citizenship, with its emphasis on a strong state and on communal public-spiritedness. A central dilemma for the relatively secular Ashkenazi Jews who pursue the promise of liberal citizenship, however, is how to address the conflict between individual rights and the role played by Orthodox Judaism in the public sphere. Until recently the option of separating state and religion was rarely raised, because it would have meant doing away with Israel's character as a Jewish state and would have threatened most Jews' conception of their self-identity. Instead, a piecemeal approach of gradually eroding the religious "status quo" through liberal legislation, judicial action, and commercial practices was taken. This approach was supplemented with a struggle for official recognition of non-Orthodox streams of Judaism as legitimate religious communities for the purpose of public law. In the last few years, emboldened by the arrival of almost one million secular immigrants from the FSU (many of them non-Jews by Orthodox criteria), Israeli liberals have been increasingly willing to entertain the idea of the separation of state and religion. Their most important organ, the liberal daily *Haaretz*, has already taken an editorial position in support of this move (February 15, 1999).

Palestinians, both citizens and non-citizens, are also keenly interested in the liberal discourse. If the liberal discourse replaced the republican one as the central narrative of Israeli citizenship, this would go a long way toward sustaining the peace process and equalizing the citizenship status of Jews and Palestinians. One key issue, however, that still divides citizen Palestinians from most Jewish liberals is the latter's continued commitment to the preservation of Israel's character as a Jewish state (Gavison 1995). This has led many citizen Palestinians to demand national–cultural autonomy, that is, recasting the Israeli state as a multicultural or consociational democracy.

Since Palestinian culture is deeply imbued with religious Islamic elements, their demand for cultural autonomy may widen the rift between the Palestinians and Jewish liberals, who have become very impatient with religion. At the time of writing, a crisis atmosphere prevails between Israel's Jewish and Palestinian citizens, because of the killing by police of thirteen citizen Palestinians during the first two weeks of the al-Aksa intifada. Beyond the immediate crisis, however, the key issue is still whether the Palestinian citizens will be given the option of liberal citizenship – integration as individuals into the society and citizenship in a state that is nationally neutral and redefined as belonging to all of its citizens. As mentioned, even Jewish liberals are currently reluctant to give up Israel's definition as a Jewish state, but they may overcome their reluctance as they realize that this is the price to pay for the separation of state and religion.

The idea of recognizing the Palestinian citizens as a national minority, with corresponding effective multicultural citizenship rights, namely, cultural autonomy, is gaining popularity among Palestinians, who are very skeptical about the possibility of truly liberal integration into Israeli society. Most Jews are quite strongly opposed to that, which may be another reason that would make them acquiesce to the liberal option.

As long as the republican discourse predominated, the political efficacy of groups that were excluded or marginalized by it was necessarily limited: They could tilt the political balance by providing the support needed by a particular section of the core group to prevail politically (religious Zionists and the LSM in 1948–77; Mizrachim and Likud between 1977 and 1999; citizen Palestinians and Labor in 1992), but they could never become dominant themselves. Consequently, these peripheral groups were unable to take effective political initiatives, and the rewards they gained from supporting sections of the core group were inevitably frustratingly small.

After 1967 various forms of synthetic citizenship discourses had emerged, with the intention of reigniting the flickering flame of colonial expansion. Gush Emunim claimed the mantle of republicanism and accented it with its own messianic religious convictions. Private enterprise, which in the West Bank assumed the form of liberal colonialism (in fact, still heavily subsidized), was attempted as the preferred method of settlement. Ultimately, however, liberalism proved more suitable for criticizing colonization than for enhancing it. At any rate, neither religio-republicanism nor liberal-colonialism could match the effectiveness of republican pioneering as a colonial strategy.

Since the outbreak of the first intifada the would-be pioneers of Gush Emunim came to be regarded by most of the original bearers of republican virtue, who had been quite ambivalent about them in the past, as usurpers. The battle over decolonization of the OT, which has raged primarily between these two groups, has already claimed the life of Yitzhak Rabin, an archetypal representative of the original beneficiaries of the republican discourse.

For Mizrachim, the (Jewish) state, which has traditionally treated them as secondary to Ashkenazim, is assuming ever-growing importance now, as the republican discourse continues to decline. They seek in the state protection against the adverse effects of economic liberalization and an affirmation of their privileged status as Jews. They cling ever more strongly to the ethno-national discourse of citizenship, increasingly infusing it with religious content and, somewhat inconsistently, with demands for the protection and extension of social citizenship rights. It is much debated whether a Mizrachi secular cultural alternative to religious identification is available, but it is quite obvious that the fulfillment of social rights through membership in religious institutions, in a manner similar to Islamic fundamentalism, does not allow class interests to be properly expressed or defended. This has been strikingly attested to in the parliamentary voting record of Shas, a party that sublimated Mizrachi identity and grievances into a religious world-view. Shas has cast the crucial votes against Basic Law: Social Rights, opposed the law entitling tenants of public housing to purchase their apartments at greatly reduced prices, and supported out-of-pocket payments for medical services. Needless to say, these positions have not been taken out of hostility to the interests of poor Mizrachim, who form the bulk of Shas's constituency. They have been taken, rather, out of a clear interest that social services to this sector be funneled through the party itself and its affiliated institutions (in a way not too dissimilar to the *modus operandi* of the historic LSM).

While the settlers and the Mizrachim share an essentially traditionalist outlook and oppose liberalization, the former are interested primarily in keeping the OT, whereas the latter favor preserving the state as both provider of welfare services and the primary avenue of social mobility open to them. Their *charedi* allies are devoted less to either territory or the state than they are to maintaining the Orthodox Jewish character of public life. This, after all, is the basis of their privileges, which they see being threatened by liberalization and by the use of civic criteria of membership. Thus, this ethno-national coalition, no less than the liberal one, is subject to internal tensions and contradiction.

Given the acrimony of the normative struggle and the conflict over the centrality of the institutions that dispense citizenship rights and duties – the marketplace and judicial system for the liberals, the welfare state and religious institutions for the ethno-nationalists – the battle between them sometimes appears as a total war. The question posed by this conflict is whether a single universal and "assimilationist" liberal citizenship, extended to groups that previously did not enjoy its full benefits, would become the dominant model, or whether ethno-nationalist citizenship would prevail by absorbing certain themes previously associated with the competing discourses, such as republican pioneering and social citizenship. Given the deep cleavages in the society it is more probable that, rather than a single discourse driving out its rival, a new but still multifaceted citizenship discourse will emerge. The incorporation regime based on such a discourse is unlikely to have a systemic character, which in the past was assured by the hegemony of republicanism and, consequently, will probably be repeatedly renegotiated.

The peace process, especially the future of the occupied Palestinian territories, is the main axis around which liberals and ethno-nationalists contend. Although predictions, especially in the Middle East, are notoriously difficult and risky, we will venture to say that, as the forces that shape Israeli society are becoming more global, the prospects of the liberals to prevail seem to be improving. For the more limited demands of liberal citizenship cohere better with international trends than either the republican or the ethno-national discourses. Certainly Rabin, and his hand-picked successor, Barak, but even some of the leaders of the ethno-nationalist camp, especially Benjamin Netanyahu, have been committed to a liberal economic vision. It would be very difficult to square this vision with the interventionist state and repressive military practices required for maintaining the occupation and defending Jewish settlers on the West Bank and in Gaza.

But the evolution of civil society in the Lockean sense of the term would not, in our view, prove a panacea for Israeli society. As we have witnessed already, liberalization has resulted in ever-costlier efforts to keep growing economic inequality within bounds, a diminution of social rights, and a decline of social solidarity. The purported inclusiveness of the liberal discourse is market-dependent: it applies only to those who can benefit from the opportunities presented by the market. While, in an ethnically stratified society such as Israel, this could mean an improvement for some members of previously subjugated groups, the distribution of market-relevant resources is quite consonant with ascriptive affiliation. Thus the low socio-economic standing of Mizrachim, citizen Palestinians, and women could be perpetuated, not through discriminatory state policy, but through the "objective" outcomes of market competition. In addition, *charedim*, whose poor standing in the market is now mitigated by generous state subsidies, legitimated through the ethno-national discourse, would sink much lower, economically, if liberalism became the hegemonic narrative of citizenship.

Furthermore, the liberal ideal of state neutrality is likely to remain constrained by Jewish dominance of the society, even if Israel's official designation as a Jewish state were to be discarded. With the disappearance of the remaining vestiges of republican citizenship, economic, political, and cultural dominance would become the final line of defense of Jewish privileged citizenship. The emphatic rejection of the Palestinian refugees' "right of return" underscores this conclusion. As many citizen Palestinians fear, even the contracted, liberal Israeli state will continue to privilege Jews and Judaism, perhaps even Orthodox Judaism, at least in the foreseeable future. Given that, and given the reality of a market society and the country's ethnic composition, what form of citizenship would be most likely to promote equal universal membership in the society and the state?

In answering this question we would like to propose a non-hegemonic citizenship discourse and a redistributive incorporation scheme that recognize what Nancy Fraser has termed "multiple public spheres" (Fraser 1992). As distinct from liberal multiculturalism (Kymlicka 1989; 1995; 1997), such a democratic multiculturalism would embody social citizenship and be concerned not only with the right of minority groups to seek the preservation of their cultures, but with all citizenship rights and with all aspects of the incorporation of individuals and groups in the society. In Fraser's words, this type of multiculturalism would be cognizant not only of issues of "recognition," but of issues of "redistribution" as well (Fraser 1995). The most worthy incorporation regime achievable under present conditions, according to this discourse of citizenship, would be one that combined universal civil, political, and social rights of individuals, regardless of ascriptive affiliation, with group cultural rights for different cultural minorities.

According to Fraser, in stratified societies that have no formal exclusionary rules, and with "only a single, comprehensive public sphere," that public sphere will inevitably be hegemonically dominated (as opposed to being coercively dominated, as in societies where formal exclusions do exist) by the privileged group(s). While subordinate groups have every (formal) right to organize and express their preferences, they can do so only in the hegemonic language that prevails in the single public sphere, and that language already incorporates the interests and values of the dominant group(s). Thus subordinate groups are at a structural disadvantage when they seek to promote their interests in the public sphere. If, on the other hand, subordinate groups are able to form their own "subaltern publics... [where they can] invent and circulate counter-discourses to formulate oppositional interpretations of their identities, interests, and needs," then they can approach the dominant group(s) in the general public sphere on a more equal footing (Fraser 1992: 122–4). These "subaltern counterpublics," Fraser argues,

> have a dual character. On the one hand, they function as spaces of withdrawal and regroupment; on the other hand, they also function as bases and training grounds for agitational activities directed toward wider publics. It is precisely in the dialectic between these two functions that their emancipatory potential resides. This dialectic enables subaltern counterpublics partially to offset, although not wholly to eradicate, the unjust participatory privileges enjoyed by members of dominant social groups. (Fraser 1992: 124; cf. Bishara 2001)

The recognition of the legitimacy of multiple groups and the advocacy of multiple public spheres is usually suspected of undermining the actuality or possibility of a single public sphere where alone, as the republican and liberal citizenship traditions hold, citizens' search for the common good is capable of being pursued. But, as Fraser has stressed, by being public, and engaged in contestation with other discourses in the general public sphere, these counterpublics militate against separatism and contribute to the cohesiveness of society, rather than undermining it. To illustrate the difference in this regard between a counterpublic and a cultural enclave, we may point to the campaign for cultural autonomy for Israel's Palestinian citizens conducted by secular Palestinian intellectuals, as opposed to the autonomous institutions being actually set up by the Islamic Movement, without engaging in dialogue with any other social group.

Combining the two principles – of universal individual rights and group-based rights – in the construction of multiple public spheres is not necessarily an inherently contradictory project. John Rawls's conception of justice (or social contract, in the traditional language of political theory) famously combines two principles according to which political and economic institutions of a fair modern liberal democracy may be set up: The possession, by individuals, of (1) "a fully adequate scheme of equal basic rights and liberties"; and (2) equal opportunity combined with the "difference principle," namely, that "social and economic inequalities" would be acceptable only in so far as they operate "to the greatest benefit of the least advantaged members of society." Rawls attempted to solve the potential conflict between these principles by listing them in order of priority. In practical terms, this means that of the alternative social orders that safeguard the individual's basic liberties, we should select the one that provides the most equal access to those positions that provide unequal rewards, and in which social and economic inequalities work to the advantage of society's least advantaged members. In other words, once basic liberties, or what Marshall called "civil citizenship rights," are guaranteed, the "social citizenship rights" of the least advantaged should be our main consideration in contracting for a just society.

For Rawls's theory of justice as fairness to work, as he repeatedly stresses, it has to be viewed as a political theory for a democratic citizenry. For, unlike their private or communal life, the political life of citizens in a liberal democracy is not dominated by a single comprehensive moral – whether religious, nationalist, or other – vision. According to Rawls, justice as fairness itself is not intended as a comprehensive moral doctrine, but rather as a practical order which allows the emergence of an overlapping consensus of moral principles between opposing comprehensive doctrines (Rawls 1971; 1993).

Although Rawls was concerned with individual rights only, the way he reconciled apparently conflicting principles of justice by prioritizing them could be applicable for reconciling individual and group rights as well. Following Rawls, we would argue that a democratic multicultural society would first see to it that individual civil and social rights are firmly guaranteed and, subject to that, would recognize the rights of different cultural groups to autonomous management of their communal affairs. This, in Fraser's terms, could result in the ordering of different public spheres, based on an overlapping consensus regarding the very principle of reconciling individual and group rights.[1]

In the remaining pages of this conclusion we would like to try and sketch the contours of such a democratic multiculturalist incorporation regime for Israeli society. In arguing for the adoption of democratic multiculturalism we will naturally turn to the normative aspect of citizenship, which has always constituted an integral part of any citizenship discourse. But our discussion of the normative aspects and prospects of Israeli citizenship will be grounded in social–historical processes we have identified through the empirical analysis presented in this volume.

While a Lockean Israeli civil society would fall short of leading to an equitable incorporation regime, the rejuvenation of the republican virtue framework, besides being impossible, would be a step backwards. The call for a return to the LSM's hegemonic regime would require the undoing of the competing public spheres that groups which had never been part of the LSM developed over the past two decades or so. The common good at the heart of republican virtue was the national goal of colonial state building, and this conception of the good has outlived both its usefulness

---

[1] For a critique of previous liberal attempts to reconcile individual and group rights and a proposal for applying a Rawlsian analysis to Jewish–Palestinian relations, see Brunner and Peled 1996; Peled and Brunner 2000.

and its effectiveness, as we have seen, and has also changed its character. Its contemporary version, anchored in ethno-nationalist religious beliefs, is more extreme in every way. Thus, revived republicanism would bring back not the solidarity of the LSM and the Histadrut, but the militant particularism of Jewish Orthodoxy.

As the al-Aksa intifada has demonstrated, Israel is deeply implicated in the fate of the "invisible" Palestinian refugees beyond its borders. As the first step in the institution of democratic multicultural citizenship Israel will have to acknowledge, therefore, its moral responsibility for the catastrophe, its creation, and the ensuing war inflicted on the Palestinians. It will then have to open the possibility for the return of at least a symbolic number of refugees, and offer compensation to all other refugees and their descendants. These are indispensable preconditions if Jewish–Palestinian relations within the state of Israel are to have a new start (Pappe 1999; Rabinowitz et al. 2000; Rabinowitz 2001). The partial decolonization of the West Bank and full decolonization of the Gaza Strip, combined with divided sovereignty over Jerusalem (which should not necessarily entail either physical or municipal division of the city) and Palestinian sovereignty over the Temple Mount/Haram al-Sharif compound, would go a very long way towards blunting the dangerous edge of the Israeli–Palestinian conflict.

In a non-conflictual context, citizen Palestinians would no longer be suspected of sympathy to the enemy, and with the decline in the importance of the military, perhaps even its transformation into a professional force, they could no longer be accused of not fulfilling their duty by not being called up for service. In that situation, where ties between social rights and military service still exist, such as in the area of housing, they could no longer be justified. The same would be true for all state budgetary allocations, urban planning policies, investments in infrastructure, land and water issues, employment opportunities, etc. Compensatory measures, such as affirmative action, would help heal past wrongs in this realm.

But, as Fraser has pointed out, equality of individual citizenship rights, and even affirmative action programs, will not make the Palestinians equal citizens with the Jews. In order to ameliorate this problem, a wide-ranging Palestinian autonomy in the cultural sphere, beginning with autonomous control over the already existing Arabic school system, would be required to supplement formal rights. An elected representative Palestinian council should be established to manage this cultural autonomy, but a common education administration would be required to ensure that Palestinians students meet the educational requirements that will enable them to compete with Jews in the labor market.

Ehud Barak apologized to the Mizrachim, before the 1999 elections, for the "mistakes" made in their treatment by the Mapai-dominated governments of the 1950s and 1960s. This was a symbolic act of great importance, but it is still a long way from a serious attempt to decrease the inequality in the social standing of Ashkenazim and Mizrachim. Two areas at which efforts should be particularly directed are social rights and cultural autonomy.

As a group, Mizrachim are likely to be the biggest net losers from the liberalization of the Israeli economy (Smooha 1998). They are disproportionately concentrated at the bottom of the occupational ladder among Jews, and they form a very large share of the workforce in traditional industries, which the liberalization of trade relations has rendered obsolete. To improve the aggregate situation of Mizrachim, continued social investment in providing quality education and more adequate housing and infrastructure in development towns and poor urban neighborhoods will be ever more important. Every diminution of social rights hurts mostly the poor, and in Israel this means Palestinians and Mizrachim. With the decoupling of social rights from republican citizenship, their reassertion as universal rights is not an easy task. A democratic multiculturalist incorporation regime requires that the state diligently safeguards social rights and invests seriously in the provision of social services.

Culturally, Mizrachim have suffered from two closely related problems: denigration of Mizrachi culture by the Ashkenazim and by Ashkenazi-controlled institutions, and lack of sufficient resources to maintain and develop their own culture by themselves. The main reason for the negative attitude towards Mizrachi culture was its origins in Arab and other Muslim societies. With the resolution of the Arab–Israeli conflict, the similarity between Mizrachi Jewish and Arab culture will no longer be seen as sufficient reason to denigrate the former. Some of this attitudinal change is already evident, particularly in the field of music. The preservation and revival of Mizrachi culture, an effort that will have to be undertaken by autonomous Mizrachi institutions of culture and education, will also require considerable investment. As a matter of fact, the state already expends large sums of money in supporting the autonomous Mizrachi education system of Shas, but similar efforts will have to be directed towards secular Mizrachi institutions (Levy and Barkai 1998). Ultimately, the issue of Palestinian and Mizrachi citizenship is connected to the much broader question of the dominant groups and institutions of Israeli society accepting the fact that Israel is located in the Middle East and eschewing their Orientalist attitude towards this region and its cultures.

Democratic multiculturalist arrangements could be extended to the Jewish religious sphere as well. Short of the separation of state and religion, religious pluralism could be encouraged by extending official recognition to non-Orthodox streams of Judaism, particularly in the area of family law. If non-Orthodox Jewish communities are allowed to conduct marriage and divorce by their own rules, this would remove most of the difficulties facing "marriage refusniks" – Jews who are not allowed to marry each other for various religious reasons, and interreligious couples. At the same time, it would also improve the position of women in the sphere of family law. Ideally, non-religious, civil marriage should also be available, but even if this is not to be, religious pluralism among Jews will go a long way towards relieving the burden imposed on many people by the Orthodox monopoly in the administration of marriage and divorce. The Orthodox Rabbinate and political parties themselves would rather have civil marriages than non-Orthodox ones, because the latter, in their eyes, pose as Jewish ceremonies, which in reality they are not. But whether or not civil marriage and divorce are instituted alongside the Orthodox ones, so long as the state continues to recognize religious ceremonies as binding, it should recognize a plurality of Jewish religious traditions, not just one. In general, any depoliticization, or privatization, of Jewish ethno-nationalism will contribute to the promotion of pluralism.

To conclude, a democratic multiculturalist incorporation regime would combine equal individual rights with multicultural autonomy. To compensate the second- and third-class citizens of the past, it will be crucial to build up a network of state-sponsored and institutionally provided social citizenship rights and collective cultural rights. Most importantly, in order to prevent the pluralist and democratic multiculturalist regime from reverting to the hierarchical practices of its predecessors, it will be essential to base citizenship on a foundation of equal, universal, and effective individual rights.

Bibliography

Abramov, Zalman S. 1976. *Perpetual Dilemma: Jewish Religion in the Jewish State.* Rutherford, NJ: Fairleigh Dickinson University Press

Abramson, P. R. 1990. "Demographic Change and Partisan Support," in A. Arian and M. Shamir (eds.), *The Elections in Israel – 1988.* Boulder: Westview, pp. 173–88

Achdut, Lea 1993. *Income Inequality and Income Composition: Israel 1979–1991.* National Insurance Institute (Discussion Paper No. 50), Jerusalem (Hebrew)

1996. "Income Inequality, Income Composition and Macroeconomic Trends: Israel, 1979–93," *Economica*, 63: S1–S27

Adalah 1998. *Legal Violations of Arab Minority Rights in Israel.* Shfaram: Adalah the Legal Center for Arab Minority Rights in Israel

Adler, Hayim and Nahum Balas 1997. "Inequality in Education in Israel," in Yaakov Kop (ed.), *The Allocation of Resources for Social Service in Israel, 1996.* Jerusalem: Center for the Study of Social Policy in Israel, pp. 121–55 (Hebrew)

Adler, Shmuel 1997. "Israel's Absorption Policy since the 1970s," in Lewin-Epstein et al. (eds.), pp. 135–44

Adva Center 1993. *Recommendations of the Gafny Commission (October 1993) and the Wilkansky Commission (August 1993)* (written by Yossi Dahan and Barbara Swirski), Tel Aviv: Adva Center (Hebrew)

1995. *Inequality among Jews in Israel* (written by Barbara Swirski). Tel Aviv: Adva Center

1996a. *The National Health Insurance Law: Its Equality, Efficiency, and Cost.* Tel Aviv: Adva Center (Hebrew)

1996b. *A Look at the Ministry of Education Budget, 1990–1996* (written by Shlomo Swirski, Meirav Sun-Zangi, and Adi Dagan). Tel Aviv: Adva Center (Hebrew)

1996c. *The State Budget for 1997: A Look at the Arab Sector.* Tel Aviv: Adva Center (Hebrew)

1998a. *Government Budgetary Allocations to the Charedi Jewish Sector* (written by Shlomo Swirski, Etty Connor, and Yaron Yechezkel). Tel Aviv: Adva Center (Hebrew)

1998b. *The Allocation of the Ministry of Education's Fostering Hours in Arab Localities and in Development Towns* (written by Shlomo Swirski and Joseph Houri). Tel Aviv: Adva Center (Hebrew)

1998c. *Place of Residence and Wage Level, 1995* (written by Shlomo Swirski and Yaron Yechezkel). Tel Aviv: Adva Center (Hebrew)

1999. *Eligibility for Matriculation Certificates by Locality, 1996–1998* (May) Tel Aviv: Adva Center (Hebrew)

2000a. *Eligibility for Matriculation Certificates by Locality, 1997–1999* (written by Shlomo Swirski). Tel Aviv: Adva Center (Hebrew)

2000b. *A Social Snapshot 2000* (written by Shlomo Swirski and Etty Connor). Tel Aviv: Adva Center (Hebrew)

2000c. *Infant Mortality in Israel, 1993–1997* (written by Barbara Swirski). Tel Aviv: Adva Center (Hebrew)

Aharoni, Yair 1991. *The Israeli Economy: Dreams and Realities.* New York: Routledge

1998. "The Changing Economy of Israel," *Annals of the American Academy of Political and Social Science,* 555 (*Israel in Transition*): 127–46

Allon, Gideon 1995. *Direct Election.* Tel Aviv: Bitan (Hebrew)

1997. "Another Detour around the High Court of Justice?" *Haaretz,* September 30 (Hebrew)

Almog, Shulamit 1996. "On Women, the Military and Equality," *Mishpat u-mimshal,* 3, 2: 631–47 (Hebrew)

Amir, Delila 1995. "'Responsible,' 'Committed' and 'Reasonable': The Construction of Israeli Womanhood in the Committees for the Termination of Pregnancy," *Teorya u-vikoret,* 7: 247–54 (Hebrew)

Amir, Delila and David Navon 1989. *The Politics of Abortion in Israel.* Tel Aviv: Tel Aviv University, Pinhas Sapir Center for Development (Hebrew)

Amor, Meir 1999. "State Persecution and Vulnerability: A Comparative Historical Analysis of Violent Ethnocentrism," Ph.D. thesis, University of Toronto

Arendt, Hannah 1973. *The Origins of Totalitarianism,* new edn. San Diego, Harcourt Brace & Co.

Arian, Asher 1980. "The Israeli Electorate, 1977," in Asher Arian (ed.), *The Elections in Israel – 1977.* Jerusalem: Academic Press, pp. 253–76

1995. *Security Threatened: Surveying Israeli Public Opinion on Peace and War.* Cambridge: Cambridge University Press

1998. *The Second Republic: Politics in Israel.* Chatham, NJ: Chatham House

Arian, Asher and Michal Shamir 1995. "Two Reversals: Why 1992 was not 1977," in Asher Arian and Michal Shamir (eds.), *The Elections in Israel – 1992.* Albany: SUNY Press, pp. 17–53

1999 (eds.). *The Elections in Israel – 1996.* Albany: SUNY Press

2001a (eds.). *The Elections in Israel – 1999.* Jerusalem: Israel Democracy Institute (Hebrew)

2001b. "Candidates, Parties and Blocs: Israel in the 1990's," in Arian and Shamir (eds.), pp. 15–46

Aridor, Edna 1993. "The Thirteenth Proposal for National Health Insurance," *Haaretz,* July 5 (Hebrew)

Arlosoroff, Chaim 1969 [1926]. "Class Struggle in the Context of Palestine," in S. N. Eisenstadt et al. (eds.), *Israel's Social Structure.* Jerusalem: Academon (Hebrew), pp. 66–74

Aronsohn, Shlomo 1997. "Zionism and Post-Zionism: The Historical–Ideological Context," in Weitz (ed.), pp. 291–309 (Hebrew)

Aronson, Geoffrey 1987. *Creating Facts: Israel, Palestinians, and the West Bank.* Washington: Institute for Palestine Studies

2000. "Palestinian Revolt Centers around Settlements," *Report on Israeli Settlements in the OT*, 10, 6

Arrighi, Giovanni and Jessica Drangel 1986. "The Stratification of the World-Economy: An Exploration of the Semiperipheral Zone," *Review*, 10, 1 (Summer): 9–74

Asa-El, Amotz 1997. "Koor Grabs the Future," *Jerusalem Post*, February 19

Association for Civil Rights in Israel 1985. *The Judicial and Administrative System* (Studies in Civil Rights in the Occupied Territories). Jerusalem: Association for Civil Rights in Israel (Hebrew)

Atashe, Zeidan 1995. *Druze and Jews in Israel – A Shared Destiny?* Brighton: Sussex Academic Press

Aviad, Janet 1983. *Return to Judaism: Religious Renewal in Israel.* Chicago: University of Chicago Press

Avineri, Shlomo 1980. *The Variety of Zionist Ideas.* Tel Aviv: Am Oved (Hebrew)

1994. "Zionism and Jewish Religious Tradition: The Dialectic of Redemption and Secularization," in Shmuel Almog, Jehuda Reinharz, and Anita Shapira (eds.), *Zionism and Religion.* Jerusalem: Zalman Shazar Center for Jewish History, pp. 1–9 (Hebrew)

Avneri, Uri 1993. "Return, Return, O Shulamit," *Zeman Tel Aviv (Maariv)*, January 1 (Hebrew)

Avnon, Dan 1996. "The 'Enlightened Public': Jewish and Democratic or Liberal and Democratic?" *Mishpat u-mimshal*, 3: 417–51 (Hebrew)

Avruch, Kevin A. 1978/79. "Gush Emunim: Politics, Religion, and Ideology in Israel," *Middle East Review*, 11, 2 (Winter): 26–31

Awad, Yasser and Nirit Israeli 1996. "Poverty and Inequality of Income Distribution: An International Comparison," in *Annual Survey 1995/96.* Jerusalem: National Insurance Institute, Research and Planning Administration, pp. 209–38 (Hebrew)

Ayalon, Hanna, Eliezer Ben-Rafael and Stephen Sharot 1988. "The Impact of Stratification: Assimilation or Ethnic Solidarity?" *Research in Social Stratification and Mobility*, 7: 305–26

Azmon, Yael and Dafna N. Izraeli 1993a (eds.). *Women in Israel* (Studies of Israeli Society, no. 4). New Brunswick, NJ: Transaction

1993b. "Introduction," in Azmon and Izraeli (eds.), pp. 1–13

BADIL Resource Center 2001. "Remarks and Questions from the Palestinian Negotiating Team Regarding the United States Proposal," info@BADIL.ORG, January 4

Bank Hapoalim 1996. "Poverty and Inequality of Income Distribution in Israel," *Economic Survey*, 82 (Hebrew)

2000. *Economic Survey*, 131 (Hebrew)

Bar, Aryeh 1990. "Industry and Industrial Policy in Israel: Landmarks," in David Brodet et al. (eds.), *Industrial–Technological Policy for Israel.* Jerusalem: Institute for Israel Studies, pp. 22–46 (Hebrew)

Barak, Aharon 1992. "The Constitutional Revolution: Protected Fundamental Rights," *Mishpat u-mimshal*, 1: 9–35 (Hebrew)
1993. "Judicial Philosophy and Judicial Activism," *Tel Aviv University Law Review*, 17: 475–501
1998. "Israel's Economic Constitution," *Mishpat u-mimshal* 4: 357–79 (Hebrew)
Barak, Eitan 1999. "Under Cover of Darkness: The Israeli Supreme Court and the Use of Human Lives as 'Bargaining Chips," *International Journal of Human Rights*, 3: 1–43
Barkai, Hayim 1988. *The Military Industry's Watershed*. Jerusalem: Maurice Falk Institute for Research on the Israeli Economy (Research Publication No. 197) (Hebrew)
Barkey, Henri J. 1994. "When Politics Matter: Economic Stabilization in Argentina and Israel," *Studies in Comparative International Development*, 29 (Winter): 41–67
Barnett, Michael N. 1992. *Confronting the Costs of War: Military Power, State, and Society in Egypt and Israel*. Princeton: Princeton University Press
1996 (ed.). *Israel in Comparative Perspective: Challenging the Conventional Wisdom*. Albany: SUNY Press
Bartram, David V. 1998. "Foreign Workers in Israel: History and Theory," *International Migration Review*, 32: 303–25
Barzilai, Gad 2000. "Parliamentarism and its Rivals: The Politics of Liberal Law," in Hanna Herzog (ed.), *Reflection of a Society: In Memory of Yonathan Shapiro*. Tel Aviv: Ramot, pp. 359–77 (Hebrew)
2001. "Arabs? Only in the Singular," *Mishpat Nossaf*, 1: 55–63 (Hebrew)
Barzilay, Amnon 1996. *Ramon: A Political Biography*. Tel Aviv: Schocken (Hebrew)
Bechor, Guy 1996. *Constitution for Israel*. Jerusalem: Keter (Hebrew)
Begin, Zeev B. 1996. "Primaries – the Cost to Democracy," in Doron (ed.), pp. 207–13
Beilin, Yossi 1985. *The Price of Unification*. Tel Aviv: Revivim (Hebrew)
1999. *Touching Peace: From the Oslo Accord to a Final Agreement*. London: Weidenfeld & Nicolson
Beit-Hallahmi, Benjamin 1991. "Back to the Fold: The Return to Judaism," in Zvi Sobel and Benjamin Beit-Hallahmi (eds.), *Tradition, Innovation, Conflict: Jewishness and Judaism in Contemporary Israel*. Albany: SUNY Press, pp. 153–72
Bellisari, Anna 1994. "Public Health and the Water Crisis in the Occupied Palestinian Territories," *Journal of Palestine Studies*, 23: 52–63
Ben-Ami, Shlomo 1998. *A Place for All*. Bnei-Brak: Hakibbutz Hameuchad (Hebrew)
Ben-David, Dan and Haim Ben-Shachar 2000. "The Third World is Already Here," *Haaretz*, June 11 (Hebrew)
Ben-Eliezer, Uri 1993. "The Meaning of Political Participation in a Nonliberal Democracy: The Israeli Experience," *Comparative Politics* (July): 397–412
1998a. *The Making of Israeli Militarism*. Bloomington: Indiana University Press
1998b. "Is a Military Coup Possible in Israel? Israel and French-Algeria in Comparative Historical-Sociological Perspective," *Theory and Society*, 27: 311–49

Ben-Israel, Ruth 1997. "From Collective Justice to Individual Justice: Changing Employment Relationships in Israel," in J. R. Bellace and M. G. Rood (eds.), *Labour Law at the Crossroads: Changing Employment Relationships. Studies in Honor of Benjamin Aaron.* The Hague: Kluwer Law International, pp. 27–55

Ben-Meir, Dov 1978. *The Histadrut.* Jerusalem: Carta (Hebrew)

Ben-Porath, Yoram 1986. "Introduction," in Yoram Ben-Porath (ed.), *The Economy of Israel: Maturing through Crises.* Cambridge, MA: Harvard University Press, pp. 1–23

Ben-Rafael, Eliezer and Stephen Sharot 1991. *Ethnicity, Religion and Class in Israeli Society.* Cambridge: Cambridge University Press

Ben-Rafael, Eliezer, Elite Olshtain, and Idit Geijst 1997. "Identity and Language: The Social Insertion of Soviet Jews in Israel," in Lewin-Epstein et al. (eds.), pp. 364–88

Ben-Shahar, Haim 1995. "Highlights of the Report of the Economic Advisory Team to the Political Negotiations, July 1993," *Rivon lekalkala,* 42: 135–54 (Hebrew)

Ben-Simon, Daniel 1999. "The Russian Heart Belongs to Bibi," *Haaretz,* April 9 (Hebrew)

Benski, Tova 1993. "Testing Melting-Pot Theories in the Jewish Israeli Context," *Sociological Papers* (Bar-Ilan University, Sociological Institute for Community Studies), 2: 1–46

Benvenisti, Eyal 1990. *Legal Dualism: The Absorption of the Occupied Territories into Israel.* Jerusalem: West Bank Data Base Project; Boulder: Westview

Benvenisti, Meron 1984. *The West Bank Data Project: A Survey of Israel's Policies.* Washington: American Enterprise Institute

   1986a. *1986 Report: Demographic, Economic, Legal, Social and Political Developments in the West Bank.* West Bank Data Base Project and Boulder: Westview

   1986b (with Ziad Abu-Zayed and Danny Rubinstein). *The West Bank Handbook: A Political Lexicon.* Boulder: Westview

Benvenisti, Meron and Shlomo Khayat 1988. *The West Bank and Gaza Atlas.* Jerusalem: West Bank Data Project

Ben-Yaakov, Yochanan 1978 (ed.). *Gush Etzion.* Kfar Etzion: Hakibbutz Hadati (Hebrew)

Ben-Zadok, Efraim 1993. "Oriental Jews in Development Towns: Ethnicity, Economic Development, Budgets and Politics," in Efraim Ben-Zadok (ed.), *Local Communities and the Israeli Polity: Conflict of Values and Interests.* Albany: SUNY Press, pp. 91–122

Benziman, Uzi and Attalah Mansour 1992. *Subtenants: Israeli Arabs, their Status, and State Policy towards them.* Jerusalem: Keter (Hebrew)

Ben-Zvi, Shmuel 1994. "The Overt and Covert Security Burden," *Rivon lekalkala,* 41: 227–32 (Hebrew)

Bergesen, A. and R. Schoenberg 1980. "Long Waves of Colonial Expansion and Contraction, 1415–1969," in A. Bergesen (ed.), *Studies of the Modern World-System.* New York: Academic Press, pp. 231–77

Berkovitch, Nitza 1997. "Motherhood as a National Mission: The Construction of Womanhood in the Legal Discourse of Israel," *Women's Studies International Forum,* 20: 605–19

Berler, A. 1970. *New Towns in Israel*. Jerusalem: Israel Universities Press
Berman, Eli and Ruth Klinov 1997. "Human Capital Investment and Nonpartic-
ipation: Evidence from a Sample with Infinite Horizons (Or: Jewish Father
Stops Going to Work)." Jerusalem: Maurice Falk Institute for Economic
Research in Israel (Discussion Paper No. 97.05)
Bernstein, Deborah S. 1992 (ed.). *Pioneers and Homemakers: Jewish Women in
Pre-state Israel*. Albany: SUNY Press
   1993. "Economic Growth and Female Labour: The Case of Israel," in Azmon
   and Izraeli (eds.), pp. 67–96
   2000. "Challenges to Separatism: Joint Action by Jewish and Arab Workers in
   Jewish-owned Industry in Mandatory Palestine," in Shafir and Peled (eds.),
   pp. 17–41
Bernstein, Deborah and Shlomo Swirski 1982. "The Rapid Economic Develop-
ment of Israel and the Emergence of the Ethnic Division of Labour," *British
Journal of Sociology*, 33: 64–85
Beyer, Peter 1994. *Religion and Globalization*. London: Sage
Biale, David 1983. "Mysticism and Politics in Modern Israel: The Messianic
Ideology of Abraham Isaac ha-Cohen Kook," in Peter H. Merkel and Ninian
Smart (eds.), *Religion and Politics in the Modern World*. New York: New York
University Press, pp. 191–202
Bilsky, Leora forthcoming. "'J'Accuse': The Deri Trial, Political Trial and Col-
lective Memory," in Peled (ed.)
Bishara, Azmi 1993. "On the Question of the Palestinian Minority in Israel,"
Teorya u-vikoret, 3: 7–20 (Hebrew)
   2001. "Between Nation and Nationality: Reflections on Nationalism," in Peled
   and Ophir (eds.), pp. 35–72
Bloom, Anne R. 1991. "Women in the Defense Forces," in Swirski and Safir
(eds.), pp. 128–38
Bonacich, E. 1972. "A Theory of Ethnic Antagonism: The Split Labor Market,"
American Sociological Review, 37: 547–59
Borukhov, Eliyahu 1988. *Industry in Development Towns and its Problems*. Sapir
Center for Development, Tel Aviv University (Hebrew)
   1998. "The Absorption of the Immigration in Housing and its Effects on the
   Housing Industry," in Sikron and Leshem (eds.), pp. 207–31
Brodet, David 1994. "Economic Might and Military Might," *Rivon lekalkala*, 41:
223–7 (Hebrew)
Brubaker, Rogers 1992. *Citizenship and Nationhood in France and Germany*.
Cambridge, MA: Harvard University Press
Brunner, Jose and Yoav Peled 1996. "Rawls on Respect and Self-Respect: An
Israeli Perspective," *Political Studies*, 44: 287–302
Bruno, Michael 1986. *Generating a Sharp Disinflation: Israel 1985*. Cambridge,
MA: National Bureau of Economic Research
Brynen, Rex 1991 (ed.). *Echoes of the Intifada: Regional Repercussions of the
Palestinian–Israeli Conflict*. Boulder: Westview
B'tselem 1994. *Law Enforcement on Israeli Citizens in the [Occupied] Territories*.
Jerusalem: B'tselem – the Israeli Information Center for Human Rights in
the Occupied Territories (Hebrew)

Bulmer, Martin and Anthony M. Rees 1996 (eds.). *Citizenship Today: The Contemporary Relevance of T. H. Marshall.* London: UCL Press

Carmon, Naomi and Oren Yiftachel 1994. *Israel's Population: Basic Data and Projections for Spatial Policy.* Haifa: Center for Urban and Regional Research, the Technicon (Hebrew)

Carnegy, Hugh 1991. "Koor Optimistic after Struggle for Survival," *Financial Times,* October 1

Central Bureau of Statistics 1987. *Classification of Geographical Units According to the Socio-economic Characteristics of the Population (1983 Census of Population and Housing Publications, 15).* Jerusalem: CBS (Hebrew)

  1993. *Results of the Elections to the Thirteenth Knesset,* vol. I. Jerusalem: CBS (Hebrew)

  1994. *Special Supplement to Statistical Yearbook.* Jerusalem: CBS (Hebrew)

  1995a. *Characterization and Ranking of Local Authorities According to the Population's Socio-economic Level in 1995.* Jerusalem: CBS (Hebrew)

  1995b. *Statistical Abstracts of Israel,* vol. XLVI. Jerusalem: CBS

  1996a. *Statistical Abstracts of Israel,* vol. XLVII. Jerusalem: CBS

  1996b. *Population in Localities: Demographic Characteristics by Geographical Divisions.* Jerusalem: CBS (Hebrew)

  1997. *Income Survey 1996.* Jerusalem: CBS (Hebrew)

  1998. *Women in the Statistical Mirror.* Jerusalem: CBS (Hebrew)

  1999a. *Statistical Abstracts of Israel.* vol. L. Jerusalem: CBS

  1999b. "Percentage of College Graduates in Urban Localities," www.cbs/gov.il/hodaot1999/99 20tb2.htm (press release, Hebrew)

Chernichovsky, Dov and David Chinitz 1995. "The Political Economy of Health System Reform in Israel," *Health Economics,* 4, 2: 127–41

Chetrit, Sami Shalom 2001. "Mizrahi Politics in Israel: Between Identification and Integration to Protest and Alternative," Ph.D. thesis, Hebrew University n.d. "New State, Old Land: The East and the Easterners in the Jewish State of Theodor Herzl," unpublished

Cohen, Erik 1983. "Ethnicity and Legitimation in Contemporary Israel," *Jerusalem Quarterly,* 28: 111–24

  1989a. "The Changing Legitimations of the State of Israel," *Studies in Contemporary Jewry,* 5: 148–65

  1989b. "Citizenship, Nationality and Religion in Israel and Thailand," in Kimmerling (ed.), pp. 66–92

Cohen, Jean and Andrew Arato 1992. *The Political Theory of Civil Society.* Cambridge, MA: MIT Press

Cohen, Stuart A. 1997a. *The Scroll or the Sword? Dilemmas of Religion and Military Service in Israel.* Amsterdam: Harwood Academic Publishers

  1997b. "Towards a New Portrait of the (New) Israeli Soldier," *Israel Affairs,* 3: 77–114

Cohen, Yinon 1998. "Socioeconomic Gaps between Mizrachim and Ashkenazim, 1975–1995," *Israeli Sociology,* 1: 115–34 (Hebrew)

Cohen, Yinon and Yitzhak Haberfeld 1998. "Second-Generation Immigrants in Israel: Have the Ethnic Gaps in Schooling and Earnings Declined?" *Ethnic and Racial Studies,* 21: 507–28

Coordinating Bureau of the Economic Organizations 1992. "Autonomy in the Territories – Economic Implications: Interim Report," Committee for Studying the Economic Implications of the Autonomy and the Peace Process, October 29 (Hebrew)

1993. "Economic Implications of the Establishment of Autonomy in the Territories and Ways for its Integration with the Israeli Economy," report of the Special Committee chaired by Dan Gillerman of the FCC, February (Hebrew)

Corbin, Jane 1994. *The Norway Channel: The Secret Talks that Led to the Middle East Peace Accord.* New York: Atlantic Monthly Press

David, Yossi 2000 (ed.). *The State of Israel: Between Judaism and Democracy.* Jerusalem: Israel Democracy Institute (Hebrew)

Dayan, Arie 2000a. "Marcia Freedman Raises a 'Funny Issue,'" *Haaretz*, May 9

2000b. "Want to go to Israel? Get a Divorce First," *Haaretz*, May 22

Dayan, Moshe 1969. *New Map – New Relations.* Tel Aviv: Maariv (Hebrew)

Dehter, Aaron 1987. *How Expensive are West Bank Settlements?* Boulder: Westview

Deshen, Shlomo 1994. "The Religiosity of the Mizrachim: Public, Rabbis and Faith," *Alpayim*, 9: 44–58 (Hebrew)

Deutsch, Karl W. 1985. "Introduction," in Ernest Krausz (ed.), *Politics and Society in Israel* (Studies of Israeli Society, no. 3). New Brunswick, N J: Transaction

Dillman, Jeffrey D. 1989. "Water Rights in the Occupied Territories," *Journal of Palestine Studies*, 19: 46–71

Diskin, Abraham 1998. "The Decline of the Parties and the Direct Election of the Prime Minister," in Korn (ed.), pp. 67–77

Dominitz, Yehuda 1997. "Israel's Immigration Policy and the Dropout Phenomenon," in Lewin-Epstein et al. (eds.), pp. 113–27

Don-Yehiya, Eliezer 1979. "Stability and Change in a 'Camp-Party': The NRP and the Youth Revolution," *Medina, mimshal veyachasim benleumiyim*, 14: 26–39 (Hebrew)

1984. "Jewish Orthodoxy, Zionism, and the State of Israel," *Jerusalem Quarterly*, 31: 10–29

1990. "Religiosity and Ethnicity in Israeli Politics: The Religious Parties and the Elections to the Twelfth Knesset," *Medina, mimshal veyachasim benleumiyim*, 32: 11–54 (Hebrew)

1997a. *The Politics of Accommodation: Settling Conflicts of State and Religion in Israel.* Jerusalem: Floersheimer Institute for Policy Studies (Hebrew)

1997b. "Religion, Ethnicity, and Electoral Reform: The Religious Parties in the 1996 Elections," *Israel Affairs*, 4: 73–102

Doron, Gideon 1996 (ed.). *The Electoral Revolution: Primaries and Direct Election of the Prime Minister.* Tel Aviv: Hakibbutz Hameuchad (Hebrew)

Dotan, Yoav 1997. "Constitution to Israel? – The Constitutional Dialog after the Constitutional Revolution," *Mishpatim*, 28: 149–210 (Hebrew)

Drobless, Mattityahu 1978. *Master Plan for the Development of Settlement in Judea and Samaria, 1979–1983.* Jerusalem: World Zionist Organization, Department for Rural Settlement (October) (Hebrew)

1981. *Settlement in Judea and Samaria: Strategy, Policy, and Plans.* World Zionist Organization, Settlement Division (January) (Hebrew)

Druyan, Nitza 1981. *Without a Magic Carpet: Yemenite Settlement in Eretz Israel (1881–1914)*. Jerusalem: Ben-Zvi Institute (Hebrew)

Economic Advisory Team for the Political Negotiations 1995. "Report" (mimeo), July; subsequently published in *Revaon lekalkala*, 42 (1995): 135–79 (also known as the Ben-Shahar Committee)

Economic Models 1993. *The Israeli Economy: Outlook*. Ramat Gan: Economic Models (August) (Hebrew)

Efrat, Elisha 1987. *The Establishment of Development Towns in Israel and their Status*. Sapir Center for Development, Tel Aviv University (Hebrew)

Ehrlich, Avishai 1987. "Israel: Conflict, War and Social Change," in Colin Creighton and Martin Shaw (eds.), *The Sociology of War and Peace*. London: Macmillan, pp. 121–42

Eilam, Yigal 2000. *Judaism as Status Quo*. Tel Aviv: Am Oved (Hebrew)

Eisenstadt, S. N. 1947. *Introduction to the Study of the Sociological Structure of Oriental Jews*. Jerusalem: Szold Institute (Hebrew)

1948. "The Sociological Structure of the Jewish Community in Palestine," *Jewish Social Studies*, 10: 3–18

1950. "The Oriental Jews in Israel (A Report on a Preliminary Study in Culture Contacts)," *Jewish Social Studies*, 12: 199–222

1954. *The Absorption of Immigrants*. London: Routledge & Kegal Paul

1968. *Israeli Society*. London: Weidenfeld & Nicolson

1969. "Introduction," in Ofra Cohen (ed.), *The Integration of Immigrants from Different Countries of Origin in Israel: A Symposium Held at the Hebrew University on October 25–26, 1966*. Jerusalem: Magnes Press, the Hebrew University, pp. 6–13 (Hebrew)

1985. *The Transformation of Israeli Society*. London: Weidenfeld & Nicolson

1986. *The Development of the Ethnic Problem in Israeli Society: Observations and Suggestions for Research*. Jerusalem: Jerusalem Institute for Israel Studies

Eisenstadt, S. N., Moshe Lissak, and Yaacov Nahon 1993 (eds.). *Ethnic Communities in Israel – Socio-economic Status*. Jerusalem: Jerusalem Institute for Israel Studies (Hebrew)

Elboim Dov 1997. "Ne'eman is Right, but we are Afraid," *Yediot achronot*, September 5 (Hebrew)

Eliash, Shai 2000. "Sellers Only," *Maariv Business*, November 10 (Hebrew)

Eliav, Binyamin 1988 (ed.). *The Jewish National Home: From the Balfour Declaration to Independence*. Jerusalem: Keter (Hebrew)

Elmusa, Sharif S. and Mahmud al-Jaafari 1995. "Power and Trade: The Israeli–Palestinian Economic Protocol," *Journal of Palestine Studies*, 24: 14–32

Enchin, Harvey 1992. "Koor's Survival an Epic Tale," *Globe and Mail*, November 2

Eraqi-Klorman, Bat-Zion 1997. "Settlement of Yemeni and Ashkenazi Workers: From Rishon le-Zion to Nahalat Yehuda and Back," *Cathedra*, 84: 85–106 (Hebrew)

Erez, Yossi, Yossi Shavit, and Dorit Tsur 1993. "Is there Ethnic Inequality in Promotion Opportunities in the IDF?" *Megamot*, 35: 23–37 (Hebrew)

Eshet, Gideon 2001. "Non-Affirmative Action, *Mamon*, *Yediot achronot*, May 4 (Hebrew)

Etner-Levkovitch, Gal 1997. "The Politics of Marriage: Legitimation Crises and the Rabbinate in Israel," MA thesis, Tel Aviv University (Hebrew)

Etzioni, Amitai 1959. "Alternative Ways to Democracy: The Example of Israel," *Political Science Quarterly*, 74: 196–214

Ezrahi, Yaron 1993. "Democratic Politics and Culture in Modern Israel: Recent Trends," in Ehud Sprinzak and Larry Diamond (eds.), *Israeli Democracy under Stress*. Boulder: Lynne Rienner, pp. 255–72

1997. *Rubber Bullets: Power and Conscience in Modern Israel*. New York: Farrar, Straus & Giroux

Farjoun, Emanuel 1983. "Class Divisions in Israeli Society," *Khamsin*, 10: 29–39

Fein, Aharon 1995. "Voting Trends of Recent Immigrants from the Former Soviet Union," in Asher Arian and Michal Shamir (eds.), *The Elections in Israel – 1992*. Albany: SUNY Press, pp. 161–74

Fieldhouse, D. K. 1966. *The Colonial Empires from the Eighteenth Century*. New York: Weidenfeld & Nicolson

Filk, Danni 2000. "The Neo-Liberal Project and Privatization Processes in the Healthcare System," in Mautner (ed.), pp. 375–88 (Hebrew)

Fischer, Stanley et al. 1993 (eds.). *The Economics of Middle East Peace*. Cambridge, MA: MIT Press

Fogiel-Bijaoui, Sylvie 1992a. "From Revolution to Motherhood: The Case of Women in the Kibbutz, 1910–1948," in Bernstein (ed.), pp. 211–33

1992b. "One Way to Equality: The Struggle for Women's Suffrage in the Jewish Yishuv, 1917–1926," in Bernstein (ed.), pp. 261–82

Fraser, Nancy 1992. "Rethinking the Public Sphere: A Contribution to the Critique of Actually Existing Democracy," in Craig Calhoun (ed.), *Habermas and the Public Sphere*. Cambridge, MA: MIT Press, pp. 109–42

1995. "From Redistribution to Recognition? Dilemmas of Justice in a 'Post-Socialist Age,'" *New Left Review*, 212: 68–93

Fredrickson, George 1988. "Colonialism and Racism: The United States and South Africa in Comparative Perspective," in George Fredrickson, *The Arrogance of Race*. Middletown, CT: Wesleyan University Press, pp. 216–35

Frenkel, Michal, Yehuda Shenhav, and Hanna Herzog 2000. "The Ideological Wellspring of Zionist Capitalism: The Impact of Private Capital and Industry on the Shaping of the Dominant Zionist Ideology," in Shafir and Peled (eds.), pp. 43–69

Friedberg, Rachel M. 1998. "The Impact of Mass Migration on the Israeli Labor Market." Jerusalem: Maurice Falk Institute for Economic Research in Israel (Discussion Paper No. 98.01)

Friedland, Roger and Robert R. Alford 1991. "Bringing Society Back in: Symbols, Practices, and Institutional Contradictions," in Powell and DiMaggio (eds.), pp. 232–65

Friedman, Menachem 1986. "Charedim Confront the Modern City," *Studies in Contemporary Jewry*, 2: 74–96

1987. "Life Tradition and Book Tradition in the Development of Ultraorthodox Judaism," in Harvey E. Goldberg (ed.), *Judaism Viewed from Without and from Within*. Albany: SUNY Press, pp. 235–55

1988a. *Society and Religion: The Non-Zionist Orthodox in Eretz-Israel – 1918–1936*, 2nd edn. Jerusalem: Ben-Zvi Institute (Hebrew)

1988b. "History of the Status Quo: State and Religion in Israel," in Varda Pilawski (ed.), *Transition from Yishuv to State, 1947–1949: Continuity and Changes*. Haifa: University of Haifa, pp. 47–79 (Hebrew)

1989. "The State of Israel as a Theological Dilemma," in Kimmerling (ed.), pp. 165–215

Friedman, Robert 1979. "The Gush Emunim," *Present Tense*, 7: 25–30

Friedman, Thomas L. 1997. "Exodus," *New York Times*, April 21

Gabay, Yoram and Avi Lavon 1996. "Universalism and Selectivity of Transfer Payments in Israel." Jerusalem: Maurice Falk Institute for Economic Research (Discussion Paper No. 96.11) (Hebrew)

Gal, Johnny and Elazar Leshem 1999. "'Absorption Basket' – Lessons for the Social Security System," *Chevra u-rvacha*, 19: 99–119 (Hebrew)

Galili, Israel 1971. "The Minister's Speech at the Congress of the Labor Party, 1971." Information Department of the Labor Party (mimeo) (Hebrew)

Gaon, Benjamin D. 1992. "The Re-emergence of Koor: A New Way of Doing Business in Israel," remarks to the British–Israel Chamber of Commerce, London, June 25

1993. "Remarks at the Washington Institute's October Policy Conference's Session on 'Beyond Politics: The Potential for Economic Cooperation,'" Washington, DC, October 15–17

1994a. "Remarks at a Reception in Washington and at the Waldorf-Astoria NYC to Celebrate the Conclusion of the International Banking Chapter in the Story of Koor's Restructuring," April 20

1994b. "The Business Opportunities of Peace," written for Giora S. Meyuhas, Israel's economic minister in North America

Gaon, Boaz 1999. "Disillusioned with Sharansky," *Maariv Weekend Magazine*, December 17 (Hebrew)

Gavison, Ruth 1986. *The Ideology of Meir Kahane and his Followers*. Jerusalem: Van Leer Institute (Hebrew)

1995. "A Jewish and Democratic State – Political Identity, Ideology and Law," *Tel Aviv University Law Review*, 19: 631–82

1997. "The Constitutional Revolution: A Reality or a Self-Fulfilling Prophecy?" *Mishpatim*, 28: 21–147

1999. *Can Israel be Both Jewish and Democratic? Tensions and Prospects*. Jerusalem: Hakibbutz Hameuchad (Hebrew)

Gavison, Ruth, Mordechai Kremnitzer, and Yoav Dotan 2000. *Judicial Activism: For and Against; the Role of the High Court of Justice in Israeli Society*. Jerusalem: Magnes (Hebrew)

Gazit, Shlomo 1988. "Policies in the Administered Territories," in Stephen J. Roth (ed.), *The Impact of the Six-Day War: A Twenty-Year Assessment*. London: Macmillan, in association with the Institute of Jewish Affairs, pp. 53–68

Gelber, Yoav 1994. "The Consolidation of Jewish Society in Eretz-Israel, 1936–1947," in *The Period of the British Mandate*, part 2 of *The History of the Jewish Community in Eretz-Israel since 1882*, ed. Moshe Lissak. Jerusalem: Israeli Academy for Sciences and Humanities, pp. 303–463 (Hebrew)

Ghanem, As'ad 1996 (ed.). *Arabs and Jews in Israel: Multi-annual Comparative Data*. Jerusalem: Sikkuy

Ghanem, As'ad and Sarah Ozacky-Lazar 1999. *The Arab Vote to the Fifteenth Knesset* (Studies of Israeli Arabs, no. 24).Givat Haviva: Center for Peace Research (Hebrew)

Ghanem, As'ad, Nadim Rouhana, and Oren Yiftachel 1999. "Questioning 'Ethnic Democracy,'" *Israel Studies*, 3: 253–67

Ghanem, As'ad and Sammy Smooha 2001. Press release. Givat Haviva: Center for Peace Research (mimeo) (Hebrew)

Giladi, Dan 1969. "Private Initiative, National Capital, and the Political Crystallization of the Right-Wing," in S. N. Eisenstadt et al. (eds.), *The Social Structure of Israel*. Jerusalem: Academon (Hebrew), pp. 86–98

Gitelman, Zvi 1995. *Immigration and Identity: The Resettlement and Impact of Soviet Immigrants on Israeli Politics and Identity*. Los Angeles: Susan and David Wilstein Institute of Jewish Policy Studies

Gitelman, Zvi and Ken Goldstein 2001. "The 'Russian' Revolution in Israeli Politics," in Arian and Shamir (eds.), pp. 203–29

Golan, Avirama 1998. "The New Soldiers," *Haaretz New Year's Supplement*, September 20 (Hebrew)

Golan, Matti 1982. *Peres*. Jerusalem: Schocken (Hebrew)

Goldberg, Giora and Efraim Ben-Zadok 1988. "Ethnic Rebellion against the Machine: The Case of Oriental Jews in Israel," *Ethnic Groups*, 7: 205–26

Goldberg, Harvey 1984. *Greentown's Youth: Disadvantaged Youth in a Development Town in Israel*. Assen: Van Gorcum

Gonen, Amiram 2000. *From the Yeshiva to the Workplace: The American Experience and Lessons for Israel*. Jerusalem: Floersheimer Institute for Policy Studies (Hebrew)

Gorni, Yosef 1968. "The Ideology of the Conquest of Labor," *Keshet*, 10, 2: 66–79 (Hebrew)
  1974. "Continuity and Transformation," in *The Raphael Mahler Book*. Merchavia: Sifriat Hapoalim pp. 89–112 (Hebrew)
  1983. *From Rosh Pina and Degania to Dimona: Conversations about the Zionist Settlement Project*. Tel Aviv: Ministry of Defense (Hebrew)

Gramsci, Antonio 1971. *Selections from the Prison Notebooks*, trans. Quintin Hoare and Geoffrey Nowell Smith. New York: International Publishers

Greenberg, Stanley B. 1980. *Race and State in Capitalist Development: Comparative Perspectives*. New Haven: Yale University Press

Greenfeld, Liah 1992. *Nationalism: Five Paths to Modernity*. Cambridge, MA: Harvard University Press

Grinberg, Lev L. 1991. *Split Corporatism in Israel*. Albany: SUNY Press
  1993a. "Peripheral Ethnicity: Trends in Local Representation," in Eisenstadt et al. (eds.), pp. 103–19 (Hebrew)
  1993b. "Ethnic Representation in the Histadrut: Distinct Tracks," in Eisenstadt et al. (eds.), pp. 120–30 (Hebrew)

Gross, Aeyal M. 1998a. "The Politics of Rights in Israeli Constitutional Law," *Israel Studies*, 3: 80–118

1998b. "Property as a Constitutional Right and Basic Law: Human Dignity and Liberty," *Tel Aviv University Law Review*, 21: 405–47 (Hebrew)

2000a. "Democracy, Ethnicity, and Constitutionalism in Israel: Between the 'Jewish State' and the 'Democratic State'" *Israeli Sociology*, 2: 647–73

2000b. "How did 'Free Competition' Become a Constitutional Value? Changes in the Meaning of the Right to Freedom of Occupation," *Tel Aviv University Law Review*, 23: 229–61 (Hebrew)

Gross, Joseph 1994. *Koor Industries Inc.: The Reorganization Process and the Capital Market*. Tel Aviv: Tel Aviv University, School of Management (Hebrew)

Gross, Revital and Shuli Barmali 1996. *Supplementary and Commercial Health Insurance in Israel, 1996*. Jerusalem: Brookdale

Grossman, David 1992. *Present Absentees*. Tel Aviv: Hakibbutz Hameuchad (Hebrew)

Gvati, Chaim 1981. *A Hundred Years of Settlement*, vol. II. Tel Aviv: Hakibbutz Hameuchad (Hebrew)

Gwirtzman, Hayim 1993. "Two in the Same Bath," *Haaretz*, May 16 (Hebrew)

Habib, Jack, Brenda Morginstin, and Allan Zipkin (1998). *Jobs versus Income Support: Integrating Soviet Immigrants into the Israeli Job Market*. Jerusalem: National Insurance Institute (Hebrew)

Haidar, Aziz 1991. *Needs and Welfare Services in the Arab Sector in Israel*. Tel Aviv: International Center for Middle East Peace (Hebrew)

1995. *On the Margins: The Arab Population in the Israeli Economy*. London: Hurst & Co.

al-Haj, Majid 1995. *Education, Empowerment, and Control: The Case of the Arabs in Israel*. Albany: SUNY Press

al-Haj, Majid and Elazar Leshem 2000. *Immigrants from the Former Soviet Union in Israel: Ten Years Later: A Research Report*. Haifa: University of Haifa

al-Haj, Majid and Henry Rosenfeld 1989. "The Emergence of an Indigenous Political Framework in Israel: The National Committee of Chairmen of Arab Local Authorities," *Asian and African Studies*, 23: 205–44

1990. *Arab Local Government in Israel*. Boulder: Westview

Hajar, Lisa 1995. "Authority, Resistance and the Law," Ph.D. thesis, American University

Halevi, Nadav and Ruth Klinov-Malul 1968. *The Economic Development of Israel*. New York: Praeger

Hall, Peter 1986. *Governing the Economy: The Politics of State Intervention in Britain and France*. New York: Oxford University Press

Hamed, Osama A. and Radwan A. Shaban 1993. "One-Sided Customs and Monetary Union: The Case of the West Bank and Gaza Strip under Israeli Occupation," in Fischer et al. (eds.), pp. 117–48

Hammar, Tomas 1990. *Democracy and the Nation State: Aliens, Denizens and Citizens in a World of International Migration*. Aldershot: Avebury

Hareven, Aluf and As'ad Ghanem 1996 (eds.). *Equality and Integration: Annual Report on Progress for 1994–1995*. Jerusalem: Sikkuy

Harris, William Wilson 1980. *Taking Root: Israeli Settlement in the West Bank, the Golan, and Gaza–Sinai, 1967–1980*. New York: Research Studies Press

Hassan, Manar 1991. "Growing up Female and Palestinian in Israel," in Swirski and Safir (eds.), pp. 66–74

Hasson, Shlomo 1981. "Social and Spatial Conflicts: The Settlement Process in Israel during the 1950s and the 1960s," *L'Espace Geographique*, 3: 169–79

  1993. *Urban Social Movements in Jerusalem: The Protest of the Second Generation.* Albany: SUNY Press

Hazan, Reuven 1996. "Presidential Parliamentarism: Direct Popular Election of the Prime Minister, Israel's New Electoral and Political System," *Electoral Studies*, 15: 21–37

  1997a. "The 1996 Intra-party Elections in Israel: Adopting Party Primaries," *Electoral Studies*, 16: 95–103

  1997b. "Executive–Legislative Relations in an Era of Accelerated Reform: Reshaping Government in Israel," *Legislative Studies Quarterly*, 22: 329–50

Hecht, Dina and Nira Yuval-Davis 1978. "Ideology without Revolution: Jewish Women in Israel," *Khamsin*, 6: 97–117

Heilman, Samuel C. 1990. "The Orthodox, the Ultra-Orthodox, and the Elections for the Twelfth Knesset," in Asher Arian and Michal Shamir (eds.), *The Elections in Israel – 1988.* Boulder: Westview, pp. 135–53

Heimberg, (Shitrit) Soli and Isachar Dor 1994. *Characterization and Ranking of Local Authorities by the Socio-economic Level of their Population in 1992.* Jerusalem: Ministry of Construction and Housing and Ministry of the Interior (Hebrew)

Held, David 1989. *Political Theory and the Modern State.* Cambridge: Polity Press

Hemdat 1996. *Free Choice in Marriage.* Jerusalem: Hemdat (Council for Freedom of Science, Religion, and Culture in Israel) (Hebrew)

Herman, Simon N. 1970. *Israelis and Jews: The Continuity of an Identity.* New York: Random House

Herman, Tamar and Ephraim Yuchtman-Yaar 1998. "The Peace Process and the Secular–Religious Cleavage," *Peace in Short*, 1, Tel Aviv University, Tami Steinmetz Center for Peace Studies (Hebrew)

Hershkovitz, Shlomo 2000. "Women in the Senior Staff at the Universities," *Academia*, 7/8: 32–44 (Hebrew)

Herzl, Theodor 1946. *The Jewish State*, ed. Alkow M. Jacob. New York: "Herzl"

Herzog, Hanna 1984. "Ethnicity as a Product of Political Negotiation: The Case of Israel," *Ethnic and Racial Studies*, 7: 517–33

  1985. "Social Construction of Reality in Ethnic Terms: The Case of Political Ethnicity in Israel," *International Review of Modern Sociology*, 15: 45–61

  1986. "Political Factionalism: The Case of Ethnic Lists in Israel," *Western Political Quarterly*, 39: 285–303

  1990. "Midway between Political and Cultural Ethnicity: Analysis of the 'Ethnic Lists' in the 1984 Elections," in Daniel J. Elazar and Shmuel Sandler (eds.), *Israel's Odd Couple: The 1984 Knesset Elections and the National Unity Government.* Detroit: Wayne State University Press, pp. 87–118

  1995. "Penetrating the System: The Politics of Collective Identities," in Asher Arian and Michal Shamir (eds.), *The Elections in Israel – 1992.* Albany: SUNY Press, pp. 81–102

Hess, Amira 1998. "The Water-Carrier's Cellphone does not Stop Ringing," *Haaretz*, July 31 (Hebrew)

Hirschl, Ran 1997. "The 'Constitutional Revolution' and the Emergence of a New Economic Order in Israel," *Israel Studies*, 2: 136–55

    2000a. "The Political Origins of Judicial Empowerment through Constitutionalization: Lessons from Four Constitutional Revolutions," *Law and Social Enquiry*, 25: 91–149

    2000b. "The Great Economic–Judicial Shift: The Legal Arena and the Transformation of Israel's Economic Order," in Shafir and Peled (eds.), pp. 189–215

Histadrut 1993. "The Implications of the Autonomy Agreement on the Economies of Israel and the Territories." Institute for Economic and Social Research (mimeo), December (Hebrew)

Hoffman, Charles 1989. *The Smoke Screen: Israel, Philanthropy and American Jews.* Silver Spring, MD: Eshel Books

Hofnung, Menachem 1991. *Israel – Security Needs versus the Rule of Law.* Jerusalem: Nevo (Hebrew)

    1997. "Authority, Influence, and Separation of Powers – Judicial Review in Israel in Comparative Perspective," *Mishpatim*, 28: 211–38 (Hebrew)

    1998. "The Candidate, the Investor and the Voter: Party Financing and Primaries in the 1996 Elections," in Korn (ed.), pp. 91–115

Horkin, Amir 1993. "Political Mobilization, Ethnicity, Religiosity and Voting for the Shas Movement," MA thesis, Tel Aviv University (Hebrew)

Horovitz, Moshe 1989. *Rabbi Schach.* Jerusalem: Keter (Hebrew)

Horowitz, Dan 1975. *Israel's Concept of Defensible Borders* (Papers on Peace Problems, no. 16). Jerusalem: Hebrew University, Leonard Davis Institute for International Relations

    1993. *The Heavens and the Earth: A Self-Portrait of the 1948 Generation.* Jerusalem: Keter (Hebrew)

Horowitz, Dan and Moshe Lissak 1978. *Origins of the Israeli Polity: Palestine under the Mandate.* Chicago: University of Chicago Press

    1989. *Trouble in Utopia: The Overburdened Polity of Israel.* Albany: SUNY Press

Horowitz, Tamar and Elazar Leshem 1998. "Immigrants from the Soviet Union in the Cultural Space in Israel," in Sikron and Leshem (eds.), pp. 291–330 (Hebrew)

Ikenberry, G. John 1988. "Conclusion: An Institutional Approach to American Foreign Economic Policy," in G. John Ikenberry et al. (eds.), *The State and American Foreign Economic Policy.* Ithaca: Cornell University Press, pp. 219–43

Ilan, Shahar 2000a. *Haredim Ltd.* Jerusalem: Keter (Hebrew)

    2000b. "Going back to Russia, to get Married," *Haaretz*, March 16 (Hebrew)

Immergut, Ellen 1992. "The Rules of the Game: The Logic of Health Care Policy-Making in France, Switzerland, and Sweden," in Steinmo et al. (eds.), pp. 57–89

Inbar, Efraim 1996. "Contours of Israel's New Strategic Thinking," *Political Science Quarterly*, 111: 41–64

Institute for Social and Economic Policy in the Middle East 1993. *Securing Peace in the Middle East: Project on Economic Transition.* Cambridge, MA: John F. Kennedy School of Government, Harvard University

International Management 1974. "Union-Owned Firm Stresses Profits" (February)

Isaac, Rael Jean 1976. *Israel Divided*. Baltimore: Johns Hopkins University Press
    1981. *Party and Politics in Israel*. New York: Longman
Israel Religious Action Center 1992. *Budgeting the Religious Sector in Israel*.
    Jerusalem: Israeli Movement for Progressive Judaism (Hebrew)
    1996. *Hush Money*. Jerusalem: Israel Movement for Progressive Judaism
    (Hebrew)
Israel Women's Network 1997. *Women in Israel: Information and Data*. Jerusalem:
    IWN (Hebrew)
    1998. *Women in the Mirror of the Fiftieth [Anniversary]*. Jerusalem: IWN
    (Hebrew)
Izraeli, Dafna 1992. "The Women Workers' Movement: First Wave Feminism in
    Pre-State Israel," in Deborah S. Bernstein (ed.), *Pioneers and Homemakers:
    Jewish Women in Pre-State Israel*. Albany: SUNY Press, pp. 183–209
    1997. "Gendering Military Service in the Israeli Defense Forces," *Israel Social
    Science Research*, 12: 129–66
Jamal, Amal A. 2000. "Israel's Political Regime: Ethnic Democracy and the
    Critique of Reality," *Israeli Sociology*, 2: 631–45
    forthcoming. "Abstention as Participation in Democratic Elections: On the
    Machinations of Arab Politics in Israel," in Asher Arian and Michal Shamir
    (eds.), *The Elections in Israel – 2001*
Jepperson, Ronald L. 1991. "Institutions, Institutional Effects, and Institution-
    alism," in Powell and DiMaggio (eds.), pp. 143–59
Jerby, Iris 1996. *The Double Price: Women Status and Military Service in Israel*. Tel
    Aviv: Ramot (Hebrew)
Jerusalem Post 1996. Internet edition, November 18 (http://www.jpost.co.il/news/
    news_main_4.html)
Jiryis, Sabri 1976. *The Arabs in Israel*. New York: Monthly Review Press
Jones, Clive 1996. *Soviet Jewish Aliyah, 1989–1992: Impact and Implications for
    Israel and the Middle East*. London: Frank Cass
Jones, Kathleen 1990. "Citizenship in a Woman-Friendly Polity," *Signs*, 15:
    781–812
Kalor, Istvan 1997. "Family Size and Income Inequality in Israel." Jerusalem:
    Maurice Falk Institute for Economic Research in Israel (Discussion Paper
    No. 97.12) (Hebrew)
Kamen, Charles 1987/88. "After the Catastrophe: The Arabs in Israel,
    1948–1951," *Middle Eastern Studies*, 23: 453–95; 24: 68–109
Kaplan, Steven and Hagar Salamon 1998. *Ethiopian Immigrants in Israel:
    Experience and Prospects*. London: Institute for Jewish Policy Research
Kashti, Ur 1997a. "The Ethnic Gap," *Haaretz*, various dates, April–October
    (Hebrew)
    1997b. "The Ethnic Gap: A Clear Class Division," *Haaretz*, May 13 (Hebrew)
    1997c. "The Ethnic Gap: The Melting Pot is not Functioning," *Haaretz*, May
    14 (Hebrew)
    1997d. "The Ethnic Gap: Still a Curiosity," *Haaretz*, June 1 (Hebrew)
    1997e. "The Ethnic Gap: More Units, More Ashkenazim," *Haaretz*, June 17
    (Hebrew)
    1997f. "The Ethnic Gap: First to go Home," *Haaretz*, July 15 (Hebrew)

1997g. "The Ethnic Gap," *News from Within*, 12, 8: 23–7

1997h. "The Ethnic Gap: The Secure Center," *Haaretz*, July 8 (Hebrew)

Kaufman, Ilana 1997. *Arab National Communism in the Jewish State*. Gainesville: University Press of Florida

Kaufman, Ilana and Rachel Israeli 1999. "The Odd Group Out: The Arab-Palestinian Vote in the 1996 Elections," in Arian and Shamir (eds.), pp. 85–115

Kazin, Orna 1998. "Feminism Ltd.," *Haaretz*, March 17 (Hebrew)

Keane, John 1988 (ed.). *Civil Society and the State: New European Perspectives*. London: Verso

Kedar, Alexandre (Sandy) 1998. "Majority Time, Minority Time: Land, Nation and the Laws of Adverse Possession in Israel," *Tel Aviv University Law Review*, 21, 3: 665–746 (Hebrew)

2000. "'A First Step in a Difficult and Sensitive Road': Preliminary Observations on *Qaadan v. Katzir*," *Israel Studies Bulletin*, 16: 3–11

Kelman, Herbert 1998. "Israel in Transition from Zionism to Post-Zionism," *Annals of the American Academy of Political and Social Science*, 555 (*Israel in Transition*): 46–61

Kemp, Adriana, Rebeca Raijman, Julia Resnik, and Silvina Schammah Gesser 2000. "Contesting the Limits of Political Participation: Latinos and Black African Migrant Workers in Israel," *Ethnic and Racial Studies*, 23: 94–119

Keren, Michael 1995. *Professionals against Populism: The Peres Government and Democracy*. Albany: SUNY Press

Khalidi, Raja 1988. *The Arab Economy in Israel: The Dynamics of a Region's Development*. London: Croom Helm

Khanin, Vladimir 2000. "The Rise of 'Russian' Politics in Israel: Elites, Institutions, and Cleavages in the New Immigrant Community," paper presented at the 2000 annual meeting of the Association for Israel Studies, Tel Aviv

forthcoming. "Israeli 'Russian' Parties and the New Immigrant Vote," *Israel Affairs*, 7, 2/3

Khenin, Dov 2000. "Discourse and Hegemony in Mapai and the British Labour Party: Patterns of Change and Continuity," Ph.D. thesis, Tel Aviv University

Kimmerling, Baruch 1983. *Zionism and Territory*. Berkeley: Institute of International Studies

1985a. *The Interrupted System: Israeli Civilians in War and Routine Times*. New Brunswick: Transaction

1985b. "Between the Primordial and the Civil Definitions of the Collective Identity: Eretz Israel or the State of Israel," in Erik Cohen, Moshe Lissak, and Uri Almagor (eds.), *Comparative Social Dynamics: Essays in Honor of S. N. Eisenstadt*. Boulder: Westview, pp. 262–83

1989a (ed.). *The Israeli State and Society: Boundaries and Frontiers*. Albany: SUNY Press

1989b. "Boundaries and Frontiers of the Israeli Control System: Analytical Conclusions," in Kimmerling (ed.), pp. 265–84

1992. "Sociology, Ideology, and Nation-Building: The Palestinians and their Meaning in Israeli Sociology," *American Sociological Review*, 57: 446–60

1994. "Religion, Nationalism and Democracy in Israel," *Zemanim*, 13, 50–1: 116–31

1998. "The New Israelis: Multiple Cultures without Multiculturalism," *Alpayim*, 16: 263–308 (Hebrew)

Kleiman, Ephraim 1967. "The Place of Manufacturing in the Growth of the Israeli Economy," *Journal of Development Studies*, 3, 3 (April): 226–48

1993. "Some Basic Problems of the Economic Relationship between Israel, the West Bank, and Gaza," in Fischer et al. (eds.), pp. 305–55

1997. "The Waning of Israeli *Etatisme*," *Israel Studies*, 2, 2 (Fall): 146–71

Klein, Claude 1997. "After the *Bank Hamizrahi* Case – the Constituent Power as Seen by the Supreme Court," *Mishpatim*, 28: 341–58 (Hebrew)

Klein, David 1996. "Evolving Markets and Institutions in the Wake of Financial Deregulation: The Israeli Case," paper presented at the conference of the Bank for International Settlements, Basle, February 14–15

Klinov, Ruth 1989. "Integrating Private Financing in the Elementary Educational System," *Rivon lekalkala*, 40 (July): 132–6

Klusmeyer, Douglas B. 1996. *Between Consent and Descent: Conceptions of Democratic Citizenship*. Washington: Carnegie Endowment for International Peace

Knesset 1950. *Divre ha-Knesset*, vols. IV–V. Jerusalem: Knesset (Hebrew)

1985. "Bill [to Amend] Basic Law: The Knesset (Amendment No. 12); Penal Code Bill (Amendment No. 24) – 1985," *Divre ha-Knesset*, XLII: 30 (Hebrew)

Kolatt, Israel 1994a. "Ideology and the Impact of Realities upon the Jewish Labor Movement in Palestine, 1905–1919," dissertation, Hebrew University (Hebrew)

1994b. "Religion, Society and State in the Period of the National Home," in Shmuel Almog, Jehuda Reinharz, and Anita Shapira (eds.), *Zionism and Religion*. Jerusalem: Zalman Shazar Center for Jewish History, pp. 329–71 (Hebrew)

Kondor, Ya'acov 1997. *Foreign Workers in Israel: The Problem and its Political–Economic Solution*. Jerusalem: National Insurance Institute, Research and Planning Administration (Hebrew)

Kook, Rebecca 2000. "Towards the Rehabilitation of 'Nation-Building' and the Reconstruction of Nations," in Shlomo Ben-Ami, Yoav Peled, and Alberto Spektorowski (eds.), *Ethnic Challenges to the Modern Nation State*. Basingstoke: Macmillan, pp. 42–64

Koor 1992. "The Making of the New Koor." Tel Aviv: Koor president's office (mimeo)

1994. "Koor Industries 1993 Profits Rose 43 Percent to $124 Million," news release, March 30 (mimeo)

Kop, Yaakov et al. 1986. "Government Expenditure on Social Services," in Yaakov Kop (ed.), *Changing Social Policy: Israel 1985–86*. Jerusalem: Center for Social Policy Studies in Israel, pp. 3–107

Koren, Yehuda 1997. "The Yeshivot Have Turned into Havens for Idlers," *Yediot achronot*, August 15 (Hebrew)

Korn, Dani 1998 (ed.). *The Demise of Parties in Israel*. Tel Aviv: Hakibbutz Hamuechad (Hebrew)

Krasner, Stephen D. 1983. *International Regimes*. Ithaca: Cornell University Press
  1984. "Approaches to the State: Alternative Conceptions and Historical Dynamics," *Comparative Politics*, 16: 223–46
Kraus, Vered and Robert W. Hodge 1990. *Promises in the Promised Land*. New York: Greenwood
Krausz, Ernest 1986. "Edah and 'Ethnic Group' in Israel," *Jewish Journal of Sociology*, 28: 5–18
Kretzmer, David 1990. *The Legal Status of the Arabs in Israel*. Boulder: Westview
  1992. "The New Basic Laws on Human Rights: A Mini-Revolution in Israeli Constitutional Law?" *Israel Law Review*, 26: 238–49
  1997. "The Path to Judicial Review in Human Rights Cases: From *Bergman* and *Kol Ha'am* to *Mizrachi Bank*," *Mishpatim*, 28: 359–85 (Hebrew)
Kurland, Samuel 1947. *Cooperative Palestine: The Story of Histadrut*, foreword by Joseph Schlossberg. New York: Sharon Books; published for the National Committee for Labor Palestine
Kuttab, Jonathan 1988. "Beyond the Intifada: The Struggle to Build a Nation," *The Nation*, October 17
Kuznets, Simon 1963. "Quantitative Aspects of the Economic Growth of Nations: Distribution of Income by Size," *Economic Development and Cultural Change*, 11, 2, part 2
Kymlicka, Will 1989. *Liberalism, Community and Culture*. Oxford: Oxford University Press
  1995. *Multicultural Citizenship*. Oxford: Clarendon Press
  1997. "Do we Need a Liberal Theory of Minority Rights?" *Constellations*, 4: 72–87
Lahav, Pnina 1993. "Rights and Democracy: The Court's Performance," in Ehud Sprinzak and Larry Diamond (eds.), *Israeli Democracy under Stress*. Boulder: Lynne Rienner, pp. 125–52
  2000. "Up against the Wall: Women's Legal Struggle to Pray at the Western Wall in Jerusalem," *Israel Studies Bulletin*, 16: 19–22
Lamar, Howard and Leonard Thompson 1981. *The Frontier in History: North America and Southern Africa Compared*. New Haven: Yale University Press
Landau, David 1993. *Piety and Power: The World of Jewish Fundamentalism*. New York: Hill & Wang
  1996. *Who is a Jew? A Case Study of American Jewish Influence on Israeli Policy*. Jerusalem: American Jewish Committee; Ramat Gan: Bar-Ilan University
Landau, Jacob 1993. *The Arab Minority in Israel*. New York: Oxford University Press
Lane, Yechezkel 1998. "The State, the Business Elite and Coalitions: The Stock Exchange Tax as a Parable," MA thesis, Hebrew University
Lavy, Victor 1988. *Unemployment in Israel's Development Towns*. Jerusalem: Jerusalem Institute for Israel Studies (Hebrew)
Law Yone, Hubert and Rachel Kalush 1995. "Housing Policy," *Israel Equality Monitor*, 4 (Tel Aviv: Adva Center, April) (Hebrew)
Lerman, Robert and Shlomo Yitzhaki 1991. "Income Stratification and Income Equality," *Review of Income and Wealth*, 3 (September): 313–29

Lerner, Abba P. and Haim Ben-Shahar 1975. *The Economics of Efficiency and Growth: Lessons from Israel and the West Bank*. Cambridge, MA: Ballinger

Leshem, Elazar 1994. "Jewishness, Religious Lifestyle and Attitudes on State and Religion Issues among FSU Immigrants," in the *State and Religion Yearbook 1993*. Tel Aviv: Hakibbutz Hameuchad, pp. 36–53 (Hebrew)

  1998. "The Policy of Immigration Absorption and the System of Services for the Immigrants: The Initial Absorption Stage," in Sikron and Leshem (eds.), pp. 41–125 (Hebrew)

Levinsohn, Hanna, Elihu Katz, and Majid al-Haj 1995. *Jews and Arabs in Israel: Common Values and Reciprocal Images*. Jerusalem: Sikkuy

Levy, Gal 1995. "'And Thanks to the *Ashkenazim* . . .': The Politics of *Mizrachi* Ethnicity in Israel," MA thesis, Tel Aviv University (Hebrew)

  (forthcoming). "Ethnicity and Education: Nation Building, State Formation and the Construction of the Israeli National Education System," Ph.D. thesis, London School of Economics

Levy, Gal and Tamar Barkai 1998. "*Yom Hashoah* in Progressive Eyes: Ethnicity, Class and Education in Israel," *Politika*, 1: 27–46

Levy, Shlomit, Hanna Levinsohn, and Elihu Katz 1993. *Beliefs, Observances and Social Relations among the Jews in Israel*. Jerusalem: Guttman Institute for Applied Social Research (Hebrew)

  1997. "Beliefs, Observances and Social Interaction among Israeli Jews," in Liebman and Katz (eds.), pp. 1–37

Levy, Yagil 1995. "How Militarization Drives Political Control of the Military: The Case of Israel," *Political Power and Social Theory*, 11: 103–33

  1997. *Trial and Error: Israel's Route from War to De-escalation*. Albany: SUNY Press

Lewin-Epstein, Noah and Moshe Semyonov 1993. *The Arab Minority in Israel's Economy*. Boulder: Westview

  2000. "Inequality in Home Ownership in Israel: Effects of Migration and Intergenerational Reproduction," paper presented at the Second Taiwan–Israel Sociology Workshop, Taipei

Lewin-Epstein, Noah, Yuval Elmelech, and Moshe Semyonov 1997. "Ethnic Inequality in Home Ownership and the Value of Housing: The Case of Immigrants in Israel," *Social Forces*, 75: 1439–62

Lewin-Epstein, Noah, Yaacov Ro'i and Paul Ritterband 1997 (eds.). *Russian Jews on Three Continents: Migration and Resettlement*. London: Frank Cass

Lewis, Arnold 1985. "Phantom Ethnicity: 'Oriental Jews' in Israeli Society," in Alex Weingrod (ed.), *Studies in Israeli Ethnicity*. New York: Gordon & Breach, pp. 58–133

Liebman, Charles S. 1983. "Extremism as a Religious Norm," *Journal for the Scientific Study of Religion*, 22: 75–86

  1987. "The Religious Component in Israeli Ultra-Nationalism," *Jerusalem Quarterly*, 41: 127–44

  1993. "Attitudes toward Democracy among Israeli Religious Leaders," in Edy Kaufman, Shukri B. Abed, and Robert L. Rothstein (eds.), *Democracy, Peace, and the Israeli–Palestinian Conflict*. Boulder: Lynne Rienner, pp. 135–61

  1995. "Introduction," in Gitelman, *Immigration and Identity*, pp. 5–10

1997a. "Religion and Modernity: The Special Case of Israel," in Liebman and Katz (eds.), pp. 85–102

1997b. "Cultural Conflict in Israeli Society," in Liebman and Katz (eds.), pp. 103–18

Liebman, Charles and Eliezer Don-Yehiya 1983. *Civil Religion in Israel: Traditional Judaism and Political Culture in the Jewish State*. Berkeley: University of California Press

1984. *Religion and Politics in Israel*. Bloomington: Indiana University Press

Liebman, Charles S. and Elihu Katz 1997 (eds.). *The Jewishness of Israelis: Responses to the Guttman Report*. Albany: SUNY Press

Lifshitz, Yaacov 1995. *The Military Industries: Asset or Burden?* Jerusalem: Jerusalem Institute for Israel Studies (Hebrew)

2000. *Defense Economics: The General Theory and the Israeli Case*. Jerusalem: Jerusalem Institute for Israel Studies (Hebrew)

Lisiza, Sabina and Yochanan Peres 2000. "Identity and Integration among Russian Immigrants," *Israeli Sociology*, 3: 7–30 (Hebrew)

Lissak, Moshe 1990. "The Intifada and Israeli Society: An Historical and Sociological Perspective," in Reuven Gal (ed.), *The Seventh War: The Effects of the Intifada on Israeli Society*. Tel Aviv: Hakibbutz Hameuchad, pp. 17–37 (Hebrew)

1995. *Immigrants from the CIS: Between Separatism and Integration*. Jerusalem: Center for the Study of Social Policy in Israel (Hebrew)

1996. "'Critical' Sociology and 'Establishment' Sociology in the Israeli Academic Community: Ideological Struggles or Academic Discourse?" *Israel Studies*, 1: 247–94

1999. *The Mass Immigration in the Fifties: The Failure of the Melting Pot Policy*. Jerusalem: Bialik Institute (Hebrew)

Lustick, Ian 1980. *Arabs in the Jewish State: Israel's Control of a National Minority*. Austin: University of Texas Press

1988. *For the Land and the Lord: Jewish Fundamentalism in Israel*. New York: Council on Foreign Relations

1989. "The Political Road to Binationalism: Arabs in Jewish Politics," in Ilan Peleg and Ofra Seliktar (eds.), *The Emergence of a Binational Israel – the Second Republic in the Making*. Boulder: Westview, pp. 97–123

1990. "The Changing Political Role of Israeli Arabs," in Asher Arian and Michal Shamir (eds.), *The Elections in Israel – 1988*. Boulder: Westview, pp. 115–31

1993a. *Unsettled States, Disputed Lands: Britain and Ireland, France and Algeria, Israel and the West Bank–Gaza*. Ithaca: Cornell University Press

1993b. "Writing the Intifada: Collective Action in the Occupied Territories," *World Politics*, 45: 560–94

1999. "Israel as a Non-Arab State: The Political Implications of Mass Immigration of Non-Jews," *Middle East Journal*, 53: 417–33

Luz, Ehud 1985. *Parallels Meet: Religion and Nationalism in the Early Zionist Movement (1882–1904)*. Tel Aviv: Am Oved (Hebrew)

Mahler, Gregory S. 1990. *Israel: Government and Politics in a Maturing State*. San Diego: Harcourt Brace Jovanovich

Makayes, Rivka 1995. "The Law against Family Violence, 1991," in Raday et al. (eds.), pp. 307–17 (Hebrew)

Malley, Robert and Hussein Agha 2001. "Camp David: The Tragedy of Errors," *New York Review of Books*, 48: 59–65

Mann, Michael 1987. "Ruling Class Strategies and Citizenship," *Sociology*, 21: 339–54

Manpower Planning Authority 2000. *Foreign Workers without Permits in Israel: Estimate for the End of 1999*. Jerusalem: Ministry of Labor and Welfare (Hebrew)

Manufacturers' Association of Israel 1989. *Industry in Israel 1988–1989: A Portrait*. (Hebrew)

   1994. *Survey of the Implications of Autonomy for Industry (October–November 1993)*. MAI Economics and Foreign Trade Department (Hebrew)

   1996. "Globalization in the Israeli Economy." MAI Strategic Planning Committee (Hebrew)

Maor, Anat 1997 (ed.). *Women – the Rising Power: The Promotion of Women at Work – Shattering the "Glass Ceiling."* Dalya: Sifriat Poalim (Hebrew)

Mardon, Russell 1990. "The State and Effective Control of Foreign Capital: The Case of South Korea," *World Politics*, 43: 111–38

Margalit, Avishai 1991. "The Great White Hope," *New York Review of Books*, June 27, pp. 19–28

Margalit, Elkana 1994. *The Israeli Trade Union in the Past and Present: Its Status in the Histadrut and in Society*. Tel Aviv: Ramot (Hebrew)

Margolin, Ron 1999 (ed.). *The State of Israel as a Jewish and Democratic State*. Jerusalem: World Association of Jewish Studies (Hebrew)

Markovski, Nachum 1977. "Jewish Settlement in the Jordan Valley – Planning and Development," in Avshalom Shmueli et al. (eds.), *Judea and Samaria: Chapters in Settlement Geography*, vol. II. Jerusalem: Canaan (Hebrew), pp. 630–9

Marmor, Andre 1997. "Judicial Review in Israel," *Mishpat u-mimshal*, 4: 133–60 (Hebrew)

Marmorstein, Emile 1969. *Heaven at Bay: The Jewish Kulturkampf in the Holy Land*. London: Oxford University Press

Marshall, T. H. 1973 [1949]. "Citizenship and Social Class," in T. H. Marshall, *Class, Citizenship and Social Development*. Westport: Greenwood, pp. 65–122

Mashov 1981. "'Mashov' – Founding Charter." December 28 (mimeo) (Hebrew)

   1983. "First Mashov Conference." April, various documents (mimeo) (Hebrew)

   1985. "Second Mashov Conference." June, various documents (mimeo) (Hebrew)

   1986. "Positions for the Third Mashov Conference." February (mimeo) (Hebrew)

   1987. "Fourth Mashov Conference." April, various documents (mimeo) (Hebrew)

   1989. "Mashov Council on the Histadrut." July (mimeo) (Hebrew)

   1991a. "Proposals Submitted to the Fifth Conference of Mashov" (mimeo) (Hebrew)

1991b. "Resolutions of the Fifth Conference of Mashov." May (mimeo) (Hebrew)

Mautner, Menachem 1993. *The Decline of Formalism and the Rise of Values in Israeli Law*. Tel Aviv: Ma'agalay Da'at (Hebrew)

1994. "The Reasonableness of Politics," *Teorya u-vikoret*, 5: 25–53 (Hebrew)

2000 (ed.). *Distributive Justice in Israel*. Tel Aviv: Ramot (Hebrew)

Mautner, Menachem, Avi Sagi, and Ronen Shamir 1998 (eds.). *Multiculturalism in a Democratic Jewish State*. Tel Aviv: Ramot (Hebrew)

McDowall, David 1989. *Palestine and Israel: The Uprising and Beyond*. Berkeley: University of California Press

Medding, Peter Y. 1990. *The Founding of Israeli Democracy, 1948–1967*. New York: Oxford University Press

Meltz, Judy 1996. "Study: The Basic Salary in the Public Sector – 46 Percent of Total Wages," *Haaretz*, July 15

Meretz 1992. *Meretz Platform: 1992 Elections*. Tel Aviv: Meretz

Meyer, John W. 1994. "The Evolution of Modern Stratification Systems," in David B. Grusky (ed.), *Social Stratification*. Boulder: Westview, pp. 730–7

Meyer, John W. et al. 1997. "World Society and the Nation-State," *American Journal of Sociology*, 103: 144–81

Michael, B. 1984. "How and Why I Became a Settler," *Haaretz Weekly Magazine*, March 2 (Hebrew)

Michaely, Michael 1975. *Foreign Trade Regimes and Economic Development: Israel*, vol. III. New York: Columbia University Press

Migdal, Joel S. 1988. *Strong Societies and Weak States: State–Society Relations and State Capabilities in the Third World*. Princeton: Princeton University Press

Milson, Menachem 1981. "How to Make Peace with the Palestinians," *Commentary*, 71, 5: 25–35

Ministry of Industry and Commerce 1990. *Towards the 1990's: Structural Queries and Directions for Development in Industry*. Center for Planning and Economics (Hebrew)

Morris, Benny 1987. *Birth of the Palestinian Refugee Problem, 1947–1948*. Cambridge: Cambridge University Press

2000. *Jews and Arabs in Palestine/Israel, 1936–1956*. Tel Aviv: Am Oved (Hebrew)

Moskovitch, Wolf 1990. *Rising to the Challenge: Israel and the Absorption of Soviet Jews*. Wellingsborough: Institute for Jewish Affairs

Multinational Business 1989. "Koor Industries: Israel's Conglomerate Restructured," 1: 28–9

Murphy, Emma 1993. "Israel," in Tim Niblock and Emma Murphy (eds.), *Economic and Political Liberalization in the Middle East*. London: British Academy Press, pp. 237–55

Nachmias, David 1991. "Israel's Bureaucratic Elite: Social Structure and Patronage," *Public Administration Review*, 5: 413–20

Nachmias, David and Itai Sened 1999. "The Bias of Pluralism: The Redistributive Effects of the New Electoral Law in Israel's 1996 Elections," in Arian and Shamir (eds.), pp. 269–94

Nahon, Yaacov 1993a. "Educational Expansion and the Structure of Occupational Opportunities," in Eisenstadt et al. (eds.), pp. 33–49 (Hebrew)
  1993b. "Occupational Status," in Eisenstadt et al. (eds.), pp. 50–75 (Hebrew)
  1993c. "Self-Employed Workers," in Eisenstadt et al. (eds.), pp. 76–89 (Hebrew)
  1993d. "Women: Education, Employment and Wages," in Eisenstadt et al. (eds.), pp. 90–102 (Hebrew)
Nairn, Tom 1977. *The Break-up of Britain*. London: New Left Books
Nakdimon, Shlomo, Shaul Maizlish, and Amos Carmel 1988. *On the Way to the Ballot Box: Elections to the Twelfth Knesset – Views and Candidates*. Ramat Gan: Seven Days (Hebrew)
National Insurance Institute 1990. *Annual Survey 1989/90*. Jerusalem: NII, Research and Planning Administration (Hebrew)
  1995. *Annual Survey 1994/95*. Jerusalem: NII, Research and Planning Administration (Hebrew)
  1996. *Annual Survey 1995/96*. Jerusalem: NII, Research and Planning Administration (Hebrew)
  1997. *Annual Survey 1996/97*. Jerusalem: NII, Research and Planning Administration (Hebrew)
  1998. *Annual Survey 1997/98*. Jerusalem: NII, Research and Planning Administration (Hebrew)
  2000. *Annual Survey 1998/99*. Jerusalem: NII, Research and Planning Administration (Hebrew)
Neipris, Joseph 1996. "Some Origins of Social Policy in a New State: The Formation of Policy Concerning Aged Immigrants in Israel, 1948–1955," dissertation, University of California, Berkeley
Neuberger, Benyamin 1991. *Political Parties in Israel*. Tel Aviv: Open University of Israel (Hebrew)
Nini, Yehuda 1996. *Were you Real, or was it a Dream? The Yemenites of Kinneret – the Story of their Settlement and Uprooting, 1912–1930*. Tel Aviv: Am Oved (Hebrew)
Nir, Ori 2001. "A Family Tree of Diseases," *Haaretz*, May 11 (Hebrew)
Nissani, Ezra 1996. "Teach the Children of the Poor to Fish," *Haaretz*, August 11 (Hebrew)
Nordau, Max 1929. *Zionist Writings*, trans. C. Goldberg, ed. P. Lachover. Jerusalem: Mizpah (Hebrew)
North, Douglass C. 1990. *Institutions, Institutional Change, and Economic Performance*. Cambridge: Cambridge University Press
  1998. "Economic Performance through Time," in Mary C. Brinton and Victor Nee (eds.), *The New Institutionalism in Sociology*, New York: Russell Sage, pp. 247–56
Nudelman, Rephael 1997. "In Search of Ourselves," *Soviet Jewry in Transition*, 3, 18: 19–40 (Hebrew)
O'Dea, Janet 1976. "Gush Emunim: Roots and Ambiguities," *Forum on the Jewish People, Zionism, and Israel*, 2, 25: 39–50
Oded, Y. 1964. "Land Losses among Israel's Arab Villages," *New Outlook*, 7: 10–25

Oldfield, Adrian 1990. *Citizenship and Community: Civic Republicanism and the Modern World*. London: Routledge

"One-Hundred-Thousand Plan for the Year 1985 (Part of the Master Plan for Settlement Development in Samaria and Judea: A Conceptual Framework)." World Zionist Organization – Settlement Division, October 1981 (Hebrew)

Ophir, Adi 2001. *Real Time: Al-Aqsa Intifada and the Israeli Left*. Jerusalem: Keter (Hebrew)

Oren, Michal 1983. "Horseshoe in the Glove: Milson's Year in the West Bank," *Middle East Review*, 16: 17–29

Ottolenghi, Emanuele 2001. "Banning Torture in Israel: A New Trend in Human Rights Jurisprudence," *Hagar*, 2: 93–117

Oz, Amos 1984. *In the Land of Israel*, trans. Maurie Goldberg-Bartura. New York: Vintage

Ozacky-Lazar, Sarah and As'ad Ghanem 1996. *Arab Voting Patterns in the Fourteenth Knesset Elections, 29 May 1996*. Givat Haviva: Center for Peace Research (Studies of Israeli Arabs, no. 19) (Hebrew)

Ozanne, Julian 1995. "Koor Raises Almost $120m in Successful IPO," *Financial Times*, November 14

Palgi, Michal 1991. "Motherhood in the Kibbutz," in Swirski and Safir (eds.), pp. 261–7

Paltiel, Ari M., Eitan F. Sabatello, and Dorith Tal 1997. "Immigrants from the Former USSR in Israel in the 1990s: Demographic Characteristics and Socio-economic Absorption," in Lewin-Epstein et al. (eds.), pp. 284–321

Pankhurst, Richard D. 1997. "Beta Israel (the Falasha) in their Ethiopian Context," in Shalva Weil (ed.), *Ethiopian Jews in the Limelight*. Jerusalem: School of Education, the Hebrew University (Hebrew), pp. 13–48

Pappé, Ilan 1992. *The Making of the Arab–Israeli Conflict, 1947–1951*. London: I. B. Tauris

  1999 (ed.). *The Israel/Palestine Question*. London and New York: Routledge

Passell, Peter 1992a. "Zionist Dreams, Capitalist Reality," *New York Times*, January 1

  1992b. "Need Zionism Equal Socialism?" *New York Times*, July 2

Peace Now n.d. "Building in the Settlements during the Labor–Meretz Government." Settlement Tracking Report, No. 8 (mimeo) (Hebrew)

Pedatzur, Reuven 1992. "The Influence of 'Decision Kitchens' on National Security Decision Making: The Eshkol Government and the Territories, 1967–1969," Ph.D. thesis, Tel Aviv University (Hebrew)

Peled, Yoav 1989. *Class and Ethnicity in the Pale: The Political Economy of Jewish Workers' Nationalism in Late Imperial Russia*. Basingstoke: Macmillan

  1990. "Ethnic Exclusionism in the Periphery: The Case of Oriental Jews in Israel's Development Towns," *Ethnic and Racial Studies*, 13: 345–67

  1992. "Ethnic Democracy and the Legal Construction of Citizenship: Arab Citizens of the Jewish State," *American Political Science Review*, 86: 432–43

  1998. "Towards a Redefinition of Jewish Nationalism in Israel? The Enigma of Shas," *Ethnic and Racial Studies*, 21: 703–27

  2001 (ed.). *Shas – the Challenge of Israeliness*. Tel Aviv: Yediot Achronot (Hebrew)

Peled, Yoav and José Brunner 2000. "Culture is not Enough: A Democratic Critique of Liberal Multiculturalism," in Shlomo Ben-Ami, Yoav Peled, and Alberto Spektorowski (eds.), *Ethnic Challenges to the Modern Nation State.* Basingstoke: Macmillan, pp. 65–92

Peled, Yoav and Adi Ophir 2001 (eds.). *Israel: From Mobilizational to Civil Society?* Tel Aviv: Hakibbutz Hameuchad (Hebrew)

Peled, Yoav and Gershon Shafir 1987. "Split Labor Market and the State: The Effects of Modernization on Jewish Industrial Workers in Tsarist Russia," *American Journal of Sociology,* 92: 1435–60

1996. "The Roots of Peacemaking: The Dynamics of Citizenship in Israel, 1948–93," *International Journal of Middle East Studies,* 28: 391–413

Peleg, Dov 1999. *Social Security for Foreign Workers: The International Experience.* Jerusalem: Ministry of Labor and Welfare, Manpower Planning Authority (Hebrew)

Pempel, T. J. 1992. "Restructuring Social Coalitions: State, Society, Regime," in Rolf Torstendahl (ed.), *State Theory and State History.* London: Sage, pp. 118–48

Peres, Shimon 1993. *The New Middle East.* New York: H. Holt

Peres, Yochanan 1995. "Religious Adherence and Political Attitudes," in Shlomo Deshen, Charles S. Liebman, and Moshe Shokeid (eds.), *Israeli Judaism: The Sociology of Religion in Israel* (Studies of Israeli Society, no. 7). New Brunswick: Transaction, pp. 87–106

Peretz, Don 1986. *The West Bank: History, Politics, Society, and Economy.* Boulder: Westview

1990. *Intifada: The Palestinian Uprising.* Boulder: Westview

Peri, Yoram 1993. "Two Worlds, Two Planets," *Davar,* May 3 (Hebrew)

Piore, Michael J. 1979. *Birds of Passage: Migrant Labor and Industrial Societies.* Cambridge: Cambridge University Press

Plotzker, Sever 1997. "Ne'eman: I will Stop the Parasitism of *Yeshiva* Students," *Yediot achronot,* August 29 (Hebrew)

Pocock, J. G. A. 1998. "The Idea of Citizenship since Classical Times," in Shafir (ed.), pp. 31–41

Pope, Juliet J. 1991. "Conflict of Interest: A Case Study of Na'amat," in Swirski and Safir (eds.), pp. 225–33

Powell, Walter W. and Paul J. DiMaggio 1991 (eds.). *The New Institutionalism in Organizational Analysis.* Chicago: University of Chicago Press

"Protocol on Economic Relations between the Government of Israel and the PLO. Representing the Palestinian People" 1995. *Rivon lekalkala,* 42: 160–79 (Hebrew)

Raanan, Tsvi 1980. *Gush Emunim.* Tel Aviv: Sifriat Poalim (Hebrew)

Rabin, Yitzhak 1979. *Service Diary.* Tel Aviv: Maariv (Hebrew)

Rabinowitz, Dan 1997. *Overlooking Nazareth: The Ethnography of Exclusion in Galilee.* Cambridge: Cambridge University Press

Rabinowitz, Danny 2001. "Opening the Debate on the Refugee Issues," *Haaretz,* January 4 (Hebrew)

Rabinowitz, Dan, As'ad Ghanem, and Oren Yiftachel 2000 (eds.). *After the Rift: New Directions for Government Policy towards the Arabs in Israel.* Tel Aviv: Inter-University Research Group

Raday, Frances 1996. "Religion, Multiculturalism and Equality: The Israeli Case," *Israel Yearbook on Human Rights*, vol. XXV, pp. 193–241

Raday, Frances, Carmel Shalev, and Michal Liban-Kooby 1995 (eds.). *Women's Status in Israeli Law and Society*. Jerusalem: Schocken (Hebrew)

Rahat, Gideon and Neta Sher-Hadar 1999. "The Party Primaries and their Consequences," in Arian and Shamir (eds.), pp. 241–68

Ram, Uri 1993. "Emerging Modalities of Feminist Sociology in Israel," *Israel Social Science Research*, 8, 2: 51–88

   1995. *The Changing Agenda of Israeli Sociology: Theory, Ideology, and Identity*. Albany: SUNY Press

   1996. "Memory and Identity: The Sociology of the Historians' Debate in Israel," *Teorya u-vikoret*, 8: 9–32

Ravitzki, Aviezer 1993. *Messianism, Zionism and Jewish Religious Radicalism*. Tel Aviv: Am Oved (Hebrew)

Rawls, John 1971. *A Theory of Justice*. Cambridge, MA: Belknap Press

   1993. *Political Liberalism*. New York: Columbia University Press

Razin, Assaf and Efraim Sadka 1993. *The Economy of Modern Israel: Malaise and Promise*. Chicago: University of Chicago Press

Reiff, Marian Freda 1997. "Immigration and Medicine: Stress, Culture and Power in Encounters between Ethiopian Immigrants and their Doctors in Israel," Ph.D. thesis, Columbia University

Reiner, Efraim 1992. "Separate and Coordinated Economies," *Haaretz*, July 8 (Hebrew)

Report on Israeli Settlement in the Occupied Territories, various dates

Rinawi, Halil 1996. "Structural Obstacles to Education amongst the Palestinian Population in Israel," *Israel Equality Monitor*, 6. Tel Aviv: Adva Center

Robinson, Jacob 1947. *Palestine and the United Nations: Prelude to Solution*. Washington, DC: Public Affairs Press

Roche, Maurice 1987. "Citizenship, Social Theory and Social Change," *Theory and Society*, 16: 363–99

   1992. *Rethinking Citizenship: Welfare, Ideology, and Change in Modern Society*. Cambridge: Polity Press

Roediger, David R. 1991. *The Wages of Whiteness: Race and the Making of the American Working Class*. London: Verso

Rolnik, Guy 1995. "Ten Years after the Reform – the Public Discovered it," *Haaretz*, February 2 (Hebrew)

Rosen, Howard 1991. "Economic Consequences of the Intifada in Israel and the Administered Territories," in Robert O. Freedman (ed.), *The Intifada: Its Impact on Israel, the Arab World, and the Super-Powers*. Miami: Florida International University Press, pp. 370–95

Rosenhek, Zeev 1996. "The Historical Roots of the Israeli Welfare State and the Zionist–Palestinian Conflict," paper presented at the conference of the Association for Israel Studies, Boston University, June 1–3, 1996

   1998. "New Developments in the Sociology of Palestinian Citizens in Israel: An Analytical Review," *Ethnic and Racial Studies*, 21: 558–78

   2000. "Migration Regimes, Intra-state Conflicts, and the Politics of Exclusion and Inclusion: Migrant Workers in the Israeli Welfare State," *Social Problems*, 47: 49–67

Rosenhek, Zeev and Michael Shalev 2000. "The Contradictions of Palestinian Citizenship in Israel: Inclusion and Exclusion in the Israeli Welfare State," in Nils A. Butenschon, Uri Davis, and Manuel Hassassian (eds.), *Citizenship and the State in the Middle East: Approaches and Applications.* Syracuse, NY: Syracuse University Press, pp. 288–315

Rosental, Ruvik 2000 (ed.). *Kafr Kassem: Events and Myth.* Bnei-Brak: Hakibbutz Hameuchad (Hebrew)

Ross, Tamar 1996. "Between Metaphysical and Liberal Pluralism: A Reappraisal of Rabbi A. I. Kook's Espousal of Toleration," *AJS Review*, 21: 61–110

Rossant, John 1989. "Israel has Everything it Needs – Except Peace," *Business Week*, December 9

Rouhana, Nadim 1987. "Collective Identity and Arab Voting Patterns," in Asher Arian and Michal Shamir (eds.), *The Elections in Israel – 1984.* Tel Aviv: Ramot, pp. 121–49

    1989. "The Political Transformation of the Palestinians in Israel," *Journal of Palestine Studies*, 18: 38–59

    1991. "Palestinians in Israel: Responses to the Uprising," in Brynen (ed.), pp. 97–117

    1997. *Palestinian Citizens in an Ethnic Jewish State: Identities in Conflict.* New Haven: Yale University Press

Rubinstein, Amnon 1977. *To be a Free Nation.* Tel Aviv: Schocken (Hebrew)

    1980. *From Herzl to Gush Emunim and Back.* Jerusalem: Schocken (Hebrew)

    1982. *A Certain Political Experience.* Jerusalem: Idanim (Hebrew)

    1996. "The Cost of *Yeshiva* Students," *Haaretz*, December 26 (Hebrew)

    1997a. "More Earners Less Poverty," *Haaretz*, January 6 (Hebrew)

    1997b. "Under the Guise of Equality," *Haaretz*, August 28 (Hebrew)

Rubinstein, Danny 1982. *On the Lord's Side: Gush Emunim.* Tel Aviv: Hakibbutz Hameuchad (Hebrew)

Saban, Ilan 1996. "The Influence of the Supreme Court on the Status of the Arabs in Israel," *Mishpat u-mimshal*, 3: 541–69 (Hebrew)

Sachar, Howard M. 1987. *A History of Israel*, vol. II: *From the Aftermath of the Yom Kippur War.* New York: Oxford University Press

el-Sadat, Anwar 1977. *In Search of Identity.* New York: Harper & Row

Sa'di, Ahmad H. 1996. "Minority Resistance to State Control: Towards a Re-analysis of Palestinian Political Activity in Israel," *Social Identities*, 2: 395–412

    1997. "Poverty among Arab Children in Israel: A Question of Citizenship," in Johnny Gal (ed.), *Poor Children in Israel.* Jerusalem: National Council for Child Welfare, pp. 29–38 (Hebrew)

    2000. "Israel as Ethnic Democracy: What are the Implications for the Palestinian Minority?" *Arab Studies Quarterly*, 22: 25–37

Safir, Marilyn P. 1991a. "Religion, Tradition and Public Policy Give Family First Priority," in Swirski and Safir (eds.), pp. 57–65

    1991b. "Was the Kibbutz an Experiment in Social and Sex Equality?" in Swirski and Safir (eds.), pp. 251–60

Sandel, Michael J. 1982. *Liberalism and the Limits of Justice.* Cambridge: Cambridge University Press

1984. "The Procedural Republic and the Unencumbered Self," *Political Theory*, 12: 81–96

Sandler, Shmuel 1981. "The National Religious Party: Towards a New Role in Israel's Political System," in Sam N. Lehman-Wilzig and Bernard Susser (eds.), *Public Life in Israel and the Diaspora*. Jerusalem: Bar-Ilan University Press, pp. 158–70

Sarvasy, Wendy 1997. "Social Citizenship from a Feminist Perspective," *Hypetia*, 12: 54–73

Savir, Uri 1998. *The Process behind the Scenes of an Historic Decision*. Tel Aviv: Yediot Achronot (Hebrew)

Schecter, Stephen B. 1972. "Israeli Political and Economic Elites and Some Aspects of their Relations," Ph.D. thesis, London School of Economics

Schiff, Gary 1977. *Tradition and Politics: The Religious Parties of Israel*. Detroit: Wayne University Press

Schmelz, Uziel O., Sergio Delapergola, and Uri Avner 1991. *Ethnic Differences among Israeli Jews: A New Look*. Jerusalem: Institute of Contemporary Jewry, the Hebrew University

Schnell, Isaac forthcoming. "The Crystallization of a Foreign Workers' Space in South Tel Aviv," *Ofakim Begeografia* (Hebrew)

Schwartz, Dov 1996. *The Theology of the Religious Zionist Movement*. Tel Aviv: Am Oved (Hebrew)

Schwartz Greenwald, Carol 1972. *Recession as a Policy Instrument: Israel 1965–1969*. London: C. Hurst & Co.

Seligman, Adam 1992. *The Idea of Civil Society*. New York: Free Press

1995. "Animadversions upon Civil Society and Civic Virtue in the Last Decade of the Twentieth Century," in John Hall (ed.), *Civil Society: Theory, History, Comparison*. Cambridge: Polity Press, pp. 200–23

Semyonov, Moshe and Noah Lewin-Epstein 1987. *Hewers of Wood and Drawers of Water: Noncitizen Arabs in the Israeli Labor Market*. Ithaca: ILR Press

Semyonov, Moshe and Ephraim Yuchtman-Yaar 1992. "Ethnicity, Education, and Occupational Inequality: Jews and Arabs in Israel," *International Perspectives on Education and Society*, 2: 215–24

Shachar, Arie and Maya Choshen 1993. "Israel among the Nations: A Developed World and the Developing World," *Mechkarim begeografia shel Eretz-yisrael* [Studies in the Geography of the Land of Israel), 14: 312–24 (Hebrew)

Shachar, Ayelet 1993. "The Sexuality of Law: The Legal Discourse about Rape," *Tel Aviv University Law Review*, 18, 1: 159–99

Shafir, Gershon 1984. "Changing Nationalism and Israel's 'Open Frontier' on the West Bank," *Theory and Society*, 13: 803–27

1989. *Land, Labor and the Origins of the Israeli–Palestinian Conflict, 1882–1914*. Cambridge: Cambridge University Press

1990. "The Meeting of Eastern Europe and Yemen: 'Idealist Workers' and 'Natural Workers' in Early Zionist Settlement in Palestine," *Ethnic and Radial Studies*, 13: 172–97

1995. "Zionist Immigration and Colonization in Palestine until 1948," in *Cambridge Survey of World Migrations*. Cambridge: Cambridge University Press, pp. 405–9

1996a. "Preface to the Paperback Edition," in Gershon Shafir, *Land, Labor and the Origins of the Israeli–Palestinian Conflict, 1882–1914*, updated edn. Berkeley: University of California Press, pp. ix–xix

1996b. "Israeli Society: A Counterview," *Israel Studies*, 1, 2: 189–213

1996c. "Zionism and Colonialism: A Comparative Approach," in Barnett (ed.), pp. 227–42

1998 (ed.). *The Citizenship Debates: A Reader*. Minneapolis: University of Minnesota Press

1999. "The Jarring Mission," in Adi Ophir (ed.), *Fifty to Forty-Eight: Critical Moments in the History of the State of Israel*. Jerusalem: Van Leer Institute, pp. 205–13 (Hebrew)

Shafir, Gershon and Yoav Peled 1986. "'Thorns in your Eyes': The Socioeconomic Basis of the Kahane Vote," in Asher Arian and Michal Shamir (eds.), *The Elections in Israel – 1984*. Tel Aviv: Ramot, pp. 115–30

1998. "Citizenship and Stratification in an Ethnic Democracy," *Ethnic and Racial Studies*, 21: 408–27

2000 (eds.). *The New Israel: Peacemaking and Liberalization*. Boulder: Westview

Shalev, Carmel 1993. "Justice in the Family and the Principle of Gender Equality against the Background of the Proposed Basic Law: Human Rights," *Ha-mishpat*, 3: 40–5 (Hebrew)

Shalev, Michael 1984. "Labor, State and Crisis," *Industrial Relations*, 23: 362–86

1990. "The Political Economy of Labor Party Dominance and Decline in Israel," in T. J. Pempel (ed.), *Uncommon Democracies: The One-Party Dominant Regimes*. Ithaca: Cornell University Press, pp. 83–127

1992. *Labour and the Political Economy in Israel*. Oxford: Oxford University Press

1993. "The Death of the 'Bureaucratic' Labor Market? Structural Change in the Israeli Political Economy," unpublished paper, Department of Sociology, Hebrew University, Jerusalem

1996. "The Labor Movement in Israel: Ideology and Political Economy," in E. J. Goldberg (ed.), *The Social History of Labor in the Middle East*. Boulder: Westview, pp. 131–61

2000. "Liberalization and the Transformation of the Political Economy," in Shafir and Peled (eds.), pp. 129–59

Shalev, Michael, with Sigal Kis 2001. "Social Cleavages among Non-Arab Voters: New Analysis," in Arian and Shamir (eds.), 2001, pp. 91–134

Shalit, David 1996. "Even Menachem Begin Opposed it," *Haaretz Weekly Magazine*, August 30, pp. 46–50 (Hebrew)

Shamir, Jacob and Michal Shamir 2000. *The Anatomy of Public Opinion*. Ann Arbor: University of Michigan Press

Shamir, Michal and Asher Arian 1997. "Collective Identity and Electoral Competition in Israel," *American Political Science Review*, 93: 265–77

Shamir, Ronen 1990. "Landmark Cases and the Reproduction of Legitimacy: The Case of Israel's High Court of Justice," *Law and Society Review*, 24: 781–805

1994. "The Politics of Reasonableness: Reasonableness and Judicial Power at Israel's Supreme Court," *Teorya u-vikoret*, 5: 7–23 (Hebrew)

Shapira, Anita 1977. *Futile Struggle: Hebrew Labor, 1929–1939*. Tel Aviv: Tel Aviv University and Hakibbutz Hameuchad (Hebrew)

1984. "Gedud ha-Avodah: A Dream that Failed," *Jerusalem Quarterly*, 30: 62–76

1991. "The Religious Motifs of the Labour Movement," in Rina Shapira and Arye Kasher (eds.), *Reshafim – Historical, Philosophical, and Social Aspects of Education*. Tel Aviv: Tel Aviv University (Hebrew)

1992. *Land and Power: The Zionist Resort to Force*, trans. William Templer. New York: Oxford University Press

Shapiro, Yonathan 1976. *The Formative Years of the Israeli Labour Party: The Organization of Power, 1919–1930*. London: Sage

1977. *Democracy in Israel*. Ramat Gan: Massada (Hebrew)

1980. "Epilogue," in Shira (ed.), pp. 100–192 (Hebrew)

1984. *An Elite without Successors: Generations of Political Leaders in Israel*. Tel Aviv: Sifriat Poalim (Hebrew)

1985. "Political Sociology in Israel: A Critical Review," in Ernest Krausz (ed.), *Politics and Society in Israel: Studies in Israeli Society*, vol. III. New Brunswick: Transaction, pp. 6–16

1989. *Chosen to Command: The Road to Power of the Herut Party – A Socio-political Interpretation*. Tel Aviv: Am Oved (Hebrew)

1996a. *Politicians as a Hegemonic Class: The Case of Israel*. Tel Aviv: Sifriat Poalim (Hebrew)

1996b. "Where Have the Liberal Movements and the Liberal Idea in Israel Gone?" *Zemanim*, 55: 92–101 (Hebrew)

Shapiro, Yonathan and Lev L. Grinberg 1988. "The Full Employment Crisis: A Chapter in Israel's Political Economy." Tel Aviv: Tel Aviv University, Golda Meir Institute for Social and Labour Research (Discussion Paper No. 45) (Hebrew)

Sharoni, Simona 1995. *Gender and the Israeli–Palestinian Conflict: The Politics of Women's Resistance*. Syracuse, NY: Syracuse University Press

Shavit, Ari 1997. "The Last European," interview with Shlomo Ben-Ami, *Haaretz Weekly Magazine*, May 23 (Hebrew)

Shavit, Yossi 1990. "Segregation, Tracking, and the Educational Attainment of Minorities: Arabs and Mizrahi Jews in Israel," *American Sociological Review*, 55: 115–26

1992. "Arabs in the Israeli Economy: A Study of the Enclave Hypothesis," *Israel Social Science Research*, 7–8: 45–66

Shavit, Yossi, Yinon Cohen, Haya Steier, and Svetlana Bulotin 2000. "Ethnic Inequality in University Education in Israel," in Mautner (ed.), pp. 391–408 (Hebrew)

Shavit, Yossi and Ephraim Yuchtman-Yaar 2000. "Self-Employment and Social Mobility in Israel," paper presented at the Second Taiwan–Israel Sociology Workshop, Taipei

Shelef, Leon 1993. "Activism Stops at the Green Line: In the Highways and Byways of the High Court of Justice Adjudication in the [Occupied] Territories," *Tel Aviv University Law Review*, 17: 757–809

Shifer, Shimon 1984. *Snow Ball: Secrets of the Lebanon War*. Tel Aviv: Yediot Achronot (Hebrew)

Shifman, Pinhas 1995. *Civil Marriage in Israel: The Case for Reform*. Jerusalem: Jerusalem Institute for Israel Studies (Research Series no. 62) (Hebrew)

Shira, Ben-Zion 1980 (ed.). *The Shinuy Movement: From Protest to Party*. Tel Aviv: Shira Public Relations (Hebrew)

Shklar, Judith N. 1991. *American Citizenship: The Quest for Inclusion*. Cambridge, MA: Harvard University Press

Shochat, Orit 1998. "The Beautiful, Wasted Years," *Haaretz New Year Supplement*, September 20 (Hebrew)

Shohat, Ella 1988. "Sephardim in Israel: Zionism from the Point of View of its Jewish Victims," *Social Text*, 7: 1–35

Shokeid, Moshe 1984. "Cultural Ethnicity in Israel: The Case of Middle Eastern Jews' Religiosity," *AJS Review*, 9: 247–71

1993. "Ethnic Identity and the Position of Women among Arabs in an Israeli Town," in Azmon and Izraeli (eds.), pp. 423–41

Sikkuy 1996. *Equality and Integration: Retrospect and Prospects, 1992–1996*. Jerusalem: Sikkuy, the Association for the Advancement of Equal Opportunity

2000. *Sikkuy's Report on Equality and Integration of the Arab Citizens in Israel 1999–2000*. Jerusalem: Sikkuy (Hebrew)

Sikron, Moshe 1998. "The Immigrants' Human Capital and the Processes of their Labor [Market] Integration," in Sikron and Leshem (eds.), pp. 127–81 (Hebrew)

Sikron, Moshe and Elazar Leshem 1998 (eds.). *Portrait of an Aliyah: The Processes of Absorbing the Immigrants from the Former Soviet Union, 1990–1995*. Jerusalem: Magnes (Hebrew)

Silberstein, Laurence J. 1996. "New Historians and Critical Sociologists between Post-Zionism and Postmodernism," *Teorya u-vikoret*, 8: 105–22 (Hebrew)

1998. *The Postzionism Debate: Knowledge and Power in Israeli Culture*. New York: Routledge

Silver, Beverly 1990. "The Contradictions of Semiperipheral 'Success': The Case of Israel," in William G. Martin (ed.), *Semiperipheral States in the World-Economy*. New York: Greenwood, pp. 161–81

Smith, Rogers M. 1988. "The 'American Creed' and American Identity: The Limits of American Citizenship in the United States," *Western Political Quarterly*, 41: 225–51

1997. *Civic Ideals: Conflicting Visions of Citizenship in US History*. New Haven: Yale University Press

Smooha, Sammy 1978. *Israel: Pluralism and Conflict*. Berkeley: University of California Press

1984a. "Three Perspectives in the Sociology of Ethnic Relations in Israel," *Megamot*, 28: 169–206 (Hebrew)

1984b. "Ethnicity and the Military in Israel: Theses for Discussion and Study," *Medina, mimshal veyachasim benleumiyim*, 22: 5–32 (Hebrew)

1989. *Arabs and Jews in Israel*, vol. I: *Conflicting and Shared Attitudes in a Divided Society*. Boulder: Westview

1990. "Minority Status in an Ethnic Democracy: The Status of the Arab Minority in Israel," *Ethnic and Racial Studies*, 13: 389–413

1992. *Arabs and Jews in Israel*, vol. II: *Change and Continuity in Mutual Tolerance*. Boulder: Westview

1993a. "Class, Ethnic, and National Cleavages and Democracy in Israel," in Ehud Sprinzak and Larry Diamond (eds.), *Israeli Democracy under Stress*. Boulder: Lynne Rienner, pp. 309–42

1993b. "Class, Ethnic and National Cleavages and Democracy in Israel," in Uri Ram (ed.), *Israeli Society: Critical Perspectives*. Tel Aviv: Breirot, pp. 172–202 (Hebrew)

1994a. "Arab–Jewish Relations in Israel in the Peace Era," *Israel Affairs*, 1: 227–44

1994b, "An Outline for Discussion of the Impact of the Mass Immigration from the Commonwealth of Independent Nations on Israeli Society," *Sociologiya*, 13: 6–7 (Hebrew)

1995. "Ethnic Democracy as a Mode of Conflict-Regulation in Deeply Divided Societies," paper delivered at the conference on the New Politics of Ethnicity, Self-determination, and the Crisis of Modernity, at the Morris E. Curiel Center for International Studies, Tel Aviv University, May 30–June 1, 1995

1997. "Ethnic Democracy: Israel as an Archetype," *Israel Studies*, 2: 198–241

1998a. "The Implications of the Transition to Peace for Israeli Society," *Annals of the American Academy of Political and Social Science*, 555 (*Israel in Transition*): 26–45

1998b. "Israelization of the Collective Identity and the Political Orientation of the Palestinian Citizens of Israel – a Re-examination," in Eli Rekhes (ed.), *The Arabs in Israeli Politics: Dilemmas of Identity*. Tel Aviv: Tel Aviv University, pp. 41–53 (Hebrew)

1999. *Autonomy for the Arabs in Israel?* Raanana: Institute for Israeli Arab Studies (Hebrew)

2000. "The State of Israel's Regime: A Liberal Democracy, a Non-democracy, or an Ethnic Democracy?" *Israeli Sociology*, 2: 535–630

Sofer, Sasson 1998. *Zionism and the Foundations of Israeli Diplomacy*. Cambridge: Cambridge University Press

Sommers, Margaret R. 1993. "Citizenship and the Place of the Public Sphere: Law, Community, and the Political Culture of the Transition to Democracy," *American Sociological Review*, 58: 587–620

Sontag, Deborah 2001. "Quest for Middle East Peace: How and Why it Failed," *New York Times*, July 26

Soysal, Yasemin Nuhoglu 1994. *The Limits of Citizenship: Migrants and Postnational Membership in Europe*. Chicago: University of Chicago Press

1997. "Changing Parameters of Citizenship and Claims-Making: Organized Islam in European Public Spheres," *Theory and Society*, 26: 509–27

Spilerman, Seymour 1996. "Bequest of Economic Assets – Apartment Ownership," in Yaakov Kop (ed.), *The Allocation of Resources for Social Services, 1996*. Jerusalem: Center for the Study of Social Policy in Israel, pp. 99–119 (Hebrew)

Sprinzak, Ehud 1991. *The Ascendance of Israel's Radical Right*. New York: Oxford University Press

Spulber, Nicolas 1997. *Redefining the State: Privatization and Welfare Reform in Industrial and Transitional Economies*. Cambridge: Cambridge University Press

Starr, Paul 1982. *The Social Transformation of American Medicine*. New York: Basic Books

State Comptroller 1995. *Annual Report [No.] 45*. Jerusalem (Hebrew)

   1998. *Annual Report [No.] 48, for 1997 and the Accounts of Fiscal Year 1996*. Jerusalem (Hebrew)

State Revenue Administration 1994. *Annual Report*. Jerusalem (Hebrew)

   1995. *Annual Report*. Jerusalem (Hebrew)

Steinberg, Gerald M. 2000. " 'The Poor in your own City Shall Have Precedence': A Critique of the Katzir–Qaadan Case and Opinion," *Israel Studies Bulletin*, 16: 12–18

Steinmo, Sven, Kathleen Thelen, and Frank Longstreth 1992. *Structuring Politics: Historical Institutionalism in Comparative Analysis*. Cambridge: Cambridge University Press

Stendel, Ori 1996. *The Arabs in Israel*. Brighton: Sussex Academic Press

Sternhell, Zeev 1998. *The Founding Myths of Israel: Nationalism, Socialism, and the Making of the Jewish State*, trans. David Maisel. Princeton: Princeton University Press

   1999. "Yonathan Shapiro: Father of Critical Research," *Israeli Sociology*, 2: 11–21 (Hebrew)

Susser, Baruch and Eliezer Don-Yehiya 1994. "Israel and the Decline of the Nation State in the West," *Modern Judaism*, 14: 171–92

Sussman, Zvi 1974. *Equality and Inequality in the Histadrut*. Ramat Gan: Massada (Hebrew)

   1996. "More Budget, More Poor People," *Haaretz*, February 2

   1998. "The Effect of the Immigration from the Soviet Union on the Economic Situation of the Veteran Israeli Population," in Sikron and Leshem (eds.), pp. 182–206 (Hebrew)

Sussman, Zvi and Zakai, Dan 1985. *Changes in the Wage Structure of the Civil Service and Rising Inflation – Israel: 1974–81*, Jerusalem: Bank of Israel Research Department

Swirski, Barbara 1991a. "Israeli Feminism New and Old," in Swirski and Safir (eds.), pp. 285–302

   1991b. "Jews Don't Batter their Wives: Another Myth Bites the Dust," in Swirski and Safir (eds.), pp. 319–27

   2000. "The Citizenship of Jewish and Palestinian Arab Women in Israel," in Suad Joseph (ed.), *Gender and Citizenship in the Middle East*. Syracuse, NY: Syracuse University Press, pp. 314–44

Swirski, Barbara and Marilyn P. Safir 1991 (eds.). *Calling the Equality Bluff: Women in Israel*. New York: Pergamon

Swirski, Barbara, Hatem Kanane, and Amy Avgar 1999. "Health Services in Israel," *Information on Equality*, 9

Swirski, Shlomo 1984. "The Mizrachi Jews in Israel: Why Many Tilted Toward Begin," *Dissent*, 31, 134: 77–91

   1989. *The Oriental Majority*. London: Zed

   1990. *Education in Israel: Schooling for Inequality*. Tel Aviv: Breirot (Hebrew)

   1995. *Seeds of Inequality*. Tel Aviv: Breirot (Hebrew)

   1998. "Zionist 'Micro-Societies,' Ethnicity and Nationalism in the Shaping of the Israeli Welfare State," paper presented to the conference on the Welfare State and the End of the Century: Current Dilemmas and Possible Futures, Tel Aviv University, January 5–6, 1998

  1999. *Politics and Education in Israel (Comparisons with the US)*. New York: Garland

Swirski, Shlomo and M. Shoushan 1986. *The Development Towns of Israel: Towards a Brighter Tomorrow*. Haifa: Breirot (Hebrew)

Tal-Shir, Anat 1995. "Rabin's Friends," *Yediot achronot Weekly Magazine*, February 3 (Hebrew)

Taylor, Charles 1989. "Cross-Purposes: The Liberal–Communitarian Debate," in Nancy L. Rosenbaum (ed.), *Liberalism and Moral Life*. Cambridge, MA: Harvard University Press, pp. 159–82

  1990. "Modes of Civil Society," *Public Culture*, 3: 95–118

Tel Aviv University Law Review [Iyunei mishpat] 1995. 19, 3 (special issue: Jewish and Democratic State) (Hebrew)

Tessler, Mark 1991. "The Impact of the Intifada on Israel's Political Thinking," in Brynen (ed.), pp. 43–96

Tessler, Riki 2001. "Public Finance in the Service of the Religio-social Revolution of Shas," in Peled (ed.)

Thelen, Katheleen and Sven Steinmo 1992. "Historical Institutionalism in Comparative Politics," in Steinmo et al., pp. 1–31

Tilly, Charles 1995. "Democracy is a Lake," in G. R. Andrews and H. Chapman (eds.), *The Social Construction of Democracy, 1870–1990*. New York: New York University Press, pp. 365–87

  1996 (ed.). *Citizenship, Identity and Social History*. Cambridge: Cambridge University Press; also published in *International Review of Social History*, supplement 3

Torgovnik, Ephraim 1980. "A Movement for Change in a Stable System," in Asher Arian (ed.), *The Elections in Israel – 1977*. Jerusalem: Jerusalem Academic Press, pp. 75–98

Touval, Saadia 1982. *The Peace Brokers: Mediators in the Arab–Israeli Conflict, 1948–1979*. Princeton: Princeton University Press

Tsahor, Zeev 1997. "History between Politics and Academe," in Weitz (ed.), pp. 209–17

Tsur, Yaron 1997. "Carnival Fears: Moroccan Immigrants and the Ethnic Problem in the Young State of Israel," *Journal of Israeli History*, 18: 73–103

Tsur, Zeev 1982. *From the Partition Dispute to the Allon Plan*. Ramat-Ephal: Tabenkin Institute (Hebrew)

Turner, Bryan S. 1993 (ed.). *Citizenship and Social Theory*. London: Sage

Turner, Frederick Jackson 1956. "The Significance of the Frontier in American History," in George R. Taylor (ed.), *The Turner Thesis*, rev. edn. Boston: Heath, pp. 17–33

Urieli, Nachman and Amnon Barzilay 1982. *The Rise and Fall of the Democratic Movement for Change*. Tel Aviv: Reshafim (Hebrew)

Van Steenbergen, Bart 1994 (ed.). *The Condition of Citizenship*. London: Sage

Varhaftig, Zerach 1988. *Constitution for Israel – Religion and State*. Jerusalem: Messilot (Hebrew)

Vital, David 1982. *Zionism: The Formative Years*. Oxford: Clarendon Press

Waldman, Peter 1991. "Big Brother is Shown the Door, Giving Israel's Largest Company a Boost," *Wall Street Journal*, July 3

Wallerstein, Immanuel M. 1979. *The Capitalist World-Economy: Essays*. Cambridge: Cambridge University Press

Weingrod, Alex 1965. *Israel: Group Relations in a New Society*. New York: Praeger; published for the Institute of Race Relations

Weintraub, Jeff 1979. "Virtue, Community, and the Sociology of Liberty: The Notion of Republican Virtue and its Impact on Modern Western Social Thought," Ph.D. thesis, University of California (Berkeley)

Weitz, Yechiam 1997 (ed.). *From Vision to Revision: A Hundred Years of Historiography of Zionism*. Jerusalem: Zalman Shazar Center (Hebrew)

Werczberger, Elia 1991. "Privatization of Public Housing in Israel." Tel Aviv University, Sapir Center for Development (Discussion Paper No. 5–91) (Hebrew)

  1995. "The Role of Public Housing in Israel: Effects of Privatization," *Scandinavian Housing and Planning Research*, 12: 93–108

Wertheimer, Mozi 1993. "Don't Err with too Rosy Dreams," *Hataasiyanim*, 25 (April) (Hebrew)

Willis, Aaron P. 1993. "Sephardic Torah Guardians: Ritual and the Politics of Piety," Ph.D. dissertation, Princeton University

  1995. "Shas – the Sephardic Torah Guardians: Religious 'Movement' and Political Power," in Asher Arian and Michal Shamir (eds.), *The Elections in Israel – 1992*. Albany: SUNY Press, pp. 121–39

Wolffsohn, Michael 1987. *Israel: Polity, Society, Economy, 1882–1986: An Introductory Handbook*, trans. Douglas Bokovoy. Atlantic Highlands, NJ: Humanities Press

World Bank 1993. *Developing the Occupied Territories: An Investment in Peace*, vol. II: *The Economy*. Washington, DC: World Bank

  2000. *World Development Indicators*. Washington, DC: World Bank

Yaar, Ephraim 1986. "Private Enterprise as an Avenue of Socioeconomic Mobility in Israel: Another Aspect of Ethnic Stratification in Israel," *Megamot*, 29: 393–412 (Hebrew)

Yadlin, Omri 2000. "Good Faith in Israeli Labor Law: From the Collective to the Individual," in Mautner (ed.), pp. 341–72 (Hebrew)

Yaniv, Avner and Yael Yishai 1981. "Israeli Settlements in the West Bank: The Politics of Intransigence," *Journal of Politics*, 43 (November): 1105–28

Yiftachel, Oren 1992. *Planning a Mixed Region in Israel: The Political Geography of Arab–Jewish Relations in the Galilee*. Aldershot: Avebury

  1996. "The Internal Frontier: The Territorial Control of Ethnic Minorities," *Regional Studies*, 30: 493–508

  1997. "Between Two Nations: Regionalism among Palestinian Arabs in Israel," paper presented at the annual conference of the Association of American Geographers, Forth Worth, Texas, April

  2000. "'Ethnocracy,' Geography, and Democracy: Comments on the Politics of Judaizing the Country," *Alpayim*, 19: 78–105 (Hebrew)

  forthcoming. "The Making of an Ethno-Class: Policy, Protest and Identity in Israeli Development Towns." Beer Sheva: Negev Center for Regional Development, Ben-Gurion University (Working Paper No. 10)

Yiftachel, Oren and Alexandre (Sandy) Kedar 2000. "Landed Power: The Making of the Israeli Land Regime," *Teorya u-vikoret*, 16: 67–100

Yiftachel, Oren and Avinoam Meir 1998 (eds.). *Ethnic Frontiers and Peripheries: Landscapes of Development and Inequality in Israel*. Boulder: Westview

Yiftachel, Oren and Michaly D. Segal 1998. "Jews and Druze in Israel: State Control and Ethnic Resistance," *Ethnic and Racial Studies*, 21: 476–506

Yiftachel, Orenn and Erez Tzfadia 1999. *Policy and Identity in the Development Towns: The Case of North-African Immigrants, 1952–1998*. Beer Sheva: Ben-Gurion University (Hebrew)

2000. "Political Mobilization in Development Towns: Struggle for Local Control," paper presented at the annual meeting of the Israeli Political Science Association, Jerusalem (Hebrew)

Yishai, Yael 1997. *Between the Flag and the Banner: Women in Israeli Politics*. Albany: SUNY Press

Yishuvi, Naama 1997. *Rights, not Privileges: Social Rights in Israel*. [Tel Aviv:] Association for Civil Rights in Israel (Hebrew)

Yonah, Yossi and Ishak Saporta 2000. "Land and Housing Policies in Israel: The Discourse about Citizenship and its Limits," *Teorya u-vikoret*, 16: 129–51

Young, Iris Marion 1998. "Polity and Group Difference: A Critique of the Ideal of Universal Citizenship," in Shafir (ed.), pp. 263–90

Younis, Mona N. 2000. *Liberation and Democratization: The South African and Palestinian National Movements*. Minneapolis: University of Minnesota Press

Yuchtman-Yaar, Ephraim 1993. "The Israeli Public and the Intifada: Attitude Change or Entrenchment?" in Ehud Sprinzak and Larry Diamond (eds.), *Israeli Democracy under Stress*. Boulder: Lynne Rienner, pp. 235–51

Zameret, Zvi 1997. *Across a Narrow Bridge: Shaping the Education System during the Great Aliya*. Sede Boker: Ben-Gurion University Press (Hebrew)

Zilberg, Narespi and Elazar Leshem 1996. "Russian-Language Press and Immigrant Community in Israel," *Revue Européenne des Migrations Internationales*, 12: 173–89

1999. "Imagined Community and Real Community: The Russian-Language Press and Renewal of Community Life among CIS Immigrants in Israel," *Chevra u-revacha*, 19: 9–37 (Hebrew)

Ziv, Neta and Ronen Shamir 2000. "'Politics' and 'Sub-Politics' in the Struggle against Land Discrimination," *Teorya u-vikoret*, 16: 45–66 (Hebrew)

Zucker, Norman L. 1973. *The Coming Crisis in Israel: Private Faith and Public Policy*. Cambridge, MA: MIT Press

Zureik, Elia T. 1979. *The Palestinians in Israel: A Study in Internal Colonialism*. London: Routledge & Kegan Paul

Interviews

The interviewees' titles and positions appear as they were at the time of the interview.

Arnon, Dr. Ariyeh, research department, Bank of Israel (January 17, 1995)

Bahiri, Simcha, economic consultant (January 13, 1995)

Barak, Mandy, head of the desk of Islamic countries, Federated Chamber of Commerce (January 13, 1995)

Beilin, Yossi, deputy foreign minister (June 15, 1995)

Ben-Ami, Professor Shlomo, chairman of the board of directors of KOOR's peace projects (January 25, 1995)

Benvenisti, Meron, former deputy mayor of Jerusalem (March 24, 1998)

Biton, Shlomo, assistant to Deputy Foreign Minister Yossi Beilin and coordinator of Labor Party's Chug Mashov (April 3, 1995)

Blizovsky, Yoram, general director of the MAI (January 19, 1995)

Efroni, Dr. Linda, labor lawyer (April 4, 1995)

Fischer, Professor Stanley, chief economist World Bank (November 5, 1996)

Fishelson, Professor Gideon, Department of Economics, Tel Aviv University and associate of the Armand Hammer Fund for Economic Cooperation in the Middle East (January 31, 1995)

Gaon, Benny, CEO Koor Industries (July 7, 1995)

Gottlieb, Daniel, research department, Bank of Israel (February 3, 1995)

Grinberg, Dr. Lev Louis, advisor to chairman of New Histadrut (April 9, 1995)

Hirsch, Professor Zeev, School of Business Administration, Tel Aviv University and associate of the Armand Hammer Fund for Economic Cooperation in the Middle East (January 3, 1995)

Hurvitz, Eli, president and CEO Teva and former chairman of the MAI (July 9, 1995)

Kamenitz, Haim, director, Israeli Management Center (February 27, 1995)

Kaufman, Dr. Ehud, director, Department of Foreign Trade, Ministry of Finance (December 30, 1994)

Klein, David, senior director, monetary operation and exchange control, Bank of Israel (March 26, 1998)

Kotz, Gideon, correspondent, Kol Israel (February 10, 1995)

Kreimer, Sarah, co-director, Center for Jewish–Arab Economic Development, Tel Aviv (February 15, 1995)

Lautman, Dov, CEO, Delta Textiles and former chairman of the MAI (February 16, 1995)

Lerner, Dr. Miri, School of Business Administration, Tel Aviv University (February 12, 1995)

Menashe, Uri, CEO, Kargal (March 29, 1995)

Nachum, Moshe, head of foreign trade department, MAI (December 28, 1994)

Nachum, Nurith, general director, Yaad Business Development, part of Kesselman & Kesselman, Public Accountants, a subsidiary of Coopers & Lybrand (February 3, 1995)

Peres, Shimon, former prime minister (August 23, 1996)

Pundik, Dr. Ron, director, Economic Cooperation Foundation and negotiator with PLO delegation in secret Oslo talks (March 30, 1995)

Raban, Dr. Yoel, economist, MAI (December 28, 1994)

Reiner, Efraim, former CEO of Chevrat Haovdim (June 25 and December 24, 1995)

Sagi, Dr. Eli, Economic Models Inc. (Klal) (January 30, 1995)

Index

1948 war, 26, 53, 160
1967 war, 2, 19, 26, 59, 89, 90, 160, 164, 187, 217, 218, 337
1973 war, 19, 90, 160, 164, 165, 168, 233, 234, 263

Abu Ala, 229
Achdut Haavoda Party, 29, 50, 69, 107, 145
African Workers' Union (AWU), 331, 332
Agudat Yisrael Party (AY), 60, 61, 85, 92, 93, 139, 140, 141, 147, 149, 167
al-Aksa intifada, 128, 129, 133, 134, 183, 203, 205, 336, 340, 346; *see also* intifadas
aliya see immigration
Allon, Yigal, 160, 165 fn, 169, 184
Aloni, Shulamit, 221
Allon Plan, 160, 162, 163, 170, 172, 175, 180, 220
Amir, Yigal, 145, 172
Amit, Meir, 246
Amor, Meir, 134
Arab boycott (primary and secondary), 238, 251, 253, 258, 259
Arab Democratic Party, 130, 131
Arab Revolt, 52, 69–70
Arafat, Yassir, 256, 315
Aranne, Zalman, 149
Arendt, Hannah, 71–2
Arlosoroff, Chaim, 44
Aronson, Geoffrey, 179
Ashkenazim, 2, 17, 18, 30–2, 33, 45, 74, 79, 84, 88, 154, 213, 220, 310, 339, 347
    and education, 86, 295
    as elite, 88, 94, 219, 269, 317
    and republican citizenship, 22
    self-identification of, 318
    women, 98

Bank Hapoalim, 48, 57, 58, 239–40, 244, 250
Bank of Israel, 19, 20, 185, 217, 232, 240, 241–2, 244, 246, 269
Barak, Aharon, 1 fn, 132, 263, 267, 268, 270, 271, 273, 275, 277
Barak, Ehud, 21, 134, 152, 153, 180, 181, 182, 202, 203, 205, 206, 207, 266, 315, 338, 342, 347
Barkai, Hayim, 291–2
Barnett, Michael, 235, 238
Bartram, David, 325
Basic Law: Cabinet, 264
Basic Law: Freedom of Occupation, 227, 263, 267, 275
Basic Law: Human Dignity and Freedom, 227, 263, 267, 270, 271
Basic Law: The Knesset, 126–7, 262–3, 264
Basic Law: Social Rights, 277, 341
Bedouins, 113, 124, 281
Begin, Menachem, 171, 172, 192, 198, 220
Beilin, Yossi, 224, 225, 227, 229
Ben-Ami, Shlomo, 248, 249
Ben-David, Dan, 328, 331
Ben-Eliezer, Uri, 32, 51–3,
Ben-Gurion, David, 18, 19, 40 fn, 61, 64, 69, 77–8, 140, 147, 165 fn, 218, 219 fn, 261, 269
Ben-Porath, Yoram, 214–15
Ben-Shahar, Haim, 54, 185, 187, 189, 282, 291, 328, 330
Ben-Shahar Commission and Report (1993), 185–6, 187, 189
Benvenisti, Eyal, 194, 196, 197
Benvenisti, Meron, 174, 176
Berkovitch, Nitza, 98
Beta Israel *see* immigrants from Ethiopia
Bishara, Azmi, 135

Cambridge Middle East Studies 16

Printed in the United States
119982LV00003B/166-204/A

9 780521 796729